Fortune
Is a Woman

Fortune Is a Woman

Gender and Politics in the Thought of Niccolò Machiavelli

With a New Afterword

Hanna Fenichel Pitkin

THE UNIVERSITY OF CHICAGO PRESS

Chicago and London

Hanna Fenichel Pitkin, professor emerita of political science at the University of California, Berkeley, is one of political science's premier theorists. She is a member of the American Academy of Arts and Sciences and recipient of the APSA award for lifetime achievement. Her latest book, *The Attack of the Blob: Hannah Arendt's Concept of the Social,* is also available from the University of Chicago Press.

The University of Chicago Press, Chicago 60637
The University of Chicago Press, Ltd., London
© 1984, 1999 by Hanna Fenichel Pitkin
University of Chicago Press edition 1999
All rights reserved.
Printed in the United States of America

08 07 06 05 04 03 02 01 00 99   1 2 3 4 5
ISBN: 0-226-66992-0 (paperback)

Pitkin, Hanna Fenichel.
     Fortune is a woman : gender and politics in the thought of Niccolò Machiavelli ; with a new afterword / Hanna Fenichel Pitkin.
          p.   cm.
     Originally published: Berkeley : University of California Press, ©1984.
     Includes bibliographical references and index.
     ISBN 0-226-66992-0 (pbk. : alk. paper)
     1. Machiavelli, Niccolò, 1469–1527—Contributions in political science.
     2. Machiavelli, Niccolò, 1469–1527—Political and social views.   3. Autonomy (Psychology)   4. Gender identity.   5. Sex role.   I. Title.
JC143.M4P57   1999
320.1'092—dc21   99-28728
                                                                                              CIP

⊗ The paper used in this publication meets the
minimum requirements of the American National Standard
for Information Sciences—Permanence of Paper for
Printed Library Materials, ANSI Z39.48-1992.

For my mother, Clare Fenichel

Contents

Acknowledgments

Many people have helped me make this book, and I am deeply grateful to them. Norman Jacobson read an early draft and gave me useful advice and encouragement. Peter Euben aided me by several conversations about sex roles and heroism in ancient Greece. Gene Brucker read an early version of Chapter 8 and supplied useful references. Such references came also from Louise G. Clubb, Natalie Zeman Davis, Richard C. Trexler, and an anonymous referee for *Signs*.

I am also profoundly indebted to the students in my various classes on Machiavelli and heroism: from Frank Circiello, whose delight in a lecture first launched this project, to George Shulman, whose insights and enthusiasm graced its completion; and including the many others in between, who led, pulled, and pushed the work forward. George Shulman and John Leonard also read the whole manuscript with patient care, saving me from many errors.

Finally, I want to but cannot adequately thank four people whose thinking has influenced my own so deeply that I can no longer distinguish where their contribution leaves off, and whose gifts to me of love, criticism, and support sustained the writing of this book at every stage: Sara M. Shumer, Deborah Rogin, Michael Paul Rogin, and John H. Schaar.

PART I

Introduction

CHAPTER ONE

Autonomy—Personal and Political

Niccolò Machiavelli may well be the most political of all the great political theorists; and, like politics itself, Machiavelli horrifies and repels us, yet also attracts and fascinates. We do not know what to make of him, or how to think rightly about political life. We know that politics matters profoundly, perhaps more in our time than ever before; we suspect that somehow we have gotten it terribly wrong; but we feel powerless to change, or even fully to understand our situation. For me, thinking about politics and thinking about Machiavelli have become interconnected enterprises, each illuminating and obscuring the other. That is the reason for this book.

The book thus has a dual intent: the narrowly specific one of interpreting a particular thinker on the basis of a body of texts and the more general one of understanding the subject matter those texts address: ourselves as political creatures.

Neither task is simple, for Machiavelli's thought is as problematic as politics itself, presenting a different face to each observer. Thus, he is also one of the most misunderstood of political theorists, or at any rate the most subject to conflicting interpretations. Some see him as a tough-minded advocate of *raison d'état*, others as a romantic who idealized ancient Rome; some see him as a passionate patriot, others as a cynic; some as a detached, objective observer, others as a teacher of evil; some as a republican, others as worshiping strong leaders and military might. Each reading claims foundation in the texts, yet none has ever succeeded in displacing the others. What, then, could be the point in adding yet another interpretation to the list?

But it is not exactly the intent of this book to add yet another interpretation, nor even to proffer a new defense of a familiar interpretation. I do have a favored interpretation, which will emerge in due time, but the focus of this book is the very difficulty of interpreting Machiavelli; it seeks to understand the tensions and ambiguities in the texts that give rise to, or at least permit, so diverse an array of readings. Often the problem of interpreting Machiavelli is formulated in terms of a conflict between his two best-known works, *The Prince* and *The Discourses on the First Ten Books of Titus Livius.* The former is seen as favoring one-man rule, the latter a republic; the former is seen as cynical, the latter idealistic. But although there are important differences of tone and intent between these two works, the fundamental tensions in Machiavelli's thought lie not between these works but within each of them, and indeed within all his writings. *The Discourses*, too, are studded with cynical advice to princes and disparaging remarks about human nature; *The Prince*, too, gives indications of a devoted, patriotic concern for republican virtue.

In my understanding, Machiavelli was a committed, lifelong republican and Florentine patriot. He served the republic loyally in office, mourned its fall, and meditated on ways to restore it or to create a more viable version of it for the whole of Italy. Unemployed, he also tried to get a job with those who had overthrown the republic; that may or may not be considered cynical or evil. But Machiavelli also despised utopian idealism, and relished the tough, reeking realities of political power. He admired success, skill, strength, power; he revered the ruthless, heroic leader, the effective military force, the conquering empire of ancient Rome. He was, then, both a republican and something like a protofascist.

How should one understand that combination? Is it to be regarded as fortuitous and idiosyncratic? As laying bare the dangers of popular participation in public life? Or as indicating something about the nature of politics itself? The matter is not without significance for our own time. Contemporary efforts to mobilize the mass of ordinary people for political action—the heirs, as it were, of Renaissance republicanism—are understood in precisely this dual way: by some as promoting, and by others as preventing, fascist authoritarianism. The political insurgency of the 1960s has faded, but questions about its meaning linger on: Do we need more popular political involvement or less? More apathy and "benign neglect" or less? More political idealism or less? A higher or a lower "profile" for politics? Or are these apparent choices wrongly formulated?

With respect to Machiavelli himself, some have suggested that the tensions and ambiguities in his thought simply indicate the carelessness of a second-rate mind. Others regard them as evidence of duplicity, of an effort to convey simultaneously an esoteric and an exoteric message. The initial suggestion of this book will be that the apparent contradictions in Machiavelli's thought arise neither from ineptitude nor from manipulative cleverness, but from ambivalence—intense but incompatible feelings that can be neither given up nor reconciled. The focus of ambivalence in Machiavelli's texts, as I shall suggest, is manhood: anxiety about being sufficiently masculine and concern over what it means to be a man.

In due time that suggestion leads to Machiavelli's images of women and relations between the sexes, of family life and relations between generations. Here, too, there are issues of contemporary concern. Machiavelli raises the problem of the relationship of republican, activist politics not merely to fascism, but also to misogyny and what we now call *machismo*: the anxious and defensive effort of men to prove their manliness.[1] It is an issue that no one interested in human liberation—political or personal—can afford to ignore. Why is it that so many of the theorists of republican or participatory politics appeal specifically to patriarchal values and are fearful of and hostile toward the "feminine"? From the political ideals of ancient Athens to their recent revival by Hannah Arendt, republican activism seems to be linked to "manly" heroism and military glory, and to disdain for the household, the private, the personal, and the sensual. Is this a fortuitous or a significant linkage, and how is it to be understood?

In proposing to study Machiavelli in terms of ambivalence about manhood, this book may seem to share in the current withdrawal from the public, the political, and the objective to the personal and inward. That is not its intent. Interpreters have often claimed that Machiavelli's thought is characterized precisely by the distinction between personal ethics and *raison d'état*, the recognition of politics as a distinct sphere of life with its own unique rules. Yet Machiavelli nowhere says that politics is or should be different from the rest of human life, or that political action is governed by different principles than personal conduct.

1. In my understanding, this is the meaning now attached to *machismo* in American English. It is not what the term means in Spanish, the language to which it owes its origin. To members of hispanic cultures, *machismo* means an ideal of true manliness, as *virtù* does in Machiavelli's works. Whether their pursuit of that ideal is nevertheless anxious and defensive, I do not presume to say; whether the pursuit of *virtù* is so in Machiavelli's thought constitutes a central problem for this book.

He does indeed say that what is morally good in normal life may have terrible consequences in the long run and on the larger scale, especially in corrupt or immoral times. Apparent kindness may turn out to be cruel, and apparent generosity may have different consequences with public than with private funds. But such claims do not amount to making politics a distinct realm with a special morality, or with none. The rules of conduct for private life displayed in Machiavelli's fiction and letters are much the same as those advanced for public life in his political theory.

Nevertheless, applying the categories of personal life and psychology to Machiavelli's thought may all too easily de-politicize the teachings of this most political of theorists, preventing our access to what is of most value in his thought. Though this book will refer to biographical materials and employ psychoanalytic categories, it is not psychohistory or psychobiography. It will not offer a causal explanation of the origins of Machiavelli's ideas, reducing their "apparently" political content to some underlying, "real" psychic significance, claiming that they concern manhood rather than citizenship, Oedipal rather than factional rivalry, psychic rather than political conflict. Instead, this book proposes to *investigate* the relationship—in Machiavelli's thought and in our own— between inner and outer reality, private and public life, "the personal" and "the political." And that investigation will seek not causal links of dependent and independent variables, but interrelationships of meaning. If this book succeeds, the issues of gender and citizenship should illuminate rather than displace each other.

The categories and concepts through which we comprehend our shared social world are not mere epiphenomena—deceptive superstructures on some psychic or economic base. Ideas *can* be used to conceal, deny, or distort reality: hypocritically, ideologically, defensively. But they can also be used to reveal and understand reality and ourselves. And all of these categories and concepts have both public and personal significances, which are inevitably interrelated. Authority, membership, freedom, justice—our experience of such categories begins in childhood, long before we have mastered the words; and our first encounters with, say, parental authority or injustice among siblings continue to inform our adult, political understanding of these categories. That does not mean that a male political leader is "merely" a father-figure; on the contrary, our early encounters with parents already begin to teach us what authority is, and perhaps how it can fail. As Erik H. Erikson wrote about Martin Luther:

The theological problems which he tackled as a young adult of course reflected the peculiarly tenacious problems of the domestic relationship to his own father; but this was true to a large extent because both problems, the domestic and the universal, were part of one ideological crisis: a crisis about the theory and practice, the power and responsibility, of the moral authority invested in fathers: on earth and in heaven; at home, in the market-place, and in politics; in the castles, the capitals, and in Rome.[2]

Although this book approaches Machiavelli in terms of ambivalence and manhood, it will center not on authority but on a different, though related, concept: autonomy. Autonomy, it will argue, is Machiavelli's central preoccupation, the thread that unifies the contradictions and tensions in his works, enlarging the seemingly personal issue of *machismo* and tying it to his meditations on political themes.

The word *autonomy* derives from the Greek *auto*, meaning "self" or "own," and *nomos*, meaning "law, rule, binding custom, way of life." Autonomy thus means having or making one's own laws or principles: independence, self-control, self-government, freedom. It begins with the infant's first struggles to become a separate self despite its conflicting yearning to return to blissful unity with the mother. Autonomy extends into every aspect of social, cultural, religious, and political life—our relations with others, with the past, with nature. Autonomy concerns borderlines, found or made; it concerns the question of how and to what extent I (or we) have become or can become a separate self (or community). In an important sense, then, autonomy is a problem in the living of any human life, the workings of any human community.

For the child, it may mean development of its own powers, mastery of its body, but also independence from the constraints of parents and other authorities. For the adult, it may mean something like an independent life: a source of livelihood, a degree of personal security, and some room for significant choices. It may also be interpreted in more Kantian terms, as the capacity and willingness to take responsibility for one's own conduct and for the moral principles by which one lives. Politically, autonomy means something like a self-governing polity: one free of foreign domination, but also perhaps one that is internally self-governing —what Machiavelli would have called a republic. Citizenship in such a community may extend the Kantian notion of personal autonomy into a shared public freedom, that is, participation in the political activity by which the community makes decisions and shapes its collective principles and way of life, its *nomos*.

2. Erik H. Erikson, *Young Man Luther* (New York: W. W. Norton, 1962), 77.

Autonomy, then, evokes a wide range of meanings, some public and some personal, interdependent but also in mutual tension. And at every level and in every sense, the idea of autonomy is itself problematic, implying both a connection and a separation: a separation that challenges, denies, or overcomes a connection. Thus, autonomy may be conceived either as a kind of sovereign isolation or, paradoxically, as the rightful acknowledgment of interdependence.

Against the background of the concept of autonomy, the seemingly more personal and pyschological idea of manhood can be seen also to have public and political dimensions. For what it means to be a man, what it "really" means to be a "real" man, will vary depending on the context in which the question is raised and the contrasts to which manhood is juxtaposed. For example, to be a man may mean not to be a woman, to be male rather than female, masculine rather than feminine, manly rather than effeminate. But alternatively, to be a man may mean not to be a child, to be adult rather than childish, mature rather than infantile—that is, independent, competent, potent. But then again, being a man may mean something like being human; the Italian *uomo* is ambiguous in the same way here as the English *man*. In this sense, being a man might be contrasted to being inhuman or bestial, but also to being superhuman, immortal, or divine. In Aristotle's terms, being a man means being neither a beast nor a god. Unlike the beasts, a man is part of a historically created civilization, a person, capable of choice, judgment, action, responsibility; unlike divinities, a man is mortal and fallible, simply one among others who have fundamentally equal rights and claims. This last sense of being a man might also suggest, as it did to both Aristotle and Machiavelli, being a "political animal," a creature whose potential is fully realized only in a *polis* as an active citizen among peers.

These various senses of manhood, like the various senses of autonomy, are both interrelated and sometimes mutually in conflict. The details of their relationships remain to be explored. For now, the point is only that approaching Machiavelli from the idea of ambivalence about manhood is meant not to deny but to illuminate the political content of his teaching.

❖ ❖ ❖

In an important sense, autonomy is problematic in any human life or community; but there is another, equally important sense in which the problem is a historical product, specifically characteristic of modernity. Individualism, liberation, national self-determination are modern concerns, and they first become salient in the Renaissance. If one may be permitted some broad stereotypes as a way of getting started, in the medieval world people understood themselves as embedded in a hierarchical network of mutual obligation—the feudal order of fealty, which also reflected the natural and sacred order of the universe. In that understanding, the social, like the natural order, is essentially given to man, not made. Just as an individual is born into a particular social rank rather than achieving his status in a competitive market, so too the customs and rules of the social order are not subject to choice. Of course, particular individuals make decisions applying law or custom in particular situations; and people are fallible and can make bad or wrong decisions. But the law that men should be seeking to apply—that good men do seek to apply—is eternal, universal, absolute, and ultimately of divine origin. Law is not made, but found, by men.

Moreover, the finding, interpretation, and application of the community's law and custom are the work of particular ranks in the social hierarchy. Every rank is understood as bound by obligations and subordinated to a still higher rank—a hierarchy culminating in God. There may well be wicked rulers who misapply the law, but there is no right of rebellion against them; neither law nor authority depends upon consent. *Passive Submission (?)* Thus, the pervasive medieval attitude might be put this way: "Certainly I have my tasks and obligations, but someone else is in charge of the whole—the lord in his castle, the Lord in Heaven." God will judge sinners, both high and low. And although God is implacable and inscrutable in his righteousness, he is surrounded by a company of angels and saints, the Virgin and Jesus, who can intercede on the individual's behalf, as indeed can priests and pope. Finally, the individual is embedded in a network of rituals that ratify and renew his connections with others, with nature, the past, and the sacred.

In the medieval understanding, then, interconnectedness and dependence were taken for granted almost as the definition of the human condition. They were neither shameful nor constricting but were assumed to be natural and even sacred. This acceptance of dependence, this sense that someone else was in charge, is what made medieval people seem, to later ages, childish, as if they had never grown up. Henry Adams captures this outlook in the prayer he imagines a medieval artisan directing to the Virgin: "Gracious Lady, what ought I to do? . . . without your help, I am lost."[3] In such a world people felt neither an aspiration nor

3. Henry Adams, *Mont-Saint-Michel and Chartres* (1913; reprint, Boston: Houghton Mifflin, 1936), 176.

an obligation to be autonomous; mutual dependence was the very nature of the universe.

This image of the Middle Ages is a distortion, as sterotypes invariably are. Yet no one can deny that there is a difference between the medieval and the Renaissance outlook. To sense the difference, set the prayer of Adams's artisan alongside a line from Machiavelli's *Prince*: "Those defenses alone are good, are certain, are durable, that depend on yourself and your own abilities."[4] Society had changed profoundly, and so had human self-understanding. Far from being natural and sacred, dependence had now become both contemptible and dangerous; autonomy was the goal. The aspiration to autonomy was, as Ernst Cassirer has said, "increasingly central" to "the Renaissance ideal of humanity."[5]

An urban and market society gradually supplanted feudal agriculture, leaving men free (but also forced) to make their own way in life. Instead of being born into a social station, men might achieve or lose wealth, power, and status in a single generation. Rather than as parts of a universal, "given" social order, men now understood themselves as members of a particular, historically located state and language group; the universal Latin had been replaced by local vernaculars. And states, too, like individuals, were understood to be in competitive conflict, their relative positions constantly shifting as a result of skill, boldness, resources, or luck.

Along with these social, economic, and political developments, there were changes in family structure and child-rearing practices. In times of rapid social change, the authority of the older generation is inevitably undermined to some extent. What the parents know and can teach no longer functions well in the child's world. There is no longer just one traditional and unquestioned right way to do things. In the Renaissance, the medieval extended family and communal life were increasingly fragmented; the family was privatized and became more nuclear. Traditional sex roles also underwent challenge and change. There emerged a whole new genre of literature on family and child rearing, as well as a flourishing literary topic of the "battle between the sexes." The Renaissance imagination dwelled on domesticity and sweet childhood, on the one hand, and on patriarchal power, on the other. Painters depicted *putti*, nursing mothers, and domestic scenes, but they also re-

4. Niccolò Machiavelli, *The Prince*, ch. 25, in *Machiavelli: The Chief Works and Others*, 3 vols., tr. Allan Gilbert (Durham, N.C.: Duke University Press, 1965), 89 (hereafter cited as G).

5. Ernst Cassirer, *The Individual and the Cosmos in Renaissance Philosophy*, tr. Mario Domandi (New York: Harper & Row, 1963), 98.

vived the ancient hero, Hercules, who was portrayed as dominating various female figures. In religious art, they depicted the infant Jesus, but replaced the cult of the Virgin with a new emphasis on Joseph.[6]

In personal as in public life, mastery had become problematic. Autonomy and dependence had become the issues. Authority was no longer experienced as embedded in a sacred hierarchy, and the rituals that once guaranteed and renewed its legitimacy were increasingly empty and incapable of generating meaning. Anxiety and remnants of piety alternated with the growing suspicion that the ancient forms served only to disguise the new realities of power and wealth.

The Renaissance recovery of ancient documents, artifacts, and ideas also played a part in this transformation. On the one hand, it was a triumph for the human intellect, for independent critical inquiry. Much that had been taken for granted in the medieval tradition was now exposed as a distortion or even a falsification of original sources. For instance, Lorenzo Valla's exposure of the "Donation of Constantine" as a forgery revealed the false foundation on which papal authority rested. Yet, on the other hand, the challenge to traditional medieval authorities and beliefs was also based partly on the recovery of a still earlier authority, the original sources—classical or biblical—to which the independent intellect reached back. Thus, the Renaissance was simultaneously a recovery of origins and a discovery of the independent self; a new humility and deference toward the ancients, and yet, as Erikson has said, "the ego revolution *par excellence*."[7] In reviving ancient authority and pitting it against the medieval, men felt liberated to exercise their own powers here and now.

For the medieval sense that dependence is natural and that "someone else is in charge," the Renaissance substituted a lively consciousness of human self-creation—both the individual shaping his character and career, and the community shaping itself through history. The community and its laws, its *nomos*, were now understood as human artifacts, the products of choice, subject to further action. Individuals increasingly

not "givens"

6. Ibid., 77; Erwin Panofsky, *Hercules am Scheidewege* (Leipzig: B. G. Teubner, 1930), 57, 84, 165n; Millard Meiss, *Painting in Florence and Siena After the Black Death* (Princeton: Princeton University Press, 1951), 61, 151; Aldo S. Bernardo, *Petrarch, Scipio and the "Africa"* (Baltimore: Johns Hopkins Press, 1962), 57, 60; Richard A. Goldthwaite, *Private Wealth in Renaissance Florence* (Princeton: Princeton University Press, 1968), 262; Christiane Klapisch, "L'enfance en Toscane au début du XVe Siècle," *Annales de Démographie Historique* (1973): 118–19. The quotation is from John Gerson (1363–1429), cited in Meyer Schapiro, "'Muscipula Diaboli,' the Symbolism of the Mérode Altarpiece," in *Renaissance Art*, ed. Creighton Gilbert (New York: Harper & Row, 1970), 29.

7. Erikson, *Young Man Luther*, 193; see also Cassirer, *Individual*, 99.

felt required to create order for themselves and for each other, to master themselves and take charge of their communities. In short, authority was becoming internalized. The change seems to have been both exhilarating and frightening. As Pico della Mirandola, a contemporary of Machiavelli's in Florence, put it, although God assigned every other species its particular place and role in nature, man alone was gifted with the capacity to be and do whatever he wished.

> To him it is granted to have whatever he chooses, to be whatever he wills. On man when he came to life, the Father conferred the seeds of all kinds and the germs of every way of life. . . . Who would not admire this chameleon?[8]

Man is the unique species that was made by God to make itself. Pico concludes, "What a work of art is man!" God is the creator, but by making man in his own image he has also made a creator, almost a rival to divinity. Marsilio Ficino, a Florentine of Machiavelli's father's generation, said, "Man possesses as it were almost the same genius as the Author of the heavens"; man, too, is an author and he could even make the heavens, "could he only obtain the instruments and the heavenly material."[9] Such bold claims were bound to entail a corresponding level of anxiety and doubt; there was still a God in the heavens who would judge, but the maintenance of human life and *nomos* was now up to man himself.

Italy was always a partial exception to some of these generalizations, feudalism never having been as strongly established there as in the north of Europe; still the city of Florence seems to have undergone such a shift in self-understanding. As historical records show, Florence in the late Middle Ages was a self-governing commune, a republic that made its own decisions and administered its own rules. Yet the Florentine conception of the city was characteristically medieval: Florence was understood as part of a timeless, sacred, universal order, monarchical and hierarchical in structure. Having struggled successfully in practice to win local civic autonomy from the Holy Roman Empire, the Florentines nevertheless thought of their city as part of, and a concrete symbolic replica of, that higher order.

J. G. A. Pocock has pointed out that Florentines still thought in these terms about their civic order as late as the fourteenth century.[10] Thus

---

8. Pico della Mirandola, "On the Dignity of Man," quoted in Erikson, *Young Man Luther*, 192.

9. Quoted in ibid., 193. Cf. Richard C. Trexler, "Florentine Religious Experience: The Sacred Image," *Studies in the Renaissance* 19 (1972): 35–41.

10. J. G. A. Pocock, *The Machiavellian Moment* (Princeton: Princeton University Press, 1975), 50.

Dante, despite his "memorably intense" Florentine patriotism, still "saw the delivery of Florence from faction rule as part of the restoration of Italy to political and spiritual health within a universal empire." Though he knew Florence to be in practice self-governing, he understood "secular rule as the empire in which the eternal order was repeated and restored, not as the republic in which a particular group of men resolved what their particular destiny should be." It is, of course, not unusual for a society's understanding of what it is doing to lag behind its practice. As long as Florence's practical self-government seemed to be working, Pocock suggests, it did not require theoretical investigation or reconceptualization. Florentines "felt no need to manufacture a dramatic symbolism for the republic (as such), or clothe it in prophetic declamation," because they already had that republic, and it worked.[11] Its actual practice was gradually articulated by the practitioners in the course of their activities, in an untheoretical, concrete, and "singularly realistic" way. But that newer articulation calmly coexisted with the older, more abstract theory of universal sacred hierarchy.

By the fifteenth century, however, this had begun to change, for reasons partly local and fortuitous, but also reflecting general trends. The city-states in the Italian peninsula were ranged in two opposing alliances: an alliance of republics led by Florence and one of princedoms and dukedoms led by Milan. Under the stimulus of this struggle, as Hans Baron has shown, Florence began to rethink its own character and to define itself as essentially a republic in opposition to monarchical and princely rule, connected symbolically with ancient republics rather than with the Empire.[12] For early fifteenth-century thinkers like Coluccio Salutati and Leonardo Bruni, the republic of Florence was no longer subsumed in a universal, sacred empire, but was presented instead

as a high ideal but existing in the present and in its own past, . . . affiliated only with other republics and with those moments in past time at which republics had existed. . . . The republic was more political than it was hierarchical; it was so organized as to assert its sovereignty and autonomy, and therefore its individuality and particularity.[13]

Accordingly, the understanding of Florentine origins shifted from the Roman Empire to the Roman Republic. A figure like Brutus was transformed from a despicable traitor into a heroic rebel, and—even more

11. Ibid., 51–52.
12. Hans Baron, *The Crisis of the Early Italian Renaissance*, 2d ed. (Princeton: Princeton University Press, 1966).
13. Pocock, *Machiavellian Moment*, 53.

fundamentally—there was a new emphasis on secular, historical founding as such. The civic order was now a human creation in secular time
that had to be sustained by continued human activity.

The first third of the fifteenth century, then, was a time of optimism,
activism, and civic pride in Florence, as John Rigby Hale has recently
reminded us. Having prevailed in its struggle against Milan, Florence
controlled almost half of Tuscany, and "intellectual life had never been
more vital, nor classical studies more stimulatingly attuned to problems of individual and public life."[14] Above all, "the most widely felt
source of pride" was the apparently excellent health of Florentine self-
government. Florence was a genuine republic, spreading "political
power among a large group of responsible citizens," its institutions "fil-
igreed with legal devices to prevent . . . domination" by any one group.
Citizenship was restricted, to be sure, and actual participation confined
to an elite of wealthy, influential male citizens. The one serious effort to
widen participation and alter its class base, the Ciompi Rebellion of
wool workers in 1378, was fiercely suppressed. Yet even among the excluded classes,

the chronicles and memoirs of the time show the liveliest interest in political
issues and personalities, and . . . the sense of involvement in public affairs,
through gossip, through sheer physical proximity, penetrated into all sections
of society.[15]

There were frequent meetings of local *gonfalone* groups in each district
of the city for a variety of purposes.[16] Thus Florence had "what was
proportionately the largest politically conscious class in Europe," as well
as "something like an ideal of public service, a political ethos which took
for granted the collaboration of responsible citizens as equals in the
conduct of public affairs."[17]

As the century progressed, however, Florence's international position
and economy became unsteady, and the republic less successful. A single
family, the Medici, came increasingly to dominate, and together with a
small circle of other families of great wealth they formed a ruling elite.
Increasingly often, the ideal of public service was only a pretense, behind which operated self-interest, particularly of a financial kind. It was
the inner circle of the elite

14. J[ohn] R[igby] Hale, *Florence and the Medici* (London: Thames and Hudson,
1977), 9.
15. Ibid., 15.
16. Francis William Kent, *Household and Lineage in Renaissance Florence* (Princeton:
Princeton University Press, 1977), 173.
17. Hale, *Florence*, 18.

who decided how much money [the city] needed; they or their friends who put up the cash for war loans; they who imposed taxes as security for the sum; they who made sure that repayment of their loans would be given precedence and at what interest. . . . The gap between the self-protecting rich and the heavily taxed majority was growing.[18]

Thus Florence gradually developed its own, secular version of the Renaissance legitimation problem: an increasing ossification of ceremonial forms into sham and ideology. In Florentine politics in the latter half of the fifteenth century, as in the late medieval Church all over Europe, the gap widened between ideals and practice.

Meanwhile, although the Italian peninsula remained divided into a multitude of local political units, northern European nation-states were consolidating their power and military force. In 1494 France invaded Italy. After Piero de' Medici fled Florence at the approach of the French army, a widely participatory republic was restored to the city, despite efforts by the elite to protect their privileges. The attempt was once more made to close the gap between doctrine and practice. "Florence was loud with political debate. . . . It became clear that the old ideals of widely shared participation in government had merely been hibernating."[19] It was in this restored republic—after a brief eschatological period under the charismatic leadership of Savonarola—that the young Machiavelli took office and made his career. It was the fall of this republic fifteen years later that ended his career and made him a political theorist.

From its inception, the restored Florentine republic that Machiavelli served was beset with profound military, economic, and political troubles; it was, one might say with the benefit of hindsight, bucking the tide of history. The French invasion of 1494, which had brought the republic into existence, was only the first of a series of highly destructive, north European military intrusions into the Italian peninsula. In this connection, Machiavelli's friend and contemporary, Francesco Guicciardini, called 1494 "a year most unhappy for Italy and, indeed, the year which headed all the following years of misery because it opened the door to an endless number of terrible calamities."[20] European intervention meant a continual series of wars and threats of war, accompanied by severe social dislocations and suffering. The small and poor

18. Ibid., 80.
19. Ibid., 87.
20. Francesco Guicciardini, *Storia d'Italia*, bk. 1, ch. 6, quoted in Felix Gilbert, "Machiavelli: The Renaissance of the Art of War," in *Makers of Modern Strategy*, ed. E. M. Earle (Princeton: Princeton University Press, 1944), 8.

Italian city-states were at the mercy of the northern powers. The techniques of warfare were becoming more deadly. The invasions ruined the north Italian industrial centers; population and production both declined drastically. For example, in Florence between 1500 and 1540, population fell by one-sixth, and production fell even more. The number of wool shops decreased by three-fourths in this period.[21]

These militarily induced hardships, moreover, merely contributed to a longer-range economic decline in the Italian peninsula—the shift of Europe's economic, commercial, and industrial center from the Mediterranean basin to the north and west. The roots of this change lay in the fifteenth century, but in the sixteenth century the Florentine economy faced the greatest difficulties. Textile production was still high, but foreign competition was mounting and the margin of profit was declining, especially in the wool industry. There was still much wealth in Florence, and at first the biggest merchants actually gained ground.[22] Florentines also held important positions as bankers abroad, but increasingly the northern powers made themselves independent of these sources, and Florentine bankers, including the Medici, were forced to retrench.[23]

In Florence as elsewhere, then, the new Renaissance sense of human power—the understanding that "man makes himself," as individual, as community, as species—was experienced as both a promise and a threat, the emphasis shifting with the city's fortunes. But in terms of objective social and historical development, the opportunities for successful autonomous human action were diminishing even as the desire for autonomy increased. Both personally and politically, individuals and communities wished to be free and self-governing. Men feared dependence and regarded it with contempt, as a dangerous failure of their already embattled manhood. But these increasing demands for independence came at a time when economic, military, social, and political conditions made their fulfillment increasingly difficult. No longer subject to feudal restraints, the new economic man—whether craftsman, merchant, or banker—found himself more and more at the mercy of the market, which in Florence meant being at the mercy of a declining mar-

21. Harry A. Miskimin, *The Economy of Later Renaissance Europe, 1460–1600* (Cambridge: Cambridge University Press, 1977), 118.

22. Arthur K. Rabb, *The Struggle for Stability in Early Modern Europe* (New York: Oxford University Press, 1975), 88.

23. Rudolf von Albertini, *Das Florentinische Staatsbewusstsein im Uebergang von der Republik zu dem Prinzipat* (Bern: A. Francke, 1955), 15–16; Rabb, *Struggle*, 88; Mis-

ket. No longer embedded in the extended family, in communal cere-
mony, in hierarchical networks of mutual obligation, the individual was
free to define and develop himself; but what could such freedom mean
in the face of devastating invasions by north European armies? No
longer conceiving their city as the epitome of a monarchical hierarchy,
the Florentines were free for the self-conscious, collective directing of
their republic, but at a time when external conditions made success in
that venture virtually unattainable.

Autonomy was thus a problem in Machiavelli's time as it had never
been before. It had already been a goal and an active concern a century
earlier, in the time of Bruni and Salutati. Indeed, the thinkers of that
time wrote more eloquently—if less systematically and extensively—
than Machiavelli in praise of human self-creation and self-government.
But they were able to do so partly because the theme had not yet
emerged in its full complexity. It was still easy to identify Florentine
with Roman republicanism and expect its speedy and lasting triumph.
Writers like Bruni still had, as George Holmes has put it,

a natural self-confidence which contrasts with the tortured analyses of Machiavelli and Guicciardini at the beginning of the sixteenth century, when the
existence of bourgeois society and republican institutions was threatened and
the problem of their preservation was uppermost.[24]

Florence and republicanism had been under threat in Bruni's time, too,
from the alliance of monarchical states led by Milan; but that threat
served as a stimulus to optimistic republican theory. The threats in Machiavelli's time were deeper and more complex. Although the civic humanists of the earlier period anticipated Machiavelli's republicanism,
his invocation of ancient greatness, and his praise of a civic militia, they
were quite unlike him in their untroubled patriotic fervor and their easy
assimilation of the Florentine to the Roman republic.[25] Thus, they could
occasionally fairly "revel in the idea of patriotic massacre," as Ernst
Kantorowicz has pointed out, adopting the Roman *dulce et decorum
est pro patria mori*. Kantorowicz cites as example Coluccio Salutati,
who wrote of the "sweetness" of patriotic fervor:

If such would be expedient for the fatherland's protection or enlargement [!], it
would seem neither burdensome and difficult nor a crime to thrust the axe into

---

kimin, *Economy*, 119–20; Richard A. Goldthwaite, *The Building of Renaissance Florence* (Baltimore: Johns Hopkins University Press, 1980), 52.

24. George Holmes, *The Florentine Enlightenment, 1400–1450* (London: Weidenfeld
and Nicolson, 1969), 137.

25. On earlier humanist anticipations of Machiavelli, see F. Gilbert, "Machiavelli: The
Renaissance," 21.

one's father's head, to crush one's brothers, to deliver from the womb of one's wife the premature child with the sword.[26]

Though Machiavelli was perfectly capable of advocating cruelty and bloodshed, of issuing patriotic appeals, and of practicing a kind of humanist dissociation, he never wrote such a passage, with its almost salacious combination of patriotism and familial mayhem. Indeed, the only comparably gory passage in his works expresses the horrors of war—probably those he had observed at Verona in 1509.[27]

It is not just that, as Richard C. Trexler has said, the humanists were "intellectuals with a vengeance," while Machiavelli and his contemporaries had seen the realities of war.[28] For Salutati had been a Florentine chancellor, as Machiavelli was to become later, and this passage stems from his early rhetorical and activist period rather than from his later years of Stoic and Christian withdrawal.[29] But the world had changed during the intervening century. Although there had been war in Salutati's and Bruni's time, Machiavelli and his contemporaries had actually seen the horrors of defeat in war on a large scale, and in a warfare far more brutal and bloody than any known in the preceding centuries. On the whole, Machiavelli refused to permit himself the dissociated so-called detachment of the intellectual, but insisted that abstract ideals like autonomy be tied to the reality of body and feeling. His was to be a theory self-consciously relevant to the harsh practicalities of political life; and the practicalities of his time precluded any simple division of the world into "good guys" and "bad guys." The autonomy that had once been an unproblematic goal was now itself a theoretical problem.

Furthermore, the humanists of the earlier period had largely construed human activity on the model of production—the making of objects out of physical material, *technē* rather than *praxis*. Ficino's glorification of man as potential artificer of the heavens has already been mentioned; and indeed, these humanists presented God himself as epitomizing what he gave to man: the power of creation, understood as power over objects.[30] As long as human power and creativity were con-

26. Coluccio Salutati, *Epistolario*, ed. Francesco Novati (Rome, 1891), 1: letter 10, quoted in Ernst Kantorowicz, *The King's Two Bodies* (Princeton: Princeton University Press, 1957), 245.

27. Niccolò Machiavelli, "Tercets on Ambition," lines 133–59 (G 738, 735n).

28. Trexler, "Florentine Religious Experience," 36. See also Benjamin G. Kohl and Ronald G. Witt, eds. *The Earthly Republic* (Philadelphia: University of Pennsylvania Press, 1978), 5–9.

29. Kantorowicz, *King's Two Bodies*, 245n; Alfred Wilhelm Otto von Martin, *Coluccio Salutati und das humanistische Lebensideal* (Leipzig: B. G. Teubner, 1916); Jerrold Seigel, "Rhetoric and Philosophy in Renaissance Humanism from Petrarch to Valla" (Ph.D. diss., Princeton University, 1963).

30. Trexler, "Florentine Religious Experience," 36–37.

ceived in this way, the full theoretical problems of autonomy could not be confronted. They emerged only when human power was understood not as making or manipulating objects, but as arising out of relationships among *persons*, each of whom has his own needs, interests, and way of seeing the world, yet all of whom must live together.

From the perspective of Machiavelli's time, the earlier humanists seem naively optimistic, dangerously abstracted, and theoretically superficial. It now seemed that humanist republican ideals were no more relevant to the requirements of practice than the otherworldly, medieval Christian ideals they had replaced. Meanwhile, practice continued down its own untheorized and evidently disastrous path. Some people were fiercely active, but for selfish and ultimately destructive ends; others withdrew into privacy or passivity, seeing no hope for public action; still others succumbed to millenarian enthusiasms, like that led by Savonarola. Such diverse people were both the subject matter and the audience for Machiavelli's political theorizing. Through and for them, he sought to reformulate republican ideals in terms that took political reality into account, even though political reality by this time seemed almost hopeless. He was a republican for hard times, seeking to encourage men to action, but to action that would not be destructively self-interested or blindly self-defeating.

Machiavelli never directly addressed the topic of autonomy; the term does not figure significantly in any of his writings. Yet something like the problem of autonomy and dependence appears with obsessive persistence in all his works in a variety of guises. The value of self-sufficiency and the dangers inherent in needing others fascinate and haunt Machiavelli; his mind returns to them again and again, seeking resolution of the problems they pose. Autonomy thus forms a unity behind the apparent inconsistencies in the texts, not by resolving and making them consistent, but by providing a clear overview of the unresolved tensions and their sources. *synthetic approach*

To begin with the theme's most obvious form, Machiavelli poses autonomy as a goal for states. He will judge only those states strong, he says, that are "capable of maintaining themselves alone," while weakness is defined as "always [having] need of others."[31] It is always best to "repel attack" by your "own strength," if possible; external assistance is the last and most dangerous resort. Particularly alliances with powers stronger than yourself, which might at first glance seem the most useful,

31. Niccolò Machiavelli, *The Prince and the Discourses*, tr. Luigi Ricci (New York: Modern Library, 1940), 39. I use the Ricci translation of this passage because it is more accurate for my purposes; cf G 42 and Niccolò Machiavelli, *Opere*, 8 vols. (Milano: Feltrinelli Editore, 1960–1965), 1: 48.

are in fact to be avoided because they leave you the "prisoner" of your ally and at his mercy.[32]

Machiavelli's advice to states merges, particularly in *The Prince*, with his advice to new rulers who want to maintain their power. "Wise princes avoid as much as they can being in other men's power."[33] The prince should "take care to base himself on what is his own, not on what is another's."[34] While Machiavelli does urge the prince to seek the support of the common people, this is precisely because such support allows the ruler to stand "solitary"; he can "command" and "manage" his popular support at will, while a ruler relying on a few rich nobles is dependent on them.[35] For the same reason, it is always "much safer for a prince to be feared than loved," since fear, unlike love, is reliable in adversity.[36] "He who is too eager to be loved, gets despised."[37] This is particularly true for the innovator, because introducing new ways is always risky. That is Machiavelli's famous point about the "armed" and the "unarmed" prophet: only those innovators succeed who "stand by their own strength," while those who "depend on others" fail.[38] Similarly, when Machiavelli advises the prince about taking advice from others, the danger he stresses is not that of taking bad advice from knaves or fools, but that of falling into the advisor's power. The wise ruler allows counsel only "when it suits him and not when it suits somebody else," and having taken counsel, he always "decides for himself, at his own pleasure."[39]

This insistence on princely self-reliance becomes, in *The Discourses*, the theme of the solitary founder. Leadership in difficult crises must, above all, be by one man acting alone; that is why Romulus must be excused for having slain his brother, Remus, and why Cleomenes succeeded in reforming Sparta where Agis had failed. Like Moses, Lycurgus, and Solon, each had made himself "the only one in authority."[40] The same requirement of course applied to commanding an army.[41] In successful conspiracy, as well, the number of participants should be kept to a minimum; best of all is a solitary plotter who involves others only at the last moment.[42] The *Discourses* begin, more-

32. *Prince*, ch. 10 (G 42–43); ch. 21 (G 84); cf. Letter to Vettori [29 April 1513] (G 908).
33. *Prince*, ch. 21 (G 84).   34. Ibid., ch. 17 (G 64).
35. Ibid., ch. 9 (G 39–40).
36. Ibid., ch. 17 (G 62). See also Niccolò Machiavelli, *Discourses on the First Decade of Titus Livius* 3: 21 (G. 477).
37. *Discourses*, 3: 21 (G 478).
38. *Prince*, ch. 6 (G 26). Cf. *Discourses* 1: 1 (G 190).
39. *Prince*, ch. 23 (G 86–87).
40. *Discourses* 1: 9 (G 217–19). See also 1: 17 (G 40); 3: 1 (G 420–21).
41. Niccolò Machiavelli, *The Art of War*, bk. 1 (G 577).
42. *Prince*, ch. 19 (G 68–69); *Discourses* 3: 6 (G 435–36).

over, with the crucial distinction between cities that originate "with free men" and those that originate with men "who depend on others." Those that have "a free beginning, without depending on anyone" are likely to succeed; those with dependent beginnings have difficulty ever getting out from "under the control of others."[43]

A closely related theme, appearing in many of Machiavelli's works and occupying much of his practical energy while he was in office, is the citizen militia, which enables a state to rely only on "its own arms." As the biblical David discovered in trying on the armor of King Saul, the "armor of another" will not let a man "make good use of" his strength, for it never fits him right.[44] A prince cannot succeed without an army of his own, for "being disarmed . . . makes you contemptible," and using a foreign or mercenary army, like having a powerful ally, puts you in the hands of others.[45] Indeed, no one who hopes to succeed can "use as a foundation forces other than" his own, and his "own forces can be organized in no other way than in a citizen army."[46]

But the theme of autonomy is not confined to Machiavelli's military and political advice. It is equally evident in his own intellectual stance. Trust, the intellectual form of dependence, is also a sign of weakness and a cause of failure; strength comes from doubt, skepticism, the refusal to be taken in by appearances. Only a child or a fool trusts in the conventional surface of things; it is always safer to assume the worst. Thus a legislator who wants to found a state on the basis of virtue and good laws should begin by assuming "that all men are evil," and that even when they seem to be good, this must be due to some "hidden cause" to be discovered later.[47] Only then will the legislator be protected against disappointment. Machiavelli's comedies, too, are intended to teach the dangers of trust, to reveal "*la poca fede di tutti li uomini.*"[48] As one of the characters in *Clizia* remarks, "there would be no deceit if there were no trust"; it is the victim's own fault if he is taken in, for naiveté invites exploitation.[49] Thus, it is wise to take nothing on faith and to question everything anew. "I do not intend that any authority should move me without reason," Machiavelli writes to a friend; and in

43. *Discourses* 1: 1 (G 193, 195); 1: 49 (G 296).

44. *Prince*, ch. 13 (G 53).

45. Ibid. (G 51); Machiavelli, *Prince*, tr. Ricci, 53 (the Ricci translation of the second passage seems better); cf. G 55 and Machiavelli, *Opere* 1: 62.

46. *Art of War*, bk. 1 (G 587).

47. *Discourses* 1: 3 (G 201).

48. Niccolò Machiavelli, *Clizia*, prologue (*Opere* 8: 117).

49. Martin Fleischer, "Trust and Deceit in Machiavelli's Comedies," *Journal of the History of Ideas* 27 (1966): 373. Fleischer's translation of the passage in *Clizia*, act 3, sc. 7, seems more accurate than Gilbert's (G 846); cf. Machiavelli, *Opere* 8: 145.

the *Discourses*, he claims that "it is well to reason about everything."[50]
It is no "sin" for a man "to defend any opinion with arguments" rather
than relying on either "authority" or "force."[51]

Triumph in war and realpolitik, honor and liberty in civic life, independent critical thought and manliness in personal relationships are all
bound up together in autonomy; they coincide and require one another.
Yet, depending on how these concepts are understood, they may also
conflict with one another. If personal autonomy is construed as either
sovereign solitude or cynical distrust, for instance, it becomes incompatible with the mutuality of citizenship and thus undermines community autonomy; and an individual has great trouble surviving, let alone
being autonomous, without a reasonably stable and peaceful community. But the alternative understanding of autonomy, in terms of mutuality and interdependence, is problematic as well. The origins of autonomy and its relationship to dependence are mysterious, and they invite
endless theoretical reflection.

Finally, the concern for autonomy is clearly reflected in Machiavelli's
activism, his constant effort to move men out of resignation and apathy
into energetic effort. "He who does not act when he has time, then re-
pents and prays in vain."[52] Those who "decay in laziness" invite destruction; the only safety lies in timely, energetic movement.[53] Resignation is self-fulfilling; God helps those who help themselves.[54] It is in
principle better to act even if no favorable consequences are to be expected, because there is more at stake than the consequences of any particular action—namely, an active, autonomous stance toward life. As
Machiavelli writes to a friend, quoting Boccaccio, "It is better to act
and repent than not to act and repent."[55] The context of the remark is
sexual rather than political, yet it could serve as an emblem of Machiavelli's political teaching, for autonomy is intertwined with manhood. Dependence is characteristic of women, children, and animals;
for men it is despicable and fatally dangerous.

50. Letter to [Vettori, 29 April 1513] (G 906); *Discourses* 1: 18 (G 240). But of course
some topics turn out to be too delicate to write about, if not to reason about: e.g., *Prince*,
ch. 6 (G 25); ch. 10 (G 44); *Discourses* 3: 35 (G 508); Niccolò Machiavelli, "Life of Castruccio Castracani of Lucca" (G 533). Three of these passages concern religion, and the
fourth concerns the difficulties of leading a new and important undertaking. Yet elsewhere Machiavelli writes openly on these themes. Leo Strauss diagnoses conspiratorial
intent to seduce the (half) pious reader into sinful thoughts (*Thoughts on Machiavelli*
[Chicago: University of Chicago Press, 1978]).
51. *Discourses* 1: 58 (G 313–14).
52. Niccolò Machiavelli, "Carnival Song by Lovers and Ladies Without Hope" (G
879).
53. *Art of War*, bk. 7 (G 724).
54. Niccolò Machiavelli, "The [Golden] Ass," ch. 5, lines 124–27 (G 764).
55. Letter to Vettori, 25 February 1513–[1514] (G 941).

PART II

Manhood

CHAPTER TWO

The Fox and the Forefathers

Though his explicit concerns are overwhelmingly political and public, Machiavelli's writings show a persistent preoccupation with manhood. What matters for both security and glory, for both individuals and states, is autonomy; and autonomy constantly refers back to psychic and personal concerns. Beginning with the obvious, Machiavelli's most characteristic, central, and frequently invoked concept is that of *virtù*, a term by no means regularly translatable by "virtue," and certainly not equivalent to virtue in the Christian sense. Though it can sometimes mean virtue, *virtù* tends mostly to connote energy, effectiveness, virtuosity. Burckhardt described it as "a union of force and ability, something that can be summed up by force alone, if by force one means human, not mechanical force: will, and therefore force of ability."[1] The word derives from the Latin *virtus*, and thus from *vir*, which means "man." *Virtù* is thus manliness, those qualities found in a "real man." Furthermore, if *virtù* is Machiavelli's favorite quality, *effeminato* (effeminate) is one of his most frequent and scathing epithets. Nothing is more contemptible or more dangerous for a man than to be like a woman or, for that matter, a baby or an animal—that is, passive and dependent.

The themes are political and public, yet the imagery in which they are expressed is often personal and sexual. Political, military, and sexual achievement are somehow merged. Political power and military conquest are eroticized, and eros is treated as a matter of conquest and domination. In Machiavelli's plays, love is discussed in the military and political terms of attack and defense, the rousing of troops, and the

---

1. John H. Whitfield, *Machiavelli* (New York: Russell and Russell, 1966), 94, who cites Gentile, who, Whitfield says, was citing Burckhardt.

mastery of states. The city is a woman and the citizens are her lovers. Commentators often see Italy, in the famous last chapter of *The Prince*, as a woman "beaten, despoiled, lacerated, devastated, subject to every sort of barbarous cruelty and arrogance," who will welcome a rescuing prince as "her redeemer," but also as her lover, "with what gratitude, with what tears!"[2] And of course fortune is explicitly called "a woman," favoring the young, bold, and manly, to be confronted with whatever *virtù* a man can muster.

But what does being a man really mean, and how does one go about it? Machiavelli's writings are deeply divided on these questions, presenting conflicting images of manly autonomy. I shall begin by delineating two such images, one founded mainly in his own political experience, the other in his reading and fantasy about the ancient world: "the fox" and "the forefathers."

At the outset of both of his most important political works, Machiavelli ascribes his knowledge to two sources: "lengthy experience with recent matters" and "continual reading of ancient ones."[3] To begin with the former and the vision of manliness to which it gives rise, what can be learned from experience depends of course on the nature of that experience (just as what can be learned from reading depends on the works read). Machiavelli was a public servant, for fifteen years second chancellor to the city of Florence, and thus secretary and factotum to those who governed the city, particularly with respect to foreign affairs. This meant both that he did their paperwork, drafted decrees and documents, and kept records, and that he traveled as a diplomat—observing, negotiating, making arrangements, and sending home dispatches and reports. Machiavelli's own experience of political life was not of election campaigns, or of budgeting negotiations, legislative committee work, or deliberation in the *polis* marketplace. He was a counselor and servant to those in power at home, an observer and negotiator at the courts of the powerful abroad.

Thus Machiavelli was always in but not of the world of power, an insider and yet an underling. This was his professional world. He did what could and had to be done under the circumstances, and he did it well, but the circumstances were difficult. He was a low-ranking diplomat, never an ambassador. Full ambassadors at that time were men of higher social standing and greater wealth than Machiavelli, men "of

2. *Prince*, ch. 26 (G 96): cf. G 93. Machiavelli does not, however, explicitly call Italy a woman; use of the feminine pronoun in English is of course the translator's choice.
3. Ibid., dedication (G 10); *Discourses*, dedication (G 188).

sufficient birth to impress foreign governments, and enough wealth to supplement their meagre allowances."[4]

Often Machiavelli was second in command on his diplomatic missions, and even where his skill made the mission successful, the credit went to others.[5] Diplomatic agents of such lesser rank were not welcomed or feted like ambassadors, but were "regarded as spies, tolerated because they were accredited representatives of their government, but cold-shouldered by the court and forced to pester and bribe their way to information."[6]

Machiavelli's diplomatic correspondence vividly reflects the difficulties of this role. He continually pleads for the money he needs to do his job right, for sufficient authority to make decisions, or simply for someone of higher rank to replace him. In 1502, already an experienced diplomat, he writes that he "would not be and am not sufficient" to the task he has been assigned,

on account of the need for a man with more discretion, more reputation than I have, and who understands the world better. I have all the time believed that it would be a good thing to send here an ambassador—which would have gained as much from this Lord in all the things that needed to be dealt with as any other means that could have been used.

And he adds—one imagines with great sadness—that on this point "everybody here thinks the same as I do."[7] When it is not prestige he lacks, it is funds; sometimes there is not even enough money for a courier to carry his dispatches home to Florence.[8] "Courts always include different kinds of busybodies, alert to find out what is going on," and part of the diplomat's job is to cultivate the friendship of such men, if not by outright bribes, then "by pleasing them with banquets and entertainments."[9] This kind of diplomacy costs more than the Florentine government seemed to realize. But Florence could not afford to give him more money; Florence itself was of little power and low rank among the cities of Italy and the nations of Europe.[10] "The French respect only those

---

4. J[ohn] R[igby] Hale, *Machiavelli and Renaissance Italy*. (New York: Collier Books, 1963), 18–19. See also Lauro Martines, *Lawyers and Statecraft in Renaissance Florence* (Princeton: Princeton University Press, 1968), 314.

5. Giuseppe Prezzolini, *Machiavelli* (New York: Farrar, Straus and Giroux, 1967), 149.

6. Hale, *Machiavelli*, 19.

7. Dispatch from the court of Borgia, 14 December 1502 (G 139).

8. Niccolò Machiavelli, *The Historical, Political, and Diplomatic Writings of Niccolò Machiavelli*, ed. Christian E. Detmold (Boston: J. R. Osgood, 1891), 3: 86, cited in Charles Tarlton, *Fortune's Circle* (Chicago: Quadrangle Books, 1970), 43.

9. Letter to Firolami, October 1522 (G 117).

10. Tarlton, *Fortune's Circle*, 43, 40.

who are willing to fight or to pay," Machiavelli wrote to the Florentine government in 1500, "and, since you have shown yourselves incapable of either, they consider you *ser*, zero."[11]

Himself lowly, Machiavelli represented a state low in the diplomatic pecking order. Charles Tarlton sums up Machiavelli's experience,

> He worked in an environment peopled by powerful princes, the nobility, large and wealthy merchant families, and high clergy. In that environment he lacked status and the power and reputation that accompany status. . . . He was always the hireling, the messenger . . . he was forced to stand by while others acted out the drama of politics.[12]

Yet he was not free to be merely a bystander and observer. It was vital to the interests of Florence and essential to his task that he should produce results in this world of power to which he did not really belong, whose resources he lacked. He was "an onlooker somehow expected to have an effect." Perpetually "at his wit's end to make the most" of whatever means were available to him, he had to accomplish with the resources of his mind and character what others accomplished with "armies, and money, and prestige."[13] His work depended, therefore, on his personal ability to gain intimate, behind-the-scenes access to the great, to see and understand what they were really up to, and to manipulate, cajole, dissemble, flatter, and trick them into doing what he could not force them to do.

Though his experience at home did not depend on manipulation and deceit in the same way, it was equally a matter of service behind the scenes, of access and knowledge far exceeding his power or prestige. Initially probably a protégé of Florence's first chancellor, Machiavelli became the friend and confidant of the city's *gonfaloniere*, its chief executive eventually appointed for life, Piero Soderini. He was sufficiently Soderini's man so that enemies spoke of him as the *gonfaloniere's* "*mannerino*," his lackey or puppet.[14] When the republic was overthrown and the Medici returned to power, Soderini fled from the city, and Machiavelli was removed from office. Forcibly retired to his farm outside Florence, he became a theorist. His exile from the world of history, action, and politics was torture to him. All that he had most valued had collapsed, and he himself was left without any means of sup-

11. Quoted in Ralph Roeder, *The Man of the Renaissance* (Cleveland: World Publishing, 1967), 157.

12. Tarlton, *Fortune's Circle*, 39, 61.

13. Ibid., 39.

14. Roberto Ridolfi, *The Life of Niccolò Machiavelli* (Chicago: University of Chicago Press, 1954), 99. They also suggested that he was illegitimate (Machiavelli, *Opere* 6: 207–8).

port or anything to do, without even access to information, "useless to myself, to my relatives, and to my friends."[15] Nor did this seem likely to change again for the better: "I do not believe I can ever [again] do good to myself or to others."[16] Things could only get worse as the family fortune diminished.

> I shall be one day forced to leave home and hire out as a tutor or a secretary . . . and leave my family here, which could reckon that I am dead, and would get on much better without me, because I am an expense to them.[17]

Personally as well as politically, practically as well as symbolically, Machiavelli had been unmanned. This was the context in which he began to rebuild in theory what had collapsed in practice.

Thus, the frustrations of political exile and idleness were in important ways not new to Machiavelli, but merely intensifications of what he had experienced all along in his professional life. He had known the world in terms of power, action, and history, yet he had perceived himself and those with whom he was identified as bereft of resources other than those of the mind. In his career, as later in his exile, Machiavelli was able to use the latter resources with consummate skill. Considering the difficulties he faced, he had been an excellent and widely praised agent for Florence.[18] For fifteen years this had been his vocation, and it was this complex of inside access and impotence, arrogance and humiliation, that made up the world of his experience.

Within this world, one can discern an ideal that becomes centrally (though not, as will emerge, exclusively) formative of Machiavelli's understanding of politics and autonomy. The ideal is of a manliness aiming not toward the actual, overt rewards of power, but rather toward indirect gratifications: the pleasures of identification with great men, the secret pride of being smarter than they and able to manipulate them. *Ligurio*

One way to make that ideal of manliness accessible is through an examination of Machiavelli's greatest play (and the only one that is entirely original), *Mandragola*. It is a bawdy comedy, whose young hero, Callimaco, has lost his heart to the beautiful Lucretia. Unfortunately, she is already married to a foolish and aged lawyer, Nicia. But Callimaco's friend, Ligurio, invents a plot to help him win Lucretia. The marriage is childless, and Nicia desperately wants a son and heir.

15. Letter to Vernacci, 15 February 1515–[1516] (G 964).
16. Letter to Vettori, 20 December 1514 (G 960).
17. Letter to Vettori, 10 June 1514 (G 945).
18. Ridolfi, *Life*, 56, 59, 77, 97, 108, 230; Sydney Anglo, *Machiavelli: A Dissection* (New York: Harcourt, Brace & World, 1969), 31–32; Orestes Ferrara, *The Private Correspondence of Nicolo Machiavelli* (Baltimore: Johns Hopkins Press, 1929), 103–16.

Ligurio convinces him that his wife will conceive if she drinks a potion of mandrake root, but that the first man to sleep with her after she drinks it will surely die. So Nicia is tricked into letting Callimaco sleep with Lucretia after she drinks the potion. The plot is successful, Lucretia falls in love with Callimaco, and the lovers agree to continue their illicit relationship, and to marry after old Nicia dies. It is a sordid story, without a single really admirable character; yet in the end everyone is, in a sense, better off. Nicia will have an heir, Callimaco and Lucretia have each other. As Ligurio says, contemplating his plan unfolding, "I believe that good is what does good to the largest number, and with which the largest number are pleased." [19]

If one were to select one character in this play with whom Machiavelli might best be identified, the choice seems clear enough. It is not, despite the possible pun on his name, Nicia, nor, as one might conventionally suppose, the hero Callimaco. Instead, it is Ligurio, the author of the plot. Ligurio is an erstwhile "marriage broker" who has fallen on hard times and taken to "begging suppers and dinners"; he has become "a parasite, the darling of Malice." [20] Not only are both Ligurio and Machiavelli authors of the play's plot, and both of them negotiators and go-betweens, but the play's prologue stresses the parallel by identifying the playwright as a man now constrained to "play the servant to such as can wear a better cloak than he," writing comedies only because he "has been cut off from showing other powers with other deeds." Like Ligurio, he is on intimate terms with malice, which was "his earliest art"; he is an expert at "how to find fault" and "does not stand in awe of anybody" in the Italian-speaking world. [21]

The suggestion that *Mandragola* in some ways parallels *The Prince*—with Machiavelli as counselor in the latter resembling Ligurio in the former—has been made repeatedly by Machiavelli scholars. [22] Like Ligurio, Machiavelli seeks to manipulate the prince into seizing power —for both the prince's glory and the good of Italy. If he were to succeed, the prince would get the actual power just as Callimaco gets the girl: poor despoiled Lady Italy as she appears in the last chapter of *The Prince*, eager to receive him so that on her he may father a new state and perpetuate his name. Machiavelli himself is pimp to the union, rearrang-

19. Niccolò Machiavelli, *Mandragola*, act 3, sc. 4 (G 798).
20. Ibid., act 1, sc. 1 (G 781).
21. Ibid., prologue (G 778).
22. For instance, Gilbert, G 775; Theodore A. Sumberg, "*La Mandragola*: An Interpretation," *Journal of Politics* 23 (1961): 338; Mera J. Flaumenhaft, "The Comic Remedy: Machiavelli's 'Mandragola,'" *Interpretation* 7 (1978): 39.

ing present disorder and conflicting desires in a way that leaves all concerned better off; the real credit should be his.

The point, however, is not establishing the parallel between Ligurio and his creator, so much as exploring its meaning and what it can teach about their shared role or character. One might, for instance, pose this naive question: why would someone creating a fantasy imagine himself in a subordinate role rather than that of the hero who gets the girl? At the close of her night with the hero, Lucretia tells him that she loves him, having been tricked into doing what she would never otherwise have consented to do—tricked by "your cleverness, my husband's stupidity, my mother's folly, and my confessor's rascality."[23] But it was not Callimaco's cleverness that won him access to his lady; actually he isn't very bright. Ligurio is the clever one who deserves the credit, and thus the lady's love. Why, then, does he not take her for himself? Why is he content to serve Callimaco?

Or, to put the question in a different way, instead of calling Callimaco the hero, should one not say the play is thoroughly problematic with respect to heroism? Callimaco gets the material reward, and gets the credit in the heroine's eyes, but Ligurio deserves the credit and receives it in the eyes of the audience. Yet Machiavelli also mocks and abuses Ligurio in the play, calling him a parasite and a glutton. It would not be difficult to read *Mandragola* as an Oedipal tale, like a hundred other bedroom farces in which a foolish old husband is cuckolded. The old man is bested by the young man, his wife becomes the young man's lover. In this vein, one might even suggest that the real point of the young man's victory is symbolic rather than physical—the conquest not of Lucretia but of her husband. Such a reading finds support in the fact that the old man is, like the playwright's own father, a lawyer. But is it not remarkable that in Machiavelli's Oedipal tale it takes *two* young men to do the job? It is as if the hero of this play were split into a matched pair, two halves of a hero, each incomplete without the other: the clever but somehow sexless adviser, agent of the victory, and the physically virile but rather dull advisee. Indeed, Ligurio tells Callimaco that they are (figuratively) of one blood, twins.[24] Is such splitting the price paid for an Oedipal victory in Machiavelli's world?

Perhaps such speculations seem irrelevant and excessively psychological. The more precise question of why Ligurio might be content to serve Callimaco instead of furthering his own cause is addressed explicitly

23. *Mandragola*, act 5, sc. 4 (G 819).
24. "Your blood is in accord with mine" (Machiavelli, *Opere* 8: 67).

within the play. Callimaco's trustworthy servant, wise in the ways of underlings, warns his master about the danger of trusting a shifty, greedy character like Ligurio:

Watch out that he doesn't trick you; these gluttons usually aren't very reliable.

So Callimaco clumsily confronts Ligurio with the question, simultaneously threatening Ligurio and trying to reassure himself:

I know that such as you live by cheating men. Yet I believe I can't be counted among your dupes, for if you did cheat me and I found it out, I'd try to get revenge for it, and at once you'd lose the use of my house and the hope of getting what I've promised you in the future.[25]

Again, one can draw parallels to *The Prince*, where Machiavelli advises princes to keep their counselors loyal by rewarding their greed—giving them their "share of honors and offices" and sufficient wealth to make them "wish no more riches."[26] But if greed for wealth or public honor were the motive, it is not clear why a really clever and ambitious counselor should accept any limit on either. Ligurio, however, is quick to reassure Callimaco:

Don't be afraid that I'm not reliable, because even if there weren't as much profit in the business as I think and hope, you and I have a natural affinity, and I want you to carry out your wish almost as much as you want to yourself.[27]

Ligurio does not seem to be speaking of friendship here, so much as of the kind of identification that a servant or adviser may feel with his master, in which his own prestige is enhanced by his master's and his master's success perceived as his own. What Ligurio does not mention is the pleasures of spinning a plot and manipulating and deploying people in accord with it—the gratification of outsmarting all the others.

Despite the disparaging things said in *Mandragola* about Ligurio, he represents a character type, a pattern of skill and achievement that is familiar and much admired in Machiavelli's world. It is a pattern characteristic of Machiavelli himself in important ways, though never exhausting his aims and ideals as a man. To make this suggestion more plausible, we might tentatively revive the old cliché of national character, as it is treated, for instance, in John Clarke Adams and Paulo Barile's *The Government of Republican Italy*.[28] Opening, as many such

25. *Mandragola*, act 1, sc. 1 (G 781).
26. *Prince*, ch. 22 (G 85–86).
27. *Mandragola*, act 1, sc. 1 (G 781). On translation of this passage see Flaumenhaft, "Comic Remedy," 39; Machiavelli, *Opere* 8: 67.
28. John Clarke Adams and Paulo Barile, *The Government of Republican Italy*, 3d ed. (Boston: Houghton Mifflin, 1972). Machiavelli himself remarks that people vary "accord-

texts do, with sections on the Italian land and people, it then lists as one of the "main characteristics of the Mediterranean culture . . . an inordinate desire to be a '*furbo*' coupled with an obsessive fear of being '*fesso*.'"[29] *Furbo* is described as "an untranslatable word," characterizing Renard the Fox in medieval French stories and Jeha in Arab tales, and meaning something like "skill in employing ruses that are usually, but not necessarily, dishonest." In such a culture, everybody wants to be outstandingly *furbo*, and a man may be scrupulously moral in his relations with family and friends, yet take pride in his ability to cheat someone outside his intimate circle or, better still, to defraud an organization or public agency.

In *Cristo se è fermato a Eboli* Carlo Levi tells of a highly respected man in a hamlet in southern Italy whose prestige came from the fact that he was living off a pension acquired dishonestly from the United States government. The basis of his prestige was not his relative wealth but that he was *furbo* enough to cheat so powerful an institution as the United States government.

Even small trickery can be a source of pride if it is done with particular skill or against a worthy opponent. "A *furbo* often gets more satisfaction out of taking an unfair advantage in a single business deal than from making an honest profit in a series of deals with the same man."[30]

The counterpart of the desire to be *furbo* is the fear—perfectly reasonable in a society where each is trying to outfox the others—of being a *fesso*: the person whom the *furbo* cheats, someone whose lack of character or ability condemns him to be a victim. The fear of being *fesso*, the textbook adds, "leads to an inordinate amount of mutual suspicion and naturally makes amicable or honest relations . . . exceptional" outside of the immediate family.[31] If such a sociopsychological pattern is indeed characteristic in the Mediterranean area, one would like to know more about when it arose. It is surely not the image we hold of Roman culture, nor of medieval Christianity. Was it nevertheless already there, or did it orginate in late medieval and Renaissance times? Certainly something like the pattern of *furbi* and *fessi* seems an important element of Machiavelli's world.

---

ing to the nature of the training from which the people acquire their manner of life. Future things are also easily known from past ones if a nation has for a long time kept the same habits, being either continuously avaricious or continuously unreliable, or having some other similar vice or virtue." (*Discourses* 3: 43 [G 521]).

29. Adams and Barile, *Government*, 14.
30. Ibid., 15.
31. Ibid.

❖   ❖   ❖

Call him the fox, then, after Renard—this *furbo* who runs the show from behind the scenes through his cleverness; who never himself wins the girl or the glory but takes his pleasure in the secret knowledge of his own surpassing foxiness; and whose pride and skill lie in the ability to deceive without being deceived. Cynic and doubter, nobody's fool, inside dopester, master of maneuver, the fox struggles to survive and even to do good in a world where no one can be trusted. The metaphor of the fox is not central in Machiavelli's writing, though it does appear occasionally. There is a fox among the animals in "The [Golden] Ass," "malicious and annoying" but sufficiently wily so that he has not yet encountered "a net that could catch him."[32] In other works, the fox appears paired with his metaphorical counterpart, the lion. Writing to a friend, Machiavelli cites the parable of the fox who sees a lion for the first time and is "ready to die for fear" but gradually overcomes his initial awe at the beast's overwhelming appearance: "Encountering him a second time he stopped behind a bush to look at him; the third time he spoke to him."[33] And in *The Prince*, the fox appears in the famous passage asserting that a successful prince must know how to fight corrupt men with the weapons of corruption, to fight animals like an animal when necessary. Since a prince must sometimes

> play the animal well, he chooses among the beasts the fox and the lion, because the lion does not protect himself from traps; the fox does not protect himself from the wolves. The prince must be a fox, therefore, to recognize the traps and a lion to frighten the wolves.[34]

Despite this unequivocal recommendation, much of the rest of the book suggests that Machiavelli intends not for the prince to be a fox himself but for him to employ a foxy counselor (Machiavelli himself is available). The fox is the clever one without overt power or glory. He remains inconspicuous.

But images of foxes are not frequent in Machiavelli's writing; let the fox serve simply as *our* metaphor for the pattern of conduct and character described in this chapter, a pattern esteemed and admired in Machiavelli's time and place, and central to his professional activity. That Machiavelli valued his own foxiness, though no doubt ambivalently, is evident in all of his works. Above all, he does not want to be, or to be

32. "[Golden] Ass," ch. 7, lines 31–32 (G 767).
33. Letter to Vettori, 26 August 1513 (G 922).
34. *Prince*, ch. 18 (G 65). See also Niccolò Machiavelli, "First Decennale," lines 448–50 (G 1455).

thought of as, gullible. He is an unmasker and demystifier, one who knows the ways of the world and is not taken in by the surfaces that fool others. He is an inverter of conventions and assumptions, a realist often to the point of cynicism. Never will he be like that "generality of men" who "feed themselves as much on what seems to be as on what is" and are often moved "more by the things that seem than by the things that are." [35]

Against this widespread gullibility, Machiavelli relies on those weapons of the intellect that had sustained him in his career. As an insider, he had come to know the reality of power from up close; he had made his way "up and down so many stairs in this world" as to know the true "nature of every mortal," even those called great. [36] Everyone can see from a distance, but he was one of the few who got close enough to touch with his hands. [37] Most people see from a single point of view and have no perspective on themselves, no awareness of perspective. Machiavelli cultivated against gullibility "the eyes of Argus": he would see not merely through his own eyes but through the "truly many eyes that from Christian princes everywhere I have extracted." [38] That is, he brought to his wide experience among the great an insatiable curiosity and a passion for observation as a way of appropriating their power. Yet it was a matter not merely of external observation but of identification, the capacity to put himself in the place of another and regard the world from that location. He must become the other yet remain himself.

Such plural vision helps a diplomat to foresee what political leaders are likely to do, but it also helps a theorist to understand the nature of politics, and his own task. Politics presupposes human plurality: our conflicting perspectives must constantly be reconciled sufficiently to sustain the common life. [39] Politics provides a major avenue for such reconciliation; where it systematically fails, political theory may be required. Politics fails systematically when people become "corrupt," by which Machiavelli means shortsightedly vengeful in a way that is ultimately destructive of both public life and the self. Unless one had "the eyes of Argus," one is bound in such a "grudging and evil" age to "see bad more quickly than good," and therefore to act in ways that pro-

---

35. *Discourses* 1: 25 (G 252).
36. "[Golden] Ass," ch. 1, lines 103–5 (G 752).
37. *Prince*, ch. 18 (G 67).
38. "Epigrams" (G 1463). Note the grisly metaphor: the fox takes, he does not receive.
39. See Hannah Arendt, "Truth and Politics," in *Philosophy, Politics and Society*, ed. Peter Laslett and W. G. Runciman, 3d series (Oxford: Basil Blackwell, 1969), 115; and *The Human Condition* (Chicago: University of Chicago Press, 1974), 57, 175–76.

mote bad and defeat good.[40] The theorist, understanding the plurality of human perception and the complex relationship between appearance and reality in political life, may be able to provide perspective, a synthetic overview of the whole. One sees the plains best from the mountaintop, but can take in the mountain as a whole only from the plains.[41] The theorist understands that subjects see differently from princes, that the view from "the palace" needs to be supplemented by the view from "the piazza," and perhaps by even more distant views, such as those of antiquity.[42]

Perhaps most important of all, Machiavelli prided himself on a special sort of courage, by which he resisted the temptation to deny or gloss over disagreeable realities and escape to more attractive imaginary worlds. The weak man turns away from harsh reality and is therefore vulnerable to shocks and disappointments; the strong man protects himself against such blows by "taking the world as it really is."[43] Thus, "many who have written about politics have fancied for themselves republics and principalities that have never been seen or known to exist in reality." But Machiavelli would strive always "*andare drietto alla verita effettuale della cosa*," to go straight to the effective reality of the matter.[44] This is the least a city can expect of its diplomatic agents; it is not helped by false optimism or the veiling of facts. Machiavelli would bring to his political theorizing the same capacity he had developed in office: to look fearlessly at the way things really are, and to report what he saw without evasion.

When young, one is told and believes in all kinds of fairy tales. Growing up means finding out how things really work and giving up childish illusions. The truth may be less attractive than fairy tales, but understanding truth is prerequisite to acting effectively in the world. Illusions make one vulnerable, infantile, *fesso*. This had been the fate of Soderini, who had trusted in legal forms and the good intentions of those who were his enemies, thereby bringing down the Florentine Republic, himself, and Machiavelli as well. Machiavelli's epigram on Soderini condemns him by the criteria of the fox:

That night when Piero Soderini died, his spirit went to the mouth of Hell. Pluto roared: "Why to Hell? Silly spirit, go up to Limbo with all the rest of the babies."[45]

40. "[Golden] Ass," ch. 1, lines 97–99 (G 752).
41. *Prince*, dedication (G 10).   42. *Discourses* 1: 27 (G 294).
43. "Tercets on Ambition," lines 1–3 (G 735).
44. *Prince*, ch. 15 (G 57); Machiavelli, *Opere* 1: 65.
45. "Epigrams" (G 1463).

To be naive in politics is to consign yourself and all who depend on you to destruction. Conversely, to know and teach *la verita effettuale*, to unmask hypocrisy and undo naiveté, is beneficial. Comedies, for instance, can benefit rather than merely amuse their audience by exposing the corrupt ways of the world. "It is certainly helpful for anyone, and especially for young men," to be shown the true workings of "avarice," "gluttony," "ambition," "flatteries," "tricks," and "all men's unreliability [*la poca fede di tutti li uomini*]."[46] In his *Florentine Histories*, Machiavelli says that, rather than telling elevating tales of bravery and patriotism, he will describe

the things that happen in this corrupt world . . . with what deceptions, with what tricks and schemes, the princes, the soldiers, the heads of the republics, in order to keep that reputation which they did not deserve, carried on their affairs.

Whereas edifying tales of bravery and patriotism may inspire imitation, the truthful depiction of things that happen in this corrupt world "will kindle [free] spirits to avoid and get rid of present abuses."[47]

But a diplomatic agent must do more than see the real truth behind appearances and report it; he must also be a master of the weapons of the powerless, the most important of which is *fraude*, deception or fraud. The fox not only sees through the deceptions of others, he is himself a consummate deceiver, and these two abilities together are the measure of his manly achievement.

Among the many things which prove what a man is, not the least important is to note how easily he believes what he is told or how cautious he is in feigning what he wishes others to believe: so that whenever a man believes what he should not or feigns badly what he would have others believe, he may be said to be shallow and devoid of all prudence.[48]

The capacity for "fraud and cleverness" is the only reliable weapon by which one can "free himself from . . . all the troubles and evils to which men are subject."[49] And it is of particular importance for a man "placed in humble fortune," for fraud is more powerful than force in helping those of low estate to rise "to great authority." Machiavelli does not believe "that force alone will ever be enough, but fraud alone certainly will [sometimes] be enough."[50] Even mighty and admirable Rome had hum-

---

46. *Clizia*, prologue (G 824); Machiavelli, *Opere* 8: 117.
47. Niccolò Machiavelli, *Florentine Histories* 1: 1 (G 1233).
48. Letter to a Chancellor of Lucca, 1 October 1499, cited in Roeder, *Man*, 143; Machiavelli, *Opere* 6: 49.
49. "Belfagor" (G 870–71).
50. *Discourses* 2: 13 (G 357).

ble beginnings, and forced to use "all methods needed for attaining to greatness . . . did not fail to use this one too."[51]

Other concepts closely related to *fraude* show up frequently in Machiavelli's thought. There is *ingegno*, which means "exceptional wit or inventiveness, cunning, ingenuity." It is related to our word *engineer*, suggesting technical ability. Others include *prudenza*, "prudence or practical reason," and *inganno*, "skill at plotting and deceiving."[52] One of Machiavelli's plays includes a hymn to *inganno*, that high and rare remedy that "takes one out of distress and makes sweet every bitter thing."[53] Brute force may well succeed, and indeed the innovator who neglects to secure its protection (the "unarmed prophet") is sure to fail; yet for the fox, wit is finally the more powerful weapon. "The one who knows best how to play the fox comes out best, but he must understand well how to disguise the animal's nature and must be a great simulator and dissimulator."[54]

An important aspect of foxy cunning, therefore, is the capacity to hide one's intentions, to disparage oneself and flatter others, to "play the fool" or even "pretend idiocy." If a man is powerful enough to act openly against his enemies, that course is "less dangerous and more honorable."[55] But if he lacks the resources for open warfare, he must pretend friendship with the powerful, "praising, speaking, seeing, and doing things contrary to [his] purposes" to please them, adapting himself to their pleasures and preferences.[56]

Here the ambiguities of the ideal of the fox begin to emerge. The fox prides himself on his ability to see the unsavory truth and on the courage to tell it. But he also prides himself on his ability to dissemble. Is there a conflict here? Perhaps not if he is employed as a diplomat for a government of his choice and in a city he loves, for then the world is divided between friends and (potential) enemies. The diplomat must convey *la verita effettuale* to his superiors and deceive enemies abroad. In modern terms, one might say that diplomacy can provide a relatively stable level of gratification for a fox's conflicting psychological needs, which makes possible a "partially sublimated discharge" of drives and impulses and allows a "corresponding reduction in the warding-off ac-

51. Ibid. (G 358).
52. Martin Fleischer, "A Passion for Politics: The Vital Core of the World of Machiavelli," in *Machiavelli and the Nature of Political Thought* (New York: Atheneum, 1972), 134, 138.
53. *Mandragola*, canzone before act 4 (G 804).
54. *Prince*, ch. 18 (G 65); See also "Life of Castruccio," (G 555).
55. *Discourses* 3: 2 (G 423).
56. Ibid. (G 424).

tivities of the ego."[57] That is, when employed as a diplomat for a government he supports, a fox can both unmask and dissemble, know when to do each, and achieve both personal satisfaction and external rewards. And so it may have been for Machiavelli: through his diligence and skill, he supported his dependents and served both the Florentine Republic and his friend and leader.

Yet even then there were ambiguities, for the Florentine Republic was beset with faction and intrigue. Even at home there were always friends and enemies, whether the issue was personal, such as an increase in salary, or public, such as a change in Florentine policy. Always Machiavelli had to think not merely about the facts, but also about how to convey them most efficaciously in order to produce the best policy. Furthermore, he always had to speak in an appropriately indirect and humble tone. "To put your judgment in your own mouth" when writing diplomatic dispatches home can often "be offensive" to your government, Machiavelli explains in a letter to a new ambassador. It is best to use phrases like "prudent men here judge that. . . ."[58] Machiavelli's own dispatches often employ expressions such as "I beg that Your Lordships will not impute this to me for advice or for presumption, but. . . ."[59] When the diplomat's own polity suffers factional conflict, so that the government and city he serves are not a single focus of loyalty but are divided into friends and enemies, and potential friends and enemies, the problem is worse still. Machiavelli's friends in the chancellery repeatedly had to warn him in letters about the machinations against him of his enemies at home, or about someone taking offense at his dispatches.[60]

Ultimately, having perfected the capacity to conceal the self and see through enemy eyes, the fox may be in danger of identifying too fully with an enemy and altogether losing track of his loyalties—and indeed, his real self. This danger might be particularly great if he faces an opponent who is outstanding precisely in the skills of foxiness, tempting him to admiration and identification beyond the proper limits. Something of this sort may well have befallen Machiavelli at the court of Cesare Borgia, that "very skillful dissembler" and enemy of Florence whom he so admired.[61] Ralph Roeder calls Machiavelli's mission to Borgia "mor-

57. Allen B. Wheelis, *The Quest for Identity* (New York: W. W. Norton, 1958), 206.
58. Letter to Girolami, October 1522 (G 118–19).
59. Legation from the court of Borgia, 15 October 1502 (G 127).
60. Machiavelli, *Opere* 6: 191, 207; Roeder, *Man*, 203, 239, 241.
61. "A Description of the Method Used by Duke Valentino in Killing Vitalozzo Vitelli, Oliverotto da Fermo, and Others" (G 165); cf. *Prince*, ch. 7 (G 30–31); Legation from Imola, 13 October 1502 (G 125); Legation from Imola, 20 October 1502 (G 127); Legation from Imola, 3 November 1502 (G 129); Legation from Imola, 20 November 1502

ally the most dangerous . . . of his life."[62] Friends in the chancellery at home had to warn Machiavelli repeatedly to moderate his glowing dispatches about Borgia, lest his own loyalty become suspect.[63]

There exists a copy of a letter of Borgia's to his vassals, copied out in Machiavelli's own handwriting and signed with a painstaking imitation of Borgia's signature. Interpretations of the meaning of this remarkable document vary, but one serious possibility is that suggested by Renzo Sereno: that Machiavelli wrote the letter out because he enjoyed imagining himself as Borgia, a powerful and cruel conqueror rather than a humble civil servant.[64]

The point is not that Machiavelli might have betrayed, or even been tempted to betray Florence in his diplomatic career; he was loyal and devoted in his service. Nor do I mean to speculate about what he might have felt or fantasied, since in the end we cannot know. The real point is that the character of the fox is intrinsically liable to a conflict, an ambivalent tension, between the desires to reveal ruthlessly and to conceal artfully—an ambiguity over the limits of the self and its loyalties.

Once Machiavelli was out of office, his situation must have been even more difficult, both psychologically and in external circumstances. It was now even less clear who was friend and who was enemy; the opportunities for affirming the self by effective action had disappeared; and the psychological conflicts to be handled must have been greatly heightened as frustrations mounted and gratifications dwindled. Who now were the friends to be told the truth, who the enemies to be deceived? Surely the Medici who had overthrown the republic and arrested and tortured him were enemies; yet, now in power, they controlled his access to the resources he needed—not just for himself and his family, but

---

(G 135); Legation from Imola, 26 December 1502 (G 142). Machiavelli's praise of the cruel, hated, and feared Borgia in *The Prince* is a major basis for Garrett Mattingly's contention that the work must be satirical and ironic in intention ("Political Science or Political Satire?" in *Machiavelli, Cynic, Patriot, or Political Scientist?*, ed. De Lamar Jensen [Boston: D. C. Heath, 1960], 103). Yet Machiavelli praises Borgia in much the same way in his private letters, and even in his otherwise thoroughly respectable *Art of War*, the only nonliterary work he published in his own lifetime (Letter to Vettori, 31 January 1514–[1515] [G 962]; *Art of War*, bk. 7 [G 712]). Machiavelli's diplomatic dispatches about Borgia not only shift gradually from early admiration to ultimate contempt as Borgia's fortunes decline, but shift vehemently almost from one day to the next, in a manner very suggestive of ambivalence. And of course Borgia not only was Florence's enemy, but also had made a fool of Machiavelli at an early point in the latter's diplomatic career.
    62. Roeder, *Man*, 179.
    63. Ibid., 203; See also René König, *Niccolò Machiavelli* (Erlenbach-Zürich: Eugen Rentsch, 1941), 164, 179, 186–87.
    64. Renzo Sereno, "A Falsification by Machiavelli," in *Psychoanalysis and History*, ed. Bruce Mazlich (New York: Universal Library, 1971), 108–14.

for whatever good he might hope to accomplish. Soderini, on the other hand, was not just absent and powerless, but also responsible for the present debacle: thus a false friend. Or was he? Perhaps it was Machiavelli's beloved Florence and the republic that were at fault? Or even he himself, who had been adviser to them? Perhaps he had given the wrong advice, or had given the right advice but not in the most persuasive way. Whom could he trust now, and to whom should he tell the truth, when almost anyone might turn out to be an enemy or, alternatively, to be a source of help and employment? And precisely in this situation of ambivalence and frustration, Machiavelli is deprived of the opportunity to do anything effective to help himself or his dependents and former allies. He is desperate for work, not merely as a source of income but as a source of self-respect, in order to distinguish himself from the country bumpkins among whom he must now live—"these lice" with whom he "sink[s] into vulgarity for the whole day."[65] He has become "useless" to everyone, unable to "do good either to myself or to others."[66] If only, he writes to a friend, he could once more be "employed at *something*," if not in behalf of Florence, then in some other cause. In idleness he feels worthless and increasingly uncertain of his own self. He complains of being "sometimes [for] a month together forgetful of my true self."[67] And later he mocks himself:

Quite a while ago I trained myself in such a way that . . . for a long time I have not said what I believed, nor do I ever believe what I say, and if indeed sometimes I do happen to tell the truth, I hide it among so many lies that it is hard to find.[68]

One might almost paraphrase: I hide among so many lies that I am hard to find. I am the consummate *furbo*, adapting to power for my own hidden purposes and those of my side. Yet who is on my side, and who am I?

One thinks of Pico della Mirandola: "Who would not admire this chameleon?" But now the costs of the human capacity for self-fashioning are more in evidence. The mistrustful self, it seems, stands in danger of losing its self altogether. Uncertain of its own identity, it profoundly needs external confirmation from its friends, yet it can never securely define anyone as friend. And it is powerfully tempted to identify pre-

65. Letter to Vettori, 10 December 1513 (G 929).
66. Letter to Vernacci, 15 February 1515–[1516] (G 964); letter to Vettori, 20 December 1514 (G 960).
67. Letter to Vettori, 16 April 1513 (G 902), my italics. The last quotation is Ridolfi's translation (*Life*, 164); cf. G 966; Machiavelli, *Opere* 6: 380.
68. Letter to Guicciardini, 17 May 1521 (G 973).

cisely with its most impressive enemies. "The best remedy that can be used against a design of the enemy is to do willingly what he intends you shall do by force."[69] The remark is lifted out of a rather specialized context, yet Machiavelli there calls it a "general rule"; and it could easily stand as emblem for the danger to the self in foxy cynicism. Though a strategy to achieve manly autonomy, foxiness ends up threatening a loss of self and implying contempt for self. In the name of self-reliance, the fox becomes impotent.

The fox is an underling, and it is characteristic of underlings both to despise and to glorify their masters. They are likely to resent their subordination to "such as can wear a better cloak," and to entertain fantasies of revenge or of displacing the master; but they may also derive gratification from their association with "so great a master," or at least from fantasies of serving some imaginary great master. To be an underling means to endure continual frustration and deprivation, and thus to have continual reason for envy and resentment. The resentment born of frustrated ambition is what makes Ligurio "the darling of Malice," and no doubt it is also what makes "the author" of *Mandragola* so skilled at "finding fault," his "earliest art."[70] But underlings cannot afford too much of such angry feelings, or at least they must learn to contain and disguise them through self-control, and through the safe and indirect devices of humor and wit, paradox and ambiguity.

The device of humor and "playing the fool" can be particularly useful here, as a safe and even rewarding outlet for malice. For the fool, as everyone knows, is exempt from the usual rules of decorum and courtesy; he is not a serious competitor and therefore can say what is forbidden to others: the fool may insult the king and be praised for his wit to boot. Indeed, the court fool's special license is traditionally symbolized by the jester's cap, whose jagged points figure an inverted crown. Machiavelli himself was noted among his friends as a jokester and raconteur, and his writings frequently display a mordant, satirical wit. Commentators often have difficulty deciding when Machiavelli is being serious and when satirical. He himself comments in a letter to a friend by quoting Petrarch: "If sometimes I laugh or sing, I do it because I have just this one way for expressing my anxious sorrow."[71]

Playing the fool, moreover, can lead to better things; it can be a prudent form of self-concealment while one awaits the right time for revenge or even for an open seizure of power. Thus the jester can not only

---

69. *Art of War*, bk. 4 (G 656).
70. *Mandragola*, prologue (G 778).
71. Petrarch, *Cesare poi che*, quoted in letter to Vettori, 16 April 1513 (G 902).

express his anger indirectly in the present, but can also comfort himself with fantasies of later, more direct expressions. Lucius Junius Brutus, who overthrew the Roman kings and established the Roman Republic, was in a position to seize power, Machiavelli says, because earlier he had known how to pretend foolishness. In a rare, direct challenge to Livy, Machiavelli denies that Brutus did this merely to protect himself and his property; from the first, he only played the fool in order "to have more chance for overcoming the king and freeing his country." Those who are "discontented with a prince can learn something" from Brutus's "example."[72] But underlings are often likely to be discontented with their princes or masters, and the foxy jester's role adopted as an expedient can become a way of life. The deceit once reserved for potential enemies can spread, the perimeter of friends contract, until the very self that was hoping to act becomes diffused in its roles and pretenses. The underling may become habituated to the safety and security of his status, captive to his own skills, and permanently resentful.

Themes and fantasies of inversion, of reversing convention or established authority, are pervasive in Machiavelli's work, both in its substantive content and in its style. Again and again he takes up an established form, a conventional assumption, a familiar doctrine, only to reverse it. *The Prince* inverts the moralistic outlook of the medieval "mirror of princes" literature it culminates, teaching the opposite of conventional moral precepts: that apparent kindness can turn out to be cruel, that apparent stinginess in a prince amounts to liberality, that the conventional keeping of faith can be a betrayal of public trust.[73] The passage about the lion and the fox already cited appears to be a similar reversal of a passage in Cicero.[74] More generally, Machiavelli often makes use of Christian themes for his own secular or anti-Christian purposes, speaking of "redemption," "rebirth," "sin," all in transmuted form. Late in his life Machiavelli wrote to a friend that while "on the privy seat" he had imagined a suitable preacher for Florence. Most people, he wrote,

would like a preacher who would show them the road to Paradise, and I should like to find one who would teach them the way to go to the house of the Devil . . . because I believe that the true way of going to Paradise would be to learn the road to Hell in order to avoid it.[75]

72. *Discourses* 3: 2 (G 423).
73. Felix Gilbert, "The Humanist Concept of the Prince and *The Prince* of Machiavelli," *Journal of Modern History* 11 (December 1939): 449–65.
74. John Higginbotham, *Cicero on Moral Obligation* (Berkeley: University of California Press, 1967), 54.
75. Letter to Guicciardini, 17 May 1521 (G 971–72).

The inversion of conventional hierarchies or established rule is also a familiar theme in many of Machiavelli's literary works. In *Belfagor* one finds a kingdom of devils, in "The [Golden] Ass" a kingdom of women ruled by a woman, and in *Mandragola* Ligurio calls Lucretia "fit to rule a kingdom."[76] The rules Machiavelli draws up for a hypothetical "pleasure company" are direct reversals of conventional fashion and manners: no member may tell the truth or speak well of another; the minority is to win in any vote; whoever reveals a secret must do so again within two days or incur "the penalty of always having to do everything backwards"; and none

> is ever to show by external signs the thoughts in his mind; rather the contrary shall be done, and he who best knows how to pretend or to tell lies merits most commendation.[77]

Even more significant, though less obvious, is the role of imitation and inversion in Machiavelli's literary style; he often prefers adapting or reversing an inherited form to following it or creating a new one. Besides *The Prince*, there is his play *Clizia*, essentially a translation of a play by Plautus, though its prologue explicitly reverses the announced theme of the ancient play.[78] *The Art of War* derives its form from Ciceronian dialogue, its content from ancient writers on warfare like Vegetius, yet with a new twist.[79] "The [Golden] Ass" owes its form to Apuleius and Plutarch, and many of its lines play off of Dante. *Mandragola* is probably an inversion of an incident central to Livy's history of Rome. And of course the *Discourses on Livy* themselves take the form of a commentary on an ancient authority, though Machiavelli often uses Livy to prove his own, somewhat different doctrines. It is a thoroughly foxy way of both disguising and presenting the self, promoting its goals from behind another ostensible authority; simultaneously serving and assaulting authority, identifying with the master's power and prestige while scheming to manipulate and use him for one's own purposes. The fox may wish to overthrow authority, but it may never come to that, for he adapts for survival in his situation. Whether or not Machiavelli sometimes imagined himself as Cesare Borgia or Brutus, in his life and in his writing he remained an underling, a go-between who transmitted the ideas and adopted the forms of others for his own purposes—an intellectual Ligurio, as it were.

76. *Mandragola*, act 1, sc. 3 (G 783).
77. Niccolò Machiavelli, "Articles for a Pleasure Company," (G 865–68).
78. *Clizia*, prologue (G 824); Plautus, *Casina*, in *The Comedies of Plautus*, tr. Henry Thomas Riley (London: George Bell and Sons, 1895), 2: 303.
79. Niccolò Machiavelli, *The Art of War*, ed. and tr. Neal Wood (Indianapolis: Bobbs-Merrill, 1965), xx–xxii.

And yet Machiavelli the playwright speaks of Ligurio with contempt. But of course he often speaks of himself with contempt as well, and of those associated with him, those concerning whom he might want to say "we": we Florentines, we Italians, we modern men. "The present age in every way is degenerate," he says, over and over; the Italians have become the "scorn of the world."[80] Machiavelli surveys Europe in 1513 and concludes:

We have a Pope who is wise, and therefore serious and cautious; an Emperor unstable and fickle; a King of France inclined to anger and timid; a King of Spain stingy and avaricious; a King of England rich, fiery, eager for glory; the Swiss brutal, victorious and arrogant; we in Italy poor, ambitious, cowardly.[81]

I and my kind—we are poor, ambitious, cowardly. Perhaps it is only an objective assessment in a list that is, after all, flattering to hardly any European nation. But perhaps it is also a scornful self-assessment by a fox in a world of foxes; as Hale has suggested, Machiavelli's letters indicate "some core of reserve, some disappointment or self-disgust."[82]

If a person, an action, or a pattern of character seems contemptible, that implies the existence of some standard against which it has been measured and found wanting. By what standard might Machiavelli have judged his best skill, his pride and delight, as also a source of shame, a sign of degeneracy or a lack of manhood? That standard is found in Machiavelli's second great source of knowledge, his reading, and particularly his reading in ancient works. What his reading of the ancients meant to Machiavelli is powerfully expressed in that letter to a friend already cited, in which he recounts his life on the farm and describes retiring in the evening to his study:

At the door I take off the day's clothing, covered with mud and dust, and put on garments regal and courtly; and reclothed appropriately, I enter the ancient courts of ancient men, where, received by them with affection, I feed on the food which only is mine and which I was born for, where I am not ashamed to speak with them and to ask them for the reason for their actions; and they in their kindness answer me; and for four hours at a time I do not feel boredom, I forget every trouble, I do not dread poverty, I am not frightened by death; entirely I give myself over to them.[83]

What makes Machiavelli worthy to speak with them, of course, is his intelligence and experience, his *furbo* insight into the realities of politi-

80. *Mandragola*, prologue (G 778); *Art of War*, bk. 7 (G 724).
81. Letter to Vettori, 26 August 1513 (G 922).
82. Hale, *Machiavelli*, 16.
83. Letter to Vettori, 10 December 1513 (G 929).

cal affairs. But what almost makes him unworthy, what suggests that perhaps he should be "ashamed to speak to them" and makes of their willingness to answer a "kindness," is not simply that they once held power. Machiavelli would not and did not speak this way about the powerholders of his own time. What suggests the possibility of shame and requires kindness is precisely his corruption, an essential element in the very skill that also makes him worthy. He does not merely know the ways of the fox; he *is* one. Confronting the ancient leaders, he feels like a mere mortal among gods, a clever little fox among real men.

On the basis of what has been said earlier, it may seem that the rival to the fox must be the lion (brawn to brain, Callimaco to Ligurio, prince to counselor, frightening force to inconspicuous cleverness). But though the lion in some ways presents a competing image of character, the lion is not a standard of manhood Machiavelli ever takes seriously, either for himself or for those he admires. Indeed, if one reads the passage about these two beasts in *The Prince* attentively, one sees that they are both juxtaposed to something wholly different in kind. The context of the passage is established by the declaration that "there are two ways of fighting," one appropriate to "animals" and the other "suited to man."[84] At first Machiavelli calls the former fighting "with force," but then he immediately differentiates it to include both the force of the lion and the cunning of the fox. But both together contrast with another, less forceful way of fighting that is suited to man: fighting "according to laws." Though Machiavelli says that success in corrupt times depends on knowing how to "play the parts" of fox and lion, he nevertheless implies that fighting by laws is a superior achievement, suited to our true nature.[85] Thus the real rival to both the lion and the fox is a different sort of world, a world that is not corrupt.

Returning to *Mandragola*, one can now see that Machiavelli has there created a circumscribed world—a world of foxes and their prey, of *furbi* and *fessi*, a world devoid of *virtù*. For that reason, it is a mistake simply to identify *Mandragola* with *The Prince* and both with the whole of Machiavelli's teachings, as some commentators do. In the play, it is true that

the "other person" is constituted in a simple and straighforward way . . . as the means or object of one's desires. . . . The satisfaction of wishes and desires requires power over external objects and other people.

84. *Prince*, ch. 18 (G 64).
85. Ibid., ch. 19 (G 73).

[margin, handwritten:] does this go for all forms of govts? tyrannies?

Social relations in the play are "in essence . . . exploitative."[86] But a world devoid of *virtù* cannot be the political world of Machiavelli's theorizing. He may well have been a fox, but he was not merely a fox. Indeed, the play's prologue says explicitly that the present age is "degenerate" by comparison with "ancient worth [*virtù*]."[87] And it is surely not pure coincidence that the play's heroine, Lucretia, bears the same name as an ancient lady central to the establishment of the Roman Republic, as described by Livy.

The ancient Lucretia, a virtuous wife, kills herself after being raped by one of the sons of the Roman king.[88] Brutus, who had been playing the fool, waiting for his opportunity, uses the occasion to arouse popular indignation against the monarchy, overthrow it, and establish a republic. In both Livy's account and Machiavelli's *Mandragola*, a virtuous wife is sexually conquered. In both, the man who takes her has first heard of her while abroad, in a conversation in which men have boasted competitively about the merits of their women. In both tales, old and formally legitimate authorities that are substantively inadequate are displaced by new, younger, and better ones. Yet nothing could be more different than the two sexual conquests, the two overthrowings of authority, the "virtues" of the ancient and modern world. In *Mandragola*, the violated wife does not kill herself but happily adapts to an adulterous life; is it for that sensible flexibility that Machiavelli (through Ligurio) calls her "wise" and "fit to rule a kingdom"? A fox would surely mock at a conception of virtue that brings a woman to suicide simply because she has been raped under the threat of death and because her husband's efforts to absolve her of blame have failed. Yet the ancient rape of Lucretia led to the transformation of a social world, the birth of a republic of true *virtù*.[89] The modern comic version leads only to the birth of a child, in a world that remains as corrupt as before. Though the cuckolded husband tells Lucretia after her adulterous night that "it's exactly as though you were born a second time," one knows that no regeneration—either Christian or classical—has taken place.[90]

---

86. Fleischer, "Trust," 377, 380.
87. *Mandragola*, prologue (G 778); Machiavelli, *Opere* 8: 58.
88. Titus Livius, *The History of Rome*, tr. B. O. Foster, 14 vols. (London: William Heinemann; Cambridge: Harvard University Press, 1967), 1.57.6–1.59.
89. Machiavelli seems contradictory on this point, saying both that "the outrage to Lucrece took their position from the Tarquins" (*Discourses* 3: 26 [G 489]) and that the Tarquins were not driven out because of the rape, but because they "broke the laws of the kingdom and governed tyrannically" (Ibid., 3: 5 [G 427]).
90. *Mandragola*, act 5, sc. 5 (G 819). But cf. p. 136, below.

Mandragola is not a recapitulation of the tale of Lucretia and Brutus in ancient Rome, but a satire on or an inversion of it.

Once again it is ancient Rome that supplies the standard by which modern times and modern people are measured and found wanting. Rome was the culture that invented the concept of *virtus* and best exemplified its pursuit. It was the very model of masculinity and autonomy. As a state, Rome kept itself strong, independent, and healthy; it grew and prospered among states and won its battles. And the Roman citizenry exemplified *virtù* as well, being courageous and public-spirited, and serving in a citizen militia that was sufficiently disciplined and effective to protect their collective autonomy. Here was an uncorrupted community of real men, competent to take care of themselves without being dependent on anyone else, sharing in a fraternal, participatory civic life that made them self-governing. Nor was their public-spiritedness a spineless, deferential uniformity; in their domestic politics, as in their relations abroad, they were strong and manly: fighters. Political conflict—that "fighting by laws" of which only true men are capable—was what made and kept Rome free, healthy, and honorable.

In this respect, Rome stands in marked contrast to modern Florence, where all is weakness and cowardice, privatization and corruption. There is plenty of domestic political conflict, but it is factional, divisive, destructive of power and manliness; it is fighting in the manner of beasts. A world of foxes and their victims is incapable of true manliness or virtuous citizenship, for its members cannot trust each other and cannot genuinely subscribe to any standards or ideals. They are essentially *privatized*—that is, absorbed in their immediate and direct relationships, unable to perceive the larger whole, incapable of sustaining a public, political life. For a public life depends on a living structure of relationships among citizens, relationships that extend beyond the personal and face-to-face to the impersonal, large-scale, and remote.

The point is familiar in the literature of modern social science, in works such as Edward C. Banfield's *The Moral Basis of a Backward Society* (which is concerned specifically with Italy) and Gabriel Almond and Sidney Verba's *The Civic Culture*.[91] Those who take as their rule of life the maximization of private advantage, who conceive of such advantage within a competitive framework, and who think in short-range terms without hope for a different future—such people make poor citizens. Feeling no positive connection between themselves and others out-

91. Edward C. Banfield, *The Moral Basis of a Backward Society* (New York: Free Press, 1958); Gabriel A. Almond and Sidney Verba, *The Civic Culture* (Boston: Little, Brown & Co., 1965).

side their immediate circle, they do not perceive themselves as part of a public. Each strives to win at the expense of others, and even those who are peaceable and well intentioned in such a society must act aggressively or lose out. Politics becomes a zero-sum game where whatever is gained by some must be lost by others; and the only rational defense becomes the preemptive strike. The desire to be *furbo* and the fear of being *fesso* may call forth great expenditures of energy and form a standard of achievement and of masculine maturity, but this desire and fear preclude citizenship in a healthy republic and are therefore incompatible with true *virtù*.

Is there any way to transform such corrupt men into citizens? Where does *virtù* come from? Who can generate manhood? It begins to seem that there is one thing even more admirable and manly than the *virtù* of the Roman Republic and its citizens: the extraordinary generative authority that could create such a state, transforming a world of foxes into one of men of *virtù*. Surely he who can father manhood is the manliest of all. As the Roman citizen out-mans the fox and shows him up as a mere beast, so the creator of Roman citizen manhood out-mans his creatures. A real man is neither an animal nor a child. Thus the fox is doubly disparaged: he can neither be a citizen nor make citizens. And the ultimate measure of manhood seems to be generative authority: the patriarchal power to create manhood.

It will help to recall the special significance that ancient Rome had for Machiavelli's time, and the distinctive character of ancient Roman society, since both are intimately bound up with paternity. The Romans, after all, were not an ideal that Renaissance Italians picked arbitrarily from the catalogue of past greatness. For Machiavelli and his audience, the Romans were literally forefathers. Where Florence stood, the Roman state had once ruled; the ancestors of the men of Florence had been Roman citizens. Rome had founded Florence. To be sure, the questions of exactly who founded Florence, when it was founded, and what relationship the city had to Rome in ancient times are a central and revealing problem for Machiavelli. But the ambiguities and problems arise within an imagery of fathers and children, not as an alternative to this imagery.

Moreover, the character and culture of the ancient Romans were such as to invite this imagery; Rome was the very essence of patriarchy, a society of fathers par excellence. As Hannah Arendt argued, the Romans invented the concept of authority, and that concept can bear its full meaning only in a context like that of ancient Rome, where origins, forefathers, and tradition form the basis of legitimacy. "At the heart of

Roman politics . . . stands the conviction of the sacredness of foundation, in the sense that once something has been founded it remains binding for all future generations."[92] But it was not just any founding that
the Romans considered sacred, as the Greeks had founded new *poleis*
here and there. For Rome, what mattered was the one, unique, unre-
peatable founding, the special beginning of the sacred tradition.

This foundation and the equally un-Greek experience of the sanctity of house
and hearth . . . form the deeply political content of Roman religion. In contrast
to Greece, where piety depended upon the immediately revealed presence of
the gods, here religion literally meant *re-ligare*: to be tied back, obligated to the
enormous, almost superhuman and hence always legendary effort to lay the
foundations, to build the cornerstone, to found for eternity. To be religious
meant to be tied to the past.[93]

The concept of authority originates in that Roman context, from the
Latin verb *augere*, to augment. What is augmented by those in authority is the original, sacred foundation; one becomes an authority by
merging with and furthering that traditional authority. An authority is
someone who is the author of other men's deeds and is himself authored
by still earlier forefathers.

All of the qualities of character central to the Roman table of virtues
had to do with this original, sacred patriarchal founding and its trans-
mission: *pietas*, which we call piety, but which to the Romans meant
reverence for the past and proper submission to ancestors; *gravitas*, the
ability to bear the sacred weight of the past, like armor, with courage
and self-mastery; *dignitas*, a manner worthy of one's task and station;
constantia, to guarantee that one never strays or wavers from the ancient path.[94] All of these together make up Roman *virtus*: that quality of
stern, serious, strong-minded, courageous manliness that despises pleasure and playfulness, cleaving to duty and strenuous effort. With their
strongly patriarchal households and ancestor-oriented religion, this society of soldiers, builders, lawyers, and administrators provides the very
model of significant (fore)fatherhood. Often on the verge of being pompous but never frivolous, perhaps stolid but never petty, they were always a little larger than life. Add to this Roman self-conception the Renaissance glorification of all things ancient, and one begins to see how

92. Hannah Arendt, "What Is Authority?" in *Between Past and Future* (Cleveland:
World Publishing, 1963), 120.
93. Ibid., 121.
94. Ibid.; Maude L. Clarke, *The Roman Mind* (London: Cohen and West, 1956),
16; Cyril Bailey, ed., *The Legacy of Rome* (Oxford: Clarendon Press, 1923), 211–22,
254, 264.

Rome and the ancients might serve as an alternative model of manhood that puts the fox to shame. By comparison with a forefather, a fox is impotent and contemptible; a forefather need not stoop to the weapons of a fox, for he can put his imprint on the world openly and directly.

Yet the model of the forefather is not really a single, coherent image but is deeply divided into two visions of manhood, as much in conflict with each other as with the image of the fox. On the one hand, there is a singular forefather as founder, whose potent generativity transforms beasts into men; on the other hand, there are the forefathers of Roman republican citizenship, the members of a self-governing community who fight by laws. The images differ as much as paternity differs from fraternity, as uniqueness differs from mutuality, as unanimity differs from conflict. It is necessary, then, to look more closely at each of the two models of manhood conflated in the concept of the forefather: the Founder and the Citizen.

CHAPTER THREE

The Founder

Machiavelli reserves his greatest praise for a different style of manhood than that of the fox. I shall call it the manhood of the Founder, using the capital letter to distinguish this image from historical human beings who have founded actual institutions or states. A Founder, as Machiavelli pictures him, is a male figure of superhuman or mythical proportions, who introduces among men something new, good, and sufficiently powerful so that it continues beyond his lifetime on the course he has set. The point is never just getting others to do what you want, but changing them, introducing new patterns of action and of relationship. Such redirection of human affairs is the most challenging task a man can undertake, for nothing is "more difficult to plan or more uncertain of success or more dangerous to carry out than an attempt to introduce new institutions."[1] And to the difficulty and danger of innovation there must be added the problem of making that innovation last. A Founder does not just "rule prudently while he lives" but must "so organize" the institution he rules "that even after he dies it can be maintained."[2] So, for instance, a general who has to "make [his] own army good and well disciplined . . . without doubt deserve[s] much more praise" than one who merely commands troops organized by others.[3] The Founder's achievement increases, however, with the scope of what he introduces: "Among all famous men those are most famous who have been heads and organizers of religions. Next after them are those who have founded either republics or kingdoms." Then come the great

---

1. *Prince*, ch. 6 (G 26). See also *Art of War*, bk. 7 (G 721).
2. *Discourses* 1: 11 (G 226).
3. *Art of War*, bk. 7 (G 722).

military leaders who have "enlarged" their "dominions," and then "men of letters." Not only will men generally praise in accord with such a ranking, but Machiavelli himself judges who is "deserving of" fame accordingly.[4]

Founding, then, means creating something that lasts, but above all something great, an expansion of *virtù*, something directed toward "glory [*gloria*] in the world."[5] In *The Prince*, Machiavelli distinguishes between the mere acquisition of dominion and the earned glory appropriate to Founding; and in the *Discourses* he speaks of the "false glory" that may tempt men to "turn to a tyranny," a form of rule that leaves no lasting order among men and does not transform them for the better.[6] As a Founder deserves glory, so, conversely,

those men are infamous and detestable who have been destroyers of religions, squanderers of kingdoms and republics, enemies of virtue [*inimici delle virtù*], of letters, and of every other art that brings gain and honor to the human race.[7]

The renovation of a state or religion that has become corrupted, the restoration of right order and *virtù*, also seems to be a kind of Founding. Sometimes Machiavelli equates the two; sometimes he suggests that reform is even more difficult than initial Founding among uncorrupted men.[8] There can be no "greater opportunity for glory" than this reshaping of the corrupted.[9]

The Founder or reformer uses his own exceptional *virtù* to generate *virtù* in others, extending his will and his character into the future.[10] In this connection, Machiavelli also uses the word *principio*, which can be variously translated as "beginning," "fundamental principle," or "initial cause." The Founder of an institution is the one who "has been its *principio*," and consequently the degree to which it achieves a "marvellous [*maravigliosa*]" fortune is a function of his *virtù*.[11] A reasonable translation would be that the Founder is the initial cause of the institution, but *principio* at least suggests in addition that he *is* the origin, the basic principle (the Greeks might have said the *arche*), of the order he founds. Thus he lives on in what he has created, attaining a secular im-

4. *Discourses* 1: 10 (G 220).
5. Ibid. (G 223).
6. *Prince*, ch. 8 (G 36); *Discourses* 1: 10 (G 220).
7. *Discourses* 1: 10 (G 220). Note Machiavelli uncharacteristically uses *virtù* in the plural here; Machiavelli, *Opere* 1: 156.
8. *Discourses* 1: 10 (G 223); 1: 11 (G 225).
9. Ibid., 1: 10 (G 223); see also Niccolò Machiavelli, "A Discourse on Remodelling the Government of Florence" (G 114).
10. *Discourses* 1: 11 (G 226).
11. Ibid., 1: 1 (G 193); Machiavelli, *Opere* 1: 127. See also *Discourses* 2: preface (G 322).

mortality. Indeed, Machiavelli did not hesitate to advise a Medici Pope, Leo X, that in the opportunity to renovate the government of Florence, "God" had given him "power and material for making yourself immortal, and for surpassing by far in this way your father's and your grandfather's glory."[12]

The Founder, then, is an unmoved mover, a source of change not the product of earlier changes, a break in the causal chain of history. He stands out almost like a god among men. He is pure source, not product, one who "give[s] laws and do[es] not take them from other men."[13] Indeed, Machiavelli sometimes employs the imagery of craftsmanship and the working of physical objects here. The Founder imposes form on matter, like a sculptor modeling clay.[14] More often, however, he pictures the Founder as working on living men, yet somehow singular and distinct from them. The Founder is the essence of authority in the root Roman sense of that term, an *auctor* who initiates and induces the free actions of others, so that his project becomes what they willingly carry out, even without his enforcing presence.

Like the Romans generally, then, the Founder is the forefather par excellence, embodiment of a generative paternity so potent that it can create lasting masculinity in other men, even in a sense overcoming death. Machiavelli repeatedly employs metaphors of birth and paternity in this connection. He calls the founding of Rome a birth (*nasciamento*); for a corrupt society to be renovated means for it "to be born again" with "many perils and much blood."[15] Despite the imagery of birth in blood, however, no mother appears; it seems the issue is a purely masculine generation, singular paternity.

By itself that odd fact seems insignificant, but it is one in a series of paradoxes connected with the Founder image. That image is problematic in ways that the image of the fox is not. The foxy ideal can also be a real character type, a way of life; but the Founder is a fantasy projected by Machiavelli's imagination from his reading about ancient Rome. Though stimulated by the practical problems of Florentine politics, that fantasy was never lived, nor was it meant to be. So the difficulties of the Founder image are logical problems for the interpreter, by contrast with the psychological and practical life problems faced by a fox himself.

12. "Discourse on Remodelling" (G. 114).
13. *Art of War*, bk. 2 (G 619). The context makes clear that Machiavelli is talking not about something like sovereignty, which any ruler has, but about a special quality distinguishing some princes from the rest.
14. For instance, *Prince*, ch. 26 (G 92, 94); "Discourse on Remodelling" (G 114); *Discourses* 3: 8 (G 449); *Art of War*, bk. 7 (G 723–24).
15. Machiavelli, *Opere* 1: 125; *Discourses* 1: 17 (G 240).

In brief, the interpretive difficulties surrounding the Founder come to this: the image simultaneously embodies an almost sanctimonious piety and a murderous cruelty, both reverence and mayhem. The Founder's world is abstract and, as already suggested, disembodied, sometimes in the sense of technical artifice that denies the difficulties of human relationships, sometimes in the sense of edifying exhortation that denies passion and animal need; yet Machiavelli also insists that the Founder must be ruthless and concretely terrifying. Although the epitome of fatherhood, the Founder must kill his sons. Indeed, his relationship to both the prior and the next generation of men is highly problematic. Resolution of these paradoxes becomes accessible only after considering the question of women; this chapter merely explores the paradoxes through the texts, taking up, first, autonomy and family murder, then Machiavelli's *Art of War* as the epitome of the world of the Founder, then his extended deliberation on the choice between cruelty and kindness in authority figures.

❖   ❖   ❖

One learns about the Founder primarily from Machiavelli's specific treatment of the exemplary Founders such as Moses, Cyrus, Romulus, Theseus, Aeneas, Lycurgus, and Solon; as well as Alexander the Great, founder of cities and builder of an empire; Numa, founder of the Roman religion; and Brutus, who founded the Roman Republic. Additional information may be extracted—with due caution—from the discussions of other great men and heroes, such as Scipio Africanus, Hiero of Syracuse, and even Cesare Borgia and Castruccio Castracani. Of this last figure, Machiavelli wrote a fictionalized biography, allowing one to identify precisely those points at which myth intrudes or improves on reality in Machiavelli's image of the heroic.

Throughout all the many and complex things Machiavelli has to say about these Founders and heroes, a single theme is fundamental: the Founder's exceptional personal autonomy. He stands out, he stands alone. The first observation made about the four great Founders listed in *The Prince* as "the most admirable"—Moses, Cyrus, Romulus, and Theseus—is that they were self-made men. To the greatest extent humanly possible they were the agents of their own success, owing nothing to chance but the occasion for action, and almost everything to their own abilities and power:

They had from Fortune nothing more than opportunity, which gave them matter into which they could introduce whatever form they chose; and without opportunity, their strength of will [*virtù*] would have been wasted, and without such strength [*virtù*] the opportunity would have been useless.[16]

One can succeed by various combinations of fortune and *virtù*, but "he who depends least on Fortune sustains himself longest." And these men, as it were, reduced the contribution of factors outside themselves to the minimum; they were as personally autonomous as any man could be. Moses, Machiavelli suggests, may have been a special case who, instead of being self-made, owed everything to God. He "should not be discussed, since he was a mere executor of things laid down for him by God"; thus he is not really entitled to credit for his actions, although perhaps "for the grace that made him worthy to speak with God." Whether or not Machiavelli was sincere in this remark, he goes on to say that in any case Moses can be omitted because the other three Founders will serve his purposes well enough: they are "all amazing," and their "actions" and "methods" seem the same as those of Moses "who had so great a teacher." The other three, in any case, succeeded on their own, given only the opportunity to use their *virtù*.

What this opportunity consisted of, moreover, is not what one would conventionally consider good luck—prosperous, happy times—but precisely unusual hardships and obstacles. Thus it was essential for Moses' great act of founding, expressing his *virtù*,

that the people of Israel be in Egypt, enslaved and downtrodden by the Egyptians, so that to escape from bondage they would prepare their minds for following him. . . . It was needful for Cyrus that the Persians be disgusted with the rule of the Medes, and the Medes made soft and effeminate through long peace. It would have been impossible for Theseus to show his ability [*virtù*] if the Athenians had not been scattered.[17]

At the end of *The Prince*, Machiavelli returns to this theme to show the prince the opportunity hidden in Italy's lamentable condition: "More slave than the Hebrews, more servant than the Persians, more scattered than the Athenians."[18] A great man thrives on affliction, and when fortune wants to do him a favor, she "creates enemies for him and has them move against him, in order that he may have opportunity to conquer them and, with the very ladder that his enemies themselves bring him, may climb still higher."[19]

16. *Prince*, ch. 6 (G 25); Machiavelli, *Opere*, 1: 31.
17. *Prince*, ch. 6 (G 25–26); Machiavelli, *Opere* 1: 32.
18. *Prince*, ch. 26 (G 93).
19. Ibid., ch. 20 (G 79); but note this passage concerns a prince, not necessarily a great Founder. See also *Discourses* 2: 29 (G 408) on Rome.

If a man is destined for the utmost greatness, moreover, the afflictions that are his opportunity should commence at the beginning of his life. In opening his essay on Castruccio Castracani, Machiavelli remarks how "wonderful" it is

that all, or the larger part, of those who in this world have done very great things, and who have been excellent among the men of their era, have in their birth and origin been humble and obscure, or at least have been beyond all measure afflicted by Fortune.[20]

One thinks of Moses left in the bullrushes, or Romulus suckled by a wolf; but such an origin was also reported of Cyrus; Hiero of Syracuse was raised by bees; Theseus was abandoned by his father; and the origins of Aeneas are also obscure. Ideally, it seems, if a man is to become a Founder he should be a foundling. The legends, of course, were not invented by Machiavelli; but he stresses them. In listing the various hardships that constitute opportunity for the four great founders, Machiavelli says in *The Prince* that "it was essential" for Romulus not to have lived in Alba, and to have been "exposed at birth, if he was going to be king of Rome and founder of that city as his home."[21] This would have to be the "opportunity" that made Romulus "prosper," as Moses prospered from the Hebrews' enslavement, and Theseus from the Athenians' being scattered. Yet it is difficult to see foundling status as parallel to the other "opportunities," since it is hard to imagine an infant "seizing" such an "opportunity" to exercise its great "*virtù*." One might suppose that Machiavelli means that obscure or humble origins allow a man later, having developed his *virtù*, to claim special greatness. For the passage in *Castruccio* continues:

All of them either have been exposed to wild beasts or have had fathers so humble that, being ashamed of them, they have made themselves out sons of Jove or of some other god.[22]

Obscure origins can be converted to mythical origins by a man of sufficient skill and achievement and thus assist his reputation and power. (It is possible that Machiavelli intended to include Christ in the list, though he carefully avoids specific examples here, explaining that "since many of them are known to everybody," it would be "boring" and "little acceptable to readers" and "superfluous" to name names.) Yet Machiavelli immediately goes on to say the opposite: Fortune afflicts in

20. "Life of Castruccio" (G 533).
21. *Prince*, ch. 6 (G 25).
22. "Life of Castruccio" (G 533).

his infancy a man destined to be great precisely so that his eventual glory will come not from his *virtù* or prudence but from her power, will be set not to his credit but to hers.

I well believe that this comes about because Fortune, wishing to show the world that she—and not Prudence—makes men great, first shows her forces at a time when Prudence can have no share in the matter, but rather everything must be recognized as coming from herself.[23]

But that would mean that even a man's *virtù* is not his own. Does the great man owe "everything" to fortune, then, or "nothing more than opportunity"? And why the ambiguity?

Whatever the answer, clearly the Founder should in no way be dependent on other men. Again and again Machiavelli stresses that the organizer of a society, the renovator or reformer, the great leader, must act alone, owing nothing to others, needing no others.

A man must be alone if he is to organize a republic afresh or remodel her with complete annulment of her old laws. . . . seldom or never is any republic or kingdom organized well from the beginning, or totally made over, without respect for its old laws, except when organized by one man.[24]

With respect to the true, great Founders, Machiavelli explicitly stresses that they must act ruthlessly and shed blood to secure the singularity necessary to their role. Moses, Lycurgus, and Solon were able to "form laws adapted to the common good" only "because they appropriated to themselves sole power."[25] Concerning Moses in particular, anyone "who reads the Bible intelligently" can see that in order "to put his laws and regulations into effect, he was forced to kill countless men."[26] Similarly, King Cleomenes, wanting to reform Sparta, learned from the failure of his predecessor, Agis, "that he could not do this good to his fatherland if he did not become the only one in authority," so he "killed all the Ephors and everyone else who could oppose him."[27] Even more striking and central, however, are Machiavelli's discussions of the two Roman Founders, Romulus and Brutus. In Christian theology at least since Augustine, the story of Romulus's founding of Rome and killing of his twin brother has been symbolic of the sinful nature of all earthly power: Cain killed Abel and founded a city, and Rome similarly originated in fratricide. Accordingly, Machiavelli observes,

23. Ibid., (G 533–34).
24. *Discourses* 1: 9 (G 217–18). See also 1: 10 (G 220); 1: 17 (G 238, 240); 3: 15 (G 468).
25. Ibid., 1: 9 (G 219).
26. Ibid., 3: 30 (G 496).   27. Ibid., 1: 9 (G 219).

Many will perhaps think it a bad example that the founder of a state, such as Romulus, should first have killed his brother, and then have been party to the death of Titus Tatius, the Sabine, who was his partner in authority.[28]

Machiavelli, however, thinks that Romulus did well, did what was necessary to be a Founder. He acted "for the common good and not for his own ambition" and "deserves excuse and not blame" for his fratricide: "Though the deed accuses him, the result should excuse him."[29]

❖ ❖ ❖

It is Brutus, however, whose story defines the ultimate test of necessary ruthlessness: a Founder must kill his own sons. After leading the overthrow of the Tarquin kings and founding the republic, Livy tells us, Brutus was chosen to serve as one of the new consuls. But two of his sons, being related by blood to the Tarquins, were persuaded to take part in a conspiracy to overthrow the republic and restore the monarchy. They were found out and condemned to death, which meant that Brutus, as consul, had to preside over their execution. Livy tells how Brutus watched as his sons were stripped, flogged, and beheaded:

So that he who, of all men, should have been spared the sight of their suffering, was the one whom fate ordained to enforce it. . . . Throughout the pitiful scene all eyes were on the father's face, where a father's anguish was plain to see.[30]

Machiavelli calls the story "striking" and uses it to draw a fundamental political lesson, but a lesson that goes far beyond what would seem to be the story's actual implications.[31] A state that has only recently become "free," Machiavelli says, will inevitably have difficulties because it "makes itself partisan enemies and not partisan friends": those who profited under the previous regime desire to return to it, whereas those who are honored under the free government feel that they are only getting what they deserve and are insufficiently grateful.[32] Now, "if a state wishes to provide against these troubles . . . there is no more powerful remedy, none more effective nor more certain nor more necessary, than to kill the sons of Brutus."[33] What this means, he says, is that anyone who undertakes to found or renovate without securing himself "against those who are enemies to the new government, establishes a short-lived state," and killing is essential to this security.[34] "For he who seizes a tyr-

28. Ibid. (G 217–18).
29. Ibid. (G 218, 220).
30. Livy, *The Early History of Rome*, tr. Aubrey de Sélincourt (Baltimore: Penguin, 1969), 94. Livius, *History* 2.5.3–9.
31. *Discourses* 3: 3 (G 424).
32. Ibid., 1: 16 (G 236).   33. Ibid.   34. Ibid.

anny and does not kill Brutus, and he who sets a state free and does not kill Brutus' sons, maintains himself but a little while."[35]

The lesson that Machiavelli draws thus seems considerably fiercer than the original story. He does not say: be ready to enforce the laws against any conspirator, even your own son. Rather, he says in effect: kill those with strong motives for returning to the previous regime before they have a chance to conspire, and chief among those will be your own sons. Somehow, the true Founder must not only be a foundling, independent of the past and self-made in his origins, but he must also be ruthless toward the future, ready to sacrifice his nearest and dearest for the sake of his founding, ready to sacrifice the immortality of the blood promised through his offspring for that larger and more individual immortality promised through the glory of his founding.

Should one perhaps read Machiavelli's injunctions about the killing of Brutus's sons and Romulus's brother simply as manifestations of the fox's cynical tough-mindedness and desire to expose the harsh realities? Many commentators have so read them; some even take them as an indication of Machiavelli's generally vicious doctrine. Leo Strauss, for example, seeing Machiavelli as a "teacher of evil," takes it as a matter of historical accident that Brutus killed his sons and Romulus his brother rather than some other near relative: what matters is the willingness to murder one's nearest and dearest. "It can only be for lack of a suitable example," he remarks, "that Machiavelli did not apply to parricide what he teaches regarding fratricide" or, presumably, regarding the killing of sons.[36]

Yet Machiavelli is not recommending the murder of sons and brothers in general, nor for just any purpose. The context of the Founder clearly is very special and involves a commitment to values utterly at odds with the cynicism of the fox. The question of parricide, moreover, turns out to be instructive. For Machiavelli did not in fact entirely lack for examples of parricide. Two parricides—one real and one figurative—whom Machiavelli does discuss, Liverotto of Fermo and Giovampagolo Baglioni, he utterly condemns. To Livoretto's murder of both his foster father and his maternal uncle, acts that Machiavelli explicitly calls "parricide," he applies the term *scelleratezza*, variously translated as "wickedness" or "iniquity" or "villainy."[37] It is the same term he used earlier in the same chapter of *The Prince* in relation to Agathocles the Sicilian,

35. Ibid., 3: 3 (G 425).
36. Strauss, *Thoughts*, 9, 258.
37. *Prince*, ch. 8 (G 37); Machiavelli, *Opere* 1: 43; *Machiavelli's The Prince* tr. and ed. Mark Musa (New York: St. Martin's Press, 1964), 71; Machiavelli, *Prince*, tr. Ricci, 33.

who exemplifies wickedness and inhumanity so extreme that even where they succeed they cannot count as *virtù*.[38] To Giovampagolo, "who did not mind being incestuous and an open parricide," Machiavelli applies the term *facinoroso*, variously translated as "vicious" or "criminal."[39] But perhaps these two parricides are condemned not for their deeds but because they used them for petty and selfish ends.[40] Certainly they were not Founders. Strauss, after all, said only that Machiavelli lacked a *suitable* example of parricide.

Yet in all his cynical efforts to shock, in all his advocacy of evil means for good and glorious political ends, Machiavelli never praises parricide. He condemns a ruler too weak to punish "a parricide."[41] And the ideal Founder, being a foundling, has no father whom he might kill, unless his claim to mythical origins is construed as a symbolic parricide. But surveying the Founders and other great heroic figures in Machiavelli's thought, one finds that, far from inclining to parricide, they are in fact characterized by exceptional piety. The Founder saves and protects, rather than slays, his father. Titus Manlius, for instance, whose *virtù* lay in his great capacity for harshness and fierceness used for good ends, and who like Brutus executed his own son in the name of the fatherland, protected his own father. "A very strong man," the sort whose "strong spirit makes him command strong things," Titus Manlius was nevertheless also "devoted to his father and his native city and very respectful to his superiors."[42] When his father was accused of a crime, Manlius forced the accuser to withdraw the charge by threatening to kill him.[43] The same piety toward authority was later manifested in his obedient willingness to kill his own son. Another example is that of Scipio Africanus:

... sent from Heaven, a man divine, such that there never has been and never will be another like him.

When still a youth, in the Tesino this man with his own breast sheltered his father—the first foreshadowing of his happy destiny.[44]

38. *Prince*, ch. 8 (G 35, 36); Machiavelli, *Opere* 1: 40, 41.
39. Machiavelli, *Opere* 1: 195; *Discourses* 1: 27 (G 255); Niccolò Machiavelli, *The Discourses*, ed. Bernard Crick (Harmondsworth: Penguin, 1974), 178.
40. In the case of Giovampagolo, it is clear that Machiavelli condemns his "cowardice" in failing to kill his (spiritual) fathers, the Pope and Cardinals (*Discourses* 1: 27 [G 255]). See also Duke Galeazzo, who "killed" his mother (*Florentine Histories* 7: 33 [G 1379]).
41. *Discourses* 2: 23 (G 390).
42. Ibid., 3: 22 (G 480). See also 1: 11 (G 224); 2: 16 (G 363); 3: 22 (G 479–82); 3: 34 (G 504–6).
43. Ibid., 1: 11 (G 224).
44. Niccolò Machiavelli, "Tercets on Ingratitude or Envy," lines 77–81 (G 742).

Ordinary men, by contrast, lack not only the strength to protect their fathers in youth, but also the piety to care very much if their fathers are killed.[45] Apparently the piety and capacity to save one's own father can somehow serve as signs of the Founder's exceptional personal autonomy. Clearly they are the very opposite of parricide, yet they contrast equally with filial dependence on paternal protection.

A similar point is developed fictionally in Machiavelli's life of Castruccio, a figure whom he explicitly assimilates to Scipio.[46] Castruccio was a foundling raised by adoptive parents. Machiavelli presents him—contrary to historical fact—as never having married and ascribes to him a remarkable deathbed speech explaining why. The speech is addressed to the natural son of Castruccio's adoptive parents, a boy considerably younger than Castruccio. Machiavelli imagines that when the adoptive father died, he consigned his young natural son to Castruccio's care, to be brought up "with the same devotion as [that with which] Castruccio had been brought up," asking that any gratitude Castruccio might feel toward his adoptive father be displayed toward the boy.[47] When Castruccio himself is dying, Machiavelli imagines him telling the boy that he himself refrained from marriage out of gratitude toward his adoptive father, so that the natural son for whom Castruccio was responsible "should have not merely what was left you by your father but also what Fortune and my ability [*virtù*] have gained."[48] Here even a foundling displays filial piety toward his surrogate father and does so specifically by withdrawing from sexual competition, from actual paternity. At the same time Machiavelli presents Castruccio as having numerous illicit sexual relationships with women. It is not from sexuality but from familial procreation that Machiavelli imagines Castruccio as having withdrawn out of filial piety, as if resignation from the "immortality" of name conferred by a legal son and heir were essential to making him eligible for the more individual immortality of earthly glory.

Correspondingly, Machiavelli often says that men who attain greatness through the sponsorship of their strong fathers are weakened thereby. Unless they make extraordinary efforts to overcome this early dependence, they never attain the *virtù* of a self-made man. Sheltered by paternal power, a man does not become able to take care of himself and thus will lose what his father secured for him. Cesare Borgia is a case in point: a man who "gained his position through his father's Fortune, and

45. *Prince*, ch. 17 (G 63).
46. "Life of Castruccio" (G 559; cf. 539). See also *Art of War*, bk. 4 (G 650).
47. "Life of Castruccio" (G 537).
48. Ibid. (G 553); Machiavelli, *Opere* 7: 34.

through her lost it," though his prudence and *virtù* were such that he almost succeeded in keeping what his father had gained for him.[49] In the *Discourses*, after surveying a sequence of Roman emperors, Machiavelli observes that all but one of "the emperors who succeeded to the empire through heredity . . . were bad; those through adoption were all good . . . and when the empire was left to heirs, it went back to confusion."[50]

The Founder must not need or depend on his father; that much is clear. Yet parricide is hardly dependence. Why, then, won't Machiavelli express admiration for it? Certainly the reforming Founders like Brutus are at least spiritually parricides, overthrowing and perhaps literally murdering the previously established authority. Why on this one matter does discretion overcome Machiavelli's general desire to shock and his specific stress on the Founder's ruthlessness? Perhaps the Founder image is incompatible with parricide because it signifies the essence of patriarchy and paternity; but then, why the stress on filicide? Autonomy again seems close to the heart of the matter, but its meaning is different than in the world of the fox. Autonomy no longer implies distrust; indeed, unlimited trust is to be placed in the great Founder. But the price of that trust is something like solipsism: the Founder is the only person, the only free agent among objects. Thus, in one sense, the only problems he faces are technical; yet, in another sense, his tools are fear and inspiration, not normally categories that apply to objects. Autonomy becomes singularity, the unmoved mover.

These puzzling issues are nowhere better brought into focus than in *The Art of War*. If the play *Mandragola* may be said to present the world of the fox, *The Art of War* presents that of the Founder, in all of its paradoxicality. While not about a great Founder, the book does present a singular patriarchal authority engaged in the reintroduction of ancient Roman *virtù*. And though its topic is the technology of death, its tone is hortatory and edifying throughout, presenting a harmonious, courteous world devoid of real conflict, of cynicism, and of humor.

The Art of War was the only prose work Machiavelli chose to publish in his lifetime. It appeared in 1521, and what is known of the context surrounding its creation suggests problems of paternity and patriarchal piety.[51] Machiavelli had by then been in exile from politics for about

49. *Prince*, ch. 7 (G 28).
50. *Discourses* 1: 10 (G 222).
51. Machiavelli, *Art*, ed. and tr. Wood, xviii–xix; Albertini, *Florentinische Staatsbewusstsein*, 31–78; Felix Gilbert, "The Composition and Structure of Machiavelli's *Discorsi*," *Journal of the History of Ideas* 14 (1953): 135–56.

nine years and for several years had been involved with a circle of young patrician humanists who met to discuss philosophy and politics in the gardens of the Rucellai family. That discussion circle had initially been formed two generations earlier by Bernardo Rucellai, a conservative patrician who opposed the republic and Soderini and withdrew from public life when Soderini was made *gonfaloniere* for life. Bernardo's sons shared his political views and were among those active in removing Soderini from power. After Bernardo died in 1512, however, his grandson Cosimo revived the discussion circle, apparently with a more republican orientation, and Machiavelli joined the reorganized group probably about 1516. Among its members were three patrician, humanist friends of Cosimo's: Zanobi Buondelmonti, Battista della Palla, and Luigi Alamanni. They encouraged Machiavelli in his work on the *Discourses*, he may have read parts of that work to the group, and he dedicated it to Cosimo and Zanobi. He dedicated his biography of Castruccio Castracani to Zanobi and Luigi. And while *The Art of War* is dedicated to yet another patrician who had recently done Machiavelli a favor, Cosimo and his three friends appear as characters in the work, which is set in the Rucellai gardens in 1516. Cosimo had died in 1519, and the book opens with a eulogy to his memory, soon followed by an appreciation of the trees planted in the garden by his grandfather Bernardo, the "ancient plantings and shades" that still shelter his heirs.[52] A year after the book's publication, the three young patricians participated in an abortive conspiracy against the Medici, though there is no evidence that Machiavelli himself was involved.[53]

In terms of founding and authority, then, the biographical context of the book's creation is complex. It includes an aging and exiled Machiavelli and a group of young friends who surpass him in class status and wealth but who lack his political experience, so that he is both their teacher and their subordinate. They meet, moreover, in a setting "founded" by a "forefather" who had been hostile to the republic and to Soderini; there they discuss humanist literature, ancient virtue and its revival, and perhaps even (though probably not) republican conspiracy against established Florentine authority. This was, further, a period in which Machiavelli was much concerned with family affairs. His letters reveal his deep distress that his political exile and unemployment left him unable to help his children and a favorite nephew whom he had raised and regarded as a son.[54] Thus there is the possibility that in a per-

52. *Art of War*, bk. 1 (G 568, 570).
53. Albertini, *Florentinische Staatsbewusstsein*, 79.
54. Letters, August 1515 to April 1520 (G 963–70).

sonal sense, too, the book's context was one of concern over generational relations, authority and dependence, the power and impotence of
fathers, all in relation to the vagaries of political life and the fate of
Florence.

In form, the work is a dialogue; in content, a manual of military organization and tactics. Its chief interlocutor, who discourses with the
young patricians in the garden, is another actual figure of Machiavelli's
time, an elderly mercenary general, Fabrizio Colonna, who had fought
for both the Spanish and the French in Italy.[55] In reality he had died
shortly before; in the book he is presented as just passing through Florence and deciding to pay a visit to Cosimo Rucellai.

The book opens with a challenge to the common opinion that military and civilian life are polar opposites, the latter implying civility, the
arts, piety, while the former means brutality, destructiveness, and death.
As a result of this common opinion, good men now "hate soldiering and
avoid association with those who engage in it." The book's annnounced
purpose is "to restore some of the forms of earlier excellence [*virtù*]"
among such men, by showing that a rightly constituted army comple-
ments and protects civility.[56]

The grandfather who planted this sheltering garden, Bernardo Rucellai, was piously imitating the Romans in doing so and is to be piously
honored. Moreover, there are still plenty of humanists like him who
honor and imitate the ancients in philosophy and the arts. What is lacking is the imitation of Roman manliness rather than Roman sensibility.
Fabrizio says, with pious caution,

How much better they would have done (be it said with due respect to all) to
seek to be like the ancients in things strong and rough, not in those delicate and
soft, and in those that are done in the sun, not in the shade.[57]

For in the absence of military *virtù* and strength, all the delicate
achievements of high civilization are left defenseless, as would be "the
rooms of a splendid and kingly palace, even though ornamented with
gems and gold, when, not being roofed over, they have nothing to protect them from the rain."[58] Thus the cultivation of military fierceness is
not an abandonment, but rather a defense of civility and "the arts." He
who revives ancient *virtù* in "things strong and rough" plants (metaphorical) trees that are truly sheltering, "trees beneath whose shade

55. Machiavelli, *Art*, ed. and tr. Wood, xix n. 10.
56. *Art of War*, preface (G 566–67); Machiavelli, *Opere* 2: 326.
57. *Art of War*, bk. 1 (G 570).
58. Ibid., preface (G 566).

mankind lives more prosperously and more happily" than in any garden.[59] Nor, if the army is a citizen militia, can it be a threat to republican political liberty. A republic cannot do better than to arm its people;
a tyrant's first move, by contrast, is to disarm the people "in order to
command them more easily."[60] A republican humanist, then, should
welcome the right form of militarism and the revival of ancient *virtù* in
"things strong and rough."

Besides advocating a citizen militia in general, Fabrizio, the mercenary soldier, explicitly defends the Florentine Republic's militia, despite
its ignominious defeat at Prato, which led to the fall of the republic. We
should never condemn a militia for "having lost once," he says, "but
should believe that just as it loses, so it can conquer."[61] And later in the
book, Fabrizio conjures up and plays out before his audience an entire
imaginary battle, in which their troops easily defeat the enemy.[62] Thus
not only does he defend Machiavelli's pet project, and by implication
Machiavelli himself, against blame for the loss of Florentine freedom;
but in addition this authoritative military figure in effect allows Machiavelli to refight the battle of Prato in his imagination, with more satisfactory results than in reality.

Did Machiavelli feel responsible for the defeat of the Florentine militia he had invented and helped recruit and thus for the fall of the republic? Did the four thousand Florentines who died at Prato in "a
slaughter famous even in a period accustomed to cruelty and ruthlessness" weigh on his mind?[63] We do not know. But *The Art of War* is
framed at the outset and conclusion by the problem of the relative guilt
entailed in action—particularly military action—and in the failure to
act. In the dedication of the work, still speaking in his own *persona*,
Machiavelli says that

> though it is a rash thing to treat material with which one has not dealt profes-
> sionally, nonetheless I do not believe I err in holding with words alone an office
> that many, with greater presumption, have held with actions, because the errors
> I make as I write can without damage to anybody be corrected; but those which
> the others make as they act cannot be recognized except through the ruin of
> their governments.[64]

In the dialogue, when Fabrizio first begins to urge the revival of Roman military *virtù*, he is asked (most respectfully) by one of his young
interlocutors,

59. Ibid., bk. 1 (G 572).   60. Ibid. (G 578).
61. Ibid. (G 585).   62. Ibid., bk. 3 (G 634–35).
63. F. Gilbert, "Machiavelli: The Renaissance," 11.
64. *Art of War*, preface (G 567).

why it is that on one side you condemn those who in their acts do not imitate the ancients, and that on the other, in war, which is your profession and in which you are considered excellent, we do not see that you have used any ancient methods.[65]

Fabrizio responds readily that whereas "men who wish to do anything ought first with all diligence to make preparations," the actual use of these preparations in action depends on the right "occasion." Like the great Founders, Fabrizio is dependent on fortune for his opportunity to act. Since "no occasion has come" for him to demonstrate his preparedness to bring soldiers "back into their ancient courses," he cannot "be censured" by anyone for having failed to do so.[66] He returns to the same theme at the close of the dialogue, again stressing that "nature" and "fortune" deprived him of "the possibility for putting . . . into effect" his ideas. By this time, he adds, he is too old and must rest his hopes in "you who being young and gifted" may be able to act "at the right time, if the things I have said please you."[67] One is reminded of passages in the *Discourses*, where Machiavelli says that fortune has deprived him of the chance to put his teachings into effect himself, and so he theorizes "in order that the minds of the young men who read these writings of mine may reject the present and be prepared to imitate the past, whenever Fortune gives them the opportunity."[68] The world of the Founder honors effective action; only a lack of opportunity can excuse the failure to act.

In other respects, too, *The Art of War* is explicitly activist in its commitments. The book blames Italy's weakness on its leaders' lack of *virtù*, their unwillingness to take the trouble to act, and their ignorance of what to do.[69] Unlike earlier works on military strategy that it otherwise imitates, it stresses the importance of taking action, the centrality of battle to warfare.[70] It repeatedly emphasizes energetic self-help, skill, and discipline to supplement what nature provides. Thus courage based on discipline and training is better than natural courage, a camp secured by artful arrangement better than one naturally well situated.[71]

The book, moreover, is explicitly republican and participatory. Although the concentration of command in a single man is essential to an effective army, because of the military necessities of "sudden decision," even a general should consult advisers to get the benefit of perspectives

65. Ibid., bk. 1 (G 572).   66. Ibid., bk. 1 (G 572–73).
67. Ibid., bk. 7 (G 721, 726).   68. *Discourses*, 2: preface (G 324).
69. *Art of War*, bk. 2 (G 624).
70. F. Gilbert, "Machiavelli: The Renaissance," 6–17, 22.
71. *Art of War*, bk. 1 (G 581), bk. 2 (G 611), bk. 6 (G 679), bk. 7 (G 703, 718).

other than his own. And even a monarch should have "absolute command" only as a military leader in his army; in ruling his kingdom he should do nothing "without consultation."[72] But it is republics, above all, that produce human greatness, for the competition of outstanding men may threaten a monarch, but it can only benefit a republic. Therefore, "excellent men come in larger numbers from republics than from kingdoms, since republics usually honor wisdom and bravery [virtù]; kingdoms fear them."[73] Human excellence is increased, moreover, by plurality and rivalry among states. This was the case, for instance, among the ancient Samnites and Tuscans before the Romans came. But "when the Roman Empire later increased and did away with all the republics and princedoms of Europe . . . competent [virtuosi] men became as few in Europe as in Asia."[74] All virtù was then confined to Rome, which itself soon became corrupt for lack of competitive tension, until there was no excellence left anywhere in the empire. Having "destroyed the competence [virtù] of others," Rome "could not maintain her own."[75]

Thus Machiavelli allows this pious and patriarchal general who actually served the enemies of Florence—France and Spain—in Italy, while ostensibly making a case for the pious imitation of ancient Roman virtù, to argue that the ancient Romans in fact destroyed the virtù of the ancient Tuscans, ancestors of the modern Florentines, and ultimately thereby were responsible for the destruction of all virtù in Europe. What constitutes true piety or imitation here, and what enhances true virtù?

In the very structure of the book, moreover, lies an even greater puzzle. Its substantive message is, as we have seen, activist, military, militant, and republican. Yet the form and style in which these themes are presented convey a very different message: they are ritualized and stylized to the point of presenting a romantic idyll free of all conflict, and they constantly suggest hierarchy, authority, discipline, and self-denial. The form of The Art of War, one might say, is altogether at odds with its manifest content. We should imitate ancient warfare, the book tells us, rather than ancient forms of art; yet it is itself an imitation of ancient literary form in the best humanist tradition, and more strikingly so than any other of Machiavelli's major works. The text lauds the virtues of plurality and conflict, of consultation and competition, except in

72. Ibid., bk. 1 (G 577), bk. 4 (G 658).
73. Ibid., bk. 2 (G 622); Machiavelli, Opere 2: 393.
74. Art of War, bk. 2 (G 623); Machiavelli, Opere 2: 394.
75. Ibid.

military command itself. Yet the general who is its principal speaker and teacher takes no advice, meets no opposition, and learns nothing from the young men with whom he converses. It is not that he commands and masters them with authoritative discipline; he is exquisitely self-effacing and polite. But they defer to him throughout with equal politeness, rarely even questioning, and never challenging what he has to say.[76] Though in form dialogical, the book is in no sense a true dialogue but a mannered monologue, a courtly dance of deference and decorum. The movements of this dance are formed of military metaphors: one of the young men takes "up his duty" as Fabrizio's interlocutor as another lays his "aside"; in so doing they are "imitating good generals."[77] The current interlocutor is said to hold a "command," even a "dictatorship," in which he "tempts fortune" as generals do in battle; the discussion is a series of "struggles where he can be conquered as well as conqueror."[78] Yet there is no evidence of conquest, or even struggle, in this "military" exercise at all. As one of the young men says politely to Fabrizio, "I have allowed myself to be directed [*governare*] up to now; so I am going to allow myself to be in the future."[79]

More broadly one might say that from the opening eulogy of Cosimo and references to his grandfather's respectful imitation of the ancients, the book breathes an atmosphere of piety, submission to authority, order, and discipline. There is no cynical fox sniping at the rules here. Foxy fraud and deception are not entirely absent, for they form part of the general's weaponry against the enemy, but they are strictly contained, the distinction between friend and enemy being beyond question. In the garden of the dialogue all is edifying and hortatory; no cynicism or fraud are admitted.

No doubt all this is appropriate in a book whose central concern is to prove to humanists that good soldiers need not be uncontrollable barbarians on a murderous rampage. Yet it is a stunning contrast to Machiavelli's other works; *The Art of War* contains none of that tough-minded cynicism, that commitment to the unmasking of hypocrisy and convention, found in the other works. It also contains none of Machiavelli's humor, his satirical wit and his gleeful inversion of conventional values; indeed, it contains no humor whatever. Its style strives so hard for gravity that it often verges on pretentiousness. Or, to put it another

---

76. The single partial exception concerns the easy victory Fabrizio achieves in his imaginary battle; bk. 3 (G 636); cf. Machiavelli, *Art*, ed. and tr. Wood, 94.

77. *Art of War*, bk. 6 (G 678).

78. Ibid., bk. 4 (G 648).

79. Ibid., bk. 6 (G 679); Machiavelli, *Opere* 2: 463.

way, there is a romantic innocence about this book on warfare. It is a pastoral of the military life, characterized by what one commentator has rightly called a "Platonic remoteness" from reality.[80]

Once one has noticed this feature in the form and style of the dialogue, it is increasingly apparent in the substance of the argument as well. Not only in its mock dialogue form, but also in its content, *The Art of War* depicts a world free of internal conflict or dissent. That Machiavelli who in the *Discourses* praises "dissension" between people and nobles as the thing that "kept Rome free" is absent from this work.[81] A striking illustration of the difference can be found in Fabrizio's suggestion that troops be made to participate in the punishment of any offenders among them. Fabrizio likens this policy to the ancient Roman institution of "accusations," which Machiavelli also praises in the *Discourses* as a healthy expression of conflict, conducive to liberty.[82] But in the *Discourses*, as in fact in Rome, the institution of accusations involved citizen participation not merely in punishing a condemned criminal, but in charging and judging him. The soldiers in *The Art of War* exercise no independent initiative or judgment at all; they only are forced into complicity in carrying out the judgment of their commander, being thus bound more tightly to him. It is indeed "the *forms* of earlier *virtù*" that are being imitated here, to the detriment of their substance. *The Art of War* enacts a fantasy of perfect military discipline; it might be read as the elaboration of a single, striking sentence in the *Discourses*: "In a well disciplined army *nobody* carries out *any* activity except according to a rule."[83]

The book, moreover, is extraordinarily optimistic. Fabrizio himself teaches that the ancient customs he wants to revive "could easily fit in with our times," being "in harmony with the life of today," so that no one "counted among the leading men of a city would find it difficult to introduce" them.[84] With respect to this sanguine outlook, *The Art of War* is matched only by the exhortations of the last chapter of *The Prince*, where the book's cynical and foxy perspective utterly disappears in a hortatory appeal to the potential Founder.

Besides being devoid of internal conflict, rule-bound, and optimistic, *The Art of War* is pervaded by an almost obsessive technical rationalism. It is on account of this feature that Felix Gilbert calls the book "a

80. F. Gilbert, "Machiavelli: The Renaissance," 19.
81. *Discourses* 1: 4 (G 202).
82. *Art of War*, bk. 6 (G 690–91); *Discourses* 1: 7 (G 211–16); 1: 58 (G 313–18); 3: 8 (G 449–51).
83. *Discourses* 3: 36 (G 510), my italics.
84. *Art of War*, bk. 1 (G 572, 571).

technical exposition of Machiavelli's military ideas" and claims that in Machiavelli's mind, "success in war" depended on "the solution of an intellectual problem"; that his "belief in the supremacy of reason" made it possible for him to discuss military problems "on a scientific basis."[85] Neal Wood similarly argues that the imaginary army Machiavelli depicts is

a supremely rational mechanism. . . . Rational efficiency in terms of the best possible means to the end of victory is the criterion by which all arrangements or kinds of conduct are instituted or permitted to exist.[86]

Wood even argues that this world of technical, rational efficiency, hierarchy of command, and orderly discipline correctly represents Machiavelli's views in other works about "the nature of a well-ordered state and of able civic leadership," that this "rational military order serves as a model for his concept of civil society."[87]

Gilbert and Wood are wrong, I believe, to extrapolate in this way from *The Art of War* to Machiavelli's general views; their characterization of even this book as a whole is questionable, but they have correctly identified a powerful thread that runs through the work. It does present a world devoid of ambiguity and conflict over goals; only the means are at issue, and among these, one can identify technically correct choices.

Certainly the book does contain substantive arguments and advice about various military topics such as the use of artillery or advantageous battle formations. But along with these there are long sections of formal, technical, often quantitative material discussed in minute detail that seem to have only minimal substantive function. Striking in this regard, for instance, is the account in Book 6 of how to construct a military encampment. The camp is described in astonishing detail for many pages, down to the precise width, number, direction, and designation of its streets. Wood calls it "a triumph of functional planning and efficiency," yet the details seem to go far beyond the functionally efficient, as if by getting the technical details right, one could control the bloody and unpredictable realities of war.[88] It is as if Machiavelli felt: if only our generals made the streets in their encampments of precisely the right width and at right angles to each other, we Italians would no

85. F. Gilbert, "Machiavelli: The Renaissance," 23–24. Gilbert says only after the eighteenth century did people once more come to realize "that war is not only a science but also an art" (p. 25). Yet he recognizes that Machiavelli was no technician and named his book "The *Art* of War" (p. 3).
86. Machiavelli, *Art*, ed. and tr. Wood, lxxiii.
87. Ibid., lxxii, lxxv.   88. Ibid., lxxiv.

longer be pillaged and raped and killed by the invaders from northern Europe.

Indeed, this book conveys no sense of the realities of pain and dirt and bloodshed in warfare at all. As the opposition in the dialogue is not real but ritual, so "the enemy" too remains a fiction, safely controlled by Fabrizio's imagination. That is, Fabrizio does imagine his troops engaged in a real battle, and this scene was evidently an innovation of Machiavelli's absent from earlier works on military strategy.[89] Thus one might argue that it is meant to introduce a degree of realism and verisimilitude into the idyll. Yet in the battle scene itself there is no blood, or dust, or noise. "Our" troops kill the enemy "with great . . . safety and ease" and with "much silence," and unlike the enemy they seem to sustain no losses.[90]

One might argue that more generally, too, the book suppresses the physical side of human existence, the body, and sensuality. Women are not merely absent from the dialogue in the garden as from the military world; they are explicitly and vehemently excluded. No women must be allowed in the military camp, for they "make soldiers rebellious and useless."[91] Similarly, it is to be expected that the soldiers will be greedy for loot, so discipline must be imposed to assure that, in the ancient manner, all goods seized "belong to the public."[92] It is a measure of good military discipline and *virtù*, as Fabrizio remarks toward the end of the dialogue, "that a tree full of apples can stand in the middle of the camp and be left untouched, as we read many times happened in ancient armies."[93] The example is borrowed from Frontinus, yet for Machiavelli's time the biblical association must have been almost unavoidable: thanks to its faultless discipline, this army of disembodied virtue may live forever in the garden, without sin or bloodshed, leaving untouched the forbidden fruit.[94] The sensuality of the troops is controlled by discipline, ruthless if necessary; it is not enough to make "good rules . . . if you do not with great severity compel them to be observed."[95] Especially the rules about entering and leaving and guarding the meticulously laid-out encampment, rules that concern the possibility of betrayal to or infiltration by the enemy, "must be harsh and hard and their executor very harsh. The Romans punished with capital punishment. . . ."[96]

89. Ibid., xxi, 92n.
90. *Art of War*, bk. 3 (G 635); but cf. Machiavelli, *Art*, ed. and tr. Wood, 93–94, where one hears "What carnage! How many wounded men!"
91. *Art of War*, bk. 6 (G 691).
92. Ibid., bk. 5 (G 672).   93. Ibid., bk. 7 (G 723).
94. Machiavelli, *Art*, ed. and tr. Wood, 208 n. 42.
95. *Art of War*, bk. 6 (G 689).   96. Ibid.

For Fabrizio himself, however, and his young interlocutors, discipline is internal; they have risen above not only sensuality, but even ceremonies and the arts, to the highest and noblest manly things—virtue and glory. Although they partake of a banquet before they enter the garden to begin their discussion, it does not take up much time, for "in the presence of noble men whose minds are intent on honorable thoughts," banquets and "every sort of festivity" are "concluded quickly."[97] They are "noble" men, ruthless toward the outer enemy; fierce disciplinarians with the lesser folk—cowards and sensualists—who make up their army, and ruthless toward their own sensual impulses as well; yet to each other, courteous, pious, and deferential, facing only technical problems and ritual engagements. It is as fanciful a world of the theorist's imagination as any that Machiavelli as cynical fox elsewhere condemns.

The Art of War, then, is a puzzle to the interpreter. Perhaps the explanation is merely that, this work being intended for actual publication, Machiavelli wanted falsely to present himself in a way he thought would win approval from his intended audience, which respected both military effectiveness and ancient forms and ceremonies. Or perhaps the ambiguities are due to Machiavelli's desire to convince abstracted humanists that they should strive for and honor military effectiveness. Yet the ambiguities run so deep and are so complexly related to those in Machiavelli's other works, that neither of these explanations seems sufficient. Something more and more revelatory is going on. *The Art of War* is complexly ambiguous between piety and murder because the Founder is and must be ambiguous in just this way.

❖   ❖   ❖

This same issue is reflected in a more general and deliberative way in Machiavelli's continuing, unresolved debate with himself over the relative merits of cruelty and kindness in authority figures. No doubt one source of this debate is simply the variety of historical facts about leadership: some great leaders have in fact succeeded through cruelty and others through kindness. But Machiavelli returns to the topic so often, and twists and turns it in so many ways, that it seems more deeply troubling to him than the mere historical facts could explain.

As examples of Founders or leaders who succeed by kindness he cites Cyrus, Scipio Africanus, who "imitated Cyrus," and the Roman generals Valerius Corvinus and Quintius.[98] As examples of cruelty he men-

97. Ibid., bk. 1 (G 569).
98. *Prince*, ch. 14 (G 57); *Discourses*, 3: 19–22 (G 474–83).

tions Hannibal and the Roman generals Titus Manlius Torquatus (who, as has been mentioned, killed his own son for Rome) and Appius Claudius. The Roman general Marcus Furius Camillus is cited on both sides, first as kind and then as cruel.[99] Posing the question whether it is better "to be loved than feared, or the reverse," Machiavelli first responds in *The Prince* that while it is best to be both loved and feared, failing that it is safer to be feared, so long as one avoids being hated. This is said to be particularly true in commanding armies. Hannibal's "well-known inhuman cruelty" is cited with approval, and Scipio, although acknowledged to be "a man unusual . . . in all the record of known events," is criticized for his "too great mercy" that led to a rebellion among his troops.[100]

But when Machiavelli returns to the subject in Book 3 of the *Discourses*, he begins with the opposite proposition: that at least in commanding troops, it is often (not always) better to be kind. He attempts to resolve the apparent contradiction by distinguishing: the crucial variable, he suggests, is the commander's status vis-à-vis his troops. If the soldiers are his comrades and equals, temporarily under his command, he must be kind; but if he is dealing with "subjects," with "the multitude," then harshness is called for.[101] But then Machiavelli returns to a more general praise of kindness in any commander, only to revert once more to the example of Hannibal and the advantages of cruelty and fear. Again he appears to resolve the dilemma, asserting that method does not matter compared with *virtù*: given sufficient *virtù*, either cruelty or kindness will succeed. Here Scipio is considered as successful as Hannibal, despite the rebellion of his troops.[102] But again the resolution fails to settle the question for Machiavelli, and he complains once more of the difficulty of choosing between harshness and kindness. Thereafter he arrives at still a third formula: harshness like that of Manlius Torquatus is best in a republic, for it imposes discipline, can be used to renew public spirit, and cannot even be suspected of currying favor with some faction for private gain. Kindness, by contrast, is profitable to a prince because it will win him the loyalty of the army; such personal loyalty to a commander would be suspect in a republic but is beneficial to a prince. And there the matter is left, except, of course, that this conclusion contradicts both the doctrine of *The Prince*, that it is safer for a prince to be feared than loved, and the doctrine in both works that armies must be harshly governed.

99. *Discourses* 3: 19–22 (G 474–83); 3: 23 (G 484).
100. *Prince*, ch. 17 (G 61–62).   101. *Discourses* 3: 19 (G 474–75).
102. Ibid., 3: 21 (G 478–79).

The contrast between Scipio and Hannibal as symbols of kindness and harshness in leaders is a familiar theme in early Italian humanist literature; but for the humanists, Scipio is the model to be emulated, Hannibal condemned.[103] It seems that Machiavelli meant at least partially to challenge, if not to invert, this ready assumption that conventional virtue is best; yet evidently he also needed its hortatory appeal.

❖   ❖   ❖

In Machiavelli's preoccupation with the fate of Florence, so closely linked to his own fate, the comparison with the ancients was obviously central: why did things work out so differently in the Roman and in the Florentine republics, and how could one reintroduce the ancient achievement among modern Florentines? The task must have seemed overwhelming, almost impossible, both because it was and because Machiavelli could see in his reading of history how effect follows cause, how conditions shape outcomes. It must often have seemed as if, in the words of the old joke about the country fellow trying to give directions, "you can't get there from here." A world of *fessi* and *furbi* is a vicious circle; there seems to be no way to make citizens of them. And yet, Rome had existed, and thus must somehow have come into existence; it was the work of human beings, so human beings are sometimes capable of generating virtue and republican citizenship. But how? The image of the Founder, one might say, is a fantasy solution to this puzzle; the more attractive, the more insoluble the puzzle seems. He is the mythical hero whose magic sword slices through the Gordian knot of historical causation, once more setting men free. The difficulties of conceiving such a role are reflected in the cruelty-kindness meditations.

To his own persistent question of how one transforms *fessi* and *furbi* into citizens, Machiavelli responds that it can only be done by a great man, acting alone. In later centuries an apparently similar question is often posed, and an apparently similar answer given, by the social contract theorists: it takes a singular sovereign to make one civic body out of a plurality of atomized individuals. "It is the unity of the representer, not the unity of the represented, that maketh the person one," says Hobbes, and "unity cannot otherwise be understood in multitude."[104] There may be some admixture of this conceptual point in Machiavelli as well: that only unity can make unity. But for the most part, his out-

103. Aldo S. Bernardo, *Petrarch, Scipio and the "Africa"* (Baltimore: Johns Hopkins Press, 1962), 203.
104. Thomas Hobbes, *Leviathan*, ed. Michael Oakeshott (New York: Collier, 1962), 127.

look and the point of his Founder figure are very different from the social contract theorists' concerns. Their problem is formal, conceptual,
hypothetical, and abstract: how shall we conceive of unity in a multitude? But for Machiavelli the problem is concretely practical and political: what to do about Florence? Yet it is also psychological, particularly
insofar as the practical political problem seems insoluble.

At first it may seem as if Machiavelli, like Hobbes, requires the
Founder to stand alone and singular because isolation means strength,
and the leader's role is to frighten men into conformity. Certainly he
says that among corrupted and privatized men, "some greater force
must of necessity be established, namely a kingly hand that with absolute and surpassing power puts a check on the over-great ambition and
corruption of the powerful."[105] Original Founders as well as renovators
must inspire "terror" and "fear" of the penalty for disobedience.[106] But
unlike Hobbes, Machiavelli seeks to produce not merely obedient, disciplined subjects but men of *virtù*, active citizens. Accordingly, where
Hobbes's sovereign, king of the children of pride, is intended to overcome man's "vainglory," his self-defeating lust for heroics, Machiavelli's
Founder is intended to enhance men's pride and sense of honor, to invite
and encourage them into heroism. Machiavelli has little confidence in
the contractual or utilitarian calculation of rational self-interest; and he
does not wish to fasten narrowly self-interested men, unchanged, into a
new constitutional machinery. So whereas for Hobbes the choice of a
sovereign is essentially arbitrary, the *idea* of sovereignty being what
solves his formal problem, for Machiavelli Founding requires almost superhuman capacities.

For Machiavelli, the Founder must be a heroic figure not merely because of the magnitude of his task, but because of its specifically educational and transformative nature, not merely to frighten but also to inspire. That is one reason why the Founder's extraordinary nature is so
paradoxical. Only the "armed prophet" will win; it is not sufficient to
introduce a new teaching if you cannot protect yourself, gain power,
and enforce it. But neither is it sufficient to seize power and terrify men;
one must be both armed and a prophet. And the qualities required for
the one conflict with those required for the other. The things that one
must do to stay in power among corrupt and evil men, as Machiavelli
remarks apropos Alexander the Great, are horrible; any decent man
would prefer to live a private life "rather than to be a king who brings

105. *Discourses* 1: 55 (G 309). See also 1: 18 (G 243); *Prince*, ch. 6 (G 26); and, concerning the nobility, *Discourses* 1: 3 (G 201).
106. *Discourses* 3: 1 (G 421).

such ruin on men."[107] So decent, good men do not become such rulers; and evil men, conversely, do not transform corruption to *virtù*.

> To reorganize a city for living under good government assumes a good man, and to become a prince of a state by violence assumes an evil man; therefore a good man will seldom attempt to become prince by evil methods, even though his purpose be good; on the other hand a wicked man, when he has become prince, will seldom try to do what is right, for it never will come into his mind to use rightly the authority he has gained wickedly.[108]

But such a passage does not yet make clear the full extent of the paradox. It speaks only to the Founder's motivations: why should a man wicked enough to gain and hold power want to reform his subjects to virtue? There is a deeper problem lodged in Machiavelli's understanding of the educational, transformational task itself. Even if the wicked leader were somehow motivated to use his authority for good ends, he would be unable to do so. For fear can control men only during the ruler's lifetime; it cannot change their character so that his new laws will be obeyed in his absence. Terrifying power, cruelty, harshness, and the fear that they inspire are necessary for transforming men, but not sufficient.

The Founder must also serve as a model for imitation, must inspire admiration, respect, even love, and embody for his subjects the character they are to acquire by following him—a character not of terrifying cruelty, but of genuine virtue. Politically, what this means is that where traditional and legal authority are lacking or have degenerated to empty husks, authority can only be personal; only in their relationship to the inspiring leader can fragmented and factionalized men begin to feel their shared membership, their communality, and find the courage to trust. Psychologically what it means is that changing men's character requires more than force or cunning or power; it requires personal authority. An authority in this sense, as John Schaar has said, "is one whose counsels we seek and trust and whose deeds we strive to imitate and enlarge . . . who starts lines of action which others complete."[109] They complete those lines of action not merely out of fear of his punishment, but because he stimulates, directs, leads, organizes their actions, taking responsibility for the outcome. Significant personal change is difficult and frightening; it always contains an element of risk, as one abandons some aspects of the old self in order to become an unpredicta-

---

107. Ibid., 1: 26 (G 254).
108. Ibid., 1: 18 (G 243).
109. John H. Schaar, *Legitimacy in the Modern State* (New Brunswick and London: Transaction Books, 1981), 26.

bly different person. In this process, such an authority stands security as a guarantor of consequences, assuring those he leads that they will grow rather than diminish as they change. He gives them his word on it; but ultimately it is himself he presents as guarantee, as a model of what they might become; "he shows others the way by going there himself."[110]

It is the same in the renovation of a corrupt state, which must also be the work of a single great man. Barring a renovation precipitated by external attack, that most dangerous alternative, the only hope for a corrupt state lies in the appearance of a "good man who . . . by his example and his virtuous [virtuose] deeds" produces the same effect.[111] Even a renovating law must "be brought to life by the wisdom [virtù]" of some citizen.[112] The renovator must indeed terrify and be prepared to kill, but he must also set an "example . . . so powerful that good men wish to imitate [it]" and even "the wicked are ashamed to live a life contrary to [it]."[113]

The Founder or renovator must also cut into history all at once and alone, yet "one man cannot live so long that he has time enough" to complete the necessary transformation of men's characters; at the minimum it would take someone "of exceedingly long life or two vigorous [virtuose] reigns in succession," which is most unlikely.[114] What, then, is the likelihood of an endless series of such figures? And would such a series of shared founding by many still be Founding, capital F, with all the implications of uniqueness and solitary action the task seems to require? Would the idea of perpetual and shared founding not reveal the Founder to be a myth? Any halfway competent fox should be able to see through it and expose it. Yet in the face of the Roman forefathers, the fox is ashamed.

Behind the relatively realistic, practical problems Machiavelli explicitly explores, of what it might take to rescue a corrupt society like that of Florence from an apparently hopeless political situation, lie more abstract and symbolic difficulties, generated as Machiavelli meditates on the practical problems, reads history, and dreams. Not only is the Founder a fantasy of rescue from insurmountable practical difficulties; he also embodies the idea of founding and therefore is entangled in all the logical difficulties raised by our conceptual system in this region of

110. Ibid.
111. Machiavelli, *Discourses*, ed. Crick, 387; the Walker translation of the passage in 3: 1 seems better than Gilbert's (G 420); cf. Machiavelli, *Opere* 1: 381.
112. *Discourses* 3: 1 (G 420); Machiavelli, *Opere* 1: 381.
113. Ibid., (G 421). See also 3: 22 (G 481).
114. Ibid., 1: 17 (G 240); 1: 20 (G 246); Machiavelli, *Opere* 1: 179, 185.

thought. How is one to understand the idea of something really *new* in human affairs? What will count as new, and where does it come from? If it has a causal antecedent, *is* it really new? In particular, can freedom be created, given, imposed? If not, how does it come to be?

These puzzles push Machiavelli to construe the Founder's autonomy on the model of solitude, as if he were the only creator, the only person, among objects, animals, or children. His task is to make free men of this material. But his means are terror and emulation, and it is not clear that those are suitable to objects or to animals. Nor is it clear whether even children, if they emulate autonomy conceived in *that* way, could ever become free citizens. The Founder must be a foundling, conceptually, because he must be the unmoved mover, his autonomy construed as having no human antecedents. Yet what he must generate in his "sons" is piety toward his initiative. He must be the very opposite of a parricide because he must embody patriarchal piety for them to emulate. And he must slay his sons because if they sought to be fully alive and autonomous following his example, no lasting institution would be constructed by him. For this model, true paternity requires slaying what you generate.

Thus there is still another type of problem, another mode of explanation besides the conceptual or logical: the symbolic or psychological. The Founder's murderous cruelty is both fed and required by the rage of frustrated, hopeless, self-defeating Florentine men, such as Machiavelli himself. They must be punished for that rage, disciplined; they must be rescued from it, protected. Symbolically the Founder is a father, guardian of patriarchy, but a father required to be murderous toward his sons because his task is to guard them and the masculine enterprise against the even fiercer and more terrifying power of the feminine. But those are themes that must wait for later chapters. First comes Machiavelli's third image of manhood, the fraternal Citizen that the Founder is meant to create.

CHAPTER FOUR

The Citizen and His Rivals

As a standard of manhood, the image of the Founder puts that of the fox to shame because of the Founder's capacity to father. Yet that implies that the Founder himself is only a means to Machiavelli's real goal: the new, uncorrupted society to be created. The vision of *that* society provides yet a third model of true manhood for Machiavelli, different from the manliness of both fox and Founder. Call it the image of the fraternal Citizen, and let the capitalization of the word mark the image as an ideal type distinct from actual citizenship in this or that historical society.

The Citizen is Machiavelli's most profound and promising vision and the most political of his images of manhood. It has the potential for synthesizing what is best in his conflicting ideas about autonomy. Yet it is also the most elusive and difficult to reconstruct from the texts. No single work embodies its world, as *Mandragola* presents the world of the fox and *The Art of War* that of the Founder. It has to be constructed from scattered sections and passages, often by implication or contrast with what Machiavelli calls "corruption" or "degeneracy." Yet the edifying vision of the Founder also contrasts with corruption and degeneracy and must nevertheless be distinguished from that of the Citizen.

The manhood of Citizenship is clearly tied to Machiavelli's republicanism, his deep commitment to politics, and his passionate love of Florence. Yet it is an image drawn at least as much from his reading as from his experience, for it concerns a free and healthy collective life such as Florence never experienced in his time, a way of life to which he refers variously as civic, political, and free: a *governo politico* or *governo libero*, a *vivere libera*, *vivere politico*, or *vivere civile*.[1]

Although the Citizen is, like the fox and the Founder, an image of manhood, it embodies *virtù* in a fundamentally different way. For both fox and Founder have *virtù* through their personal, individual autonomy, understood as needing no others, having ties to no others, acting without being acted upon. For the Citizen, by contrast, *virtù* is sharing in a collective autonomy, a collective freedom and glory, yet without loss of individuality. *Virtù* is systemic or relational. Thus it not merely is compatible with, but logically requires, interaction in mutuality with others like oneself. It lies not in isolation from or domination over others, but in the shared taking charge of one's objective connections with them. "Each Man by Himself is Weak," as a chapter title in the *Discourses* announces, but "The Populace [*la plebe*] United is Strong."[2] When individuals realize this, they act together to pursue the shared public good and thereby sustain it. When they perceive as (if they were) isolated individuals, their actions become both selfish and cowardly, for "as soon as each man gets to thinking about his personal danger, he becomes worthless and weak," his *virtù* vanishes; his actions begin to undermine the community and produce his isolation.[3] Citizen *virtù* is thus a matter both of objective activity and of outlook or attitude, each affecting the other. And in both respects, such individual *virtù* is available only in a republic; it presupposes an ethos and an institutional framework. Individuals can achieve only "such excellence [*perfezione*]" as the "way of life [*modo del vivere*]" of their community "permits."[4] A rightly constituted republic, one based "on good laws and good institutions [*ordini*]," one deserving to "be called free," has no need, as "other governments" do, of "the strength and wisdom of one man [*della virtù di uno uomo*] to maintain it."[5] Rather, its institutions will "by themselves stand firm," because "everybody has a hand in them."[6] In the Citizen vision, this is the only way to achieve strength and *virtù*, for "only authority freely given is durable."[7]

---

1. The great frequency with which Machiavelli employs these terms, like the frequency of his use of *virtù*, is inevitably hidden by even the best translation.
2. *Discourses* 1: 57 (G 312); Machiavelli, *Opere* 1: 260.
3. *Discourses* 1: 57 (G 313).
4. Ibid., 3: 31 (G 500); Machiavelli, *Opere* 1: 472.
5. *Florentine Histories* 4: 1 (G 1187); Machiavelli *Opere* 7: 271.
6. "Discourse on Remodelling" (G 115).
7. *Florentine Histories* 2: 34 (G 1125). Public freedom may even be a source of strength beyond *virtù*, as in *Discourses* 1: 43 (G 286).

That a free republic has no need of the *virtù* of one man, however, by
no means implies that it has no need of the *virtù* of individual men. To
say that free institutions sustain themselves is not to deny the role of
Citizen effort. Though relational and systemic, Citizen *virtù* is nevertheless individual and active. It is no mere passive or automatic reflection
of some community attribute, in the sense in which Hobbes later argued
that the subjects of all sovereign states are equally free, no matter what
the form of government, because their state is free in relation to other
states;[8] or as an individual serving, obeying, or formed by a great
Founder might be said to share in the Founder's greatness by association. Citizen participation must be genuine, active, and independent,
with each individual exercising his own judgment and initiative.

Citizen *virtù* is not the product of a uniform solidarity of identification or obedience. Indeed, in the Citizen vision, precisely plurality, competition, diversity, rather than uniformity, are the source of manly
strength. "Where political powers are many, many able men appear;
where such powers are few, few."[9] Thus, where "there are more states,
more strong men rise up." Conversely, as already noted, when Rome
gradually conquered Europe and unified it into a single state, it thereby
diminished the quantity of *virtù* in the region.[10] Within a single state,
similarly, diversity provides resources beyond those of any individual
alone. Success depends on adapting to the times, but no one man can
change his character sufficiently to adapt to all times; the matter is different with a collectivity.

A republic, being able to adapt herself, by means of the diversity among her
body of citizens, to a diversity of temporal conditions better than a prince can,
is of greater duration than a princedom and has good fortune longer.[11]

In a collectivity, moreover, the members can keep an eye on each other,
whether that means looking after each other for mutual protection and
benefit, or checking up on each other to prevent abuses.[12]

Rather than being instilled or imposed from above, in this vision
virtù emanates from below; it is generated by the interaction of the citizens. For example, it is much easier for a virtuous army to produce a
great general from within its ranks, than for a single commander of
however much *virtù* to transform corrupt cowards into an army.[13] Ac-

8. Hobbes, *Leviathan*, 162.
9. *Art of War*, bk. 2 (G 622).   10. Ibid. (G 623).
11. *Discourses* 3: 9 (G 453). See also 1: 20 (G 246).
12. Ibid., 1: 30 (G 261); *Florentine Histories* 7: 1 (G 1337).
13. *Discourses* 3: 13 (G 463).

cordingly, whereas both the image of the fox and that of the Founder imply contempt for, or at least dismissal of, the populace at large— whether as inert matter to be shaped by the leader or as credulous fools to be manipulated by the fox—the Citizen image locates virtue and glory precisely there. Politically,

> a people is more prudent, more stable, and of better judgment than a prince . . . governments by the people are better than those by princes . . . if we consider all the people's faults, all the faults of princes, all the people's glories and all those of princes, the people will appear in goodness and glory far superior.[14]

And, assuming the restraints of law, there is "more worth [*virtù*] in the people than in the prince."[15]

Indeed, while the images of the fox and the Founder imply rule and subordination and construe public life in terms of who dominates whom, the vision of Citizenship stresses mutuality—not a strict equality in all respects, to be sure, but a mutuality of respect and a shared participation among peers, who must take each other into account in the formulation of collective policy. Here Machiavelli comes closest to the ancient Greek conception of free citizenship as meaning "neither to rule nor to be ruled," as contrasting not merely with slavery but equally with slave ownership.[16] Both the image of the fox and that of the Founder are, in these terms, fundamentally nonpolitical, even antipolitical understandings of public life and manhood. They conceive human autonomy in terms of radical isolation and sovereignty, the singular actor manipulating others to achieve goals that are his alone, as if they were inert objects and he the only person, as if of a different species. Whether his isolation is defensive and the purposes selfish, or the isolation a mark of grandeur and the purposes noble, the net result is similar. Mutuality, reciprocity, dialogue, the web of relationships that constitute a public arena and create public power, are missing from both images. In both, politics is understood as domination, whether seen by the fox from below or within, or by the Founder from above or outside. In the Citizen image, by contrast, the essential meaning of political relationships that embody true manliness is, as Machiavelli puts it, "neither arrogantly to dominate nor humbly to serve [*ne superbamente dominare ne umilmente servire*]."[17]

14. Ibid., 1: 58 (G 316–17, see also 314–15).
15. Ibid. (G 317); Machiavelli, *Opere* 1: 265.
16. See, for example, Arendt, *Human Condition*, 32; and Hanna Fenichel Pitkin, "Justice: On Relating Private and Public," *Political Theory* 9 (August 1981), 327–52.
17. *Discourses* 1: 58 (G 314); Machiavelli, *Opere* 1: 262.

❖   ❖   ❖

Citizenship in this sense is thus linked to a kind of equality. But Machiavelli's political sociology, his discussions of class differences and social equality are scattered, sketchy, and difficult to interpret. Sometimes he speaks of societies as divided into three classes, ranks, or sorts of men: the nobles, the "people [il popolo]" or middle class, and "the plebs [la plebe]" or lower class.[18] At other times he distinguishes only two classes or "humors [umori]," the rich or "great [grandi]" and "the people."[19] In Italian as in English the term people is ambiguous, meaning sometimes a particular social class, sometimes the entire membership of society, or all but the singular ruler (as in the passages just quoted in which "the people" are contrasted to "the prince"). Only the nobles or grandi are intrinsically ambitious, crave glory, and desire to dominate others. The people at large intrinsically want only security in their privacy, the absence of oppression.[20]

This much is relatively consistent throughout Machiavelli's works. But it seems to lead him to diametrically opposed conclusions. Sometimes he locates liberty and virtue in the common people and associates it with social and economic equality; at other times he locates it in the ambition of the nobility and thus in class distinctions. In the Discourses he argues that "men of the people" are generally better guardians of liberty in a republic than are the rich or the grandi, because it makes sense to appoint as guardians over anything those "who are least greedy to take possession of it."[21] The people want only "not to be ruled" and consequently "to live in freedom," while the rich and grandi want "to rule." Accordingly, Machiavelli condemns as "dangerous in every republic and in every country" those wealthy nobles or "gentlemen" who do not work but "live in luxury on the returns from their landed possessions."[22] Both the "corruption" of a people and their loss of the "aptitude for free life spring from inequality in a city."[23] The German people, by contrast with the Italians, have maintained "il vivere politico" by preserving "among themselves a complete [pari (peer-ish)] equality."[24] But Tuscany, and Florence in particular, differ from the rest of Italy; in

18. Florentine Histories, preface (G 1032). See also "Discourse on Remodelling" (G 107, 109); Machiavelli, Opere 7: 69.

19. Prince, ch. 9 (G 39); Machiavelli, Prince, tr. and ed. Musa, 76–77.

20. Prince, ch. 9 (G 39); "Discourse on Remodelling" (G 107–8); Discourses 1: 5 (G 204); 1: 16 (G 237); 1: 40 (G 282). Sometimes, however, the grandi are more "ambitious" for wealth than for glory; Discourses 1: 37 (G 274).

21. Discourses 1: 5 (G 204).

22. Ibid., 1: 55 (G 308, cf. 310).   23. Ibid., 1: 17 (G 240).

24. Ibid., 1: 55 (G 308); Machiavelli, Opere 1: 256.

that region there is great potential for "liberty" and "well-regulated government" because, like Germany, it lacks idle "lords of castles" and "gentlemen."[25]

In the *Florentine Histories*, by contrast, Machiavelli condemns the Florentine bourgeoisie precisely for having largely eradicated the city's aristocratic class and forced those few nobles remaining to adopt or pander to the "spirit" and "ways of living" of the common people.[26] This deprived the city of the special ethos a nobility can contribute: their ambition and desire for glory, their "ability [*virtù*] in arms and . . . boldness [*generosita*] of spirit."[27] The Roman Republic fared well because its conflicts always increased social inequality there, while the Florentine Republic did poorly because of ever increasing social equality.[28]

How are such blatant contradictions to be interpreted? Does equality promote or hinder liberty and *virtù*? Is Machiavelli for or against the nobility? Is his position in the *Florentine Histories* a distortion of his real views adopted to please the pope who commissioned that work? This cannot be ruled out, but perhaps one can make substantive sense of what Machiavelli says; perhaps he was trying to say something that is difficult to formulate in a consistent manner. The Citizen image of manhood at least suggests the following possible interpretation.

Each class or grouping in society has its own distinctive perspective, spirit, and way of life; all of these can contribute toward the good of the whole, yet each of them by itself, unmodified, would destroy the *vivere civile* and the *virtù* associated therewith. They all need to be modified in mutual, political deliberation and struggle. The nobles are a threat because, while they honor and desire *virtù*, they tend to construe it wrongly as the domination of others, on analogy with military prowess in the face of an enemy. Such military prowess toward foreign enemies is an essential part of republican virtue, and a contribution the nobles can make to the whole, but it is not the correct understanding of citizen *virtù* in a free state. The common people, by contrast, while they are free of the dangerous ambition to dominate others, tend to be privatized and politically passive; whether from greed or need, they are likely to sell out liberty for security in their private pursuit of material gain. That makes them not only bad soldiers, but bad citizens as well, unless they can be brought to see that public freedom, the *vivere civile*, is necessary to protect private freedom, and to that extent to lift their eyes from

25. *Discourses* 1: 55 (G 309).
26. *Florentine Histories* 3: 1 (G 1141).
27. Ibid.; Machiavelli, *Opere* 7: 213.
28. *Florentine Histories* 3: 1 (G 1140); but cf. 3: 2 (G 1142).

profit to glory. Either class can be a danger to political stability if its intrinsic cravings are outright frustrated, but their mutually transforming political interaction is conducive to stability, as well as to the most widespread correctly understood Citizen *virtù*. This is true both under a prince and in a republic: both should strive to be as inclusive as possible.[29]

A healthy political manhood, then, requires a plurality of classes and perspectives, yet it requires that they interact in a spirit of mutuality, or the necessary modifications of position will not take place. A certain measure of socioeconomic inequality is entirely compatible with this spirit of mutuality, so long as the society does not value wealth and social status too highly or in the wrong way. What is essential is a genuine mutuality of respect rather than equality of wealth and rank. Thus the exemplary Romans knew how "to honor and reward excellence" even among the lower classes; they sought out *virtù* wherever it might be found, so that poverty "did not close your road" to political power. "Evidently" that social ethos made "riches" less desirable and important.[30] Extreme disparities between classes may, however, preclude such mutuality across difference.

If Machiavelli means something like this by the *pari equalita* of Citizens, it is no wonder if he seems to be saying that both equality and inequality are essential. His arguments for equality thus must not be read as a rejection of class differences in favor of outright socioeconomic leveling. Nor should they be read as a rejection of leadership and authority in favor of anarchic spontaneity, although on this topic, too, the texts are ambiguous and problematic. Leadership is necessary even in a free republic, for "A Multitude Without a Head is Helpless."[31] A mob can be "formidable" briefly, in the heat of violence, but cannot sustain the political vision and soon disintegrates again into private isolation. "When their minds are a bit cooled . . . each man sees that he must return to his house," and they begin "to distrust themselves and think of safety either by flight or by treaty."[32] So leadership, far from threatening republicanism, is essential to it.

But how is that claim to be reconciled with the peer equality of Citi-

29. Concerning a prince, *Prince*, ch. 9 (G 39); *Discourses* 1: 16 (G 237). More generally, *Discourses* 3: 7 (G 448); "Discourse on Remodelling" (G 110, 115). Concerning vengeance and violence, *Discourses* 2: 23 (G 389). This reading is suggested by S. M. Shumer, "Machiavelli: Republican Politics and Its Corruption," *Political Theory* 7 (February 1979): 5–34.

30. *Art of War*, bk. 1 (G 572); *Discourses* 3: 25 (G 486).

31. *Discourses* 1: 44 (G 287). Cf. 3: 28 (G 492).

32. Ibid., 1: 57 (G 312–13).

zens? Furthermore, Machiavelli repeatedly speaks with apparent approval of the way skillful leaders manipulate the people. Where that manipulation is directed toward the common good, the borderline between the vision of the Founder and that of the Citizen seems to blur: the people appear like material to be used by the leader. Where the manipulation is directed merely to the leader's own interest, contrary to the common good, the borderline between the vision of the fox and that of the Citizen becomes doubtful, and republics no longer seem different from princedoms or tyrannies.

Machiavelli says clearly, however, that there are two different styles of leadership, only one of which is suitable for relations among republican Citizens. There are two different ways to "govern a multitude . . . the method [*via* (way, road)] of freedom [and] . . . that of a princedom."[33] He does not specify the difference between them, but there are some suggestions in the *Discourses*. In brief, republican authority not only must further the common good (which would be equally true of the Founder), but requires a mutuality between leaders and led. Power is "given" by the "free votes" of the led rather than seized by the leaders and imposed on the led.[34] The people have access to office regardless of wealth or class; so a father knows that if his sons have "abilities [*virtù*] they can become prominent men [*principi*] in the republic."[35] Even those who hold no office can bring public charges against corrupt officials and make public suggestions about policy; and they participate in the making of at least some public decisions after open debate. Where Citizen *virtù* prevails, it is

desirable that each one who thinks of something of benefit to the public should have the right to propose it. And it is good that each one should be permitted to state his opinion on it, in order that the people, having heard each, may choose the better.[36]

Only rarely will the people then fail "to accept the better opinion."[37] Machiavelli by no means claims that the people are always right, and one of the functions of leadership is to restrain them from hasty action when they are wrong.[38] But princes are not always right either; and the people do generally know enough to choose good leaders, making "far better" choices of magistrates "than a prince" does.[39]

---

33. Ibid., 1: 16 (G 236); Machiavelli, *Opere* 1: 174.
34. *Discourses* 1: 34 (G 267).
35. Ibid., 2: 2 (G 322); Machiavelli, *Opere* 1: 284.
36. *Discourses* 1: 18 (G 242). See also 1: 10 (G 222); 3: 28 (G 492–93).
37. Ibid., 1: 58 (G 316).   38. E.g., ibid., 1: 54 (G 305–06); 1: 58 (G 317).
39. Ibid., 1: 58 (G 316).

Finally, republican authority must be exercised in a way that further politicizes the people rather than rendering them quiescent. Its function is precisely to keep a political movement or action that the people have initiated—such as the march of the "multitude" of armed plebs to the Mons Sacer outside Rome that resulted in the establishment of the Tribunes and enhanced liberty—from disintegrating into riot, apathy, or privatization.[40] The common people know "particulars," Machiavelli says; they know their immediate world, they know how to do things in it, they can judge character, they live in the concrete. When it comes to abstraction, to "judging things in general" and at a distance, they may be deceived.[41] The function of republican leadership is to reconnect the abstract generality of policy options and political principles with the lived experience and practical skill of the led. This will "quickly and easily open their eyes" about false generalities; and it will help them see the relationship their own perceived needs bear to the needs of others, to principle, and to the common good.[42]

Machiavelli does say that when a private citizen rises to high office and becomes privy to details of policy, his views will change, so that he may seem to the people to be betraying them and the policies and principles he was elected to serve.[43] But that is a sign precisely of ordinary people's ability to govern well once they know the facts. And in a republic of *virtù* "the people are the princes"; Citizens share in political power.[44] That need not mean that all participate equally, let alone that all are constantly preoccupied only with public affairs. Not all are ambitious for honor, and that is good; it is essential that the various "humors" interact. But even those many whose primary concern is "security" crave living in "freedom" for that very reason.[45] What Machiavelli's Citizen vision implies is not a populist utopia but something like the condition of Florentine politics early in the fifteenth century, whose description by John Rigby Hale was quoted at some length in the first chapter: a condition where none can dominate, where even the nonparticipants take a lively interest in public concerns, and where all share a "political ethos which [takes] for granted the collaboration of responsible citizens as equals in the conduct of public affairs."[46]

The one topic most in conflict with this vision for Machiavelli is religion. He clearly thinks that religions—at the minimum, religious forms

40. Ibid., 1: 44 (G 287).
41. Ibid., 1: 47 (G 293, cf. 291–94). See also 1: 48 (G 295); 1: 58 (G 316).
42. Ibid., 1: 47 (G 294).   43. Ibid.
44. Ibid., 1: 58 (G 316).   45. Ibid., 1: 16 (G 237).
46. Hale, *Florence*, 18; cf. 9, 15.

and rituals, but possibly the gods, too—are human inventions; founding a religion is the greatest source of glory.[47] He also assigns religion enormous importance, frequently blaming the Church for modern Italian corruption, ascribing ancient greatness to ancient religion, and asserting that most men will be good and will keep their oaths only if they believe themselves observed by divinities who will punish or reward them.[48] The combination of these two themes—that religion is manmade yet essential to healthy public life—plays havoc with the republican egalitarianism of the Citizen vision. For it introduces one ineradicable inequality in the healthy body politic, between those who believe in the religion and those who know its fraudulence (or at least the fraudulence of its forms and rituals) and can exploit it for public or private good. If the dichotomy were merely between the Founder and later generations, it might still be compatible with the *pari equalita* of Citizens. But Machiavelli speaks with evident approval of the Roman Senate's exploitation of the religious credulity of the plebs; he often urges military leaders to exploit the religion of their troops in this way.[49] All this is meant for the common good, no doubt, though what makes the unbelieving leaders and generals public-spirited is far from clear; but it is hard to reconcile with mutuality between leaders and led and with open access to office for all. The Citizen vision seems to founder on the shoals of religion.

Yet sometimes Machiavelli does suggest other possibilities, even on this topic. "Where the fear of God is lacking," he says, a state can be sustained instead "by fear of a prince," but only during that leader's lifetime.[50] Its real "salvation" would require "so to organize it that even after he dies it can be maintained."[51] Would that require manipulating religion? Romulus founded Rome, Machiavelli points out, without having recourse to "the authority of God." But of course Numa introduced religion soon thereafter. Moreover, it is even harder to reform a corrupt state than to found a new one; and even if the latter can be accomplished in a secular manner, the former cannot.

And truly no one who did not have recourse to God ever gave to a people unusual laws, because without that they would not be accepted. Because many

47. *Discourses* 1: 11 (G 224); 1: 12 (G 227); 2: 5 (G 340). On Machiavelli's own belief see G 170–71.
48. Ibid., 2: 2 (G 331); 1: 11 (G 224 ff); "[Golden] Ass," ch. 5, lines 118–23 (G 764); *Florentine Histories* 3: 5 (G 1145).
49. *Discourses* 1: 13 (G 230–31); 1: 11 (G 224); 1: 13–15 (G 230–34); 3: 33 (G 503); *Art of War*, bk. 4 (G 661); bk. 6 (G 691); bk. 7 (G 723).
50. *Discourses* 1: 11 (G 225).
51. Ibid. (G 226).

good things are known to a prudent man that are not in themselves so plainly rational that others can be persuaded of them.[52]

❖   ❖   ❖

A plurality of classes and interests is necessary to the Citizen vision not merely because each has its unique perspective and spirit to contribute to the community, but also because internal conflict is an essential and healthy phenomenon in its own right. If relations among real men in this vision are those of peer mutuality, fraternal rather than paternal and filial, Machiavelli is not one of those romantics for whom fraternity implies a natural or automatic harmony. He never forgets that brothers hate as well as love one another. Thus, whereas the vision of the fox involves a preference for indirect methods and manipulative means, for fraud over force and both over "fighting by laws," and whereas the vision of the Founder involves a complex combination of fierce ruthlessness directed outward at the enemy with a courtly, idealized internal harmony in which no conflict can arise, the vision of manly Citizenship differs from both in the value it places on internal, political conflict and particularly on open conflict that spurns the means of deceit or indirection.

Internal conflict, aggression, ambition, directed and used in the right way, are the sources of strength, health, and growth. Roman republican political life is again the prime example. Some may say that its

methods were unlawful and almost inhuman, for the people were shrieking against the Senate, the Senate against the people, there was disorderly running through the streets, locking of shops, the people all leaving Rome. . . .[53]

But "those who condemn" these "dissensions" are in reality "finding fault with what as a first cause kept Rome free."[54] The "perfection" of her government was achieved through "discord," and "disunion between the plebians and the Senate."[55] Indeed, if Rome "had become quieter . . . it would also have been weaker," deprived of the opportunity for "greatness" and for "growth."[56]

The Roman example, furthermore, indicates a general truth: "those who believe republics can be united," meaning thereby that they can achieve a uniform cohesion without serious conflict and at the same time be strong and capable of glory, "are greatly deceived in their belief."[57] For liberty and good order "have their origin" in the very "dis-

52. Ibid. (G 225).   53. Ibid., 1: 4 (G 203).   54. Ibid. (G 202).
55. Ibid., 1: 2 (G 200). See also 1: 4 (G 202–3); 1: 17 (G 239).
56. Ibid., 1: 6 (G 209).   57. *Florentine Histories* 7: 1 (G 1336).

sensions that many thoughtlessly condemn."[58] Without this sort of challenge, men grow complacent, forgetful, and flaccid, as excessive "ease" makes them "effeminate."[59] It is the "cities and provinces that live in freedom" which "make very great gains."[60] Where the citizens are self-governing, cities "grow enormously in a very short time," and conversely, cities have "never" been able to grow and prosper in this way "except when they have been at liberty."[61]

Health, growth, prosperity, manliness all depend on the tension of internal conflict, on ambition and energy. Yet obviously conflict and ambition are no guarantees of liberty or political health; they are also dangerous forces that can easily destroy a state or undermine its liberty. "Some divisions harm republics and some divisions benefit them," but which do which?[62] The entire *Florentine Histories*, one might say, is a meditation on this topic: why did internal conflict in Rome serve to strengthen the state and enlarge liberty, while in Florence it produced only factional dissension, destructiveness, and weakness?

The enmities that at the outset existed in Rome between the people and the nobles were ended by debating, those in Florence by fighting; those in Rome were terminated by law, those in Florence by the exile and death of many citizens.[63]

The contrast is clear enough, but how is it to be explained? Machiavelli says it has something to do with principle, with the reasonableness and justness of the claims leveled by either side, and the two sides' correlated ability to retain some mutuality, some awareness of their shared membership in a joint enterprise to which each makes distinctive contributions, and hence their ability to set limits on the means they employ in the struggle.

The people of Rome wished to enjoy supreme honors along with the nobles; the people of Florence fought to be alone in the government, without any participation in it by the nobles. Because the Roman people's desire was more reasonable, their injuries to the nobles were more endurable, so that the nobility yielded easily and without coming to arms. . . . On the other hand, the Florentine people's desire was harmful and unjust, so that the nobility with greater forces prepared to defend themselves, and therefore the result was blood and the exile of citizens, and the laws then made were planned not for the common profit but altogether in favor of the conqueror.[64]

58. *Discourses* 1: 4 (G 203).   59. Ibid., 1: 6 (G 210–11).
60. Ibid., 2: 2 (G 332).   61. Ibid., 1: 58 (G 316); 2: 2 (G 329).
62. *Florentine Histories* 7: 1 (G 1336).
63. Ibid., 3: 1 (G 1140). Ultimately, to be sure, even in Rome an excess of "hatred" between the classes "led to arms and bloodshed" and finally destroyed Roman freedom (*Discourses* 1: 37 [G 274]).
64. *Florentine Histories* 3: 1 (G 1140). Cf. *Discourses* 1: 47 (G 292).

The genuine appeal to justice and the sense of mutuality and limits even within serious conflict are further correlated with this other requirement: the conflict must be open rather than clandestine and invidious. True *virtù* requires the open staking of a claim on the basis of right and justice, along with the effort to defend it through organizing power; destructive factionalism, by contrast, relies on evasion, private cabals, and secret intrigues. To "make war openly" is the "more honorable" way, though it is not available to the weak.[65] The "goodness" of the Roman people is, for example, demonstrated by the fact that confronted by what they considered an unjust financial levy imposed on them by the nobility in the Senate, they "did not think of defrauding the edict in any amount by giving less than was due," but thought only of "liberating" themselves "from the tax by showing open indignation."[66] That is the reason, also, why Machiavelli places so much stress on the Roman institution of accusations. It allowed charges to be brought lawfully against even the rich and powerful who engaged in abuses; where the charges were found valid, the abuses were countered "with public forces and means, which have their definite limits" and therefore "do not go on to something that may destroy the republic."[67] And even if the charges were invalid, the possibility of bringing them publicly, lawfully, into the open was essential to *il vivero libero*, to free political life.[68] For hidden antagonisms seek private modes of expression which divide the community into factions that prefer vengeance to the public good, that consequently may even call in foreign forces to assist their private aims, and that fail to recognize the essential civic or civil limits (*i termini civili*) distinguishing political conflict from civil war.[69] Where "hatreds do not have an outlet for discharging themselves lawfully, they take unlawful ways." Unfortunate is the city that "inside her wall" has no safe outlet through which "the malignant humors that spring up" may "find vent."[70]

The Citizen of a healthy republic uses that "way of fighting . . . according to laws" that is suited to men rather than animals: open and fearlessly direct confrontation rather than sneaky, clandestine, foxy maneuvering; but at the same time a conflict mediated by law, justice, persuasion, community, rather than resolved by naked leonine force. The fraternity of Citizens implies genuine conflict, but it rules out the fratricide essential to Founders like Romulus. There is no mere selfish or lupine factionalism here, nor any fantasy of automatic, painless unity,

65. *Discourses* 3: 2 (G 423).   66. Ibid., 1: 55 (G 307).
67. Ibid., 1: 7 (G 212).   68. Ibid., 1: 8 (G 215–16).
69. *Florentine Histories* 7: 1 (G 1337); Machiavelli, *Opere* 7: 452.
70. *Discourses* 1: 7 (G 211, 214).

but a continuing process of genuine, yet contained, conflict. Unity is achieved again and again, neither by a selfless merging with the Founder nor by submission to his repressive discipline, but collectively, in interaction. Such a city offers each Citizen, each class of Citizens, the genuine possibility of fulfilling individual needs, pursuing separate interests, expressing real passions; it does not depend on sacrifice, either voluntary or enforced. Yet the selfish and partial needs, interests, and passions brought into the political process are transformed, enlarged, brought into contact with the conflicting needs, interests, and passions of other Citizens and ultimately redefined collectively in relation to the common good—a common good that emerges only out of the political interaction of the Citizens.

Politics must deal with those things about which people genuinely care, or it will be trivial and meaningless to them, and they will turn elsewhere. It must involve a genuine confrontation, open and sometimes serious conflict, or the Citizens will not experience in it their real relatedness. Only when the Roman common people went on strike, marched out of the city, and encamped on a nearby hill were the nobles brought to realize their interdependence with that class, their common membership in a single community, and thus to concede reforms that worked "in favor of liberty."[71] Yet the ultimate resolution of conflict must be mediated by law and justice, not merely enforced; in struggle the citizens discover the value of the rules and principles that protect them all, by turns. They are enlarged by setting their private desires into relationship with considerations of principle and the common good, which they also desire.[72]

Thus in the Citizen image of manhood, not only ambition, aggression, and conflict find positive value, but so do the self and its desires, the body and its needs; they are to be accepted and transformed, civilized, rather than rejected or repressed. It is "very natural and normal," Machiavelli says, for human beings to want to aggrandize the self, "to acquire [*aquisitare*]."[73] That can be read as foxy cynicism: given half a chance all men are evil, and only the naive believe otherwise. But it can also be read in a different spirit to mean that human institutions that ennoble and civilize us require a foundation in human need and passion. This is the spirit in which Machiavelli relishes the story of Alexan-

---

71. Ibid., 1: 4 (G 203); Livius, *History* 2.32.1.–2.33.2.
72. Like many aspects of the Citizen image, justice is a largely implicit and indirect theme; but see e.g., *Florentine Histories* 3: 1 (G 1140); 3: 16 (G 1166); 5: 8 (G 1242); *Prince*, ch. 26 (G 94); *Discourses* 1: 28 (G 405); and "A Provision for Infantry" (G 3).
73. *Prince*, ch. 3 (G 18); Machiavelli, *Opere* 1: 23.

der the Great's choice of the site for the city he planned to found "for his glory," to bear his name.[74] Urged by an architect to locate the city on the slopes of Mount Athos, where it could be built to resemble "human form" and thus become "a thing marvellous and rare and worthy of his greatness," Alexander asked only one question: what would the inhabitants live on? The architect was forced to admit he hadn't considered that, so Alexander laughed and built his city on the fertile plain. A fertile site, as we shall see later, poses problems of its own, but without food and other necessities there can be no city; the "glory" of a city located where no humans can live is ludicrous.[75]

As the example suggests, the Citizen image of manhood implies a different understanding of what is real than do the images of fox and Founder. The fox, of course, prides himself on his realism, but his reality includes no ideals or principles beyond private self-interest. Ideals and principles can *only* be shams to deceive the gullible. That view, however, makes even self-justification or self-appreciation logically problematic. Though he may take a certain pride in his unmasking of sham, the fox can ultimately say no better of himself and do no better for himself than he can of and for the rest of mankind, for his reality does not include objective value or principle. The Citizen image implies a realism that includes both ideals and practice, both concepts and observed behavior. Glory, virtue, courage, civility, or the common good can be as real, as objective, as observable as hunger, pain, ambition, or greed. And these different phenomena are connected: civic glory transcends, but also presupposes, a site suitable for human habitation.

Similarly, the Citizen image implies a different understanding of the nature of the self than do the images of fox and Founder. The fox for all his pride in unmasking and being *furbo* is a profoundly self-disparaging image. The limits of the self are narrowly drawn around the individual or perhaps his immediate family and their manifest desires; extended connections and higher principles are deflated. The authentic self must almost always remain hidden and is likely to vanish altogether into the various poses the fox assumes. In contemplating the mythical Founder, we are similarly diminished; we become mere matter which he might shape, soldiers he might command, children he might sponsor. In a way, to be sure, we can then overcome this self-disparagement by identifying with his greatness, but only at the price of dissolving our separate selves in his greater glory. The Citizen image, by contrast, is neither selfish nor

74. *Discourses* 1: 1 (G 194–95).
75. But Alexandria had a "dependent" rather than a "free" origin. Like Florence, it got off to a bad start (ibid. [G 193]).

self-sacrificing, but a way to "give thought to private *and* public advantages" *together.*[76] It concerns the transformation of narrowly defined self-interest into a larger awareness of one's ties to others, one's real stake in institutions and ideals. This is a transformation not so much from self-interest to self-sacrifice, nor even from narrowly defined short-range to prudent long-range self-interest, but rather in the understanding of what the self *is*, of the limits of the self.

Accordingly, the Citizen image implies a realistic acceptance of the self and those associated with it—those about whom one might say "we"—acceptance not in the sense of unimprovable perfection, but in the sense of something improvable, worth improving, capable of being improved *by* the self. We have suggested that the manhood of the fox is drawn mainly from Machiavelli's experience and that of the Founder from reading and fantasy. The image of the Citizen is mostly from reading and fantasy too, since fraternal citizenship was not a reality in Machiavelli's Florence. Yet, though it can be used to measure current practice and find that practice woefully "unmanly," the Citizen image nevertheless suggests that "we" are worthwhile as we are—we Florentines, we Italians, we commoners, we moderns, we human beings—with our cowardice, our ambition, our greed, our envy, but also our courage, our intelligence, our capacity for creating and sustaining the *vivere civile*: human culture.

It is in this spirit that Machiavelli remarks encouragingly from time to time that even the great Romans were only human, like ourselves, and we must not despair of being able to do what they did.[77] These passages are not a disparagement of Roman greatness, but an attempt to make it accessible, *actionable*, for modern men.

Yet the same outlook can raise even more fundamental problems about ancient Roman greatness. For the forefathers of modern Florence need not be taken exclusively as the Romans; they might instead be taken to be the ancient natives of Tuscany, which "was once powerful, religious, and vigorous [*virtù*]," until the Romans came and "wiped out" all of this "achievement."[78] Perhaps it would be enough—would in important ways even be preferable—to be "merely" Tuscan and Florentine rather than Roman, to be oneself rather than bound to a mythical hero? Having withstood torture in prison, Machiavelli wrote to a friend after his release that he had borne his "distress . . . so bravely that I love

76. Ibid., 2: 2 (G 333); my italics.
77. *Prince*, ch. 26 (G 94).
78. *Discourses* 2: 5 (G 341). See also 2: 2 (G 328).

myself for it and feel that I am stronger [*da piu* (more)] than you [or I myself?] believed."[79]

Unlike the sardonic vision of the fox and the sycophantic image of the Founder, the Citizen image is fundamentally at peace with our human condition. Glory and heroism are achieved *within* that condition rather than by its transcendence. Again one may be reminded of the ancient Greek understanding of man as by nature a *polis* creature, developing his full potential only in shared responsibility for the *nomos* by which he lives.

Like Aristotle, Machiavelli suggests that this type of manhood, this development of potential *virtù*, can only be achieved in actual experience of citizen participation. Only in crisis and political struggle are people forced to enlarge their understandings of themselves and their interests. Only in crisis and struggle do they

> learn the necessity not merely of maintaining religion and justice, but also of esteeming good citizens and taking more account of their ability [*virtù*] than of those comforts which as a result of their deeds, the people themselves might lack.[80]

Only through practice in self-reliance do people become self-reliant; liberty is an acquired taste. A people that has grown accustomed to being cared for and dominated by others lacks the ability, the *virtù*, to control itself. It is like

> a brute beast, which, though of a fierce and savage nature, has always been cared for in prison and in slavery. Then, if by chance it is left free in a field, since it is not used to feeding itself and does not know the places where it can take refuge, it becomes the prey of the first one who tries to rechain it.[81]

If the ruler of such a people is somehow removed, they must promptly submit themselves to another domination; "live as free men they cannot."[82] By contrast, a people accustomed to self-government, who have become men in the Citizen image and acquired a taste for public liberty, will fight with the utmost *virtù* to keep their autonomy. If a conqueror tries to deprive them of it, they "take awful revenge" on him, as the Romans found when they moved into free, ancient Tuscany: "Nothing made it harder for the Romans to conquer the people around them . . . than the love that in those times many peoples had for their freedom."[83]

79. Letter to Vettori, 18 March 1512–[1513] (G 899); Machiavelli, *Opere* 6: 234.
80. *Discourses* 3: 1 (G 420); Machiavelli, *Opere* 1: 380.
81. Ibid., 1: 16 (G 235). See also 1: 17 (G 238, 240); 2: 4 (G 337); 3: 8 (G 451); 3: 12 (G 460).
82. *Prince*, ch. 5 (G 24).
83. *Discourses* 2: 2 (G 328, 330).

Such *virtù* and the memory of liberty can even persist through several generations of oppression, as the Florentine signors point out to the duke of Athens before the city's successful revolt against him: "One often sees [liberty] taken up again by men who never have experienced it, but merely because of the tradition that their fathers have left them they continue to love it."[84]

❖   ❖   ❖

Here one begins to see the deepest incompatibilities between the Founder and the Citizen images. It is not merely that the one vision of manhood is paternal-filial and the other fraternal; the one repressive and stressing uniformity, the other requiring plurality and conflict; the one hierarchical, the other equalitarian. Two such ideals might still co-exist, in separate but equal spheres, as it were, and at times Machiavelli tries so to place them: they are two types of manliness required in two different sets of circumstances. Founders are best at organizing, initiating, renovating; Citizens are for maintaining and carrying on what has been started. Each task has its own glory.

If princes are superior to the people in establishing laws, forming communities according to law, setting up statutes and new institutions, the people are so much superior in keeping up things already organized that without doubt they attain the same glory as those who organize them.[85]

Founders are required where the task is reforming a corrupt people or welding a dispersed one into a single community, but where a healthy civic life exists the Citizen is required.

Though one alone is suited for organizing, the government organized is not going to last long if resting on the shoulders of only one; but it is indeed lasting when it is left to the care of the many, and when its maintenance rests upon many.[86]

Founder and Citizen, then, are to appear in sequence, the one type of manhood producing the other, each performing his particular task at appropriate times.

Yet such a deployment of the images cannot fully succeed, for they have logically incompatible implications. It is essential to the Founder image that the Founder creates manhood where none had existed; but it is essential to the Citizen image that liberty be an acquired taste, learned

---

84. *Florentine Histories* 2: 34 (G 1124). See also *Prince*, ch. 5 (G 24).
85. *Discourses* 1: 58 (G 317).
86. Ibid., 1: 9 (G 218). Cf. 1: 11 (G 226); *Prince*, ch. 19 (G 76); "Discourse on Remodelling" (G 110, 115).

through actual political participation. According to the one image, authoritarian rule is essential to fit people for self-government; according to the other, authoritarian rule renders them increasingly unfit and engenders habits of dependence.[87] Can subordination to a single leader of mythical proportions both promote and destroy *virtù* in his followers?

And what of the crucial transition, from paternal Founder to fraternal self-rule? How is it to be effected, and by which image of manhood and action is it to be construed? It is, of course, a reform, a revolt, quite possibly a conspiracy—that delicate, dangerous topic which so fascinated Machiavelli that he gave it the longest chapters in each of his two primary political works. But if the Founder father is to be overthrown by the fraternal horde he has engendered, how should that act of revolt itself be construed: as a great reform by a single, outstanding Founder-reformer, or as a collective activity by Citizen peers? Machiavelli says both, construing a conspiracy to establish republican liberty now in terms of the Founder image, now in terms of the Citizen. Brutus, the prime example, certainly seems to be one of the great Founder figures, the "father" of the republic and of Roman liberty. Yet Brutus was successful only because of his good timing: had the Roman people been "corrupt" when he acted, he could perhaps have overthrown the Tarquins, but only to replace their tyranny with another.[88] That other, later Brutus, for instance, who sought to liberate Rome from Caesar and restore the republic, failed utterly because "the Roman populace loved" Caesar and therefore "avenged him." Thus, "of all the dangers" that threaten initially successful conspirators, "there is none more certain or more to be feared than when the people love the prince you have killed; for this, conspirators have no remedy."[89] Any regime's "strongest resource against conspiracies," accordingly, "is not to be hated by the masses." Those who would alter the political structure of a state

should consider the material on which they must work, and determine from that the difficulty of their undertakings. For it is as difficult and dangerous to try to set free a people that wishes to live in servitude as it is to try to bring into servitude a people that wishes to live free.[90]

The conspirator and reformer, then, is not a Founder of mythical proportions after all, despite the metaphor of a craftsman working on inanimate material in this passage, but rather very much dependent on his

---

87. Cf. Strauss, *Thoughts*, 267.   88. *Discourses* 1: 16 (G 238).
89. Ibid., 3: 6 (G 444). See also 3: 7 (G 448).
90. Ibid., 3: 8 (G 451).

human interaction with the people of his community. For a conspiracy to succeed in setting up a republic, the people at large must already be potential Citizens in character, if not yet in practice.

But the problem is not just with conspirators and renovators. In a more general sense, each of the three images of manhood constitutes a perspective on the world and on the nature of man. From the perspective of the Citizen, as from that of the fox, there can *be* no Founders, capital *F*. Men who are weak or cowardly or narrowly selfish and short-sighted may abdicate their capacity for action to some single ruler, but from the Citizen perspective, no good can come of that. Real men do from time to time found new institutions, or even whole societies, or renovate them fundamentally. But such men are not the offspring of gods; they may be foundlings, but they had ordinary human parents and were conceived in the usual way. In human affairs there are no un-moved movers; we are all shaped by our society and our childhood; yet we are all capable of action and innovation. No leader stands in relation to his followers as a craftsman to material, imposing form on inanimate matter. He must always deal with people who already have customs, habits, needs, beliefs, rules of conduct, who already live somewhere in some manner. And his power is always dependent on their very human responses.

Does Machiavelli know that the great Founder image is a myth? If he is a fox, or sees from the perspective of a fox, or even from that of the Citizen, he surely must know. Certainly he does not believe that even the greatest leaders were fathered by gods; on the contrary, they are likely to have had humble or shameful origins and precisely for that rea-son to have invented divine parentage.[91] Just so Numa "pretended that he was intimate with a nymph" because in his renovating work he had "need for the authority of God . . . because he planned to introduce new and unwonted laws into the city, but feared that his own authority would not be enough."[92] The Founder's claims to semidivine status are necessary but fradulent: fraud plays a crucial role in the rise to power from a lowly position.

Machiavelli also clearly knows that the origins of states, like those of Founders, are regularly mythologized to camouflage their seamy reality; all beginnings lack legitimacy and thus need to create their own. The conquerors try to wipe out the past and hide the bloody origin of their power.

---

91. "Life of Castruccio" (G 533).   92. *Discourses* 1: 11 (G 225).

With violence they enter into the countries of others, kill the inhabitants, seize their property, set up a new kingdom, and change the name of the country, as did Moses, and those peoples who took possession of the Roman Empire.[93]

The Christian religion tries to obliterate the memory of the pagans, as "the Pagan probably did against any sects preceding itself"; and the historians "follow Fortune," praising the conquerors and denying their guilt.[94]

Machiavelli also appears to know that founding is not accomplished in one blow by a single man acting alone. Even within the imagery of the Founder, he acknowledges that more than one generation might be required to reform corruption. Even in Rome, Romulus had to be followed by Numa; and, indeed, Rome was not organized "at the beginning in such a way that she could continue free for a long time" but had to reach "perfection" partly by "chance," partly by "the discord between the people and the Senate."[95] In the history of Rome "new necessities were always appearing," so that it was constantly necessary "to devise new laws" for dealing with them.[96] Thus, far from being created by an unmoved mover at the outset, Rome was the product of a sort of continuous founding by many men, and even by classes in interaction; its "founding" begins to sound rather like the collective, continuing maintenance of a healthy free republic after it has been "founded on good laws and good institutions."[97] Although "two successive reigns by able princes are enough to gain the world," as can be seen in the examples of Philip of Macedon and Alexander the Great, such a succession is a rare accident, but in a republic a continual supply of men of *virtù* should be available,

since the method of choosing allows not merely two able rulers in succession but countless numbers to follow one another. Such a succession of able rulers will always be present in every well-ordered republic.[98]

Yet in the very passage where Machiavelli says of Rome that it was not well organized from the beginning but had to be developed by chance and conflict, he contrasts Rome to Sparta, Romulus to Lycurgus. Even while unmasking the Roman Founder, one might say, he affirms the Spartan one: Rome failed to "gain the first fortune" but "gained the second." The first fortune, however, would have been "having a Lycur-

93. Ibid., 2: 8 (G 345).
94. Ibid., 2: 5 (G 340); *Art of War*, bk. 2 (G 622).
95. *Discourses* 1: 2 (G 200–201). See also 2: 13 (G 358).
96. Ibid., 1: 49 (G 295, cf. 297). See also 3: 49 (G 527).
97. *Florentine Histories* 4: 1 (G 1187).
98. *Discourses* 1: 20 (G 246).

gus to organize her at the beginning in such a way that she could continue free for a long time."[99] Did Machiavelli regard the story of Lycurgus as a myth?

But if Founders are merely a myth, where *does* significant historical change come from? How did the human animal ever become capable of civility? If it is a matter of human rather than mythical founders, what do they do, and what can a would-be renovator do in corrupt times?

Foxiness will suffice for survival in such times, but it cannot transform them. The fox is put to shame by the Founder precisely because of the latter's capacity as an authority, to father men by inspiring as well as terrifying them. Not only is the fox unable to offer either inspiration or terror, but his way actively undermines their possibility. He can only feed the already existing defensive cynicism of his corrupt world, where "every man will stand aside and sneer, speaking ill of whatever he sees and hears." In such a world no one would or safely could pursue an ideal like honor, liberty, or virtue; no one will "labor and strain to turn out with a thousand hardships a work that the wind will spoil and the fog conceal."[100] That "is the reason, beyond all doubt," why modern men fail to achieve what the ancients did, and no amount of unmasking and debunking will remedy it. Foxiness is the disease; it can't be the cure.

That is the reason, also, why Ligurio can only rearrange relationships in *Mandragola*, leaving all the characters better off in terms of their desires, but not really improving their lot in the larger sense, nor changing the corruption of their world. Callimaco can certainly father in the literal sense (and, one might argue, Ligurio vicariously through him), but his and Lucretia's child will grow up in an atmosphere of adultery and deceit, will be socialized into his parents' world. The prologue may speak of that world as "degenerate" from ancient greatness, but the play offers no real improvement. If the play were really to be taken as parallel to *The Prince*, as showing the begetting of a new Italy through the cooperative efforts of a Callimaco-prince and a Ligurio-counselor, then its message would be a most depressing one: you may get your prince into power, but the new Italy will be just like the old.

In a context of general virtue and public spirit, the unmasking of a deceit is salutary; but if suspicion becomes so widespread that there is no more trust, men are rendered incapable of citizenship and real manhood. Even a diplomat may be so "clever and two-faced" that he "com-

---

99. Ibid., 1: 2 (G 200).
100. *Mandragola*, prologue (G 778).

pletely" loses the "trust" of the prince he hoped to fool; and when the ancient oracles were hypocritically exploited by "the powerful" for their own interests, the people's discovery of this fraud led not to indignation but to cynicism: "Men became unbelieving and ready to upset any good custom [*ordine* (order)] whatsoever."[101] When people have been too often "deceived in the past both by things and by men, of necessity the republic is ruined," because the people then no longer "have faith" in anyone or anything. Such a condition of disillusionment is not healthy but self-destructive, leading a people to shout "Long live its own death" and "Down with its own life."[102]

So the foxy unmasking of fraud cannot, by itself, inspire corrupt men to *virtù*; and, indeed, a true or mere fox would not even conceive that project. Machiavelli may have been foxy, but he was not merely a fox. All three images of manhood are his. So now one must ask once more: if a man were not merely a fox but somehow also held a vision of manhood as Citizenship, so that he wanted to transform society and men's character toward real glory, could he do so? If there are no Founders, what does it take to found, or to renovate?

Could a fox with such a vision perhaps inspire, manipulate, and use a lion as a false Founder-figure? A lion could certainly frighten men into obedience, but since he lacks true *virtù*, how could he—or he and the fox together—inspire men? Or would the false appearance be enough? In politics, after all, appearance is everything; it is a realm where "men judge more with their eyes than with their hands, since everybody . . . sees what you appear to be; few perceive what you are."[103] Could it be after all that the great historical Founders were only lions being used by foxes who had a larger, nonfoxy vision?

Machiavelli's treatment of theorists and theorizing is particularly interesting in this regard. In discussing the great historical Founders, and the necessity that they be alone in their organizing activities, he adds: "Still more, it is necessary that one man alone give the method and that from his mind proceed all such organization."[104] The action of a Founder, then, may proceed from a mind other than his own; is the "mind" behind the Founder then the real unmoved mover? When he discusses the great Founders in *The Prince*, as we noted, Machiavelli first sets Moses aside "since he was a mere executor of things laid down

---

101. "Discourse on Remodelling" (G 116); *Discourses* 1: 12 (G 227).
102. *Discourses* 1: 53 (G 302–3). Machiavelli says that he is quoting Dante's *On Monarchy*, but Allan Gilbert points out that the passage is actually from *Convivio*, 1.11.54.
103. *Prince*, ch. 18 (G 66–67).
104. *Discourses* 1: 9 (G 218).

for him by God" and since we can learn as much from studying the other Founders, whose "actions and . . . individual methods" did not differ "from those of Moses, who had so great a teacher."[105] So Machiavelli as theorist and teacher will examine the actions and methods of past Founders in order to teach future ones; will he then stand in relation to them as God to Moses? But does the Machiavelli who knows that "all, or a large part" of great men have been so ashamed of their obscure origins and humble paternity that they "have made themselves out sons of Jove or of some other god," actually believe that God spoke to Moses? Or does he imagine some earlier fox like himself advising Moses, or perhaps Moses himself as simultaneously lion and fox in one?

Generally Machiavelli ranks theorizing, philosophy, and thought relatively low in comparison with effective action in the world. In the ranks of famous men whose fame is well deserved, as we noted, "men of letters" come only fourth, after the Founders and fighters. In the *Florentine Histories*, even more strikingly, "letters" and "philosophy" are disparaged as a sign of degeneration from "ability [*virtù*]" into corruption:

letters come after arms, and . . . generals are born earlier than philosophers. Because after good and well-disciplined armies have brought forth victory, and their victories quiet, the virtue of military courage cannot be corrupted with a more honorable laziness than that of letters; nor with a greater and more dangerous deception can this laziness enter into well-regulated cities.[106]

Theory, then, would seem to be an "honorable laziness" that corrupts and weakens, almost the opposite pole from the supreme *virtù* of the Founder. Indeed, in his letter to Pope Leo X on remodeling Florentine government, Machiavelli says that the glory of founding is so great that theorists like Aristotle, Plato, "and many others" who were "unable to form a republic in reality . . . have done it in writing," wanting "to show the world" that their failure to act was due not to "their ignorance" but only to "their impotence" for "putting . . . into practice" what they knew.[107] Machiavelli himself was impotent to act in his exile, having been forced out of action into theory; indeed, in 1509 while still in office he had written that "for holding states, studies and books are not enough."[108]

Yet perhaps what is said of philosophy and letters in general is not meant to apply to Machiavelli's own particular theorizing. In both *The Prince* and the *Discourses* he seeks to distinguish himself from the tradi-

105. *Prince*, ch. 6 (G 25).
106. *Florentine Histories* 5: 1 (G 1232); Machiavelli, *Opere* 7: 325.
107. "Discourse on Remodelling" (G 114).
108. Letter of 26 November 1509 quoted G 739n.

tion of political theory, insofar as it meant the inventing of unrealistic imaginary states. While most men act by imitation, and while nothing is more dangerous than introducing a genuine novelty, he himself as theorist is "determined to enter upon a path not yet trodden by anyone," in hopes of thereby bringing "benefit common to everybody."[109] He wants "to write something useful" for action, yet does not plan to act on his own ideas himself, hoping instead like Fabrizio in *The Art of War* that someone "with more vigor [*virtù*], more prudence and judgment" will "carry out this intention of mine."[110]

Autonomous transforming action is what is most admirable; yet who is the source of such action: the leader who carries it out, or the "author" who first imagines it? Is theory, then, impotence or power? Are Founders mere front men for theorist-counselors behind the scenes? Then whose fault was it that Machiavelli, the consummate fox, failed to find a front man (or front lion) who might reform and unify Florence or all Italy? Surely the times and conditions were unfavorable, the task too difficult. Only a heroic man of mythical proportions could do anything in conditions such as these. Even in combination, a fox and a lion cannot produce miracles, cannot turn animals into men. So the Founder has to be real after all, for he is the only hope. The Founder, one might say, is a fantasy of the impotent; and to the extent that the situation looks utterly hopeless, Machiavelli himself is drawn into the Founder image and yearns for rescue. The attraction of magic is proportional to the apparent hopelessness of action.

Though the fox tends by nature to demystify and debunk and thereby undermine the image of the Founder, he also in some way continually needs and recreates that image. The servant, the counselor, the underling may have a considerable stake in the greatness of his master or in imagining an even greater one whose greatness he could share by identification. If in addition he fantasies controlling such a master behind the scenes; and if, like Machiavelli, he yearns to transform corrupt men into Citizens of *virtù*, then he has still further stakes of his own in the Founder image, as a last hope when all else seems blocked. Thus while Machiavelli clearly did not believe in the divine parentage of Founders or the immaculate conception of cities, the image of the Founder is no mere rhetorical device detachedly used to manipulate his readers. There is much reason to think that it was also a symbolic category of his own thinking.

109. *Discourses*, preface (G 190).
110. Ibid.

In terms of manhood, the relationships among the three images we have examined are extraordinarily complex and ultimately unresolvable because they are nontransitive. Each image is in certain respects superior to, more manly than, the other two; each is in significant ways unsatisfactory, inadequate, or unmanly. And so Machiavelli's thought in effect circles over them endlessly in various juxtapositions and transformations, the contemplation of any one of the three leading him eventually back to a reconsideration of the others. The image of the fox, though an ideal of manhood in its own right and a source of pride for Machiavelli, is also somehow despicable and unmanly, for the fox acts only by indirection and shuns direct encounter. He is put to shame by the Citizen's fearless engagement in open conflict and accusation; and a world of foxes and their victims is a world incapable of free civic life. He is put to shame by the Founder's generative power; and a fox cannot father Citizens—indeed, foxiness undermines Citizen *virtù*. Thus, by comparison with both Citizen and Founder he is not a real man, but only an animal.

The Citizen is an ideal of *virtù*, "fighting by laws" like a man, rather than in the way of beasts. Yet citizenship seems incapable of generating itself; the Citizen is good at maintenance, but can he father himself? How is a corrupt world to be transformed into one of civic virtue? One who cannot fight by the way of beasts is bound to fail in a world of lions, wolves, and foxes. Only someone who can generate a virtuous world is a *real* man. By comparison with either the Founder's generativity or the fox's cynical knowledge, the Citizen is revealed as a dependent child not yet capable of manhood.

The Founder is the ultimate man in terms of paternity, yet, being only a means to the real goal, Citizens of *virtù*, he must be overthrown. And besides, he is a myth; the fox, or perhaps even the Citizen, can show him up as a mere fantasy, incompatible with the *verita effettuale della cosa*. The Founder image is thus an escape from reality and from effective action in the world, hence bound up with unmanliness. Then the generating of *virtù* must be the work of foxes, or foxes using lions, after all; and the apparently so masculine Founder is only the product of the theorist, the "mind" that stands behind him and manipulates. Why, then, is the fox again and again beset by self-contempt, by the awareness that he is hiding from something, refusing to face up to things like a man?

And so the endless circles continue. What is it that traps Machiavelli, that so divides and confounds his understanding of manhood?

PART III

Women

CHAPTER FIVE

". . . Because of Women"

The seemingly exclusively masculine world of Machiavelli's political writings, where men contend in the arena of history, is actually dominated or at least continually threatened from behind the scenes by dimly perceived, haunting feminine figures of overwhelming power. The contest among the men turns out to be, in crucial ways, their shared struggle against that power. The feminine constitutes "the other" for Machiavelli, opposed to manhood and autonomy in all their senses: to maleness, to adulthood, to humanness, and to politics.

That claim may be startling, for at least two reasons. First, women scarcely appear in the political writings. They are almost entirely confined to Machiavelli's plays and poetry, depicting private life or fantasy worlds. Aside from a few historical figures like the ancient Lucretia and the modern Caterina Sforza, in the political writings women are conspicuous by their absence. Accordingly, for the most part, those commentators with political concerns have ignored questions of sex roles and family, along with the literary works, while those specializing in literature have not given sustained attention to its political implications. This and the next chapter analyze Machiavelli's images of women and of relations between the sexes in detail from the texts, so that their political significance can be explored in later chapters.

Once one begins to look at Machiavelli's images of women, however, a second reason emerges for being startled by the claim that behind the apparently masculine world of political contention there looms hidden feminine power: nothing is more striking in Machiavelli's explicit remarks on women than his contempt for the "weaker sex." As a counterpart to his concept of *virtù*, no epithet is more frequent or more powerful in Machiavelli's vocabulary of abuse than "effeminate." What men and states must avoid at all costs is resembling women. Now, of course, "effeminate" is not the same as "feminine," and in principle one might condemn effeminate men without disparaging women. But Machiavelli's contempt for women is repeatedly expressed, and what he condemns in effeminacy is precisely what he considers typical of women. Women are dumb, fearful, weak, indecisive, and dependent. They are childishly naive and easily manipulated. As the priest in *Mandragola* remarks, "all women lack brains"; if one of them happens, exceptionally, to be sufficiently intelligent "to say two words," that is already enough to "make her famous, because in the city of the blind, a man with one eye is Duke."[1] And Machiavelli himself apparently agrees. For example, in discussing how conspiracies are betrayed, he classes women with immature boys and other such "foolish persons" in whom one must not confide.[2] Moreover, women are fearful and cowardly, incapable of defending themselves. The clever Ligurio observes that "all women are timorous," and Callimaco admonishes himself, "don't be a coward like a woman."[3] Again Machiavelli seems to agree; for instance, in opposing fortresses, he cites with evident approval the Spartans' contemptuous comment on the walls of Athens, that such walls would indeed be "splendid . . . if they sheltered women"; the Spartans themselves preferred to rely on "each man's valor [*virtù*]."[4] At least in a military context, women, like children and old people, are "useless [*inutile*] persons"; like ecclesiastics, they must "by necessity" rely on the arms of others.[5]

Yet, at the same time as they are contemptible, foolish, and weak, women also somehow possess mysterious and dangerous powers; they constitute a threat to men, both personally and politically. Looking particularly at Machiavelli's fiction, one might say that these mysterious and dangerous powers seem to be of two distinct kinds, the one corresponding to young or unmarried women or daughters, the other to older women, wives, mothers, matrons. Often the two types of women appear in linked pairs: daughter and mother, servant and queen, or beautiful virgin who is transformed into shrewish wife.

The young women or daughters are, almost without exception, de-

---

1. *Mandragola*, act 3, sc. 9 (G 800–801).
2. *Discourses* 3: 6 (G 434).
3. *Mandragola*, act 3, sc. 2 (G 794); act 4, sc. 1 (G 805).
4. *Discourses* 2: 24 (G 397); Machiavelli, *Opere* 1: 355.
5. *Discourses* 2: 29 (G 407); Machiavelli, *Opere* 1: 366. See also *Florentine Histories* 1: 39 (G 1078).

picted as sex objects, in the proper sense of that term: they are beautiful, desirable as possessions, potentially sources of the greatest pleasure for men. They are somehow simultaneously both virginal or chaste and passionate or potentially capable of sexual abandon. But they are passive, and themselves scarcely persons at all. They have no desires or plans of their own, initiate no deliberate action, are not significant agents in the world. They are objects of the men's desire, conquest, or possession. As desirable objects, however, they do have great "power" of a sort to move and hold men; without meaning to or actually doing anything, they are the central force that makes the plot more forward. Their power is like the power of gold; or, as the priest says in *Mandragola*, "he who deals with them gets profit and vexation together. But it's a fact that there's no honey without flies."[6]

Lucretia, the "heroine" of *Mandragola*, is not totally devoid of personality or characterizations, yet what we learn about her is inconsistent and puzzling. On the one hand, she is the paragon of virtue and chastity and must be so for purposes of the plot, both to make her desirable and to make her inaccessible. Thus her "beauty and manners" are so exemplary that men who hear of her are "spellbound"; she is a "cautious and good" woman, "very chaste and a complete stranger to love dealings."[7] She kneels praying for hours at night and has already successfully defended her virtue against the advances of lecherous friars.[8] Her character is so pure and steadfast that no servant in her house would dare to plot against her or take bribes; her husband is certain she would never consent to any illicit scheme.[9] Indeed, when she hears of Ligurio's plan she objects strenuously to the "sin" and "shame" of it, as well as to the idea of taking an innocent man's life.[10] In short, she is, as Ligurio says, "virtuous, courteous, and fit to rule a kingdom."[11] Yet this paragon of virtue not only turns out to be so malleable in the hands of her foolish husband, wicked mother, and a corrupt priest that she agrees to commit an obvious sin (which may still be within the bounds of credulity) but is transformed after one night with her lover into a resolute and competent adultress who, without any pang of conscience, knows just how to arrange things so that she and her lover may continue to cuckold her husband as long as he lives. As the characterization of a real person, a

6. *Mandragola*, act 3, sc. 4 (G 796).
7. Ibid., act 1, sc. 1 (G 780); act 3, sc. 9 (G 800). See also act 4, sc. 1 (G 804).
8. Ibid., act 2, sc. 6 (G 790); act 3, sc. 2 (G 794).
9. Ibid., act 1, sc. 1 (G 780); act 2, sc. 6 (G 792).
10. Ibid., act 3, sc. 10 (G 801); act 3, sc. 11 (G 803).
11. Ibid., act 1, sc. 3 (G 783).

person in her own right, this is hard to accept. As an account of an object of desire and action whose contradictory characteristics make the plot move forward, however, it makes fairly obvious sense.

This somewhat inconsistent image of the romantic heroine is not, of course, unique to Machiavelli; it is, indeed, a stock image for many comedies. Yet Machiavelli's ambiguity about Lucretia runs deeper than the convention. There is the question, already raised, of her relationship to the ancient, historical Lucretia, suggesting that *Mandragola* plays out as farce, in relation to family life, what Livy relates as heroic tragedy in relation to ancient Roman political life. The modern Lucretia is a paragon of virtue, yet easily corrupted; the ancient one, though she knows that "only my body has been violated. My heart is innocent," nevertheless kills herself as a public example and insists on taking her "punishment."[12]

In Book 3 of the *Discourses* Machiavelli cites the ancient Lucretia as illustrating the danger that women constitute for the rulers of a state; yet Lucretia's only crime was to be the victim of a rape.[13] Indeed, Machiavelli even says that the overthrow of the Tarquins resulted not from the rape of Lucretia—a mere precipitating incident—but from the king's tyrannical violations of the law.[14] Why, then, does he cite her as an example of feminine danger? Is she an agent of history or not? And when Ligurio in *Mandragola*, whose resemblance to Machiavelli himself we have noted, calls the modern Lucretia "fit to rule a kingdom," may we assume that Machiavelli himself so regards her?

The heroine of Machiavelli's other play, *Clizia*, the young woman over whom the other characters contend, is so much an object that she never appears on the stage at all nor takes any action.[15] Yet she, too, is dangerous. Indeed, *Clizia* articulates very powerfully a frequent Machiavellian topic: that love is war, a struggle for domination. *Clizia*, as we have already remarked, is a fairly close translation of Plautus's *Casina*, but for that very reason allows us to focus on those particular passages where Machiavelli diverges from the original. Central to these divergences, as Martin Fleischer has pointed out, is that *Clizia* greatly heightens the theme of conflict already present in Plautus's play, particularly the metaphor of love as a military struggle between the sexes.[16] A servant speaks of lovemaking in terms like "attacking" and "meeting

12. Livius, *History* 1.58.7, 10.
13. *Discourses* 3: 26 (G 489).
14. Ibid., 3: 5 (G 427).
15. This, however, is common in the early *Commedie Erudite* and was standard practice in the Roman theater; Flaumenhaft, "Comic Remedy," 74 n. 79.
16. Fleischer, "Trust," 371.

strong resistance"; an old man preparing to make love to a young girl speaks of "rousing up" his "brigades" and adds, "when one goes armed to war, one goes with double courage."[17] The young lover speaks a soliloquy on this theme, without parallel in Plautus, but probably derived from Ovid:

Certainly the man who said that the lover and the soldier are alike told the truth. The general wants his soldiers to be young; women don't want their lovers to be old. It's a repulsive thing to see an old man a soldier; it's most repulsive to see him in love. Soldiers fear their commander's anger; lovers fear no less that of their ladies. Soldiers sleep on the ground out of doors; lovers on the wall-ledges [under the windows of their beloved]. Soldiers pursue their enemies to the death; lovers, their rivals. Soldiers on the darkest nights in the dead of winter go through the mud, exposed to rain and wind, to carry out some undertaking that will bring them victory; lovers attempt in similar ways and with similar and greater sufferings to gain those they love. Equally in war and in love, secrecy is needed, and fidelity and courage. The dangers are alike, and most of the time the results are alike. The soldier dies in a ditch and the lover dies in despair.[18]

The young man is depressed when he makes this speech, so he does not consider the possibility of winning nor draw the one remaining parallel: victory is alike as well, a conquest, the gaining of a prize. Plautus's play also features a soliloquy about love; but it is spoken by the old man rather than the son, and it contains no references to military matters; rather, its central metaphors are of food and eating.[19]

Nor is *Clizia* unique in its military metaphors; the theme of love as war is common in the literary works. In *Mandragola*, when Ligurio sets off with his companions to effect the events that will get Callimaco into Lucretia's bed, he says,

I'm going to be captain and draw up the army for battle. On the right horn Callimaco shall be in command, myself on the left, between the two horns will be the Judge here; Siro will be rear-guard and reinforce any squadron that falls back. The battle-cry will be Saint Cuckoo. . . . Let's march on and set our ambush at this corner.[20]

In a "Serenade" evidently based on Ovid's *Metamorphoses*, a young lover weeps and surrenders before the door of his beloved:

You conquer, Anaxarte. I am happy to die, that you may . . . carry off the victory.

17. *Mandragola*, act 5, sc. 1 (G 857); act 4, sc. 5 (G 852).
18. *Clizia*, act 1, sc. 2 (G 829). See Ovid, *Amores* 1.9.1–20.
19. Plautus, *Casina*, 2: 313–14. Cf. 310, 311.
20. *Mandragola*, act 4, sc. 9 (G 813). See also "[Golden] Ass," ch. 4, lines 105–14 (G 760–61).

Deck your temples with green laurel; celebrate your triumph for the war that I waged against you.[21]

As these lines suggest, the war between the sexes is complex, for even where the man succeeds in conquering the woman he pursues, it may turn out that he has been the victim after all, overcome by her and the power of love. Love concerns domination and possession, but this need not mean that the men are always the conquerors, the women the possessed. Indeed, there is much relish in some of Machiavelli's images of romantic servitude, reminiscent of late medieval ballads of courtly love. He dwells on the abjectness of the lover's submission, the extent of his torment.

Callimaco, in *Mandragola*, says that he is "on fire with such longing to be with" his lady that he never has any peace and would rather die than continue in this state.[22] And in soliloquy he expresses the intensity of his desire:

I feel as though my whole body from the soles of my feet to my head has gone wrong [*tutto altare* (wholly altered)]: my legs tremble, my vitals are shaken, my heart is torn out of my breast, my arms lose their strength, my tongue falls silent, my eyes are dazzled, my brain whirls.

All this is for a single occasion with his beloved, even though he tells himself:

When you get her, what'll it amount to? You'll recognize your mistake; you'll regret the labor and worry you've gone through. Don't you know how little good a man finds in the things he has longed for, compared with what he expects to find?[23]

The lovers in *Clizia* experience comparable distress in their servitude to each other and to love, with its dreaded "weapons."[24]

The same notes are struck in a more exaggerated fashion in one of Machiavelli's carnival songs, where hopeless lovers are presented in their "lamentable grief" as being "in the deep center of Hell." They went there voluntarily, it seems, because they preferred the torments of devils to the "afflictions" of their loves. The song fairly bristles with terms like "rule," "powers," "escape," "sobs and sighs," "cruelty," "torment," and "servitude."[25] In his own personal letters as well, Machia-

---

21. Niccolò Machiavelli, "Serenade," lines 161–76 (G 1019).
22. *Mandragola*, act 1, sc. 1 (G 780).
23. Ibid., act 1, sc. 1 (G 805). See also act 1, sc. 3 (G 785); act 2, sc. 6 (G 793); Machiavelli, *Opere* 8: 93.
24. *Clizia*, act 1, sc. 1 (G 828); canzone before act 2 (G 830); act 3, sc. 2 (G 838–39).
25. "Carnival Song by Lovers," lines 1–14 (G 879).

velli depicts love as a power to which a man becomes helplessly or deliciously subject. Amor shoots with his bow and arrow, "possessed with anger and fury, in order to show his lofty power," which Machiavelli is forced to "confess and acknowledge." He is bound by

such strong chains that I am wholly in despair of my liberty. I cannot think of any way in which I can unchain myself; and even if chance or some human stratagem should open to me some way of getting out of them, perchance I should not wish to take it; so much now sweet, now light, now heavy do I find those chains.[26]

❖ ❖ ❖

It is against these dangerous yet seductive torments, the powers of young women as sex objects, that most of Machiavelli's explicit warnings concerning women in politics are directed. Though rarely discussed by commentators, these warnings are repeated, and sometimes very strong. "How a State Falls Because of Women" announces the title of one of the chapters in the *Discourses*. In it, amidst examples of young women who, without actually doing anything, motivate men to cause political trouble, Machiavelli writes:

Women have caused much destruction, have done great harm to those who govern cities, and have occasioned many divisions in them. . . . I say, then, that absolute princes and governors of republics are to take no small account of this matter.[27]

In Machiavelli's schematic narrative, borrowed from Polybius, of how states pass through a cycle of political forms, the degeneration of the latter "heirs" from their virtuous "ancestors" is already ascribed to avarice, ambition, and "violence against women."[28] And while Machiavelli sometimes excuses the first of these vices and even praises the second, when it comes to relations with women what this supposed immoralist seems to value in political leaders and heroes is chastity.[29] This is not because Machiavelli admires chastity intrinsically or as a Christian virtue, but because of its political significance. Though love is war and domination, it is also in some way an alternative to, hostile to, politics; and sexual conquest may demonstrate, but also threatens to undermine,

26. Letter to Vettori, 31 January 1514–[1515] (G 960–61). See also letters to Vettori, 4 February 1513–[1514] (G 937); 10 June 1514 (G 945); 3 August 1514 (G 946).
27. *Discourses* 3: 26 (G 488–89).
28. Ibid., 1: 2 (G 198). Cf. Polybius, *Histories*, tr. Evelyn S. Schuckburgh (London: Macmillan 1889), 1: 458–66, who includes in the list of offenses "the appropriation of boys," omitted by Machiavelli.
29. For instance, *Discourses* 3: 20 (G 476); *Art of War*, bk. 6 (G 701).

a man's *virtù*. Cosimo Rucellai, we learn at the outset of *The Art of War*, wrote love poetry while waiting for a chance at "higher"—that is, political—action.[30]

Indeed, Machiavelli himself writes letters from his political exile, bragging to his friends about his sexual adventures and romances. The commentators seem agreed that most of these are imaginary, invented for his friends' and his own amusement. He explains that he has

abandoned . . . the thoughts of affairs that are great and serious; I do not any more take delight in reading ancient things or in discussing modern ones; they all are turned into soft conversations, for which I thank Venus and all Cyprus.[31]

The contrast is reminiscent of the one drawn in *The Art of War* between things "strong and rough" and those "delicate and soft," between those who provide shelter and those who depend on it.[32] Since women signify the soft, delicate, and dependent things, it seems that association with them threatens to infect a man with these qualities. Though love may be conquest, it turns the womanizer into a weak and unmanly man unable to control his passions and distracted from other, "higher" concerns. Women are time off for a man, a diversion of energy and a lowering of his guard.

The personal adventures to which Machiavelli's letters allude are of two kinds, both presented in a jocular vein of male companionship. Most concern the romantic pursuit of some rapturously fair young woman, to which he is gladly and utterly devoting himself, as in the passage above. But at least one such story, although equally jocular, has an undercurrent of horror and revulsion: lured into the dark, underground shop of his laundress, Machiavelli reports, he was there solicited by a woman and began to make love to her, but when he saw her in the light, she turned out to be horrifyingly ugly; her ugliness is described in exquisite, repulsive detail.[33] With his guard lowered by sensuality, it seems, a man is in danger; male companionship involves the sharing of such fantasies of adventure, restoring distance from and control over the passions of the flesh.

Accordingly, an acceptable alternative to the heroic chastity that Machiavelli recommends for political leaders, is a contemptuous and emotionally distanced sexuality that keeps passion strictly within bounds and prevents any infectious softness from being transmitted to the man. Thus Machiavelli's Castruccio, the one significant hero who, far from

30. *Art of War*, bk. 1 (G 568).
31. Letter to Vettori, 3 August 1514 (G 946).   32. *Art of War*, bk. 1 (G 570).
33. Tarlton, *Fortune's Circle*, 132–33; Machiavelli, *Opere* 6: 204–6.

being chaste, is glorified for his sexual conquests, is admirable precisely because for him those conquests are not self-indulgence but mastery. We already noted that Machiavelli presents Castruccio—contrary to historical fact—as refraining from marriage out of loyalty to his foster father, "filial gratitude" overcoming his "love of children."[34] Masculine loyalty is pitted against sexual reproduction. And when Castruccio is reproached by a male friend for his intimate association with a certain young woman—not for its immorality but on the ground that "it was bad for him to let himself be taken by a woman"—he is described as responding, "I have taken her, not she me."[35]

The seductive danger of young women as sex objects, then, has at least two components: it threatens a man's self-control, his mastery of his own passions, and it threatens to infect him with feminine softness. Exactly the same danger lies in the acquisition of luxurious spoils as a result of military conquest: the conqueror who abandons himself to the sensuality and fertility of his conquest will be undone thereby. Thus the capture of what Livy called "fertile and delightful" Capua nearly destroyed all discipline among the Roman troops.[36] Machiavelli quotes Livy on the manner in which

Capua, a storehouse of all the pleasures, turned away the captivated spirits of the soldiers from the remembrance of their country.[37]

Small wonder that the wise Romans prohibited women in their army camps and that Machiavelli's *Art of War* follows suit.[38]

Women constitute a danger to conquerors, princes, and tyrants; they are both cause and sign of the ruler's weakness and decline, when he can no longer control his own impulses, or (like King Tarquin) those of his sons: the "heirs" who turn to "violence against women." But there is a third reason why women are a danger, still another form of their political threat. Machiavelli cites Aristotle as listing, "among the first causes for the fall of tyrants some injury in a matter of women," mentioning as examples both Lucretia and the ancient Virginia, sexual abuse of whom led to the downfall of the Decemvirs.[39] But the case of Duke Galeazzo makes the point more explicitly. He liked "to debauch noble women" and then, bragging, "make his successes public," and he also abused his

---

34. "Life of Castruccio" (G 553); J. H. Whitfield, "Machiavelli and Castruccio," *Italian Studies* 7 (1953): 13.

35. "Life of Castruccio" (G 556).

36. Livius, *History* 7.38.5–7.

37. *Discourses* 2: 19 (G 381); Livius, *History* 7.38.5. See also *Florentine Histories* 7: 34 (G 1381).

38. *Art of War*, bk. 6 (G 691).   39. *Discourses* 3: 26 (G 488–89).

mother to the point where people considered him responsible for her death; he ultimately came to grief because he "dishonored" two of his subjects "with regard to women." Through these "private injuries" he strengthened their political "resolve" to act against him and "free their country."[40]

Women are a danger for conquerors, as this example shows, because they are invested with other men's sense of honor. Each woman is attached to at least one man—husband, father, brother—whose honor is at stake in her chastity. The ruler who cannot or will not leave the women of his subjects alone is toying with one of the most dangerous sources of potential opposition. That is why the prince must never "seize upon the property and the women of his subjects"; men will put up with almost anything so long as they "are not deprived of either property or honor."[41] Property is property, but women are both property and honor.

For the same reason, women are a danger not merely to tyrants, princes, and conquerors, but also to the healthy political life of a republic. They weaken the manly self-control of citizens as they do that of princes, and they tend to privatize the republican citizen, drawing him out of the public square into the bedroom. Was not the very first "division" in the city of Florence, which had remained united in its early virtuous political health longer than other Italian cities, "caused" by two women: a "rich widow" and her "very beautiful daughter" who stirred up a family feud?[42] Internal divisions in turn are likely to produce external intervention and thus destroy the autonomous life of the body politic. Machiavelli cites the example of the city of Ardea, in which a dispute over a woman led to so profound a factional division that each side called in foreign aid, and the city was conquered.[43] So, too, the ancient Tuscan city of Chiusi lost its freedom after a citizen, whose honor had been violated by an offense to his woman, called in the French to avenge it.[44]

❖   ❖   ❖

But here we begin to arrive at the deeper, more uncanny dangers that femininity seems to constitute for political life and at the more active, intentionally malicious power of women, exercised not by attractive

40. *Florentine Histories* 7: 33 (G 1379).
41. *Prince*, ch. 19 (G 67). See also ch. 17 (G 63).
42. *Florentine Histories*, 2:2–3 (G 1083).
43. *Discourses* 3: 26 (G 488–89).
44. Ibid., 1: 7 (G 214). Machiavelli distorts the story; cf. Livius, *History* 5.33.3; Strauss, *Thoughts*, 318 n. 66.

maidens but by older women who are active persons, but hostile. Older women constitute an even greater political danger than seductive girls. For one thing, these women can be as ambitious as men, particularly for their families or for their marriageable daughters, thus in ways that privatize and tend to fragment the community. Their power to exploit the divisive effect of sexual concerns takes on legendary proportions. It caused the first internal divisions in Florence. It specifically weakens patriarchal and political bonds among men. Tarquin the Proud seized power at the urging of his ambitious wife, the daughter of the previous, legitimate king. "Moved" by the "fury" of her ambition for the throne, "against all paternal devotion," she "urged on her husband against her father to take away his life and his kingdom."[45]

The older women in Machiavelli's fiction are very different from their daughters. They are not sexually attractive or seductive, but they often control access to the young women, either blocking or facilitating the men's desires. The mother in *Mandragola* is presented from the outset as worldly wise and knowledgeable, and corrupt.[46] She is characterized as "a bitch" with a checkered past of her own; she readily accedes to Ligurio's plan for her daughter and even personally beds the girl down for the adultery.[47] Aside from her own background, the only hint we are given of her motive in doing so is a maxim she enunciates—a maxim familiar from Machiavelli's political writings: it is prudent always to "take the best among bad choices."[48] In *Clizia*, the mother is even more of an active schemer, though on the side of conventional morality rather than corruption (but that is dictated by Plautus's plot). Whereas in *Casina*, the ancient play, the mother is a shrew who has been at odds with her husband for years, the mother in *Clizia* is a good woman, an agent of virtue and order. Instead of advising "the best among bad choices," she says "one ought to do what's right at any time," and especially "when the rest are doing what's bad."[49]

Although she is an agent of morality, however, her methods are those of manipulation and deceit. There is no foxy Ligurio in this play; instead, the successful manipulator is the mother herself, who controls the outcome through her "beautiful cleverness [*bello inganno*]." In the end she tells her defeated and humiliated husband whose adulterous intentions she has foiled that it was she who "managed all those tricks that have been played on you" in order to "make you come to your

45. *Discourses* 3: 4 (G 426).
46. *Mandragola*, act 1, sc. 1 (G 780).
47. Ibid., act 3, sc. 9 (G 801); act 3, sc. 11 (G 803).
48. Ibid., act 3, sc. 1 (G 793).   49. *Clizia*, act 2, sc. 3 (G 832).

senses." He thereupon agrees to put himself "into her hands" and submit to her rule in the household: "Do what you like; I'm prepared not to
go beyond the limits you set."[50]

Is this mother, agent of morality and order, then like Lucretia "fit to
rule a kingdom"? She certainly manages the outcome of events, refusing
to submit even to fortune. At one point she and her husband agree to
leave the decision of their conflict "to Fortune" by drawing lots, but
when the lot goes against the mother, she seeks other remedies.[51] At this
point in the play, Machiavelli inserts a song with no counterpart in
Plautus, concerning the dangerous power of woman. "He who once an-
gers a woman," it says, would be "a fool" to hope for "any mercy" from
her. For woman is characterized by "pride, anger, and disregard of par-
don," as well as "deceit and cruelty." With the aid of these characteristics, woman "gains her wish" in her "every undertaking," and when she
is angry or jealous, "her strength mortal strength surpasses."[52] It is almost as if a vengeful older woman *becomes* fortune, with superhuman
power over the outcome of events in the world of men.

Many of these topics recur in yet another combination in Machiavelli's story or fable, "Belfagor: The Devil Who Married." The primary
theme is that the torments of hell are preferable to those inflicted by
"the female sex," particularly by a shrewish wife.[53] Again there are two
sorts of women: young, passive but seductive daughters, and older,
vengeful wives, though here the pairing is not of mother and daughter
but of before and after. The shy virgin turns into the dangerous shrew
once she has gotten power over the man through love and marriage.

The tale of "Belfagor" is this. So many of the men arriving in hell
complain that they had been brought there "by nothing else than by
getting married" that the devils decide to test the truth of this plea.[54]
One devil is sent back to earth to marry. He chooses a "very beautiful"
girl, the "daughter" of a rich man, but soon falls "excessively in love
with her." Once she realizes her power over him, she begins to "lord it
over him." She is more prideful than Lucifer, spends all her husband's
money on clothes, gives him orders "without any mercy or consideration," and has such an "arrogant disposition" that she cannot even keep
servants.[55] Indeed, even the devils who came with the husband from hell
as his servants prefer to return there "and live in fire rather than stay in
the world under her rule." The husband flees her and, after further adventures, is finally tricked into returning to hell by the announcement

---

50. Ibid., act 5, sc. 3 (G 861).   51. Ibid., act 3, sc. 7 (G 845).
52. Ibid., canzone before act 4 (G 847).   53. "Belfagor" (G 869).
54. Ibid.   55. Ibid. (G 871).

that his wife is coming to fetch him. At the mere sound of the word "wife," he flees in "terror," preferring "to return to Hell . . . rather than again with such great annoyance, anxiety and danger to put his neck under the marriage yoke."[56] Earlier, during his adventures on earth, the devil enters into and "possesses" a number of young women. Although one of these women is married, they are all referred to only as "girls" or "daughters," and in every case it is the woman's father who arranges for an exorcism.[57] Again these women are not persons at all; they appear only for the purpose of being possessed. A mother, by contrast, has a distinct personality and is indeed capable of action, but she is filled with fury, and more dangerous to her husband than the devil himself.

The ominous nature of that fury and danger also appear in nonfictional form in the somewhat enigmatic last chapter of the *Discourses.* Linking apparently quite disparate dangers overcome by Rome, that chapter begins to suggest the underlying antipolitical power of femininity itself. Under the title, "A Republic, If She Is To Be Kept Free, Requires New Acts of Foresight Every Day; And For What Good Qualities Quintus Fabius Was Called Maximus," the chapter speaks first of "emergencies" in which a city needs a "physician."[58] These threats to the body politic are exemplified by an occasion in ancient Rome, "when it seemed that all the Roman wives had conspired against their husbands to kill them—there were so many who did poison them and so many who had prepared for doing so." The reference is to an incident in 331 B.C. when many leading Roman men died during an epidemic, and a slave girl charged they had been poisoned by Roman matrons. Twenty patrician ladies, found brewing something over a fire, were forced to drink their brew and died. After further investigation, 170 matrons were sentenced to death.[59]

Next, Machiavelli mentions another, later, poisoning incident in Rome, in which some two thousand people were condemned. Though here both men and women were involved, the poisoning conspiracy involved Bacchic rites of an obscene character performed in Roman nightclubs. Such "emergencies" were overcome, Machiavelli then indicates, only by Rome's readiness to punish large numbers of wrongdoers in "terrible" ways, such as decimation, whose very terribleness demonstrated "the greatness of that republic and the power of her deeds."[60]

56. Ibid. (G 877).
57. Ibid. (G 874–76).   58. *Discourses* 3: 49 (G 527).
59. Livius, *History* 8.18.1–13; Leslie J. Walker, tr., *The Discourses of Niccolò Machiavelli*, 2 vols. (New Haven: Yale University Press, 1950), 2: 214.
60. *Discourses* 3: 49 (G 528).

Only at this point does the chapter turn to Quintus Fabius. He in fact
was the one to whom the slave girl denounced the matrons' plot in 331
B.C. But Machiavelli does not mention that, presenting him instead
through a later incident in his life, involving an apparently quite unrelated sort of danger. "Through the liberality practiced by the Romans in
giving citizenship to foreigners, so many children were born in new
families that soon such numbers of them obtained the right to vote that
the administration was growing uncertain" and abandoning the old
policies and the old leadership. Quintus Fabius understood the danger
of this foreign growth inside the body politic, and he isolated "all those
new families—the cause of the difficulty—into four tribes," so that they
"could not infect all Rome."[61] For this he was, and "deserved to be"
called the greatest: "Maximus."[62] Machiavelli himself calls the "emergencies" conjoined in this chapter "strange," but he does not make clear
what they mean to him. They seem to concern the introduction into the
body politic of alien substances that threaten to destroy it unless a physician intervenes with drastic measures. But sometimes the poison is literal, introduced in one case by women in conspiracy against their men,
in another by persons connected with a cult centered on female rapacious orality; sometimes the poison is symbolic, a foreign element introduced initially by Roman liberality about citizenship but immediately
interpreted in terms of fertility, the childbearing capacity of the foreign
women. This last case is remedied, as the chapter title suggests, by the
great man ready for any emergency. But in the former case, what saves
Rome is a readiness for severe and terrible punishment on a large scale,
and no "physician" or "act of foresight" seems involved. Is terrifying
punishment in some way the functional equivalent of a great man in
overcoming the corrupting poison of women? And why should a chapter about feminine and sexual dangers conclude the *Discourses*? Surely
it was not simply the last item left over after the other materials had
been arranged.

The richest but also the most confusing single source on women
in relation to politics is Machiavelli's long, unfinished poem, "The
[Golden] Ass," which again features the paired maiden and matron, and
which begins to extend the image of femininity from the merely human
to females of mythical proportions, including fortune. It relates a ver-

61. Ibid. (G 528–29).
62. Ibid. (G 529).

sion of the legend of Circe, a superhuman feminine figure who turns men into animals.[63] After an introductory chapter, the story proper begins in dark night, in a very "rough" and frightening place. The narrator says he cannot tell how he got to this place where he has "wholly lost [his] liberty"—though a little later he says "my little wit, vain hope and vain opinion have made me fall into this place."[64]

The threatening atmosphere of the place and a sudden loud blast on a horn so frighten him as to "vanquish" his "vigor [*virtù*]"; unable to stand upright, he is forced to lean against a tree trunk. While he is thus unmanned, a young woman "of the utmost beauty" appears, carrying a horn and a lantern and leading a flock of animals. The image of Diana was invoked in the first lines of the poem, but this young woman appears to be more of a herdswoman than a huntress. She explains that she is one of "many damsels" in the service of Circe, who rules over a kingdom in this forest. Circe is "an enemy to men" and turns any man who comes her way into an animal, "as soon as she looks fixedly on his face."[65] The young woman, by contrast, turns out to have a "loving countenance" that shines for the narrator "more than all other faces."[66] She warns the hero, "never does one who has come here get away," but nevertheless offers to help him do just that. She will protect him against Circe and reveal to him all of the queen's secrets. She tells him to pretend he is part of her flock, and thus, on all fours, he is led back to Circe's palace. There, unlike Diana who in mythology is always a virginal figure, the young woman proceeds to seduce the hero, summoning up his lost *virtù*.[67]

In "The [Golden] Ass," the beautiful young woman, though still the object of the hero's desire, plays a very active, even a dominant, role and has a developed personality. She encourages, teaches, feeds, and seduces him, and thereby protects him from the power of Circe that would hold him captive and unman him. She and the hero talk together "of many things, as one friend speaks with another," a degree of mutuality between the sexes that is not even approached anywhere else in Machiavelli's writings.[68] Yet even this woman holds the hero captive in her

---

63. Circe was the daughter of Helios. She poisoned her husband, a king, and went to live on the island of Aeaea. An enchantress celebrated for her knowledge of magic, evil spells, and poisonous herbs, she changed Odysseus's companions into swine but was overcome by Odysseus and slain by Telemachus, who married her daughter.

64. "[Golden] Ass," ch. 2, lines 22–24, 85–87 (G 753–54); the line is from Dante's *Inferno*.

65. Ibid., ch. 2, lines 36–37, 49–57, 5, 110–41 (G 753–55).

66. Ibid., ch. 5, lines 16–18 (G 762).

67. Ibid., ch. 2, lines 112–13 (G 755); ch. 4, lines 112, 129 (G 761).

68. Ibid., ch. 6, lines 22–24 (G 764).

room; and he, "surrendering" himself into her "power," swoons "all prostrate on her sweet bosom."[69] Her presence also keeps him from "reflection," and particularly from reflection on politics.

Indeed, "The [Golden] Ass" is a far more complex poem, of far greater interest for our purposes, than so far suggested. It not merely concerns relations between the sexes, but explicitly connects that topic with questions of political order; though its political message is far from obvious. Circe herself is a political figure, a "queen" who "rules her kingdom."[70] But much stress is also laid on the contrast between her feminine, natural world, and the world of men, which is political and the product of human artifice. Circe came to live in her palace in the forest, we are told, only after being forced "to abandon her ancient nest, before Jove seized dominion [lo stato]," and only after being unable to find refuge among human beings, "so great was the rumor of her infamy."[71] Thus she established herself in the forest, "fleeing all human society and law." And there, living as an enemy to man, she captures any men who come her way, depriving them of their "liberty," and of course literally changing them from human into animal form.[72] The men held captive by Circe live in dormitories resembling a "convent," and they are wholly dependent on feminine care in Circe's "nest," being guarded and led out to feed daily by the young servant woman.[73]

The entire Circe narrative making up the bulk of the poem, moreover, is set in a framework juxtaposing animality to political life. The introductory prologue opens with the narrator's declaration that he will relate what befell him while he was in the form of an ass. Now, this transformation into an ass never occurs, presumably because the poem is unfinished; the servant woman does at one point tell the hero that he will have to "travel to explore the world, covered with a different skin."[74]

In the prologue, however, the narrator does speak of himself as "braying" and having an ass's "nature," and then proceeds to tell a "tale" suggesting what these references might mean, what their political import might be. No other reason is given for the inclusion of this seemingly unrelated "tale." The tale concerns a young man living in Florence once upon a time, who suffered from a strange ailment: for no apparent reason, he would suddenly begin running heedlessly through the streets.

69. Ibid., ch. 4, lines 140–42 (G 761).   70. Ibid., ch. 2, lines 116, 138 (G 755).
71. Ibid., ch. 2, lines 101–5 (G 755).   72. Ibid., line 24 (G 753).
73. Ibid., ch. 6, lines 41–42 (G 765); ch. 5, line 10 (G 761).
74. Ibid., ch. 1, lines 1–2, 21 (G 750); ch. 3, lines 116–17 (G 758). The prologue seems modeled on Apuleius's "Golden Ass"; Udo de Maria, *Intorno ad un Poema Satirico di Niccolò Machiavelli* (Bologna: Zamorani e Albertazzi, 1899), 5.

His father tried many ways to cure him. Finally a "quack doctor" pretended to have cured him but ordered that for four months he not be allowed on the streets alone. This worked for a time, but then one day the youth, coming to a certain corner, could no longer "restrain himself, when he saw this street so straight and wide, from turning again to his old pleasure."[75] He dropped his cloak, ignored his companions' appeals to good sense and honor, shouted "Christ can't keep me here," and ran. "After that he always ran, as long as he lived." The moral drawn by the narrator is: "The mind of man, ever intent on what is natural to it, grants no protection against either habit or nature."[76]

But what is the significance of this tale, seemingly unrelated both to the Circe legend and to the metaphor of the braying ass? What is meant by this strange compulsion to run heedlessly through the streets of Florence? The ass, the narrator tells us, is an animal that bites and kicks and is used to receiving bites and blows in return, and it has a compulsion of its own: even "the heavens" cannot keep it "from braying." The narrator himself seems to share these characteristics, having had to learn not to "mind the slanderer's bite" and not to fear bites and blows: "for I have grown to have the same nature as he whom I sing." As the ass cannot help braying, and as the Florentine boy could not help running, the narrator says he cannot help "speaking ill" of those he knows, scattering "a bit of poison" by his revelations, seeing "bad more quickly than good" in his fellows. Like the Florentine boy, he began these evil practices in his childhood, having "early turned my thoughts to nipping this and that"; but seemed for a time to have given them up, standing "quite still and patient" like an obedient donkey, "no more observing others' defects, but seeking in some other way to get ahead so that I believed I was cured."[77] But nature will out; like the Florentine boy, the narrator relapsed, compelled by "the present age, so grudging and evil," and by the fact that he has been denied other ways of "getting ahead." Like the ass, he has "taken his course" in the world "up and down so many stairs . . . in order to see the nature of every mortal," that he cannot keep from braying out the truth, biting those around him.[78]

It seems inescapable that the ass, like the boy who ran, represents that other Florentine boy, Machiavelli himself, in his political exile; like him having been up and down so many back stairs in the palaces of the world, having learned to endure slander and other bites and blows, denied other ways of getting ahead, he will tell the malicious truth about

75. "[Golden] Ass," ch. 1, lines 18, 103–8, 30–78 (G 750–51).
76. Ibid., ch. 1, lines 79–90 (G 752).
77. Ibid.   78. Ibid.

all he knows. He presents himself in the ludicrous guise of an animal in order to have, as it were, license to bray.[79] Thus the prologue leads one to expect a satirical poem, in which various of Machiavelli's contemporaries will be ridiculed as animals. And indeed, that is how the catalogue of animals in the seventh chapter of the poem reads, though in its unfinished form one cannot identify the references.[80]

In addition, though more hesitantly, one might connect "running through the streets" of Florence with that "disorderly running through the streets" of Rome that Machiavelli praises in the *Discourses* as a manifestation of political health and a stimulant to Roman liberty, though others may condemn it as disease or craziness.[81] Or one may link it with that "promptness" with which, Machiavelli tells us in the *Florentine Histories*, the citizens of Genoa "ran together" in that city's streets when a patriot "shouted the name of liberty."[82] In Florence, by contrast, when Jacopo de'Pazzi took to the streets during the Pazzi conspiracy, "calling upon the people and liberty," because the people had been bought off by the Medici's "fortune and liberality," they had been made "deaf" so that "liberty was not known in Florence," and "he got no reply from anybody."[83] It may be, then, that while speaking malicious truths about all he has seen in the world, Machiavelli is also tempted to run heedlessly through his city's streets shouting the name of liberty; but because the people have been rendered deaf by the Medici once more, his shouts are merely the braying of an ass, the compulsion of a diseased boy. In his fury and frustration he will bite and kick at the people through a satirical poem; in his disguised form he may escape their vengeance, though unable to secure their liberty.

Besides Circe's own political or antipolitical role, and the prologue's evident references to the politics of Machiavelli's Florence, the poem links its manifest story with political themes in still a third way. Its fifth chapter is a long disquisition on politics, a meditation by the hero, left alone when the young servant woman goes off to her herding. Instructed to stay in the safety of her room, but no longer rendered "forgetful of human things" by her presence, the hero is struck by "the arrow of reflection," of whose "wound" she had temporarily "cured" him, and begins to think about the world of politics.[84] Specifically, he thinks about what causes the rise and fall of "kingdoms" and "ancient

79. In a letter from exile complaining how he has lost touch with political events, Machiavelli calls himself an ass; to Vettori, 10 August 1513 (G 921).
80. G 767n; de Maria, *Intorno*.
81. *Discourses* 1: 4 (G 203).
82. *Florentine Histories* 5: 7 (G 1241).   83. Ibid., 8: 8 (G 1393).
84. "[Golden] Ass," ch. 4, line 138 (G 761); ch. 5, lines 22–24 (G 762).

peoples," and his conclusion is: ambition, particularly ambition that knows no limit—the fact that "the powerful with their power are never sated." Everyone recognizes "this transgression" and its consequences, that "this appetite destroys our states," yet "no one flees from it." Thus Florence failed to understand that her security lay in not extending her empire too far, "that too much power was damaging." The right way for Florence to live would be like the free German cities, "secure through having less than six miles round about." But since ambition drove Florence to limitless expansion, the city now "dreads everything."[85]

Yet surely it was also ambition that drove the narrator, unable "in some other ways to get ahead," to bray and run. Is ambition always bad? The hero's meditation turns immediately to the opposite view. Ambition is a form of manly energy that promotes success: those king- ~NARRATOR~ doms "always" rise that are "pushed on to action by energy [*virtù*] or ~OF GOLDEN~ necessity," so long as they have appropriate safeguards against the dan- ~ASS~ gers ambition entails. They must be internally unified and governed by good laws and customs. And it concludes with an attack on those Christian reformers—perhaps like Savonarola—who ascribe the decline of states to "usury or some sin of the flesh" and prescribe "fastings, alms, and prayers."[86] The narrator maintains that though religion is necessary for "unity and good order" in the state, God only helps those who help themselves. "To believe that without effort on your part God fights for you, while you are idle and on your knees, has ruined many kingdoms and many states."[87] The meditation seems to call, then, for activity and effort rather than prayer and the acknowledgment of dependence, yet it recognizes that this urge to action can easily become a hunger for power after power that knows no satiety. But why are these thoughts sandwiched between two bedroom scenes in Circe's palace? What is the connection between ambition and politics on the one hand, and relations between men and women, and animality, on the other?

The agency that destroys the overextended state and the overambitious individual is feminine. The narrator calls that agency "fortune" and personifies her as a female of mythic proportions. She looms behind the entire world of the poem, as a sort of supermatriarch beyond even Circe. In the very first line of "The [Golden] Ass" fortune is invoked as the poet's muse, and both the narrator and the young servant woman acknowledge their subjection to her, though her relationship to Circe is left undefined.[88] The servant woman advises the hero not to let fortune

85. Ibid., ch. 5, lines 32–69 (G 762–63).
86. Ibid., lines 79–111 (G 763).   87. Ibid., lines 115–7 (G 764).
88. Ibid., ch. 1, line 3 (G 750); ch. 5, line 6 (G 761).

know how much her blows have hurt him, to show her a "face un-
stained with tears"; his greatest danger, it seems, is being unmanned
and reduced to mewling babyhood, for "weeping has always been
shameful to a man."[89] Against this danger, as against the power of
Circe, the servant woman seeks to protect him by summoning up his
virtù. And, like the narrator and the ass in the prologue, fortune bites:
the rise and fall of ancient peoples is characterized as the alternate ca-
ressing and "nipping" of fortune.[90] But the figure of fortune gets relatively little explicit attention in "The [Golden] Ass," and we shall
postpone further discussion of her in order to look more fully at the
complex relationships suggested in the poem between politics and nature, and between each of these and sexuality.

Machiavelli never explicitly personifies nature, yet it is clear that in
this poem the feminine world is the world of mother nature as well. Juxtaposed to the masculine world of law and liberty, we have the forest
world where men are turned into animals and held captive in permanent
dependence. Each is turned into the animal that best embodies his particular human character. So when the young servant woman takes the
hero on a tour of Circe's zoo, she shows him, by "the light she had hidden beneath her garment," the true nature of each captive man, and
thereby also the general "nature of our condition."[91] She shows him the
lions, transformed men who had "magnanimous and noble" hearts, but
adds wryly, "few of them are from your city."[92] Instead, as they proceed,
the narrator learns "how many" whom he "had once considered Fabiuses
and Catos turned out to be sheep and rams" in their transformed—
that is to say, their true—nature.[93] Finally she shows the narrator a pig
covered with "turd and mud," warning him not to try enticing the pig out
of its wallow to make it "turn into a man," for she says the pig "would not
desire" such a change. It has come to prefer its animal condition, as the
pig itself proceeds to confirm.[94]

It is only the narrator's "self-love," the pig says, that makes him consider the human condition superior to that of animals and regard it as
the sole source of value. The pig instead affirms "without the least
doubt" that "our condition" is "superior to yours."[95] For animals live
by instinct, in harmony with nature. It is "Nature who teaches us" what

89. Ibid., ch. 3, lines 85–87 (G 757).
90. Ibid., ch. 5, lines 31–33 (G 762).
91. Ibid., ch. 7, line 8 (G 767); ch. 6, line 30 (G 764).
92. Ibid., ch. 6, lines 55–57 (G 765).
93. Ibid., ch. 7, lines 100–102 (G 769).
94. Ibid., ch. 7, lines 124–125; ch. 8, lines 1–3 (G 769).
95. Ibid., ch. 8, lines 25–45 (G 770).

to do, "what any plant is, whether harmless or injurious."[96] Further, the animals are more virtuous than modern men:

Among us are done bold deeds and exploits without hope of a triumph or
  other fame, as once among those Romans who were famous. . . .
Still among us some beasts live who to escape from prison and chains, by
  dying gain both glory and liberty;
If on temperance you turn your gaze, you will plainly see that in this game we
  have surpassed your side.
On Venus we spend but short and little time, but you without measure follow
  her in every time and place.[97]

Finally, the animals are "closer friends to Nature" than is man and share in her "vigor [*virtù*]" more freely. They are content with the food nature offers them "without art," instead of hungering like man for "that which Nature cannot supply."[98] Not thus contented, man must rely on artifice for his needs; among all the animals, "only man is born devoid of all protection," naked and helpless: "in weeping he begins his life." And though nature gave man "hands and speech" as the twin tools of his art, along with them she also gave "ambition and avarice," whose evil outweighs the good of the first gifts.[99] Nature at the outset and afterwards fortune subject man to countless ills, betray countless promises they have made him. No animal has a "frailer life" or a "stronger desire" for living, "more disordered fear or greater madness." Beset with "ambition, licentiousness, lamentation and avarice," man is "slain, crucified and plundered" by his fellowman, while animals never harm other members of their own species. And the pig reiterates his refusal to be changed back into a human, saying that he lives "more happily" in his mud wallow, where he is free of "anxiety."[100]

There is, then, considerable ambivalence in this poem about the costs and advantages of being a man. Circe has fled human society and law yet rules a kingdom. The pig claims that animals not merely are more natural than man but even excel man at the civic virtues: as brave as the ancient Romans, more temperate and continent than modern man. Are ambition and *virtù* gifts of nature, or are they what raise man out of the animal world? The pig says he will not leave that world, where he is free of anxiety. Yet everything else that we are told about the animals in Circe's palace indicates that they are contemptible and de-

96. Ibid., ch. 8, lines 46–54 (G 770–71).
97. Ibid., lines 76–93 (G 771).
98. Ibid., lines 106–7, 94–96 (G 771–72).
99. Ibid., lines 121–32 (G 772). See also *Discourses* 3: 12 (G 459).
100. "[Golden] Ass," ch. 8, lines 136–51 (G 772).

generate, unwilling captives longing to return to human form. The interpretive difficulties presented by these conflicting themes have driven some commentators to the claim that there are two different categories of animals in the poem: healthy ones that have always been animals and are noble in nature, and transformed humans who are unhealthy and crippled. This would make good sense, but there is no textual evidence for it. On the contrary, the pig that defends animal nobility is explicitly identified as a former human transformed by Circe and is clearly speaking about others like himself. He tells the hero to "direct your imagination . . . on me" and uses the first person plural throughout his praise of the animal world: we (formerly human) animals are superior to men.

Machiavelli is not the only writer for whom the Circe legend has involved ambivalence about the relative desirability of being masculine and adult versus being animal and childish. Indeed, the chapter on the pig may well imitate Plutarch's dialogue on "Reason in Beasts," in which Ulysses holds discourse with Gryllus, changed into a pig by Circe.[101] In Plutarch's version, too, the general implication of the Circe legend, that being captured and turned into an animal is undesirable, is surprisingly contradicted by the pig's attitude. Plutarch's pig, like Machiavelli's, refuses restoration to human form, finding animals more courageous, more temperate, and generally more virtuous than man. We must also recall that Machiavelli's poem is unfinished. Perhaps he had not yet noticed, or at any rate not yet been able to resolve, the contradiction; perhaps, indeed, that was why the poem was left unfinished. Also, in its present form the poem tells us nothing about how the narrator was changed into an ass and later changed back: was he willing or unwilling? And by what agency was he so transformed? One suspects Circe but also that other female looming behind her who deprived the narrator of any "other way to get ahead" than malicious "observing" and asinine "braying" about the "defects" of other men. This woman, whom the narrator invokes as his muse, is the same power that "cut off" the author of *Mandragola* "from showing other powers [*virtù*] with other deeds" and that laid on the (ass's?) back of the author of *The Prince* the "burden of" her "great and steady malice": fortune.[102]

"THE GOLDEN ASS"

In any case, the themes of this poem seem clear enough. It concerns male and female, autonomy and dependence, maturity and childhood, humanity and animality, political artifice and nature, ambition, aggres-

---

101. Plutarch, *Complete Works*, 6 vols. (New York: Thomas Y. Crowell and Company, 1909), 5: 693–705.
102. "[Golden] Ass," ch. 1, lines 94–96, 108 (G 752); lines 1–3 (G 750); *Mandragola*, prologue (G 778); Machiavelli, *Opere* 8: 58; *Prince*, dedication (G 11).

sion, and anxiety. But the poem's teaching about these matters is far
from clear, at least in the absence of a coherent theoretical framework
for Machiavelli's general views on these topics.

❖   ❖   ❖

The problematic relationships of the human, masculine, artificial,
and political to the natural and feminine, and of ambition and action to
both, recur as central themes in Machiavelli's other poetry, particularly
the tercets on "Ingratitude or Envy," on "Ambition," and on "Fortune."
All of these latter abstractions are, like the concept of fortune, of feminine gender in Italian; but that by itself is insufficient to prove that
Machiavelli or anyone else personified them at all, or specifically, as
women.[103] There may be a psychological tendency among speakers of a
language with gender, if they personify an abstraction, to imagine its
sex in accord with the word's gender, other things being equal. That is
an empirical question. But other things often are not equal, and it is
quite common in gender languages for a personification to have the sex
opposite to the word's gender. Translators sometimes mislead us in
these matters. Merely by capitalizing some abstract nouns they can suggest personification which may or may not have been intended by the
original author; and by using either the masculine and general, or the
feminine pronoun in English in connection with those nouns, they are
likely to suggest the sex of a personification, which again may or may
not correspond to the author's intent. We must therefore be cautious
in our claims. In Machiavelli's case, however, it is clear from the texts
that these particular abstractions are personified as female, and specifically as powerful women of mythical proportions who threaten men or
rule them.

The "Tercets on Ingratitude" are, even more explicitly than the prologue to "The [Golden] Ass," a meditation on Machiavelli's own "afflictions." These result, of course, from the actions of particular men, but
those actions were prompted by the intervention of a force called "ingratitude," personified in the poem as feminine.[104] Ingratitude is the
"daughter" of avarice and suspicion. In addition to her parents, she appears to have had a wet nurse who profoundly influenced her character;
she was "nursed in the arms of envy." We are not told whether the infant ever bit the nurturing breast, but biting appears repeatedly in the

103. The word *virtù* itself is of feminine gender. So are nature, necessity, *occasione*, and
chance (*sorte*). Another word for chance (*caso*) is masculine, as are fate, deception (*inganno*), genius (*ingegno*), heaven, and laziness.
104. "Tercets on Ingratitude," lines 17–18, 24–25 (G 740).

poem. The wet nurse, envy, characteristically has "a tooth" with which she can "bite" men, cursing the bitten ever after to "live as a malcontent." Indeed, everything everywhere is "pierced and bitten by" the "envenomed tooth" of ingratitude's "nurse."[105] Machiavelli has been its victim. Ingratitude herself does not bite but (like love) shoots at men with arrows; her arrows, however, seem to transmit the oral aggression associated with her nurse. A man struck by ingratitude's third and most powerful arrow ever after "rends and bites his benefactor."[106]

As in "The [Golden] Ass," such images of oral aggression are directly linked with political consequences. Ingratitude makes her "nest," her "chief abode," in "the breasts of princes and kings," though in fact she "triumphs in the heart of every ruler" whatever.[107] In states where the people rule, she "takes even more delight in the heart of the populace." For the people, being ignorant of and distant from political affairs, are more liable to suspicion and therefore to ingratitude: "Where little is known, more is suspected." Machiavelli's own plight and that of his former leader, Soderini, might be cases in point, but the poem cites the ancient example of Scipio Africanus, forced into exile from public life by the ingratitude of the Roman people.[108] Scipio is characterized in extravagant language, very much as a heroic forefather of mythical proportions, yet even he was ultimately brought down by the dominant feminine power of envy, expressed both in her bite and (like the power of Circe) in her glance. Though Scipio was a man without equal, ancient or modern, she did not "fear to show him the teeth of her madness, and to look on him with the pupils of her eyes aflame."[109]

In the "Tercets on Ambition," the dangerous feminine figures are ambition and avarice. Though the images of oral aggression are absent, these figures are personified like envy and ingratitude, and like ingratitude, they are themselves formed by a still more seriously dangerous female. Ambition and avarice, the poem says, are "natural instincts" in man and were "born into the world" together with him.[110] However, the poem also maintains a later origin for them, more in accord with Christian doctrine. Ambition and avarice appeared only after God had made man and after Adam and Eve had been banished from the garden. They were created not by God, but by a "hidden power which sustains itself

105. Ibid., lines 25–26, 33, 1–2, 112–13 (G 740–42).
106. Ibid., lines 40–54 (G 741).
107. Ibid., lines 27–28, 61–62 (G 740–41). See also *Discourses* 1: 28 (G 256).
108. "Tercets on Ingratitude," lines 62–129 (G 741–43). See also *Discourses* 1: 29 (G 259).
109. "Tercets on Ingratitude," lines 112–14 (G 742).
110. "Tercets on Ambition," lines 12, 79 (G 735, 737).

in the heaven, among the stars which heaven as it whirls encloses."[111] Like Circe and others of these mythical females, this power is "to man's being by no means friendly"; it sends ambition and avarice as two "furies" to live among men. They are naked and possessed of "such grace that, to the eyes of many, in grace and happiness they abound"; but they are also said to have four faces each and eight hands, enabling "them to grip you and to see in whatever direction they turn."[112] These graceful, monstrous feminine furies are explicitly said to symbolize the limitlessness of human cravings, hence each of them carries a "bottomless urn." It was they who pitted Cain against Abel, introducing "the first violent death . . . in the world." Since then, their influence has become so widespread that by now "there is no reason for men to repent of doing evil." Among universally wicked men, wickedness is the only policy that works; goodness will lead to defeat and regrets.[113]

But is that the teaching of the poem? Not at all: it proceeds to show most eloquently why men might nevertheless "repent" of evil, and particularly of limitless ambition, as they "behold the sorrows of others" and draw the implications for themselves.[114] Quite possibly based on Machiavelli's experiences at Verona in 1509, where he observed the consequences of the war of Pope Julius II and his allies against Venice, the poem sings vividly of

. . . strange events such as never have happened before in the world! . . .
Foul with blood are the ditches and streams, full of heads, of legs, of arms,
    and other members gashed and severed.
Birds of prey, wild beasts, dogs are now their family tombs—Oh tombs
    repulsive, horrible and unnatural!
Wherever you turn your eyes, you see the earth wet with tears and blood, and
    the air full of screams, of sobs, and sighs.[115]

Thus the "natural instincts" of ambition and avarice produce results "repulsive, horrible and unnatural." As with the pig's discourse in "The [Golden] Ass," it is no easy matter to discern the costs and advantages of the natural life.

The point at which the horrors of war reach the height of "unnaturalness," moreover, is in the outraging of piety toward dead relatives, the violation of "family tombs." The whole of the poem's description of the

111. Ibid., lines 13–25 (G 735–36).
112. Ibid., lines 27–36 (G 736). Compare medieval images of fortune as multilimbed; Howard R. Patch, *The Goddess Fortuna in Medieval Literature* (New York: Farrar, Straus and Giroux, 1974), 42–44.
113. "Tercets on Ambition," lines 41–63 (G 736).
114. Ibid., lines 130–31 (G 738).
115. Ibid., lines 132–59 (G 738, 735 headnote).

horrors of war, indeed, is filled with images of violence in the bosom of
the family:

A man is weeping for his father dead and a woman for her husband; another
   man, beaten and naked, you see driven in sadness from his own dwelling.
Oh how many times, when the father has held his son tight in his arms, a
   single thrust has pierced the breasts of them both!
. . . every day many children are born through sword cuts in the womb.
To her daughter, overcome with sorrow, the mother says: "For what an
   unhappy marriage, for what a cruel husband have I kept you!"[116]

Whether these desecrations result from natural instincts untamed by
civilization or are the work of a "hidden power" in "the heaven" different from God the creator and far from "friendly" to man, either way
they would seem to derive from a dangerous, mythical female force. For
the mysterious hostile force in the heavens seems, again, to be fortune.
The poem does not explicitly make the identification, but it does say
that it is because of ambition and avarice that men's condition, and that
of states, is never stable or secure, that "one goes down and another
goes up" eternally—an image strongly reminiscent of fortune's wheel.[117]
In the face of these powers, most men resign themselves to passivity, believing that nothing can be done: "Most men let themselves be mastered
by Fortune."[118] But Machiavelli wants to teach that they need not do so;
they do have resources for controlling their own limitless ambition. If
anyone "blames Nature" for the dreadful, bloody conditions in Italy,

I say that this does not excuse or justify . . . for discipline [*educazion*] can
   make up where Nature is lacking.[119]

The remedy, then, would seem to be that same punitiveness which in the
last chapter of the *Discourses* was the Romans' remedy against the
murderous conspiracy of wives. Italy flourished in ancient times, the
poem says, precisely because "stern discipline [*fiera educazion*]" then
countered the powers of nature or fortune. The agent of these powers,
ambition, cannot be extirpated from the human soul, but it can be controlled through "grace or better government [*ordin*]." For the individual
this means that

Since no man has power to drive her out of himself, needful it is that Judgment and Sound Intellect, with Method and Vigor [*ordine e ferocia*], be her
   companions.[120]

116. Ibid., lines 113–53 (G 738).
117. Ibid., line 64 (G 736).   118. Ibid., line 177 (G 739).
119. Ibid., lines 112–14 (G 737); Machiavelli, *Opere* 8: 322.
120. "Tercets on Ambition," line 117 (G 737); lines 187, 163–65 (G 739); Machiavelli,
Opere 8: 322–24. Gilbert exaggerates the point, however, by rendering *educazion* as
"discipline."

For if ambition is joined with "a valiant [*feroce*] heart, a well-armed vigor [*virtute*]," with a manliness that verges on ferocity, it will give the individual courage, so that "for himself a man seldom fears evil." Similarly for states,

> When through her own nature a country lives unbridled, and then, by accident, is organized and established under good laws,
> Ambition uses against foreign peoples that violence which neither the law nor the king permits her to use at home.[121]

That is why in war, "home-born trouble most always ceases" as the citizenry close ranks against the foreign enemy. For states, then, the evils of ambition that are manifested in internal divisions can, through discipline and good laws, be converted into courage in warfare. But the poem at once acknowledges the costs of this solution: inflicting abroad the violence that has been eliminated at home. A state that pursues such a course

> . . . is sure to keep disturbing the sheepfolds of others, wherever that violence of hers has planted its banner.[122]

And the disturbed sheep, as the metaphor implies, are innocent victims in the slaughter, precisely like those whose sufferings the poem so eloquently describes.

Thus this poem, like "The [Golden] Ass," seems to be a desperate, circular meditation on the costs and advantages of being human rather than bestial, of being ambitious and political; and once more these are intertwined with questions of masculinity, the dangerous power of female forces, the hope of overcoming them through masculine discipline and ferocity, the horrible costs that the latter entail.

The power of femininity, then, is a complex topic for Machiavelli, centrally intertwined with political concerns. Young women are dangerous as desirable objects, threatening to debilitate men and to privatize them. Older uxorial and matronly women have personality and the capacity for agency, but their purposes are likely to be evil, particularly when they are angry, which they often are. Their powers then approach the superhuman and dwarf those of men.

Obviously the maidens must eventually turn into matrons themselves. One suspects that the transition is mediated by carnal knowledge. Once initiated into adult sexuality, the maiden becomes dangerous in a new way because henceforth she has her own desires, has become a person in her own right. And her desires soon turn out to be insatiable. Then she

---

121. "Tercets on Ambition," lines 91–99 (G 737).
122. Ibid., lines 100–102 (G 737).

appears in twofold guise: as the raging shrew, the *virago* men fear, and as the lawful matron, subdued by the bonds of patriarchal marriage. The ancient Lucretia is such a tamed female, ready to destroy herself to uphold her husband's male honor against the dangers of her own sexuality. The modern Lucretia of *Mandragola*, though in fact married, is at first in character a "maiden," no doubt because feeble old Nicia has never really initiated her into sexuality. Once initiated by Callimaco, she is as if "reborn"; she has become a person. Though not yet angry or vengeful, she is instantly a competent and willful schemer, and one suspects that the dangerous anger will follow soon enough.

But there may also be a deeper, more symbolic level of relationship between the young and the older woman, in which the maiden is preceded rather than succeeded by the matriarch. The *virago*, one might suggest, is not merely woman experienced by adult men as the resentful wife, but also woman experienced by small children as the dangerous mother, who feeds but also dominates and threatens to engulf. The mythological females Machiavelli depicts suggest this interpretation, both by their overwhelming size and power, and by their frequent association with orality (feeding, nursing, biting, poisoning) and infancy (nests). In the face of such infantilizing matriarchal peril, a sexual liaison with a younger woman might offer comparative safety, affirming the man's masculinity and his graduation from childish dependence. Only comparative safety, however; for sexual liaison, in turn, threatens to make a man the slave of love, and it threatens to transform the younger woman into yet another angry shrew.

In these images of women, Machiavelli seems to juxtapose men, autonomy, adulthood, relations of mutuality, politics, the *vivere civile*, human agency in history, and humanness itself, on the one side, to women, childhood, dependence, relations of domination, nature, the power of environment and circumstance, instinct, the body, and animality, on the other. Human autonomy and civility are male constructs painfully won from and continually threatened by corrosive feminine power. Male ambition and human sexuality, however, play ambiguous roles in this struggle, sometimes aiding and sometimes threatening the men. Indeed, the men themselves are ambivalent about the struggle, continually tempted by the contented pig rolling about "without anxiety" in his "turd and mud."[123] So the feminine power seems to be in some sense inside the men themselves. Only ferocious discipline and terrifying punishments can secure them in the male enterprise of becoming human and autonomous.

123. "[Golden] Ass," ch. 8, line 151 (G 772); lines 1–3 (G 769).

But Machiavelli's most central and politically significant personification of the female power, in whom the dangerous matriarch and the sexually attractive maiden seem combined, has not yet been explored. She is, however, a figure of such importance and derives from such a long and complex historical tradition, that she requires a chapter of her own.

CHAPTER SIX

Fortune

Machiavelli did not invent the figure of fortune, but rather inherited it from a long tradition. He did, however, transform that inheritance, and the figure became central for his thought in a new way. Machiavelli's image of fortune embodies his central teachings about the human condition, about the possibilities and limitations of human action; in Allan H. Gilbert's words, it is "the essence of his theory of life and affairs."[1]

But one must begin with the tradition he inherited. Originally, *Fortuna* was a Roman goddess, though there are still earlier antecedents in prior cultures, like the Greek *tyche*. The word *fortuna* in Latin is formed adjectivally, from the noun *fors*, which means "luck," and ultimately from the verb *ferre*, "to bring."[2] So etymologically, fortune is that which is brought, and *Fortuna* is she who brings it. In its origins, the term was neutral concerning the manner in which she brings what is brought; the idea that fortune is capricious, variable, or unpredictable was an addition made in late Roman times.[3] The Romans, moreover, already understood that variability of fortune in terms not of meaningless, chaotic fluctuations, but of the character and caprices of a person. She was identified as female, and her changeability was regarded as typifying the fickle unreliability of women.

As a goddess, fortune was open to human influence through supplication and propitiation. Yet on the whole her image in Roman thought was positive; though capricious, she was primarily the source of goods—

1. Allan H. Gilbert, *Machiavelli's Prince and Its Forerunners* (New York: Barnes and Noble, 1968), 219.
2. Thomas Flanagan, "The Concept of *Fortuna* in Machiavelli," in *The Political Calculus*, ed. Anthony Parel (Toronto: University of Toronto Press, 1972), 129.
3. Patch, *Goddess*, 10.

both of the good life and, more particularly, of external goods and possessions, fortunes. The Romans called her *bona dea*, the good goddess, and she had a great cult following.[4] By the time of the Empire, she had diversified into "one of those universal deities who gradually replaced the old Roman contingent of gods"; she became identified with Isis, for instance, or worshipped as *Fortuna Panthea* or *Fortuna Populi Romani*.[5] Three symbols were central to her image in Rome and appeared persistently when she was depicted: she was shown with a cornucopia (as the bringer of abundance), at the rudder of a ship (steering the course of our lives), or with a ball or wheel (determining the turning, the rise and fall of human destinies).[6] Already in Roman thought, the figure of fortune was often coupled with that of *virtus*, human manly energy or ability capable of confronting fortune's power. The confrontation between *virtus* and *Fortuna*, indeed, became so frequent in Roman literature even before Cicero as to be commonplace, "even so banal, that it could sink to the level of a pedagogical device for rhetorical exercises."[7] The role of *virtus* in regard to *Fortuna* appears always to have been limited and respectful, however, as is appropriate in the face of a goddess. *Virtus* was directed toward human self-control rather than toward control of the goddess. The cultivation of courage, rational wisdom, mastery of the passions, and selfless devotion either to public duty (as in middle Stoic thought) or to withdrawal from public and worldly concerns into the inner values of contemplation (as in late Stoicism) were remedies against fortune, not in the sense of reducing the realm of her power, but in the sense of withdrawing human concern from it.[8]

With the triumph of Christianity, fortune by no means disappeared, but the conception was transformed. For the early Middle Ages, the imagery was set by Boethius's enormously influential *Consolations of Philosophy*, which presents a much more somber picture. Much of the metaphor and imagery surrounding fortune disappears; there remains only the wheel, "which fortune grimly turns."[9] The wheel's movement, and fortune's character, shift from capriciousness to inexorability. And far from being propitiated or influenced by supplication, fortune—

4. Flanagan, "Concept," in Parel, *Political Calculus*, 130–31.
5. Ibid.; cf. Patch, *Goddess*, 12; A. Doren, "Fortuna im Mittelalter und in der Renaissance," *Vorträge der Bibliothek Warburg* 2 (1922–1923): 71–115.
6. Flanagan, "Concept," in Parel, *Political Calculus*, 130–31.
7. Klaus Heitman, *Fortuna und Virtus: eine Studie zu Petrarcas Lebensweisheit* (Köln: Boehlau, 1958), 18–19.
8. Patch, *Goddess*, 13.
9. Robert Orr, "The Time Motif in Machiavelli," in Fleischer, *Machiavelli*, 198; Doren, "Fortuna," 77–79.

though still personified and female—has become an agent of the Christian God, part of the universal order and hierarchy, working out divine providence. In the medieval understanding, from Boethius to Aquinas, God governs the world through his providence, which is the reason of the universe, and through fate, which is the active order of the universe exercised from above in the great hierarchy of being. This latter fate, in turn, governs fortune, who becomes ultimately "the duly appointed Intelligence in charge of the distribution of external goods," as distinct from "goods of the soul."[10]

In some ways the medieval concept of fortune parallels the cult of the Virgin.[11] Both figures are conceived as feminine and specifically maternal; fortune is frequently shown nursing an infant. Both are often shown as queens ruling over a realm, living in a palace. But the Virgin is a "good" mother, to whom one prays for intercession with God the Father, for mercy and forgiveness to temper his righteous justice. Fortune, by contrast, is often seen as a stepmother, as angry and terrifying, and as an inexorable agent of God's judgment.[12] Sometimes she is depicted as a monster, with multiple faces or limbs.[13] One does not pray to fortune, not so much because that might be idolatrous as because she is no longer subject to human influence. Men do not contend against her power over them; at most they participate in the making of their fortune by *choosing* to ride or climb her wheel. But fortune is no longer juxtaposed to the masculine energy of *virtus*; even less than in Roman thought is there "any room for maneuver against her."[14] Instead, men are to submit to her and learn from her: "she is not to be challenged, but to be studied." And what men learn from her is precisely the "consolations of philosophy": she works "to turn men's eyes away from this world where there is no justice, no correspondence between merit and reward, toward the eternal."[15] In their Christianization, both fortune and virtue have moved in the direction of transcendence and otherworldliness. "All fortune is good fortune because it can never rob the soul of virtue"; indeed, it instills virtue by teaching the acceptance of divine providence.[16]

10. Vincenzo Cioffari, "The Function of Fortune in Dante, Boccaccio and Machiavelli," *Italica* 24 (1947): 1–2.

11. Patch, *Goddess*, 61–63.

12. Ibid., 56, 61.   13. Ibid., 42–44, 52.

14. Flanagan, "Concept," in Parel, *Political Calculus*, 132; Orr, "Time Motif," in Fleischer, *Machiavelli*, 198.

15. Orr, "Time Motif," in Fleischer, *Machiavelli*, 198.

16. Boethius, *Consolations of Philosophy*, cited in Flanagan, "Concept," in Parel, *Political Calculus*, 143.

Even Petrarch's famous essay on fortune still sets out to provide "remedies" for both good and bad fortune. It consists of two dialogues, between Reason and Joy and between Reason and Sorrow. Both emotions prove vain in earthly terms, and the point is their transcendence by turning to God, the liberation from both failure and success.[17] So Petrarch's conception is still essentially medieval, though fortune has assumed a new—or revived—centrality in it and *virtus* has reappeared as her opponent. However, man is a passive object over which these forces contend. Man's role as defined by *virtus* is one not of resistant effort but of submission.[18]

Dante, too, continued the medieval pattern. He presented "Dame Fortune," the "lady of permutations," as having been assigned her post by God. No "mortal power" can influence her or even understand her ways; she does not hear those foolish mortals who want to address her.[19] By the time of Boccaccio's *Decameron*, fortune is no longer a disinterested, tranquil agency of transcendence but begins once more to be personified as an involved, mischievous, even cunning woman. She determines the outcomes of human actions, often helping to promote men's secular and even illicit intentions. Yet Boccaccio also maintains the connection between fortune and God's providence. Far from being blind, fortune works "with a view toward the ultimate end, carrying out the Divine Will."[20]

The Renaissance transformation of the figure of fortune is thus a gradual and piecemeal development. Medieval images continue alongside revived Roman themes as well as genuine innovations; there is a loosening and proliferation of images.[21] Perhaps because of the Renaissance interest in seafaring, exploration, and trade, the metaphorical connection of fortune to ships, steering, ports, and storms—probably never entirely abandoned in popular culture—is powerfully revived.[22] Indeed, by this time the Latin word *fortuna* has come in Italy to mean not just "chance" and "wealth" but also literally and specifically "storm."[23] But while in ancient renderings of seafaring fortune, she was shown at the helm of the ship, or occasionally as the storm driving it

17. Flanagan, "Concept," in Parel, *Political Calculus*, 145; Heitman, *Fortuna*, 57.
18. Heitman, *Fortuna*, 241, 249.
19. Dante, *The Inferno*, tr. John Ciardi (New York: New American Library, 1959), 74–75.
20. Cioffari, "Function," 3.
21. Cassirer, *Individual*, 75.   22. Doren, "Fortuna," 135.
23. Patch, *Goddess*, 107; Aby Warburg, *Francesco Sassettis Letztwillige Verfügung* (n.p., 1907), 140.

onward, now she appears as the ship's mast, holding the sail, while it is man who steers.[24] Thus, man is increasingly presented as active in the face of the forces that govern his life; if he is not able to control them, he can at least influence their effects or limit the extent of their power. Fortune is seen as yielding, "not to goodness, nor yet to wisdom, but to power."[25]

As the juxtaposition of *virtus* to fortune is revived, it carries an increasingly pronounced connotation of sexual conflict. In medieval depiction, *fortuna* and *virtus* were often both shown as female figures; and sometimes *virtus* was replaced by *paupertas*, so that the images presented the alternatives of wealth and poverty, rather than a conflicting of forces.[26] But in the fifteenth and sixteenth centuries, in both the plastic arts and literature and philosophy, the ancient juxtaposition of male *virtus* and female *fortuna* is revived. In addition, there appears, as an increasingly popular theme, a struggle between *fortuna* and Hercules— that figure of superhuman masculinity whose revival in the Renaissance we have already noted.[27]

In general, then, in this period fortune seems to become less grim and more promising, less inexorable and more amenable to human intervention. Indeed, some have suggested that the limits of fortune's power and the possibility of human action against her, the extent of human autonomy in history, become the central problem in Renaissance thought. Despite the conventional familiarity of the *Fortuna-virtus* theme in Roman thought, Klaus Heitmann argues that only in Italian Renaissance humanism does the question of their relationship become truly problematic, the central concern for man in this world.[28] The problem fascinated Coluccio Salutati, for instance, in the latter half of the fourteenth century, as he struggled to formulate an activist doctrine but ultimately returned to resigned acceptance of the inevitability of fortune.[29] Poggio, half a century later, essayed that the extent of human power vis-à-vis fortune changes as a man matures. The power of external forces over us is greatest when the self is still undeveloped, in childhood and youth. It recedes as the self awakens, strengthens, and becomes autonomous; it is

24. Flanagan, "Concept," in Parel, *Political Calculus*, 132; Cassirer, *Individual*, 77; Doren, "Fortuna," 134–35. Warburg cites an image with a female at the helm, though it is not clear whether the figure represents fortune (*Francesco Sassettis Letztwillige Verfügung*, 140). Doren cites an example from 1532 in which the wind turns fortune's wheel.
25. Doren, "Fortuna," 104.
26. Panofsky, *Hercules*, 164–66; Cassirer, *Individual*, 75–76.
27. Bernardo, *Petrarch*, 57, 60; Cassirer, *Individual*, 73.
28. Heitman, *Fortuna*, 21; Doren, "Fortuna," 100.
29. Doren, "Fortuna," 110.

forced to give way before the striving of man's cultural and intellectual energy. Thus, it is *virtus* and *studium* that ultimately conquer the opposing powers of the heavens, as manhood is fully achieved.[30]

Leon Battista Alberti, a quarter of a century later still, teaches that although fortune can deal heavy blows or give many rewards, she cannot take everything from a man nor give him character, virtue, or skill.[31] These ultimately depend on him. Alberti likens fortune to a river, suggesting that one must be a strong swimmer to survive the current.[32] Ficino, a generation after that, asserts boldly that fortune governs the outcome of only half our actions, our own *ingenium* governing the rest. Yet he means thereby still to refer to the ancient and medieval distinction between external goods that fortune controls, and goods of the soul that are within our own power. Thus in the end Ficino, too, counsels submission to fortune rather than struggle against her.[33] And Pico della Mirandola, just six years older than Machiavelli, writes that it is we who postulate fortune as a goddess, thereby attributing to the heavens powers that actually reside within ourselves. Man's fate is manmade; and fortune is not some force preceding and dominating man, but actually his dependent product, "the daughter of his soul [*sors animae filia*]."[34]

This, then, is the evolving and complex tradition that Machiavelli inherits, transmits, and develops. For him, too, fortune is sometimes a goddess, sometimes a river or storm, often in conflict with *virtù*, problematic in her relationship to human action. But for him, fortune is no longer, as in the medieval Christian view, the agent of divine providence in an ordered, hierarchical universe, nor is she a goddess in the Roman sense. He does occasionally link fortune with "God" or "Heaven(s)," but the former passages are usually attributed to some historical speaker rather than to Machiavelli himself, and the latter usually refer clearly to ancient rather than Christian "heaven(s)." Machiavelli's fortune is no longer a teacher of detachment or of the vanity of all external goods,

30. Cassirer, *Individual*, 76.

31. Leon Batista Alberti, *The Family in Renaissance Florence*, tr. Renée Neu Watkins (Columbia: University of South Carolina Press, 1969), 89, 148.

32. *Intercoenales. Op. Ined.*, ed. Mancini, 136 ff., cited in Cassirer, *Individual*, 77.

33. Cioffari, "Function," 10, citing Francesco Ercole, *Lo Stato nel Pensiero di Niccolò Machiavelli* (Palermo, 1917), 19 n.1. Warburg, *Francesco Sassettis Letztwillige Verfügung*, 140.

34. Pico della Mirandola, *In astrologiam libri* 12.3.27. fol. 519 cited in Cassirer, *Individual*, 120.

whether in relation to the welfare of the Christian soul or to ancient Stoic indifference. He does on rare occasions distinguish between the external "goods of fortune" and the internal goods of the soul and does sometimes use "fortune" simply to refer to wealth or possessions, but on the whole this distinction plays no significant role in his thought.[35]

Though he is far removed from the medieval conception of fortune, then, Machiavelli does not revive the ancient one either. He is not a teacher of Stoic detachment and withdrawal, but an activist. If he confronts fortune with *virtù*, it is not to inure men against her blows but to ward off or control those blows through active contention. And while he sometimes calls fortune a goddess, the means of coping with her that he suggests are not those usually applied to divinities. Specifically, although the personification of fortune as female is very old, Machiavelli appears to be the first to use that metaphor as a way of suggesting the sexual conquest of fortune, introducing into the realm of politics and history concerns about manliness, effeminacy, and sexual prowess. As Allan H. Gilbert has pointed out, references to fortune are frequent in the earlier *de regime principum* literature culminating in *The Prince*, but nowhere in that tradition is there a counterpart to the Machiavellian conception.[36]

Machiavelli's presentation is closest to the inherited tradition, as well as most metaphorical or mythical, in his tercets devoted specifically to fortune, where she is envisioned as a divinity and a queen, presiding over the wheels whose turning determines the destiny of man. She is a "cruel goddess," who is "demanding and injurious" toward men; she "gives commands and rules" them "with fury."[37] She is an "aged witch" with "two faces," one fierce and one mild, yet the poet hopes that because of his course she will look on him (presumably favorably), though with her "fierce eyes."[38] She is "shifting," "unstable," and "fickle," never keeps her promises, and acts "without pity, without law or right," often depriving "the just" and rewarding "the unjust." Like Circe, in "The [Golden] Ass," she has "dominion" over a "kingdom," sitting on a "throne" in a "palace" that is open to all men who want to come in, but difficult to escape.

---

35. *Florentine Histories* 4: 12 (G 1199); 3: 13 (G 1160); 4: 16 (G 1204); Machiavelli, *Opere* 1: 41, though the translators do not use the word *fortune* for *fortuna* here.

36. A. Gilbert, *Machiavelli's Prince*, 204–7, 234. The seizing of occasion by the hair (see below) is, however, an older theme with clear connotations of sexual conquest; the theme of fortune as a whore is also familiar in medieval literature; Patch, *Goddess*, 57.

37. Niccolò Machiavelli, "Tercets on Fortune," lines 4, 19–20, 23 (G 745).

38. Ibid., lines 19, 55 (G 745–46). Compare the medieval fortune figure with multiple limbs or faces, note 13 above.

Whoever tries to enter, she receives benignly, but at him who later tries to go
out she rages, and often his road for departing is taken from him.[39]

And again like the personified envy, she has a tendency to oral aggression:

you cannot . . . hope to escape her hard bite, her hard blows, violent and
cruel.[40]

Ultimately she raises men up only to cast them down again because
she "delights" in their fall; she is like a "raging," hungry eagle that

. . . carries a tortoise on high, that the force of its fall may break it, and he can
feed on the dead flesh.[41]

There is also a suggestion that the men who fall into her power are in
danger of castration, as she now "exalts," now "cuts off," the "splendid
horns of their fame."[42] She is herself ambitious and craves glory, liking
to make "herself splendid" and to have "her power . . . clearly seen";
she has the walls of her palace decorated with murals depicting her "triumphs"; she "turns states and kingdoms upside down as she pleases,"
and everyone sooner or later "feels her power." For this reason, many
consider her "omnipotent," but the poet advises that there is "no reason
. . . for fear" where a man is strong.[43] Among the masculine figures at
her court, the bad example is set by "anxiety," who lies "prostrate on
the floor" of the palace, "so full of fears that he does nothing" and
therefore is continually attacked by regret and envy.[44] "Audacity and
youth," by contrast, "make the highest showing," which indicates that
fortune prefers the man "who pushes her, who shoves her, who jostles
her."[45] Fortune's

reign is always violent if prowess [virtù] still greater than hers does not vanquish her.[46]

But it is not immediately clear where such prowess might be found.
"Her natural power" is "too strong" for any man and is feared "even by
Jove."[47] That she is at odds with Jove reminds us again of Circe; but
while Circe was put to flight by the god, he fears fortune, apparently an
even greater feminine power.

39. Ibid., lines 58–60 (G 746).   40. Ibid., lines 106–8 (G 747).
41. Ibid., lines 178–80 (G 749).   42. Ibid., lines 188–89 (G 749).
43. Ibid., lines 122–23, 128–29 (G 748); lines 31–32 (G 746); lines 25–27, 7 (G
745).
44. Ibid., lines 76–78 (G 747).
45. Ibid., line 75 (G 746); lines 163–65 (G 749).
46. Ibid., lines 14–15 (G 745); Machiavelli, Opere 8: 312.
47. "Tercets on Fortune," line 13 (G 745); line 45 (G 746).

In fortune's palace we find her traditional wheel, but Machiavelli has introduced an innovation: there is now more than one wheel, so that it may be possible for men to choose among them, or to jump from one to another.[48] Multiple wheels of fortune were not unknown in the Middle Ages, but they always formed an integrated system, not alternative options.[49] And while there were occasional suggestions that men climbed the wheel voluntarily, choosing to submit themselves to fortune's power, the stress on activism and human choice in Machiavelli's vision is really new.[50]

Those men will be fortunate, he says, who manage to "choose" a wheel in accord with fortune's "wish," to choose what she had intended for them.[51] But since each of the wheels turns, raising and then lowering anyone who rides it, so that no matter which wheel one chooses one must fall sooner or later, the only way to have good fortune permanently would be to change wheels periodically, at or near the crest of the turn.

A man who could leap from wheel to wheel would always be happy and fortunate.[52]

As Machiavelli makes clear, what he means by this metaphor is that success depends on a man's character being suited to his situation. If we could adapt our character to each new situation, we would always succeed. But he promptly adds that this is impossible, since "you cannot change your character," that possibility being "denied by the occult force that rules us." And what force is that? Is it fortune as well? Machiavelli does not say. His teaching in this poem is extraordinarily ambiguous. First it seems that success depends on choosing the right wheel, the one fortune intended for you; then, on the contrary, it depends on mobility from wheel to wheel, but this is again interpreted as an adaptation to fortune's changing wishes; then we are told that in fact such adaptability is humanly impossible. Thus the image of leaping from wheel to wheel, seen by some commentators as offering man "new possibilities for outwitting Fortune," in the end fails to do so, both because it is an adaptation to rather than an outwitting of fortune, and because it is revoked almost as soon as it has been presented.[53]

Like so many of Machiavelli's mature female figures, fortune is ac-

48. Ibid., lines 115–17 (G 747).
49. Patch, *Goddess*, 169–74.
50. Ibid., 165, 158; Doren, "Fortuna," 115.
51. "Tercets on Fortune," line 102 (G 747).
52. Ibid., lines 116–17 (G 747).
53. Flanagan, "Concept," in Parel, *Political Calculus*, 141.

companied in this poem by a young girl, *l'occasione*, a word variously translated as "occasion" or "opportunity" or "chance." She is "a tousel-haired and simple maiden," the only person who "finds sport" in for-tune's terrible palace, "frisking about among the wheels."[54] From an-other tercet devoted specifically to *l'occasione* we learn further that she never rests, always having one foot on her mother's wheel.[55] Following Ausonius, Machiavelli says in that tercet that *l'occasione*'s touseled hair is all in the front of her head, covering her face and breast, while the back of her head is bald. So the occasion can be seized (and fortune mastered) only by someone astute enough or lucky enough to recognize her as she approaches; once she has passed, there is no longer any way to seize her. For those who miss her, she is accompanied by her sister, *penitenzia*, regret.[56]

Besides a matriarch in a palace and the goddess of the wheel, fortune is compared in the poem about her to a natural force, specifically to a river liable to flood. Fortune is "a rapid torrent" which

> destroys whatever its current anywhere reaches, and adds to one place and lowers another, shifts its banks, shifts its bed and bottom, and makes the earth tremble where it passes.[57]

Nothing more is made of this metaphor in the poem, however, and in particular it yields no policy suggestions for human action.

Besides the tercets on fortune, there is only one other concentrated and extensive treatment of the topic in Machiavelli's work: the famous penultimate chapter of *The Prince*. It is a meditation every bit as com-plex and confusing as the tercets, developing many of the same themes in a more analytic manner.

In the final paragraph of the previous chapter, Machiavelli attacked the Italian princes of his time for ascribing the loss of their states to fortune, instead of taking responsibility for their own faults: they "should not blame Fortune, but their own laziness."[58] And then comes the analogy of natural forces. The princes' failure was that in times of good weather they never imagined the possibility that bad weather might follow, it being "a common defect in men not to reckon, during a calm, on a storm." Even when the weather did change, moreover, the princes

54. "Tercets on Fortune," lines 79–81 (G 747). On the medieval treatment of occasion, see Patch, *Goddess*, 116–17.
55. Machiavelli, *Opere* 8: 325.
56. Flanagan, "Concept," in Parel, *Political Calculus*, 147. See also Hugh G. Evelyn-White, *Ausonius, with an English Translation* (London: W. Heinemann; New York: G. P. Putnam's Sons, 1931), 2: 175.
57. "Tercets on Fortune," lines 151–56 (G 748).
58. *Prince*, ch. 24 (G 89).

did not think to "defend themselves" but ran away, vainly hoping that their subjects might later summon them back. This behavior—obviously reminiscent of Soderini's departure from Florence—Machiavelli condemns as a policy of dependence. And it is in this context that he formulates the striking maxim of autonomy cited before:

those defenses alone are good, are certain, are durable, that depend on yourself and your own abilities [virtù].[59]

At first, this train of thought seems to be a call to action and a condemnation of passivity in the familiar Machiavellian activist vein. But on closer examination, as in the "Tercets on Fortune," the activist message becomes more and more problematic, the implications increasingly obscure. Princes who blame fortune for the loss of their states are avoiding their true responsibility, for fortune is like the weather, changeable. Bad weather cannot be prevented, but it can be foreseen and prepared for. But instead of proceeding then to explain how a prince might prepare for bad weather, the passage instead distinguishes two policies available to those caught unprepared: flight with a fantasy of being loved and recalled, or autonomy in "defending oneself." But how is one to defend oneself against a storm for which one has neglected to prepare? Was it the vain hope of being loved that made the princes (and Soderini?) neglect to prepare for foul weather in the good times, neglect to erect around themselves the defensive bulwarks of autonomy? "He who is too eager to be loved gets despised," we may recall.[60] But what is the relationship between the very human issues of love and autonomy, and the almost mechanical concerns of preparing for a storm? Is fortune really as impersonal and beyond human influence as the metaphor implies? What is the real extent of fortune's power in relation to man?

These are the questions to which Machiavelli then turns in Chapter 25: "Fortune's Power in Human Affairs and How She Can Be Forestalled."[61] It opens with the question of whether to apply any metaphors at all, that is, whether there is any such agency as "fortune," other than a mere name for the consequences of what we do. And the chapter may be read as a meditation on the choice between the two metaphors introduced in the previous chapter: between fortune as a river and fortune as a woman. For though both metaphors suggest human activism, they have conflicting implications for conduct.

"Many have believed and now believe," the chapter begins, that human affairs are so much controlled by superhuman forces—"by For-

59. Ibid.; Machiavelli, Opere 1: 98.
60. Discourses 3: 21 (G 478).   61. Prince, ch. 25 (G 89).

tune and by God"—that they cannot be "managed" by men with their "prudence." This belief is particularly widespread in Machiavelli's own time because "of the great variations in affairs . . . beyond all human prediction" that have occurred and continue to occur.[62] When events in the world seem disordered and random, people tend to feel that they have no power over outcomes at all. Indeed, Machiavelli acknowledges that he himself inclines "now and then . . . in some respects to their belief." But the consequences of that belief are unacceptable to him, for it tends to make men passive; feeling unable to influence outcomes, they will "not sweat much over man's activities."[63] And then their belief becomes self-fulfilling, for when men refuse to take the initiative, "chance" really does determine what happens. So despite his occasional "inclinations" to believe in fortune's omnipotence, Machiavelli struggles to define a different position:

> Nonetheless, in order not to annul our free will, I judge it true [*potere esser vero* (that is could be true)] that Fortune may be mistress of one half of our actions but that even she leaves the other half, or almost, under our control.[64]

This last is a curious sentence, and curious in the Italian, not just in translation. For the placement of the clause about free will seems to imply that Machiavelli judges as he does because if he judged otherwise, he would by that act of judgment annul our free will. But surely that is an anxious delusion of grandeur: Machiavelli cannot strip us of free will if we have it; he can at most be wrong about free will. And the conclusion is hedged with extraordinary caution: "*may* be," *even* she," "*leaves*," "half, *or almost*." In the statement of his own judgment, moreover, the matter of God's role has disappeared, though he himself introduced it in the initial mention. Evidently the theme of human action and responsibility is fraught with great danger, and not just the social and political dangers threatening a theorist with unorthodox teachings, but also the hidden dangers threatening anyone who toys with impiety—with a prideful glorification of self and corresponding aggression toward the larger, older, senior, higher powers, be they parental, political, or divine. "Am I—are we—really autonomous?" is a question of the utmost sensitivity.

Having made his cautious yet implicitly megalomaniac declaration of his own judgment on the matter, Machiavelli returns directly to fortune as analogous to a natural force, but this time it is not the weather; it is a river, whose flooding is, however, linked to "the weather."

---

62. Ibid. (G 89–90).   63. Ibid. (G 89).
64. Ibid. (G 90); Machiavelli, *Opere* 1: 99.

I compare Fortune with one of our destructive rivers which, when it is angry, turns the plains into lakes, throws down the trees and buildings, takes earth from one spot, puts it in another; everyone flees before the flood; everyone yields to its fury and nowhere can repel it.[65]

The linking of fortune with natural forces, particularly with storms, we have seen, is very old and even encoded in Machiavelli's native language. The specific comparison to a river was made earlier, for instance by Alberti. Yet in the past the implications of these metaphors had been largely fatalistic. At most, as the Renaissance develops, there are ideas of human navigation through a storm, or of a strong swimmer surviving in the river. But Machiavelli, familiar with the flooding of the Arno in Florence and the veteran of an unsuccessful campaign to reroute that river in order to cut Pisa off from its water supply, draws a different implication from the simile. He is less interested in individual survival than in public, political control. Though fortune is like a river, he continues,

we need not therefore conclude that when the weather is quiet, men cannot take precautions with both embankments and dykes, so that when the waters rise, either they go off by a canal or their fury is neither so wild nor so damaging.[66]

There is thus the possibility to control the damaging power of fortune, if plans are made and implemented prudently early. Yet even as he develops a vision of technological mastery that might reduce the vagaries of chance in human affairs, Machiavelli continues to elaborate the alternative metaphor, that fortune is a woman. Having already spoken of the river as "angry" and in "fury" when it floods, he now suggests that fortune will not even try to harm those who have made preparations: "She . . . directs her fury where she knows that no dykes or embankments are ready to hold her."[67] The example Machiavelli immediately adduces is Italy, unprotected against invasion by the northern European states: Italy lacks embankments, which is to say, she lacks "*conveniente virtù*."[68] But concepts like anger and intent to harm are not literally appropriate to natural forces; even as Machiavelli invokes the images of flood and storm, he continues to personify the force involved.

Further, it seems that by the simile of the flooding river, Machiavelli means to suggest confidence in human foresight and capacity. Yet the image itself suggests more: it implies a way of proceeding—prudent planning, engineering skill, the erection of structures—and thereby a character type, and certain expectations about knowledge and results. It

---

65. *Prince*, ch. 25 (G 90).   66. Ibid.
67. Ibid.   68. Ibid.; Machiavelli, *Opere* 1: 99.

implies prudence and calculation, technical skill and engineering certainty, the handling of materials rather than interactions among men. And these implications turn out not to be what Machiavelli wants after all, or not to be the whole of what he wants to say. For his and Soderini's prudent planning did not work; and the militia did not succeed in protecting Florence against military aggression.

Thus, although he concludes the discussion of fortune as a river by saying he thinks it all he needs to say "in general" and so will now proceed to "particulars," in fact he proceeds instead to a reexamination or partial rejection of his own metaphor. The image of floods and dikes may imply activism, but the major question remains unsettled: not whether to act but how. The image of floods and dikes suggests prudence, but Machiavelli's experience has taught him that prudence ultimately succumbs to boldness and military might; in the end, the fox is not man enough. Thus the "particulars" to which he turns become the general observation that no one policy, even prudence itself, can successfully guide action in all situations. Prudence teaches its own insufficiency. "Men act in different ways: one with caution, another impetuously; one by force, the other with skill; one by patience, the other with its contrary. . . ."[69] And each may succeed sometimes and fail at others. Thus, no simple rule will do; neither "be prudent" nor "be bold." Rather, one can only say that to succeed, a man must adapt "his way of proceeding to the nature of the times." If a man "could change his nature with times and affairs," in effect, he would always have good fortune; for him, "Fortune would not change." This is of course the familiar idea of jumping from wheel to wheel in fortune's palace and thus never being forced to ride a wheel's downswing. But here, as before, Machiavelli is immediately forced to add that the image is a fantasy, for no man can change his basic character, which is what determines his way of proceeding. In particular, the prudent and cautious man, presumably good at planning and building dikes, will not always succeed, does not, in fact, gain technological control over outcomes. "When it is time to adopt impetuosity," this cautious man "does not know how. Hence he fails."[70]

Machiavelli then cites Pope Julius II as an example of a naturally bold and impetuous man who succeeded. And though Machiavelli insists that Julius would have failed if the times in which he lived had required prudence, apparently the advantages of boldness and impetuousness remain overwhelming in his mind, for he concludes the chapter with the

69. *Prince*, ch. 25 (G 91).
70. Ibid. (G 90–91).

second metaphor, again introduced, as was the first one, as his personal judgment:

> As for me, I believe [*iudico*] this: it is better to be impetuous than cautious, because Fortune is a woman and it is necessary in order to keep her under, to cuff and maul her. She more often lets herself be overcome by men using such methods than by those who proceed coldly; therefore always, like a woman, she is the friend of young men, because they are less cautious, more spirited, and with more boldness master her.[71]

Obviously one does not cuff, maul, and master a river in flood. Which is Machiavelli's real view: the river or the woman? The dilemma laid out in this chapter is, however, the same as that in the "Tercets on Fortune" and similar to those in "The [Golden] Ass." What commences as a rousing call to action develops into a meditation on man's helplessness in the face of fortune's power.

Much the same pattern of thought is played out again in the *Discourses*, although here all metaphors have disappeared except for fortune's femininity and the discussion is not concentrated in a single chapter or section but scattered throughout the text. At the outset of Book 2, Machiavelli challenges both Plutarch and Livy by asserting that the successful expansion of the Roman Republic was due more to *virtù* than to fortune. But in Chapter 29 of that book, entitled on the basis of a passage from Livy, "Fortune Blinds the Intellects of Men When She Does Not Wish Them to Oppose Her Plans," her powers again seem almost invincible.[72] She is equated with "heaven" and "the heavens," and even the man of *virtù* seems to be part of her arsenal, rather than her opponent. When fortune wants "to bring to pass great things," we are told, she "chooses a man . . . of so much perception [*spirito*] and so much ability [*virtù*] that he recognizes the opportunities she puts before him."[73] Conversely, when she wants to cause

great failures, she puts there men to promote such failure. And if somebody there is able to oppose her, she either kills him or deprives him of all means for doing anything good.[74]

Yet her intent to cause failure may be part of a larger plan to promote her favorites, for affliction strengthens a man of *virtù*. Thus, "in order to make Rome stronger and bring her to the greatness she attained, [fortune] judged that it was necessary to afflict her." As a result, despite the almost wholly determinist thrust of this chapter, Machiavelli is able to close on a note of hope and incongruous activism:

71. Ibid. (G 92).   72. *Discourses* 2: 29 (G 406).
73. Ibid. (G 407); Machiavelli, *Opere* 1: 366.   74. *Discourses* 2: 29 (G 408).

Men are able to assist Fortune but not to thwart her. They can weave her designs but cannot destroy them. They ought, then, never to give up as beaten, because, since they do not know her purpose and she goes through crooked and unknown roads, they can always hope, and hoping are not to give up.[75]

By the close of the following chapter, Machiavelli is once more summoning up *virtù* as a way of limiting or even overcoming fortune's power. She "shows her power much," he says, only where men lack *virtù*, and indeed he fantasizes that there might appear a man "who is so great a lover of antiquity that he will rule [*regoli*] Fortune in such a way that she will not have cause to show in every revolution of the sun how much she can do."[76]

In Book 3, the theme of adapting one's conduct to the times is re-explored. Men succeed when "their method of working" is well suited to the requirements of their time. Yet men cannot change their method, for two reasons: it is "impossible" to persuade them to abandon a policy that has worked in the past, and secondly, even if they could be so persuaded, they "cannot counteract that to which Nature inclines" them. Thus, with the aid of nature, fortune's power triumphs again.[77]

❖　❖　❖

In the many briefer references to fortune distributed throughout Machiavelli's writings, most of the inherited metaphors have disappeared. There are no more palaces or daughters with touseled hair, only one or two references to weather or fortune's wheel. What remains is the image of fortune as a woman, mostly in juxtaposition to autonomous human effort, often explicitly to *virtù*. Although still a superhuman figure of mythical proportions, fortune can no longer be regarded as a goddess in any ordinary sense. She is not to be worshipped, supplicated, treated with reverence, nor does she represent any transcendent order. Rather, she acts on the basis of familiar human motives, impulses, and desires, by no means always admirable.

Fortune wants to "command" men and keep them under her "yoke," to be "mistress of all human affairs."[78] And she craves acknowledgment of her power, to "show the world" that it is she, and not human effort, that "makes men great." Sometimes she will manipulate outcomes sim-

75. Ibid.

76. Ibid., 2: 30 (G 412); Machiavelli, *Opere* 1: 371.

77. *Discourses* 3: 9 (G 452).

78. Letter to [Soderini, January 1512–(1513)] (G 897). Niccolò Machiavelli, "The Life of Castruccio Castracani of Lucca," in *The History of Florence and Other Selections*, tr. and ed. Myron P. Gilmore (New York: Washington Square Press, 1970), 48; but cf. Gilbert's translation (G 553).

ply to demonstrate that "everything must be recognized as coming from herself."[79] Second, she is "fickle and inconstant," or "variable and unstable," changeable, capricious, unreliable, not to be trusted, sometimes downright perverse in her desire to violate expectations and alter established patterns.[80] Often she is, third, actively hostile to men, bringing them down simply because she envies, "resents," or has become "hostile" to their "fame."[81] Or she "gets tired" of or bored with the existing state of affairs and wants to make trouble just because someone is "having too much good weather."[82] Machiavelli often speaks of the man who puts himself at risk as "tempting fortune," an expression implying that she has an active desire to harm that is mostly kept in check but can from time to time be indulged.[83] She treated Machiavelli himself, he remarks in the dedication of *The Prince*, with "great and steady malice."[84] When she is in such a dominating mood, it is best to become passive and "let her do it," to lie low,

> be quiet, and not give her trouble, and to wait for a time when she will allow something to be done by men.[85]

Indeed, men may come to take a certain masochistic pleasure in such passivity; about "fate," at least, Machiavelli writes in a letter from his exile, that he is "glad to have her drive me along this road, to see if she will be ashamed of it."[86]

Such resignation is dangerous, however, for on the whole, fortune favors the young, bold, and active. She does, fourth, have benevolent impulses sometimes and selects favorites among men. Machiavelli remarks, for instance, that she and God "greatly loved" Lorenzo de'Medici, although that may have been a mere rhetorical flourish.[87] More generally, she sometimes favors fools and usually, though not inevitably, "is the friend of young men," and "more friendly to him who attacks

---

79. "Life of Castruccio," (G 534).

80. Machiavelli, *Art*, ed. and tr. Wood, 110; *Art of War*, bk. 4 (G 648). See also *Clizia*, act 5, sc. 5 (G 862); letter to Guicciardini, 17 May 1526 (G 998); *Florentine Histories* 4: 33 (G 1242) where Gilbert uses "fickle."

81. Machiavelli, *The History*, tr. and ed. Gilmore, 47; "Life of Castruccio" (G 552).

82. Letter to Soderini, January 1512–[1513] (G 896); *Mandragola*, act 1, sc. 1 (G 779); *Prince*, ch. 24 (G 89).

83. *Discourses* 2: 10 (G 350); 3: 10 (G 456); "Discourse on Remodelling" (G 110); *Art of War*, bk. 4 (G 648); *Florentine Histories* 2: 26 (G 1112); 2: 37 (G 1131); 3: 27 (G 1182); letter to [Vettori], 20 December 1514 (G 950).

84. *Prince*, dedication (G 11).

85. Letter to Vettori, 10 December 1513 (G 927).

86. Ibid. (G 929).

87. *Florentine Histories* 8: 36 (G 1433).

than to him who defends."[88] Even fortune's favorites, however, do not
have an easy time of it, for she likes to put obstacles in their way in
order to develop their capacities. "When she wishes to strengthen a new
prince," fortune sometimes

creates enemies for him and has them move against him, in order that he may
have opportunity to conquer them and, with the very ladder that his enemies
themselves bring him, may climb still higher.[89]

Further, she likes to tempt and tease men, setting before them apparent
short-range goods or dangers to seduce them into the wrong course of
action.

One might say, then, that relations between fortune and men range
for Machiavelli, like relations between the sexes, from outright hostility
and war to a kind of semiaffectionate, mutual teasing and tempting. But
at least four layers of ambiguity blur the resulting picture; fortune is
always juxtaposed to *virtù*, but what *virtù* is and can do is far from
clear. First, *virtù*'s aim is ambiguous: sometimes a matter of conquering
or mastering fortune, sometimes of pleasing her and winning her favor,
sometimes of anticipating and adapting to her will, sometimes of securing a sphere of autonomy from her power. The borderlines and relationships among these alternatives are themselves blurred; for example, sexual conquest can be construed either as a mastery of fortune or as a
winning of her favors by pleasing her. Second, most of these aims can be
accomplished sometimes by boldness, attack, audacity; at other times
by prudence, patience, and self-restraint.[90] This leads repeatedly to the
teaching that success depends on suiting one's style of action to the
times; which, in turn, is soon followed by the observation that men are
unable to change their style of action. There is, moreover, a third layer
of ambiguity about the units of analysis to be employed: *whose* fortune
is at stake, and how are the fortunes and *virtù* of some related to those
of others? Both the second and third layer of ambiguity tend to push
Machiavelli back toward the assumption he initially most wanted to
challenge: that fortune's power might be total and absolute; yet he can-

88. *Mandragola*, act 1, sc. 3 (G 783); *Prince*, ch. 25 (G 92); Letter to [Soderini, January 1512–(1513)] (G 896). But not always; cf. *Florentine Histories* 4: 5–6 (G 1192);
Clizia, act 4, sc. 1 (G 848).
89. *Prince*, ch. 20 (G 79). See also *Florentine Histories* 4: 13 (G 1200).
90. Machiavelli complicates things by talking not only about prudence and boldness,
rival aspects or ways of *virtù*, but also about a number of other qualities opposed to fortune's power: ingenuity, sagacity, judgment, intelligence, wisdom, even self-knowledge.
But perhaps these are all aspects or ways of *virtù*. In addition, in *The Prince*, ch. 8, he
mentions two alternatives to the fortune-*virtù* dyad. One is conduct so effective as to suc-

not rest content with that as a conclusion; so a final layer of ambiguity concerns the limits of fortune's power, and the whole meditation repeatedly starts over.

When the focus is primarily on the sexual conquest of fortune, Machiavelli's image seems to be neither of an outright rape nor of a romantic courtship. There is a certain mutuality between fortune and the man of *virtù*, but they are not equals. He is mortal and, one feels, life-size. She looms larger, is of course immortal and much more powerful, and, one suspects, older than he, though not aged. If he succeeds in conquering her, it is a matter of her deciding to grant her favors, to "let him master her." Yet that decision, Machiavelli repeatedly indicates, can be aided by a certain—limited—amount of physical violence: "cuffing and mauling," "beating and fighting."[91]

Where the focus is more on winning autonomy from fortune, *virtù* is less a way of relating to her power than an alternative to it. "Fortune rules everything" only where "there is little vigor [*virtù*]" and because of its absence. And "he who depends least on Fortune sustains himself the longest."[92] The passage in *The Prince* about fortune controlling the outcomes of half our actions clearly suggests this interpretation; but it leaves open the question of whether the proportion is fixed, a maximum, or a minimum, depending on human action. Other passages make clear, however, that Machiavelli's main intent is a variable proportion with a fixed minimum. Where men are lazy or apathetic, lacking in *virtù*, fortune controls all by default. Depending on the extent of their energy, ability, and manliness, they will be able to reduce that control in particular actions and, if they act rightly, even to enlarge the sphere of their autonomy for the future; but they can never totally control outcomes in a lasting way. Certain courses of action, notably battle in war and conspiratorial action in politics, tend to reduce the potential

---

ceed without or in spite of fortune, yet so thoroughly evil that it cannot be considered *virtù*. His prime example is Agthocles the Sicilian, who rose from a lowly *fortuna* to become king of Syracuse. Nothing or very little in his career was due to fortune, yet it wasn't due to *virtù* either, for

It cannot . . . be called virtue [*virtù*] to kill one's fellow-citizens, to betray friends, to be without fidelity, without mercy, without religion; such proceedings enable one to gain sovereignty [*imperio*], but not fame. (G 36).

A second exception is the man who becomes prince through popular support among his fellow citizens, creating what Machiavelli calls a "civil princedom [*principato civile*]." It is achieved neither by *virtù* alone, nor by fortune alone but rather by "a fortunate shrewdness [*una astuzia fortunata*]." Neither of these alternatives is explored further, nor do they recur in Machiavelli's other writings.

91. Depending on whether you prefer Gilbert's or Musa's translation of "*batterla et urtarla*"; (G 92); Machiavelli, *Prince*, tr. and ed. Musa, 215; Machiavelli, *Opere* 1: 101.

92. *Art of War*, bk. 2 (G 624); Machiavelli, *Opere* 2: 396; *Prince*, ch. 6 (G 25).

for human *virtù*. Choosing them means putting oneself into fortune's hands, commiting oneself to risk. No "prudent" man will do this "unless he must," but if he must, then he should boldly do his utmost."[93] If you must stake "all your fortune" on a single action or battle, then it is essential to have *virtù* enough to commit "all your forces" to it.[94] Such action is "tempting fortune," and Machiavelli advises avoiding it if possible but condemns those who avoid it when they should commit themselves to it. Yet he sees that their character may preclude a choice.

Whether in terms of seducing fortune, conquering her, or winning autonomy from her, then, the dilemma of prudence versus boldness recurs with obsessive persistence, in ways reminiscent of the dilemma we examined earlier, between kindness and cruelty in styles of leadership. Again and again Machiavelli dwells on the idea he first formulated in the initial letter he was able to send Soderini after that former leader had fled and the republic failed:

Anybody wise enough to understand the times and the types of affairs and to adapt himself to them would have always good fortune, or he would protect himself always from bad, and it would come to be true that the wise man would rule the stars and the Fates. But because there never are such wise men, since men in the first place are shortsighted and in the second place cannot command their natures, it follows that Fortune varies and commands men and holds them under her yoke.

Each man's "individual disposition" and "imagination [*fantasia*]" are given to him by nature. Hannibal, who was cruel, treacherous, and irreligious, and Scipio, who was merciful, loyal, and religious, were both "equally excellent in their military attainments," and both "won countless victories."[95] And in a marginal note presumably for expansion in the final draft, Machiavelli added:

To test Fortune, who is the friend of young men, and to change according to what you find. But it is not possible to have fortresses and not to have them, to be cruel and compassionate.[96]

At times Machiavelli is forced to take seriously the possibility that fortune's power, especially when merged with that of nature, may be total. Not only does fortune deploy men of *virtù* and those who lack it as she pleases, but she (or nature) is herself the source of character, and thus of *virtù*. Not only can she blind or mislead men, but, for instance,

93. *Discourses* 2: 27 (G 403). See also 2: 16 (G 365–66); *Art of War*, bk. 3 (G 627); bk. 7 (G 718); letter to Vettori, 5 April 1527 (G 1008).
94. *Discourses* 1: 22–23 (G 248–49); 2: 12 (G 355); 3: 37 (G 512); letters to [Vettori], 20 December 1514 (G 950); to Bartolomeo [November 1526] (G 1004).
95. Letter to [Soderini, January 1512–(1513)] (G 897); Machiavelli, *Opere* 6: 229.
96. Letter to [Soderini, January 1512–(1513)] (G 896).

"cause" a man to "become so ambitious and haughty" that he fails.[97] She can give (or deny) a man good "judgment" and "sense"; thus, it was fortune who denied Machiavelli himself any business experience and thereby "determined" that he must write about politics if he was to write at all.[98] Insofar as a man's *virtù* derives from his birth, upbringing, and experience, it is itself the product of fortune. Manly character can hardly be an autonomous force opposing destiny if character *is* destiny.

A third layer of ambiguity concerns the unit of analysis, the agent who "has" a particular fortune or whose *virtù* is mustered against fortune. Sometimes Machiavelli speaks of the fortune of a particular individual, sometimes that of a family or a state or another social group, sometimes of the whole record of history, as when he complains that historians tend to "follow Fortune" in their accounts and "honor the conquerors."[99] In any of these meanings, further, fortune may mean either the outcome of some particular action or enterprise, or the whole pattern of outcomes over the lifetimes of a man or state. These shifts are related to a fundamental tension about autonomy already noted in Machiavelli's thought: whether fortune is pitted against men individually, so that the rise of one is another's fall, or (sometimes, at least) collectively, so that their cooperatively pooled manly strength can overcome or outlast her; whether true autonomy lies in isolation or in community.

Certainly men are affected by each other's fortunes. Cesare Borgia, for instance, is said to have "gained his position through his father's Fortune and through her lost it."[100] If his career had not been cut off by his father's death and his own severe illness coinciding with it,

he would have gained such forces and such reputation that he could stand by his own strength and would no longer rely on other men's Fortune and forces, but on his own vigor and ability [*virtù*].[101]

That dependence on the armed forces of others renders one weak and subject to fortune is a familiar idea; but here Borgia is said to depend not on his own fortune but on that of another, his father. What Machiavelli might mean here becomes a little clearer when he speaks of alliances of various kinds. He who is the dependent member of an alliance or similar association will be affected by, and in that sense is dependent on, the fortune of the other member. If the side you choose to support

97. *Florentine Histories* 6: 4 (G 1288).
98. "Life of Castruccio" (G 553); Letter to Vettori, 9 April 1513 (G 900); Machiavelli, *The History*, tr. and ed. Gilmore, 48.
99. *Art of War*, bk. 2 (G 622).
100. *Prince*, ch. 7 (G 28, 29).
101. Ibid. (G 33); Machiavelli, *Prince*, tr. and ed. Musa, 58.

in a conflict loses, you will be "obliged to follow the Fortune of these others."[102] Of course they may be able to help you even though they were defeated, so that "you are the ally of a Fortune that can rise again."[103] Or your partner may save you from his fate at the last minute by returning your stake to you, dissolving the association, as Messer Jacopo returned all the goods of others he had been storing just before the Pazzi conspiracy "in order not to make others share in his adverse fortune."[104] And of course if you hitch your wagon to a successful ally, his good fortune will similarly benefit you. Thus "all who depended on" Cosimo de'Medici's fortune "grew rich."[105] But why should Machiavelli call this Cosimo's fortune rather than theirs? It seems that he means what we would mean if, for instance, we ask a friend for a tip on the horses and bet accordingly, and if that friend's horse wins not through any skillful knowledge he had but simply because he is eternally lucky in such matters. We will do well to follow such a friend, for it means sharing in his luck. Why not *our* luck? Because it was his tip and because it is the outcomes of his bets that show a pattern of consistent success independent of skill and knowledge. Without his advice, *our* bets usually lose. For Machiavelli, too, it seems that fortune is ascribed to him whose action was primarily involved, fortune being the outcome of some intended enterprise or action.

But ultimately the matter extends far beyond alliances, for what befalls others often affects me though no action or associate of mine was involved. Cosimo de'Medici's *virtù* and fortune, Machiavelli says, "destroyed all his enemies and raised up his friends."[106] The fate of his friends was that of allies who share in a principal's fortune; the fate of his enemies adds a much wider consideration. When misfortune befalls me, is that because fortune has turned against me, or am I only a pawn in a game in which she is promoting someone else? Since fortune deals in human history, no one's fortune develops in isolation. Others are always affected. Thus ultimately, although Machiavelli never makes such implications explicit, there could be said to be only one overall fortune for the whole of mankind after all.

Yet Machiavelli cannot accept the conclusion that there is no personal relation to fortune, no opportunity for *virtù* to make a difference, any more than he can accept that character is simply part of fortune's power. For if he knows anything at all from his reading and observation, it is surely that men's beliefs in these matters make a difference in

---

102. Letter to Vettori, 20 December 1514 (G 959).   103. *Prince*, ch. 21 (G 83).
104. *Florentine Histories* 8: 9 (G 1395).
105. Ibid., 7: 6 (G 1344).   106. Ibid., 7: 5 (G 1343).

how they act, and therefore in the course of events. Apathetic, dispirited men will act differently from those who have hope and energy, privatized men differently from those who feel their membership in a significant community. And their actions surely sometimes affect what happens in history. So Machiavelli returns again and again to the struggle against fortune's power by means of *virtù*. Perhaps it is that *virtù* consists neither of prudence nor of boldness, but of the extraordinary, almost superhuman power to modify one's character as the times change. Machiavelli seems to suggest that in meditating on the choice between Hannibal's cruelty and Scipio's kindness. It will not matter, he says, "which of these two roads a general travels, if only he is an able [*virtuoso*] man," for with his "extraordinary ability [*virtù*]" he can mitigate any "excess" produced by his mode of proceeding.[107] Or perhaps a republic, with a pool of citizens of *virtù* available from which to choose its leaders, can overcome the dilemma of fixed character that stymies individuals; it is "able to adapt . . . by means of the diversity among [the] body of citizens, to a diversity of temporal conditions."[108] Or perhaps there might yet arise a man whose *virtù* somehow taps that of ancient patriarchy, who is "so great a lover of antiquity" that he can not merely conquer fortune sexually or push back the limits of her power, but dominate her so that she "does not have power over" him.[109]

❖   ❖   ❖

In many respects, then, fortune is a confusing figure in Machiavelli's thought, and commentators have, accordingly, found her difficult to interpret. Most agree, however, that either Machiavelli does not take her seriously himself, or else that taking her seriously is an unfortunate lapse in his otherwise rational and disenchanted system of ideas. Those commentators, in particular, who read Machiavelli as a social scientist or proto–social scientist regard the concept of fortune as a lamentable regression to mythical, prescientific explanation. Fortune, they say, serves as a residual category for what cannot be rationally explained. Ernst Cassirer in *The Myth of the State* calls fortune "the mythical element in Machiavelli's political philosophy."[110] He argues that Machiavelli believed in "scientific principles" that implied there must be a certain and objective causal explanation for everything human just as there is in physical nature, but his political experience showed him that

107. *Discourses* 3: 21 (G 478–79); Machiavelli, *Opere* 1: 447–48.
108. *Discourses* 3: 9 (G 453). See also 1: 20 (G 246).
109. Ibid., 3: 31 (G 498).
110. Ernst Cassirer, *The Myth of the State* (Garden City, N.Y.: Doubleday, 1953), 194.

"even the best political advice is often ineffective," so that a scientific study of man seems impossible.

His logical and rational method deserted him at this point. He had to . . . have recourse to another—to a half-mythical power. "Fortune" seems to be the ruler of things.[111]

Similarly Laurence Arthur Burd maintains that Machiavelli resorts to the concept of fortune when he is "taken off the lines familiar" to him; his "natural acumen appears to desert" him then, and he shares in "the superstition of the age."[112] Federico Chabod, although acknowledging that Machiavelli sometimes regards fortune "as the force and logic of history," maintains that more often it is "as a mysterious, transcendent grouping of events, whose incoherence is unintelligible to the human mind."[113] Robert Orr says that Machiavelli treats fortune as

that which is fortuitous and therefore inexplicable—not only as that which men cannot predict, but that which they cannot retrodict, an event that they can nei- ther foresee nor account for even after it has happened.[114]

Some commentators have suggested that Machiavelli shared the wide- spread Renaissance belief in astrology and saw fortune as astrological destiny.[115] Though there are one or two passages that might support such a view, it seems inconsistent with Machiavelli's intense activism, his stress on the mutability of fortune under the impact of effort and ability.

Other interpreters, equally convinced of Machiavelli's scientific inten- tions, interpret fortune as an integral part of his science, an explanatory device whose personification is not to be taken literally. Leonardo Olschki, for instance, maintains that both *virtù* and fortune are "techni- cal terms in a rational system of political thought." For Machiavelli, he says, fortune is "an abstract and secular concept"; it is the set of sur- rounding preconditions necessary for a political action to succeed: "Fortune represents the passive condition of political success in con- quests or internal administration. *Virtù* is its active counterpart."[116]

---

111. Ibid., 196.
112. Laurence Arthur Burd, *Il Principe* (Oxford: Clarendon, 1891), 355, quoted in Flanagan, "Concept," in Parel, *Political Calculus*, 150.
113. Federico Chabod, *Machiavelli and the Renaissance*, 69–70, quoted in Flanagan, "Concept," in Parel, *Political Calculus*, 151.
114. Orr, "Time Motif," in Fleischer, *Machiavelli*, 199.
115. Flanagan, "Concept," in Parel, *Political Calculus*, 154. See also *Prince*, ch. 7 (G 29); *Discourses* 1: 56 (G 311).
116. Leonardo Olschki, *Machiavelli the Scientist* (Berkeley: Gillick Press, 1945), 37–38, quoted in Flanagan, "Concept," in Parel, *Political Calculus*, 151.

Thomas Flanagan attempts to synthesize the two views: fortune is both a scientific explanation and a mysterious residue. Machiavelli's concept, he argues, covers

the truly fortuitous and contingent single event, but also the entire context in which such events occur; and while the individual event must remain mysterious, the large-scale constellation of social forces is in principle explicable.[117]

When Machiavelli uses the concept in the latter sense, he says, it constitutes a "mystification."

Leo Strauss, while rejecting the notion of Machiavelli as a scientist in achievement or intention, agrees with Olschki that there is nothing mysterious about the concept of fortune. When Machiavelli discusses matters "at length," Strauss says, he replaces fortune with an expression like "extrinsic accident."[118] Fortune is not "a superhuman being, a being which is more powerful than man and which wills and thinks," but rather a mere shorthand expression for what befalls a man (or state) from outside, through no fault or achievement of his own. Yet Strauss by no means regards the personification of fortune in Machiavelli's thought as an irrelevancy, a careless adoption of the idiom then current. Rather, it is one step in a complex theoretical process designed for no less a purpose than to wean the reader away from God: the idea of God is first replaced with that of fortune, and only later does the latter turn out to mean no more than extrinsic accident. Just so, Strauss argues, Machiavelli first displaces the authority of the Church with that of ancient Rome and then systematically undermines the latter, in order to leave his readers ultimately at odds with all authority whatever. The concept of fortune thus is first personified and (quasi)-deified, made into a substitute for all previous deities; then it is secularized and demystified, thereby undermining all transcendent belief.[119]

Is Machiavelli's concept of fortune a protoscientific explanatory device, a lamentable lapse from his usual scientific rationalism to mystical belief, or a clever rhetorical use of mystery, in which he does not himself believe, to manipulate his audience? An earlier chapter inquired whether the great Founder is a myth, and whether Machiavelli believes in him. Now the same question must be seriously posed about the figure of fortune.

Certainly Machiavelli sometimes speaks as if he himself held no notion of a personified fortune, as if it were only a metaphor to be used in

117. Flanagan, "Concept," in Parel, *Political Calculus*, 153.
118. Strauss, *Thoughts*, 216; Machiavelli, *Opere* 1: 379.
119. Strauss, *Thoughts*, 213–18. See also Harvey C. Mansfield, Jr., *Machiavelli's New Modes and Orders* (Ithaca: Cornell University Press, 1979), 283, 292, 300.

poetry, while in political and historical works the word is a mere short-hand term for the complex pattern of events that emerges from count-less individual human choices. "Men's fortunes . . . vary," Machiavelli says, because their cravings are endless, so that they are constantly "dis-contented" with their lot; this leads to "enmity and war," which bring about "the ruin of one province and the prosperity of another"—precisely the sort of rise and fall of states Machiavelli elsewhere ascribes to fortune.[120] From time to time, moreover, Machiavelli suggests that states make their own fortune through their laws and customs: "Good laws make good fortune."[121]

And if one examines in detail the sorts of specific events that Ma-chiavelli actually ascribes to fortune, they turn out to be perfectly ordi-nary, not mysterious or inexplicable as Cassirer, Orr, and others sug-gested, but human choices or natural events of a sort that in principle are rationally comprehensible and often predictable. The examples do include outcomes of choices by lot, which might perhaps be said to be inexplicable.[122] But they also include illness and its consequences, which Machiavelli surely regarded as rationally comprehensible both cate-gorically and in particular cases.[123] A general, sweat-soaked from battle, stands in the "wind that generally at midday rises from up Arno and is almost always unhealthful," falls ill, and dies; fortune "took his life."[124] The outcomes of wars and battles are other frequent examples; Ma-chiavelli maintains that the role of fortune is relatively large compared to that of human skill and energy precisely in battle.[125] Yet would he regard the outcomes of battles and wars as in principle inexplicable, mysterious? Machiavelli also sometimes ascribes to fortune deliberate human decisions and choices, such as he would himself in another con-text explain in naturalistic and rational terms. Thus it is fortune who is said to determine whether someone is offered a job, whether someone is released from prison, that a certain individual comes to a certain city at a particular time, that an army arrives at a particular time, that a third party or state decides to intervene in a dispute, that those willing to sell are able to find a buyer, and whether friendships are made or broken.[126]

120. *Discourses* 1: 37 (G 272).
121. Ibid., 1: 11 (G 225).
122. *Clizia*, act 4, sc. 1 (G 848); *Florentine Histories* 4: 28 (G 1222).
123. *Prince*, ch. 7 (G 29, 33); *Florentine Histories* 5: 23 (G 1263).
124. "Life of Castruccio" (G 552).
125. *Discourses* 2: 10 (G 351); 2: 16 (G 365–66); *Art of War*, bk. 3 (G 627); bk. 4 (G 657); bk. 7 (G 718); *Florentine Histories* 5: 24 (G 1265); 8: 22 (G 1413); "First Decen-nale," line 222 (G 1450).
126. Letter to Vettori, 20 December 1514 (G 960); letter to Guicciardini, 17 May 1526 (G 997); *Discourses* 3: 42 (G 520); *Mandragola*, act 1, sc. 1 (G 779); *Prince*, ch. 13 (G

What makes such events, in their context, acts of fortune is not their inexplicability or mysteriousness or the apparent need for supernatural explanation of them, but simply that they could not have been foreseen by the actors involved in the particular situation Machiavelli has been describing; the principals on whom he has focused his narrative could not reasonably have been expected to anticipate and provide for *this*. To them, in this context, it was fortuitous, an act of fortune. Orr is thus right to speak of fortune as the fortuitous, but only if one understands that there is nothing *intrinsically* inexplicable or mysterious about the events ascribed to fortune; they are fortuitous only to these particular actors in this particular context. Thus one man's *virtù*, his deliberate choice, can be another man's fortune, can befall that other in a way that could not have been foreseen. Fortune is like luck or chance; indeed, Machiavelli repeatedly equates them.[127] And Strauss is right about the equation of fortune with extrinsic accident in Machiavelli. That equation, however, does not yet settle the question of how seriously Machiavelli takes his own fortune figure, whether he might nevertheless himself think in terms of a "being which is more powerful than man and which wills and thinks" and is female.

Machiavelli's teaching about fortune is not, I would suggest, primarily an explanatory device at all, if by explanation we mean the detached, scientific observation of causal sequences in the world. His concern is always action, and specifically political action. His constant question is "What shall we do?" and therefore, secondarily, "What went wrong last time?" or "What has succeeded for others in the past?" From this perspective, the point of referring certain events to fortune is that in political contexts, contexts of human choice and action, there will always be an element of the unexpected, unforeseeable, uncontrollable. But that element does not consist of events that are intrinsically beyond explanation or control wherever they occur; rather, even what is in principle capable of being explained and predicted can be unforeseeable and beyond control for a particular actor in a particular situation. And in any context of human action, there is the constant possibility of such events. Though Machiavelli urges action, energetic and prudent *virtù*, it is never with the expectation that we might ultimately

---

52); *Florentine Histories* 8: 21 (G 1411); *Discourses* 2: 30 (G 409); *Florentine Histories* 4: 27 (G 1221); Legation from court of Borgia, 23 October 1502 [24 October] (G 128); *Florentine Histories* 4: 13 (G 1200); 7: 18 (G 1360).

127. The two Italian terms sometimes translated as either "luck" or "chance" are *sorte* and *caso*; see *Prince*, ch. 25 (G 90); *Discourses* 1: 2 (G 200); 3: 31 (G 498, 499); "Tercets on Fortune," lines 91–93 (G 747); "[Golden] Ass," ch. 3, lines 81–87 (G 757).

achieve full certainty about and control over outcomes. In any context of action, that which is in that context fortuitous can be expected to play some role; the interaction between *virtù* and fortune is as inevitable as that between men and women.

Did Machiavelli, then, "believe in" fortune, or not? Surely he could not have believed literally in all the things he wrote about fortune: the palace, the wheel, that she is a goddess. Nor does he seem to have believed that there is any category of events that are in principle beyond rational, naturalistic explanation. But if by "believing in fortune" one means something like: understanding the world as if, feeling about it as if, acting as if it were mostly run by a large senior, female person, who holds men in her power to a greater or lesser extent depending on their conduct and specifically on their manliness—if that is what one means, then the textual evidence, though not conclusive, surely suggests that Machiavelli did so believe.

First, his references to fortune are so frequent and pervasive, appearing significantly in every one of his major works, most minor ones, and many letters, and thus in works addressed to the widest range of audiences, that they cannot be construed as a mere rhetorical device for manipulating some particular audience. Second, the intensity of Machiavelli's pride and pleasure in foxiness, in the cynical debunking of conventions and superstitions in which others believe, makes it likely that if he had considered fortune a mere myth for the gullible, he would sooner or later, in one or another work to one or another audience, have said so. The temptation to demystify the image—particularly an image of a female power—should have been just about irresistible. And third, as already noted, fortune does not stand alone but is surrounded by and associated with a number of other figures, all of them female and superhuman, larger than life, and threatening to men, to manliness, to politics and the *vivere civile*. Thus, whether or not Machiavelli "believed" in fortune specifically, there is much evidence he thought, or at any rate wrote, as if men confronted such a female power or group of powers in the world.

For example, fortune is sometimes equated with chance or luck but also contrasted to them. Fortune is associated with but also distinguished from nature, necessity, envy, ambition, ingratitude, opportunity, chance, heaven, fate.[128] The previous chapter already introduced various series or hierarchies of feminine power: daughters and mothers, maidens and shrews; ingratitude and her nurse, envy; opportunity and

128. See chapter 5, note 103, above.

her mother, fortune; ambition and avarice and behind them, nature or a "hidden power . . . in the heaven" that is "by no means friendly" to mankind; the Diana-like servant woman, behind her Circe, the queen, and behind her, fortune. All of them are associated with nature and with an "occult force that rules us" and prevents men from changing their natures.

Nature itself is never explicitly personified by Machiavelli but is regularly associated with fortune and other mythic female powers. Indeed, in precisely those passages where Machiavelli appears to minimize his own personification of fortune and disparage fortune's power, nature as it were looms up behind fortune (as fortune does behind Circe, Circe behind her servant), replacing the disparaged female power. The only reason why "men's fortunes" vary, says Machiavelli, is the instability of their cravings; but the source of that instability is "nature."[129] Similarly, when he claims that "good fortune" can be secured by human activity, by "order" and "*virtù*," he does so only to locate that achievement in a larger cyclical pattern determined by "nature," which will not "allow worldly things to remain fixed" but causes states to "go from order to disorder and then from disorder [to] move back to order."[130]

But it is hard to tell where fortune leaves off and nature begins. A character in *Mandragola* remarks that the good things that befall come from fortune, the bad from nature.[131] Yet in "The [Golden] Ass," nature is generous, at least to animals, whereas evil comes from human greed, the unwillingness to settle for what nature offers.[132] Then again, Machiavelli frequently suggests that nature is the source of ambition and avarice.[133] In the *Discourses* and elsewhere, we are told that human desires are natural, while fortune gives or withholds opportunities for fulfilling those desires.[134] But sometimes it is nature that gives opportunities.[135] Men "cannot be rebuked for following" nature and specifically for imitating her "variability."[136] Yet for Machiavelli the natural usually is what is fixed, given, unalterable, while fortune is the variable one.[137] And in another sense, "*all* our actions imitate nature."[138] Some-

---

129. *Discourses* 1: 37 (G 272).
130. *Florentine Histories* 5: 1 (G 1232).
131. *Mandragola*, act 4, sc. 1 (G 804).
132. "[Golden] Ass," ch. 8, lines 46–66, 94–108, 130–32 (G 771–72).
133. *Discourses* 3: 27 (G 491); "Tercets on Ambition," lines 12, 79–81 (G 735, 737); *Florentine Histories* 3: 13 (G 1160).
134. *Discourses* 2: preface (G 323).
135. *Art of War*, bk. 7 (G 726).
136. Letter to Vettori, 31 January 1514–[1515] (G 961).
137. *Discourses* 1: 11 (G 226); 1: 39 (G 278); 1: 58 (G 315); 3: 43 (G 521); *Florentine Histories* 3: 13 (G 1160); 3: 16 (G 1166).
138. *Discourses* 2: 3 (G 335), my italics.

times what is fixed is human nature, which does not change with time, place, and circumstance, while fortune determines the particular experiences that shape an individual.[139] So nature and fortune seem to correspond respectively to inborn and acquired characteristics. Accordingly, it is nature that is usually said to determine birth and death; yet sometimes fortune is said to do just that.[140] Despite the notion of a single, universal, and unchangeable human nature, each person is also said to have an individual nature, a way of proceeding that is characteristic for him and that he cannot change.[141] That is what makes him unable to adapt as fortune varies.

But perhaps one should not expect rigor or precision here; Machiavelli was neither a philosopher nor a technical scientist. Certain broad lines of difference do seem to emerge between nature and fortune. Nature tends to mean what one starts with or from, fortune what befalls, particularly what befalls as the unforeseen consequence of action. "To how many ills Nature subjects you at starting! and afterwards Fortune."[142] Nature, moreover, tends to be connected with what is fixed or long-range or, if changing, then cyclical like the seasons and the tides. Nature is the permanently given from which we begin. Though fortune herself is eternal, her actions are variable, irregular, and intermittent. Fortune is the unexpected. Nature underlies; fortune intervenes. Human *virtù* opposes them both, yet sometimes seems itself the product of nature or fortune.

Another, even more enigmatic figure in the constellation around fortune is necessity. Like nature, necessity is never explicitly personified by Machiavelli but appears together with the various abstractions he does depict as mythological females. Often it is almost identified with fortune. There are references to "fate's necessity," and it appears as that force, elsewhere called fortune or "the times," to which men must adapt if they would succeed.[143] Thus it seems the direct opponent of *virtù*. Yet the essence of fortune is variability, and we ordinarily contrast the necessary to the fortuitous or accidental. In the "Tercets on Fortune," her wheels are turned by two agencies: laziness and necessity, the latter constantly reordering (*racconcia*, from *acconciare* [to prepare for use,

---

139. *Florentine Histories* 5: 34 (G 1281–82); 7: 33 (G 1378); Niccolò Machiavelli, "The Nature of Florentine Men" (G 1436).

140. G 71n; *Art of War*, bk. 1 (G 568); *Florentine Histories* 4: 16 (G 1204); 5: 34 (G 1281).

141. *Discourses* 3: 9 (G 452–53); "Tercets on Fortune," lines 112–13 (G 747); letter to [Soderini, January 1512–(1513)] (G 896–97).

142. "[Golden] Ass," ch. 8, lines 133–34 (G 772).

143. "First Decennale," dedication (G 1444); *Prince*, ch. 15 (G 58).

adorn, attire, dress the hair of]) what the former constantly lays waste.[144] Thus necessity seems to be a part or servant of fortune, yet an ordering rather than a fickle force, and opposed to laziness, as *virtù* is. Indeed, though fortune is said, in the poem, to appreciate the man "who pushes her, who shoves her, who jostles her," *virtù* is never explicitly mentioned.[145] So it almost seems as if necessity is a substitute here for *virtù*.

That possibility gets support from other texts. Necessity is consistently opposed to human choice; they are inversely related.[146] But sometimes that is taken to imply that necessity produces *virtù*, at other times, that it precludes *virtù*. The difference seems to correspond to that between the long-run shaping of men and the short-run impact of circumstances on conduct. Men's character is weakened by luxury, and one such luxury is the opportunity for choice, having a wealth of options.[147] Thus men will develop *virtù* only under constraint; it is imposed either by natural necessity or artificially by fierce human discipline.[148] In the forming of character, then, necessity is akin to nature, yet a source rather than an opponent of *virtù*. But men and states can be "pushed on to action" by either necessity or *virtù*.[149] Weak men may be driven by necessity to perform acts of valor such as in other circumstances would be produced only by *virtù*. For example, necessity makes cowardly soldiers fight fiercely; in military affairs, it is an alternative to both discipline and natural spirit.[150] Accordingly, one should neither praise nor blame those who act out of necessity; they have no choice.[151] Necessity can justify morally what would otherwise be unjust and can justify pragmatically what would otherwise be imprudent.[152]

What is one to make of these inconsistent, shifting figures that seem to merge and separate in such unsystematic ways? They could, of course, be taken simply as indications of Machiavelli's carelessness, and the unimportance of all these figures in his thought. They could indicate a hidden plot to manipulate or confuse the reader. The suggestion of

144. "Tercets on Fortune," line 85 (G 747); Machiavelli, *Opere* 8: 314.
145. "Tercets on Fortune," lines 163–65 (G 749).
146. *Discourses* 1: 1 (G 193); 1: 3 (G 201); letter to Vettori, 10 December 1513 (G 930); *Florentine Histories* 8: 22 (G 1413).
147. *Discourses* 1: 1 (G 193); 1: 3 (G 201).
148. Ibid., 1: 1 (G 193–94).
149. "[Golden] Ass," ch. 5, lines 79–81 (G 763).
150. *Discourses* 2: 12 (G 355); 3: 12 (G 460–62); *Art of War*, bk. 4 (G 657, 662); *Florentine Histories* 5: 11 (G 1248).
151. *Discourses* 1: 28 (G 256); *Florentine Histories* 5: 11 (G 1247). Cf. *Discourses* 1: 51 (G 299).
152. *Prince*, ch. 26 (G 94); *Discourses* 3: 12 (G 461); *Florentine Histories* 5: 8 (G 1242); *Prince*, ch. 21 (G 84); *Discourses* 1: 38 (G 275); letter to [Vettori, 29 April 1513] (G 904, 908); *Florentine Histories* 3: 13 (G 1161); 6: 13 (G 1298–99).

this study, however, has been that they are, as a group, of central importance to Machiavelli's thought and that they are close to interchangeable because fundamentally they are all versions of a generalized feminine power against which men struggle. Taken in this enlarged sense together with her cohorts, fortune is neither a mere popular cliché that Machiavelli invokes unthinkingly, nor a rhetorical device he has mastered and cleverly deploys for its effect on the reader, but rather part of a vision of human reality that underlies the entire body of his thought, a vision of embattled men struggling to preserve themselves, their masculinity, their autonomy, and the achievements of civilization, against almost overwhelming odds. And while Machiavelli constantly summons men to active effort in this struggle, he also confesses to being, as he says in *The Prince*, "now and then incline[d] in some respects" to believe that the struggle is hopeless, that men "cannot manage . . . human affairs."[153]

153. *Prince*, ch. 25 (G 90).

PART IV

Families and Foundings

CHAPTER SEVEN

Psychological Theory

What is one to make of this complex constellation of images of men and women: multiple visions of manhood that are simultaneously interdependent and incompatible, and behind them a vision of woman as contemptible yet terrifying, defenseless yet dominating? The material fairly invites psychological interpretation, but along what lines and to what end? This chapter attempts to mine the resources of theoretical psychology, particularly psychoanalysis, for suggestions about the psychic meaning of such images. But first, some words of caution.

Seeking to answer such questions, one might easily be led to attempt a psychobiography of Machiavelli, perhaps on the model of Freud's pioneering and controversial work on Leonardo da Vinci, Machiavelli's contemporary and friend, or Erik Erikson's splendid study of their north European contemporary, Martin Luther.[1] But almost nothing is known about Machiavelli's childhood and personal life. There is no famous recorded dream, ready for analysis; no youthful episode like Luther's "fit in the choir" to serve as a clue. And that is just as well, since our interest is a deepened understanding of Machiavelli's thought, specifically of his political teachings, and a psychobiography is unlikely to serve that purpose. Even Freud never claimed that his investigations would deepen our comprehension or appreciation of Leonardo's art. Indeed, he felt constrained to "admit" that in general "the nature of artistic attainment is psychoanalytically inaccessible to us."[2] Psychoanalysis might explain what causes someone to become an artist, but

1. Sigmund Freud, *Leonardo Da Vinci,* tr. A. A. Brill (New York: Random House, 1961); Erikson, *Young Man Luther.*
2. Freud, *Leonardo,* 119.

not what "causes" the greatness, let alone the specific content, of his work. Here lies "a degree of freedom which can no longer be solved psychoanalytically."[3]

Erikson was more engaged with the substantive content of Luther's ideas than Freud was with Leonardo's art; and for the most part he managed to avoid reducing "ostensibly" theological doctrine to its "actual" psychological or familial significance, as if the issue for Martin Luther had not really been God the Father but Martin's own father. Instead, Erikson tried to clarify the interrelationships among psychological, sociopolitical, and theological issues; no one of them is a disguised version of another. Yet even *Young Man Luther* remains psychobiography rather than theology, or even interpretive commentary on theology.

We want to understand not Machiavelli but his ideas, not the psychic causes of those ideas but their meaning, which is simultaneously personal and public, psychic, philosophical, and political. At the minimum, we are interested as much in the psychology of Machiavelli's contemporaries—his audience and his subject matter—as in his own. But even that does not suffice. It might be tempting to propose psychoanalyzing the texts, rather than the author. But what does that mean, and what constitutes success at it? Texts do not have a psyche, and the usual criteria of successful psychoanalysis—improved functioning and feeling in relation to the world—do not apply. The aim is to clarify the psychic significance of Machiavelli's thought, not in order to unmask or displace, but to illuminate its manifest problematic political content. Keeping this goal in mind will be important as this and the next chapter draw on a variety of materials usually employed to other ends in other ways. The chapters explore widely, invoking whatever resources seem promising: psychological theory, what facts are known about Machiavelli's own life, sociological data about the family in Renaissance Florence. But they aim neither at psychological nor at sociological causal explanation of Machiavelli's ideas; they do not test, improve, or even presuppose the validity of the theories discussed. They seek the psychic meaning of the images found in Machiavelli's texts—both what these images might have meant in his time and what they mean in ours. The intent throughout is interpretive, the ultimate purpose an enriched political understanding. These materials, then, are more of a scaffolding than a foundation for my reading of the texts; the ultimate point is that reading itself, what it can teach about Machiavelli and about politics.

3. Ibid., 118–19.

❖ ❖ ❖

Both Freud and Erikson investigate something like the conception of foxiness, with its concomitant but also conflicting image of the great Founder, and interpret those images in terms of the Oedipus complex, a boy's possessive love for his mother and rivalry with his father.[4] The normal course of the Oedipus complex, of course, is for the boy to repress his libidinal—sexual—desires for his mother into the unconscious, identify with his father, and later fall in love with a woman reminiscent of his mother. But there are alternative patterns of Oedipal development, in a sense alternative "strategies" open to the psyche in Oedipal conflict; and among these, both Freud and Erikson mention one resembling our fox. The boy may withdraw from rivalry with the father by becoming an observer, investigator, knower, by investing himself in his intellect and wit. He may figuratively (though perhaps also literally) watch the father's privileged activities from behind the scenes, taking comfort in his own knowledgability, perhaps even imagining himself as the impresario who has willed and staged the whole performance.

Locating the origins of this possible pattern of development chronologically at the beginning of the Oedipal phase, both Freud and Erikson link it specifically with a boy's curiosity about sex, where babies come from, and more generally with his struggle for autonomy—social and intellectual. "Through a period beginning with the third year," Freud says, the child becomes curious about sexuality, the onset of the curiosity usually being precipitated by some "important experience, through the birth of a little brother or sister, or through fear of the same engendered by some outward experience, wherein the child sees a danger to his egoistic interests."[5] If, as is common, the child is then put off with false information, some tale about storks for instance, Freud says it "refuses to give credence to" what it is told, and "its psychic independence dates from this act of disbelief."

Erikson cites an incident illustrating how sexuality, Oedipal rivalry,

4. This chapter deals only with the psychology of little boys. That is mainly because Machiavelli and his intended audience were males, but also because, in my opinion, no very satisfactory account of the psychological development of little girls is available. While psychoanalytic therapy has helped many women, psychoanalytic theory of female development is in a state of turmoil. In addition to the promising work of Dinnerstein and Chodorow cited in this chapter, and works mentioned in notes 39 and 50 below, see also: Juliet Mitchell, *Psychoanalysis and Feminism* (New York: Pantheon, 1974); Jean Baker Miller, ed., *Psychoanalysis and Women* (New York: Penguin, 1973); Jean Strouse, ed., *Women and Analysis* (New York: Grossman, 1974); Fred Weinstein and Gerald M. Platt, *The Wish to Be Free* (Berkeley: University of California Press, 1969), ch. 6; Janet Sayers, *Biological Politics* (London: Tavistock, 1982), ch. 8.

5. Freud, *Leonardo*, 27.

and autonomy are linked here. A five-year-old boy speaks out of turn in front of guests and is reprimanded by his father, who says, "This was seven years ago, before you were born, before you were even conceived."[6] The boy bursts into violent tears, plunged, Erikson suggests, into "a grave metaphysical anxiety" by thus being forced to confront the "fundamental mystery" of a time before his own existence, in conjunction with that other fundamental mystery alluded to by his father's reference to conception. At this age, Erikson says, a boy may well be "doubtful as well as sensitive about the way in which he was created," both the "biological riddle of the act of conception" and the sociological riddle of the father's privileged role in the act, "his prerogatives in regard to the mother." Understanding sexuality, understanding human mortality and historicity, being curious and thinking independently, and coming to terms with the Oedipal problem, then, are interrelated psychic developments.

The period of early childish sexual investigation typically ends, Freud says, "through an impetus of energetic sexual repression."[7] But he catalogues a number of different possibilities for the "future fate of the investigation impulse," among which "the most rare and perfect" characterized Leonardo: "The libido withdraws from the fate of the repression by being sublimated from the outset into curiosity, and by reinforcing the powerful investigation impulse."[8] Passion is "transmuted" into "inquisitiveness," and the boy settles for knowing the mother and the world intellectually rather than carnally: "Instead of acting and producing, one just investigates."[9] In investigating and observing the boy finds mastery and gratification; he achieves an indirect victory without the dangers of an overt Oedipal challenge. Later he may, as Erikson suggests, enhance his self-esteem "by participating in the arts and sciences with all their grandiose displays of magic omnipotence," mastering the world in his mind.[10] "Deep down," he may even believe that knowing is generating, "that an Einstein creates the cosmic laws which he predicts." A closely correlated strategy is that of wit and humor: by making fun of one's rival one may achieve a sense of superiority without the risks of open conflict. Outfoxed by a boy's cleverness, observed and mocked, the father may come to seem ridiculous, yet the boy is safe from retaliation, for it is all in fun and may even amuse the father. The fool, as already noted, is free to insult the king.[11]

6. Erikson, *Young Man Luther*, 110.   7. Freud, *Leonardo*, 29.
8. Ibid., 29–30.   9. Ibid., 20, 22.
10. Erikson, *Young Man Luther*, 113.
11. Philip E. Slater, *The Glory of Hera* (Boston: Beacon Press, 1968), 193–95. Anton

Something like foxiness, then, may be seen as one possible outcome of the Oedipus complex. Clearly, however, there are both theoretical problems in the Freudian Oedipal account and difficulties in attempting to apply it to the purposes of this book. Freud links the psychic strategy of withdrawal into the intellect with Leonardo's sexual abstemiousness and homosexual tendencies, and he traces all of these to the special circumstances of Leonardo's childhood. Leonardo was an illegitimate child, raised for the first few years entirely by his mother, but then at about the age of five adopted by his father and stepmother and taken into their household.[12] Freud claims to have clinical evidence that homosexual men often emerge from a family situation in which the father is absent, and in which the mother unconsciously focuses her own erotic needs on her son.[13] This prompts an initial "very intensive erotic attachment" to the mother, but later this attachment becomes too threatening and is transformed into an identification and forgotten—or rather denied. "The boy represses the love for the mother by putting himself in her place." If as an adult he becomes actively homosexual, the boys he loves "are only substitutive persons or revivals of his own childish person, whom he loves in the same way as his mother loved him." In effect, he makes love to himself. Freud calls such love narcissistic, "for the Greek legend called a boy Narcissus to whom nothing was more pleasing than his own mirrored image."[14]

Freud does not explain why the initial erotic attachment to the mother should become repressed and transmuted into identification—a *being* her instead of *having* her. In a normal, classical Oedipal account, what causes a boy's erotic attachment to his mother to be repressed is fear of the father; but the repression does not result in identification with her. On the contrary, the boy identifies with the father and sets out to find a woman reminiscent of his mother but sufficiently different to be Oedipally "safe." In Leonardo's case one can see how the initial period alone with his mother might have produced an unusually "intensive erotic attachment" to her, and one can imagine that the reappearance of the father, and the mother's replacement by a stepmother when the boy was about five, might have forced repression or sublimation of that attachment. But Freud strongly suggests that it is the *absence* of a father that is crucial both in Leonardo's case and in male homosexuality generally. The "boldness and independence" of Leonardo's

---

Ehrenzweig, "The Origin of the Scientific and Heroic Urge (The Guilt of Prometheus)," *International Journal of Psychoanalysis* 30 (1949): 113.
12. Freud, *Leonardo*, 32.　　13. Ibid., 61.　　14. Ibid., 62.

adult scientific investigations, he says, "presupposes that his infantile sexual investigation was *not* inhibited by his father"; his inquiring spirit and questioning of all authorities "would not have been possible had he not been deprived of his father in the first years of life."[15] Similarly, male homosexuality seems to be most powerfully "furthered by" the "absence of the father during the childhood period," so that the boy grows up "entirely under feminine influence."[16]

But in the absence of a father, what fear is it that causes the sublimation of libido into the investigative impulse and the repression of erotic love for the mother into an identification with her? Freud acknowledges that he cannot answer that question. He calls it "a transformation . . . whose mechanisms we know but whose motive forces we have not yet grasped."[17] Could there be some powerful threat in the early relationship to the mother itself, quite apart from the reappearance of a father? Freud makes no such suggestion in this book, nor does he consider the impact on Leonardo of the abrupt substitution of a stepmother for the mother who nursed him.

Besides these theoretical difficulties in Freud's study, its application to the purposes of this book also raises serious problems. For to the extent that it is bound to Leonardo's special sexual proclivities and the special circumstances of his childhood, it does not seem relevant to most of Machiavelli's contemporaries or to Machiavelli himself, who as far as we know was heterosexual and grew up in a "normal" family.

Furthermore, though the Freudian account does fit some features of Machiavelli's thought, there are other important features to which it does not seem to apply. Machiavelli surely did share with Leonardo, and with a number of other outstanding Renaissance men, an "unrequited wish to understand everything surrounding him, and to fathom with cold reflection the deepest secret of everything that is perfect" or powerful.[18] All the commentators agree, and indeed Machiavelli's letters and dispatches make evident, that he was "constantly exercising with all he met, great or small, his insatiable curiosity."[19] The Oedipal theme is surely evident, moreover, in *Mandragola* and *Clizia*, as young suitors triumph over old, paternal cuckolds. Ligurio's role, in particular, might be taken to illustrate withdrawal into the intellect for an indirect Oedipal triumph. By analogy, one could argue for an Oedipal reading of *The Prince*, as the new prince displaces the ineffectual established ruler and

15. Ibid., 97, my italics.   16. Ibid., 61.   17. Ibid., 61–62.
18. E. Solmi, *Leonardo Da Vinci*, tr. Emmi Hirschberg (Berlin, 1908), 193, cited in ibid., 18.
19. Ridolfi, *Life*, 101.

is welcomed by poor, abused, unprotected Lady Italy as her "redeemer." Indeed, as commentators have pointed out, in many of Machiavelli's works there is a strong emphasis on the power and value of youth and on the conspiratorial overthrow of established paternal authority.

Yet other significant aspects of Machiavelli's thought elude Oedipal categories. There is, for instance, the heavy stress on activism and the almost obsessive concern with autonomy and the dangers of dependence. And in his life, of course, Machiavelli did not choose to withdraw from active, worldly engagement into investigation; only his forced exile from politics made him into a theorist.

❖   ❖   ❖

Some further help may be obtained from Philip Slater's fascinating study of ancient Greece, *The Glory of Hera*; for although it concerns a wholly different society than Machiavelli's, this book helps clarify the theoretical difficulties in Freud's Oedipal account by focusing attention on a boy's fear of his mother rather than his father; it also suggests social conditions that might give a general relevance to the very special circumstances of Leonardo's childhood.

Slater sets himself the problem of understanding what he calls a striking paradox about women in ancient Greece, specifically in Athens. On the one hand, we know that women were severely restricted and deprived in actual social relations, low in power and status. Yet, on the other hand, the female figures in Greek mythology and literature are prominent, powerful, dangerous, perhaps more so than in the literature of any other society. Slater's basic, Freudian premise is that since this literature was created by men, it will reflect the fantasy life of these men, and that to understand the significance of that fantasy life one must look not at their actual relations with women who were their contemporaries, but at the way they experienced relationships with women in their infancy—that is, at their relationships with their mothers. "The social position of women and the psychological influence of women are thus quite separate matters."[20] Infantile experience does depend on (though it will not accurately depict) real social relationships, but less those between adult men and women than those between women and children.

Slater describes women in ancient Greek society as despised and powerless in every respect except one: they controlled the household and young children. In fifth-century Athens, he says, "women were le-

20. Slater, *Glory*, 8.

gally powerless," and they "were excluded from political and intellectual life, uneducated, virtually imprisoned in the home, and appeared to
be regarded with disdain" by the masculine culture.[21] Marriages were
arranged, with women typically being married off at an early age to men
much older than they, men who were reluctant to wed.[22] The "ignorant
and immature" bride joining her husband's household, "moved abruptly
from the life of childhood and the security of her family" into confinement in a stranger's house, becoming "totally dependent" on him "for
all her needs."[23] Thus marriage was often a disappointing and traumatic
experience for the Athenian girl. Marriage had nothing to do with romantic love, and emotional intensity was found instead in friendships
between members of the same sex. This emotional "shallowness of the
marital bond" did not originate in the classical period but was already
characteristic of early Greece, Slater says. In the classical period, however, with the breakdown of other traditional and extended social ties,
that marital bond was in effect required to bear the burden of new needs
it could not fulfill.

In most societies or subcultures in which the marital bond is weak, the partners
are deeply invested in other relationships which are strong and enduring and
supported by a stable and permanent environment. When this external stability
breaks down, the marital bond becomes more important, and if marital roles
are still structured along the older principle, substantial misery can result. This
seems to have happened in fifth-century Athens, particularly for the wife. . . .[24]

Within her low status and her deprivation, however, the mature Athenian wife did have one realm of power and privilege: she was in charge
of the household, and that included complete control over small children.[25] The men stayed away, in the public places where women were
not welcome.

In such a society, Slater argues, a boy's relationship with his mother
will be very intense and troubled: intense, because for years she is the
entire focus of his world, the dominant power over him; troubled, because she will play out in relation to him her own ambivalent feelings
about sex roles. On the one hand, of course, the mother loves her son.
Especially with the heavy cultural valuation of masculinity, producing a
son and heir for the family is "her principal source of prestige and vali-
dation" as a woman.[26] Moreover, being dissatisfied and resentful of her
husband, she may come to experience her son as a substitute—simul-

21. Ibid., 5, 4.   22. Ibid., 25, 23–24.   23. Ibid., 25.
24. Ibid., 27–28.   25. Ibid., 7–9.   26. Ibid., 29.

taneously both as "her little man," her "hero," who loves and will take care of her, and as a masculine extension of herself, her way of penetrating into the forbidden world of men.[27] On the other hand, she also resents the boy's masculinity—the symbol of her own degradation—and constantly attacks, undermines, ridicules it. She wants him to "grow up and be a real man, not like your worthless father," yet she also wants him to be all hers, to remain a part of herself.

For a young boy, Slater argues, it is a classical "double bind."[28] His masculinity becomes the most important question there is, yet he is constantly in doubt about it, constantly afraid that he will be unable to measure up to his mother's exaggerated demands. Thus "the most grandiose self-definitions are at once fomented and punctured" in him.[29] He is made to "feel that if he is not a great hero he is nothing, and pride or prestige becomes more important than love."[30] Further, at this point his mother is still his whole world; he has as yet no clear image of his distant father. Instead, he has two conflicting projections: his mother's critical and resentful view, and his own secret wish for a really strong, powerful father who would act as "an antidote to the conflicting demands" his mother makes on him, who would "protect him against these overpowering feminine needs."[31]

In general, Slater suggests, such social patterns will tend to produce men who are narcissistic. Toward women they will feel a combination of fear, awe, and contempt, being particularly afraid of adult, motherly women; they will prefer virgins, young girls, or even boys for sexual partners. They will be haunted by a sense of the danger of maternal entrapment, of being engulfed, consumed. The fear will be the more haunting because it is half wish. Toward men they will be competitive and defensively masculine, stressing honor and the avenging of insults, prone to boasting and violence, "proving behavior" or "protest masculinity."[32] At the same time they will yearn for a strong father to rescue them, a great, supermasculine hero who would slay the maternal dragon. All of these configurations will tend to foster homosexuality.

This book need not be concerned with whether Slater's characterization of Greek society is right historically, but only with whether and

27. Ibid., 31–33. Compare Freud on Leonardo's mother (Freud, *Leonardo*, 87–88).
28. Slater, *Glory*, 49. The expression originates with Gregory Bateson and his associates, "Toward a Theory of Schizophrenia," *Behavioral Science* 1 (1956): 251–64.
29. Slater, *Glory*, 44.   30. Ibid., 33.   31. Ibid., 54, 63.
32. The phrases are, respectively, from Paul Goodman, *Growing Up Absurd* (New York: Vintage, 1962), 41–44, 191–215; and Beatrice B. Whiting, "Sex Identity Conflict and Physical Violence," *American Anthropologist* 67 (December 1965 suppl.): 126.

how his approach might apply to Machiavelli's time and thought.[33] Certainly the character pattern that Slater describes is reminiscent of the men of Renaissance Italy, who surely were narcissistic, competitive, defensive about their honor, and—some of them—prone to violence. Moreover, the general idea of parallels between Renaissance Italy and ancient Greece, with their small, self-governing, unstable city-states, their magnificent artistic and intellectual achievements, is familiar. But for a more careful assessment, the question must be divided into two distinct inquiries: Were the social and familial conditions of Renaissance Florence anything like those ascribed by Slater to ancient Greece? And how might Slater's psychological account apply to the Machiavellian texts? The former, historical question must be postponed to the next chapter, leaving the latter, theoretical question as the immediate focus of inquiry.

In Machiavelli's thought, the Slater thesis seems to give promise of illuminating the stress on action and autonomy, especially those passages where that stress seems to evince a fear more of being engulfed or of disappearing as a separate self than of being castrated or Oedipally punished. Slater's Hera is reminiscent of Machiavelli's mythologized female figures: fortune, nature, Circe. Under Slater's thesis, the ambivalent conceptions of manhood found in Machiavelli's thought would originate in the boy's fear of his mother's angry ambivalence, rather than in his fear of the father; indeed, the boy would long for a strong father to rescue him.

So far, Slater's account seems less obviously helpful, however, regarding the specific psychic strategy of foxiness, the withdrawal from overt masculine competition into investigation or manipulation. But the fox appears as Slater goes on to examine in detail a number of major figures in Greek mythology, using each of them to represent one of the character types or psychic strategies available in this culture, within the general schema he has delineated. One among these Slater associates with the mythical figure of Hephaestus, a craftsman and a clown, skilled, clever, sly, knowledgeable, and amusing. He was also lame, crippled at birth or by an angry parent; Slater takes Hephaestus's lameness to symbolize his "withdrawal from the lists of sexual and marital rivalry . . . his resignation from manhood."[34] It happens, moreover, that Hephaestus had a brother, Ares, who "seems to represent everything that He-

33. For criticism, see, e.g., Sarah B. Pomeroy, *Goddesses, Whores, Wives, and Slaves* (New York: Schocken Books, 1975), 95–96.
    34. Slater, *Glory*, 193.

phaestus is not allowed to be: he is uncrippled, virile, and aggressive."[35] On the other hand, Ares is not very bright. It is as if Hephaestus and Ares are two halves of what might, in better circumstances, have been a whole man: mind and body, intellect and feeling, thought and action. We may be reminded of Ligurio and Callimaco in *Mandragola*, and perhaps of the relationship between counselor and prince, theorist and Founder. Thus Slater seems to offer us a way of understanding at least some of what we found in Machiavelli's texts, both the activism and the foxiness; and to do so with reference to a boy's relationship to his mother.

Yet while his general theory is based on fear of the mother rather than the father, Slater's account of Hephaestus in particular is formulated in classical Oedipal terms, in terms of "self-emasculation" out of fear of the father. As Slater himself acknowledges, the pattern that Hephaestus represents almost does not belong in his book.[36] The best that he can do by way of explanation is to mention that there are conflicting Greek myths about how Hephaestus became lame: one in which he is flung from heaven by a jealous father, another by his enraged mother. Slater concludes, with some hesitation and qualification, that "it would seem reasonable to assume" such a character type would be "most likely to develop when *both* parents are intolerant of masculinity in a son." Where a boy is "persecuted by [an enraged mother] but lovingly supported and protected by [a strong father]," the pattern of development will be different.[37] But none of Slater's Greek boys is so supported in his early years; and he does not give any account of the psychodynamics of the boy facing two hostile parents.

The literature of depth-psychology does offer other accounts interpreting a character type like that of Slater's Hephaestus or our fox in relation to the fear of maternal power and engulfment. But they reach back further into infancy than most of Slater's explanations. Freud's discussion of Leonardo, we saw, although ostensibly based on Oedipal fear of the father, rested on the father's absence in the early years. Slater shifts the focus of fear to the mother, but still in terms of the Oedipal phase of development; he speaks of sexual nuances between mother and son, and of ambivalence about gender roles. A boy's relationship with his mother originates much earlier, however, in the oral rather than in the genital phase, with the infant nursing at the breast.[38] One might

35. Ibid., 202.   36. Ibid., 194–95.
37. Ibid., 197, my italics.
38. Slater does deal with this infantile period, but in a way not relevant to our concerns (*Glory*, ch. 2).

therefore supplement Slater's suggestions with some theories focusing on this earlier period.

❖ ❖ ❖

At least one branch of post-Freudian psychoanalytic theory offers an alternative understanding of something like the image of the fox and other features of Machiavelli's thought, formulated in terms of fear of the mother rather than of the father and locating its origins in earliest infancy rather than in the classical Oedipal period. This branch of theory, originating in Freud's concept of "separation anxiety," was first developed by Melanie Klein, elaborated by numerous others, and recently formulated in commonsense terms by D. W. Winnicott and Dorothy Dinnerstein.[39] For reasons of economy, this large and very complex body of literature can only be briefly summarized here, unfortunately lending a false appearance of simplicity and completeness to this account.

Our images of femininity, this theory suggests, originate in the infant's experience of the person who first nurses and tends it, in most societies almost invariably a female. Though the infant of course knows nothing of male and female, its early experience later becomes associated with persons like that one, a category that in due time turns out to be women, particularly "maternal" ones. The infantile experience that becomes associated with women in this way, the theorists speculate, must have been characterized by the following features.

First, an infant is not yet a fully separate self, nor aware of itself as such. The unborn fetus is of course literally at one with its mother, and the first step of separation is the trauma of birth. But birth is only the beginning of a long process of development, in whose early stages the infant is not yet aware of itself as a continuing unit distinct from the rest of the world—neither as a physical body nor as a person. In the beginning, self, world, and mother are one.

39. Melanie Klein, *Contributions to Psychoanalysis, 1921–1945* (London: Hogarth Press, 1948); *Envy and Gratitude* (New York: Basic Books, 1957). Melanie Klein and Joan Riviere, *Love, Hate and Reparation* (London: Hogarth Press, 1962). D. W. Winnicott, "Breast Feeding," in *The Child and the Outside World* (New York: Basic Books, 1957); "Ego Distortion in Terms of True and False Self," in *The Maturational Process and the Facilitating Environment* (London: Hogarth Press, 1965); *Playing and Reality* (London: Tavistock, 1971). Dorothy Dinnerstein, *The Mermaid and the Minotaur* (New York: Harper & Row, 1976); R. D. Laing, *The Divided Self* (Baltimore: Penguin, 1970). Although Freud introduced the concept of "separation anxiety," he did not theorize extensively on the infant's relationship to the mother in the first year of life, maintaining that clinical psychoanalytic evidence on this preverbal period was too difficult to obtain. But Freud was also generally less insightful about mothers and daughters than about fathers and sons. Sigmund Freud, *The Standard Edition of the Complete Psychological Works of Sigmund Freud*, ed. James Strachey, 24 vols. (London: Hogarth Press, 1953–74), especially "Inhibitions, Symptoms and Anxiety," vol. 20; "On Narcissism," vol. 14; "Female Sexuality," vol. 21.

Indeed, second, the young infant is not even aware of the continuity over time of objects or persons—that there is *a* mother who goes away and comes back, a self who sleeps and wakes, and so on. Here theory is by now well supported by experimental research.[40] But there is disagreement about the precise age at which infants begin to "achieve object permanence."[41]

Third, even when it does begin to recognize objects and persons as continuing entities that exist even when they are not perceived, the infant has not yet mastered language, and so cannot think conceptually. Precisely what this means is none too clear, except that the infant's thought is very primitive and concrete. Among other things, this certainly means that any account *we* give of infantile thought is bound to distort, if only because we are forced to verbalize a preverbal experience.

Fourth, the infant's experience is not yet differentiated between cognitive and affective aspects, between what is objective in the world and what is subjective emotion. Infantile emotions, further, are as yet uncontrolled, unchanneled by any psychic agency, since the psyche itself is just beginning to develop, so they are of an overwhelming intensity we cannot even imagine. The bliss of the nursing infant is total: at that moment the world-mother-self circle is as good-happy-gratifying as anything could possibly be. But the pain, rage, fear of hunger or other unpleasant experiences is equally total; the world-mother-self then is more vile-terrifying-furious than anything encountered in later life. The infant ego, beginning to emerge, is in constant danger of being overwhelmed by floods of affect. And since there is no object-continuity, what the infant actually experiences must be a sort of unconnected series of good world-mother-self configurations and bad world-mother-self configurations.

Fifth, the infant's experience is intensely physical, since its psychic and intellectual faculties are still so primitive. And its physical experience is most powerfully concentrated on the processes of nurturance, although of course it also experiences temperature, light, sound, position. In Freudian terms, the libido is in the oral phase of organization: the infant explores the world with its mouth, its greatest pleasures come from nursing at the breast, its greatest pains and fears are those of hunger and indigestion, it perceives the world-mother-self primarily in terms of eating and being eaten.

Yet, sixth, from the very beginning, the world-mother-self is also about communication, specifically human contact as distinct from mere

40. Janet Flannery Jackson and Joseph Jackson, *Infant Culture* (New York: Thomas Y. Crowell, 1978), 70–77, 100.
41. Ibid., 101.

satiation of physical needs. Here again much has been learned from experimental study and observation. Work with primates illuminates
what happens to infants experimentally "mothered" only by an inanimate object holding a bottle. Wartime orphanages taught psychologists
what happens to infants who are given nothing more than physical
care: an infant that is not handled, talked to, and otherwise given human response will withdraw from contact with the world, become apathetic, and ultimately die, even though all its physical needs are met.
Erikson says, "In the beginning are the generous breast and the eyes
that care."[42] Of course a bottle can replace the breast, and even a blind
mother can raise a healthy baby. But in ways that are objectively observable, becoming a functioning human person requires interaction with,
recognition from, at least one other human person.

In many ways, then, an integrated self and an awareness of others as
persons are hard-won and gradual achievements. Self and world, self
and other person, are in effect constructed together, in a process of dif-
ferentiation out of the original matrix, a process of simultaneously emotional and cognitive maturation. An awareness of a continuing self cannot be achieved without an awareness of a continuing, integrated
mother. This, in turn, requires the integration of the separate moments
of "good mother" and "bad mother" into a single, persisting entity; and
so beginning to separate the objective mother from the infant's feelings
about her at any moment. And that is extraordinarily difficult, for it requires the infant to develop the capacity for modifying and controlling
its emotions of the moment.[43] If good mother and bad mother are one,
then the infant can no longer afford to merge with the former in quite
the same blissful abandon nor to hate the latter with quite the same
boundless rage. Or, to put the same thing the other way around, unless
the infant can begin to control and modify its feelings in this way, it
cannot achieve the necessary cognitive awareness of continuity. The
fragments of self to be integrated are bound up with the fragments of
mother, and with the infant's relationship to her and with its feelings at
each moment.

As persons and objects begin to assume continuity, and mother, self,
and world begin to be distinct, the infant must thus begin to deal with
problems of (what we would call) first, dependency and autonomy, and
then, agency and guilt. If there is a mother who continues to exist even
when she is out of sight, and who returns periodically, this introduces

42. Erikson, *Young Man Luther*, 117.
43. Klein speaks here of the infant "splitting" the mother or the breast into good and
bad moments, as if they had already been earlier experienced as unified.

some hope into the previously limitless terror of the "bad" times, but it also introduces the possibility of loss into the "good" times— introduces anxiety. At the same time, the previously unfocused, pervasive affect that flooded world-mother-self begins to focus on emerging objects: good feelings begin to be love of the mother, rage begins to be rage at the mother, hunger begins to be a craving for her nourishing breast. But as bad mother and good mother become a single, continuing person, what happens to the one will affect the other as well. Here the dawning awareness of separation is complicated by the dawning awareness of agency to raise the possibility of something more than anxiety about loss, namely guilt.

The nursing infant is of course totally dependent on the mother; abandoned, it will die. But the infant, lacking awareness of its separateness, does not perceive it so. Freud and other psychoanalysts hypothesize that the infant's first response to discomfort or need is to dream or hallucinate relief, only when the need becomes too intense does it begin to cry. They also speak of the infantile sense of omnipotence in its oneness with the mother. Omnipotence can't really be quite the right term, since the infant has no awareness yet of itself as an agent; but no words can really be right here. Beginning to be aware of itself and the mother as separate, continuing persons, the baby must begin to experience dependence, the limits of its powers, but also the possibility of its agency. The infant sucks at the breast, and milk flows. It cries, and the mother comes. Did it cause the flow or the coming? But then, when mother disappears, did it cause that as well? A frequent infantile experience might be something like this: blissfully nursing and gazing at the mother, the infant sinks into the blankness of sleep; when it next experiences the world it is alone, and perhaps again uncomfortable. Has it driven the mother away, perhaps destroyed or consumed her? And what of the times when it is alone and cries and she does not come? It is filled with rage; but it is still only imperfectly differentiated from world and mother, so they seem filled with rage as well; perhaps she is gone because of anger—hers or the infant's, which are not distinct.

Erikson calls the infant's first dawning awareness of a continuing mother who will return and provide care, "basic trust," and "the infant's first social achievement . . . his willingness to let the mother out of sight without undue anxiety or rage," the fundamental "optimism" that lays the foundation for a later positive attitude toward the world in general as a place of human habitation.[44] It further includes, he says, the

44. Erik H. Erikson, *Childhood and Society*, 2d ed. (New York: W. W. Norton, 1963), 247; Erikson, *Young Man Luther*, 118. Cf. Klein, *Contributions*, 202, 247–51, 312, 378.

reciprocal implication of being oneself trustworthy, since mother and
infant are not yet well separated: the security "that one may trust oneself and the capacity of one's own organs to cope with urges" so that the
mother is safe, "will not need to be on guard" against one.[45] This trust
"meets its crucial test" when the infant enters the second half of the oral
stage of development by beginning teething. Teething means, first, pain
for the infant and therefore anger; second, the possibility of biting the
mother in nursing, and indeed the desire to bite to ease the pain, and the
possibility that the mother will then withdraw the breast. Third, teething is likely to coincide with weaning—the permanent withdrawal of
the breast, and a crucial stage of separation. Many babies apparently
construe weaning as a punishment for, or prevention of, damage that
they might have inflicted on the mother.

Emerging out of primal innocence, man gave in to woman's temptation, "bit into the forbidden apple," and was banished from paradise:
"He 'knew' at the price of losing innocence; he became autonomous at
the price of shame and gained independence at the price of guilt."[46]
More generally, the development of autonomy entails the discovery of
dependence and guilt because it inevitably takes place within the ambit
of the mother's power and partly in struggle and rage against her. When
the infant first begins to discover its own will, and the mother as a separate person with a potentially conflicting will, what it encounters, as
Dinnerstein says, is an overwhelming power:

the will of a being at whose touch its flesh has shuddered with joy, a being the
sound of whose footsteps has flooded its senses with a relief more total than it
can ever know again.[47]

The awareness of dependence and near impotence is a necessary first
step toward the gradual development of actual autonomy, the capacity
to take care of oneself and others in the world. The successful development of these real autonomous powers is itself a source of gratification
and pleasure. Thus, while the loss of the infantile sense of omnipotence
or oneness with the universe "is a basic human grief" never fully
allayed,

We manage in part to console ourselves for it indirectly, through mastery, competence, enterprise: the new joy of successful activity is some compensation for
the old joy of passive, effortless wish-fulfillment.[48]

45. Erikson, *Childhood*, 248.
46. Erikson, *Young Man Luther*, 121; Erikson, *Childhood*, 79.
47. Dinnerstein, *Mermaid*, 165.
48. Ibid., 60.

In short, we begin our lifelong, ambivalent oscillation between the pursuit of these two joys: bathed in security and dependence we long for adventure, achievement, begin to feel trapped; engaged in independent mastery but encountering its costs and dangers, we yearn to retreat, to crawl back into the original matrix, be cared for, and disappear. An older child, a toddler, will venture cheerfully into the world away from its mother for a time, then suddenly want and need her desperately; if she is there, a moment's contact is enough, and it is ready once more to explore independently.

Both faces of this lifelong inner conflict between dependence and autonomy have their flip sides, their costs, as well: dependent merging may be all very well when a nurturing matrix is available, otherwise it is a fantasy or hallucination that cannot provide comfort for long. Independence and mastery, however, not only are constrained by the limits of one's own fallible power but also entail the possibility of damage and guilt. They also entail the possibility of repairing the damage done, but there is always the risk that one's capacity to harm may exceed the capacity for making amends, that damage may be irreparable. Indeed, the very wish to be autonomous might anger or harm the mother.

The baby's first steps toward autonomy take place under the mother's auspices, Dinnerstein says, and within her "power to foster or forbid, to humble or respect" those strivings.[49] Without her support and approval, the child cannot grow and gain independence; she is the first and essential audience for its achievements, a comfort for its failures. But to become genuinely independent, the child must eventually begin to test its emergent will also *against* that of the mother. And in opposing her, it risks alienating that essential audience, the "other" in whose eyes achievement can be measured. Mothers characteristically support and enjoy their children's progress toward mastery and autonomy; but with the best will in the world, they cannot always do so. And since mothers have needs and emotions of their own, affected by many concerns besides the welfare of their children, most mothers also sometimes oppose and regret those developments.[50] Thus the child's ambivalent feelings

49. Ibid., 165.

50. This book examines some men's fears of maternal engulfment and fantasies of paternal rescue and deals with a society where little boys may well have had good reason to develop such fears and fantasies (as the next chapter will show). It does not advocate what it examines. See also: Jessica Benjamin, "Authority and the Family Revisited, or A World Without Fathers?" *New German Critique* 13 (September 1978): 35–57; Stephanie Engel, "Femininity as Tragedy: Reexamining the 'New Narcissism,'" *Socialist Review* 10 (September–October 1980): 77–103; Alexander Mitscherlich, *Society Without the Father* (New York: Schocken, 1970); Roy Schafer, "The Loving and Beloved Superego in Freud's Structural Theory," *The Psychoanalytic Study of the Child* 15 (1960): 163–88.

about separation and growth are always complicated by the mother's ambivalences, for instance about "losing" her "baby." The counterpart to our occasional wish to crawl back into the original matrix, then, is the fear—whether based on wish or on reality—that the matrix may pursue and engulf us against our will.

As the baby grows and its relationship to the mother changes, it also begins to develop significant other relationships, in the Western nuclear family particularly the relationship to its father. What distinguishes the father's relationship to the baby from the mother's is that it begins—or at least becomes salient—later; it is the significant "second" relationship and thus not as primitive nor as powerfully centered on basic, physical need as the relationship to the mother. Indeed, awareness of two distinct parents, the very "appearance of the father as a separate entity is a later achievement in the child's conceptualization and object relations."[51] At first fathers are simply "non-mothers, the other kind of person," the ones without breasts.[52] As "second" persons they are sometimes rivals for the mother's attention, but also an alternative resource for the baby. And because the relationship to the father develops later, when the baby is already somewhat formed as a self, he is perceived as an ally in the baby's ambivalent struggle for independence and autonomy in relation to the mother.[53] He functions, Erikson says, "somewhat like a guardian of the child's autonomous existence," inviting but also forcing the child away from its symbiosis with the mother:

For children become aware of the attributes of maleness, and learn to love men's physical touch and guiding voice, at about the time when they have the first courage for an autonomous existence.[54]

In Western culture typically, the father also represents contact with the larger world outside the family and the household. Thus the child's developing relationship with him mediates access to worldly achievement and competence and "offer[s] membership in the wider community where prowess is displayed, enterprise planned, public event organized."[55] In these respects the father may serve as "a sanctuary from maternal authority," from the threat of sinking back into the original matrix (and from the wish to do so). That sanctuary will be "passionately cherished" by that essential part of the child's self that is seeking independence and mastery, wanting to emerge

out of the drowsing sweetness of early childhood into the bright light of open day, the light of the adult realm in which human reason and human will—not

51. Schafer, "Loving," 177.   52. Erikson, *Young Man Luther*, 123.
53. Dinnerstein, *Mermaid*, 47.   54. Erikson, *Young Man Luther*, 124.
55. Dinnerstein, *Mermaid*, 48.

the boundless and mysterious intentionality, the terrible uncanny omniscience, of the nursery goddess—can be expected, at least ideally, to prevail.[56]

With father and mother available, in effect, the child can go forth into the world with the one, return for security and comfort with the other, having adult support and guidance for both halves of its ambivalent struggle over independence. When no father or equivalent "second" person is available, the emergence from infancy is more difficult. This will be even more the case if the initial relationship between mother and infant was seriously troubled, or if the mother later hinders the child's efforts at autonomy unnecessarily, out of psychic needs of her own.

Almost universally and certainly in the past Western societies, the "first" person in an infant's life has been a female. Although the infant does not yet have concepts of male and female, Dinnerstein argues convincingly that the qualities of the "first" person's skin, flesh, touch, voice, movements are later associated with others of the same sex; mother becomes central to the definition of what "woman" means. As a result, the qualities and features of infantile experience become and remain associated for all of us with women, with the concept of the feminine. Women thus have to do with: the danger of dissolution of the self, of losing boundaries between self and others, self and world; the pre- or nonverbal, nonconceptual, nonrational; overwhelming affect and the danger of being so overwhelmed; the body and its pleasures and needs, particularly those of nurturance, eating and being eaten; helpless dependence and omnipotent domination, relationships of almost total inequality.

Men, by contrast, become meaningful to the infant at a later, less primitive stage of maturation, and therefore are perceived as less engulfing, better defined, more rational and controlled, more like persons and less like magical forces. Relations with men are less bound to sheer survival; the "second" person never was the whole world, indeed, could only enter the picture after there already were separate persons in the infant's world.

These infantile impressions are never wholly lost. Of course early experience is modified by later growth and learning. But each experience helps shape the lens, one might say, through which subsequent experience is perceived; and in times of frustration and stress we tend to regress to earlier stages of psychic organization. Furthermore, the degree to which they are modified and "worked through" in subsequent experience depends both on their psychic accessibility and on the experi-

56. Ibid., 176.

ences a particular society makes available. The more rigidly infantile experience is repressed because of psychic trauma, the more it becomes insulated and entrenched in the unconscious mind and inaccessible to later modification. And the more social institutions reinforce the infantile perceptions, the less later experience is likely to modify those perceptions. If, for example, childcare is exclusively a task for women, and public life and independence are exclusively reserved for men, this will of course tend to support rather than modify the infantile association of women with inegalitarian and dominative relationships, of men with autonomy and mutuality.

❖   ❖   ❖

Some psychologists and psychoanalysts link severe disturbances in the infant's relationship with the mother to schizophrenia. That view is controversial and need not concern us here. But many also discuss milder disturbances in that relationship in terms significantly reminiscent of the images in Machiavelli's texts. They have three different ways of talking about such disturbances and subsequent character formations: as too early or too intense an identification with the mother; as a fragmentation of, or a failure to integrate, the self; and as a withdrawal from the body and the world into the mind. All three accounts concern a failure or refusal of separation, an attempt to continue the infant's initial sense of omnipotent oneness with the mother-world.

The first way of conceptualizing that failure or refusal is as an identification with the mother, so that self and mother are not separate because the mother has been internalized into the self. Now, all children partly identify with or internalize significant persons in their world, but the pathological type of internalization of the mother occurs too early, too intensely, and in a way that insulates it against modification by later experience. As a result, *what* is internalized is a very primitive image of the mother, still fragmented into "bad" and "good" parts, still suffused with intense and powerful affect, still focused on eating and being consumed, still a magical force rather than a person.[57] As a result, the child also has difficulty in becoming a person, a continual and integrated self. The healthy development of an infant toward autonomy, toward "independent existence in a world of human beings," says Winnicott, requires not merely that the mother provide successful and gratifying nurturance, but also that she "remain . . . the one person in the infant's life over a period of time until both she and (therefore also) the infant can be felt (by the infant) to be whole human beings."[58]

57. Klein, *Contributions*, 203, 268–70.
58. Winnicott, "Breast Feeding," 143.

The literature is none too clear on why an overly early or intense internalization of the mother might occur. Freud's work on Leonardo and Slater's thesis about Greece suggest the commonsense notion that if no father or "second" person is around, the mother is the only model for identification available. But that seems an insufficient explanation for pathology, especially since it would locate the problem relatively late, at the point where a "second" person would normally become significant for the baby. An earlier and more devastating internalization of the mother is suggested by Freud in his discussion of mourning. When a person significant in our lives dies, Freud says, part of the normal "work of mourning," our response to the loss, is to erect a substitute version of the lost person inside our own psyche. The "libido" formerly invested in the relationship with the lost "object"—the person who has disappeared—will now be "withdrawn into the ego," where it will serve specifically "to establish an *identification* of the ego with the abandoned object."[59] Thus if a baby's mother dies or disappears permanently, it will try "to hold on to her by becoming [her]" and internalizing "both partners of [the] lost relationship."[60] In effect, the lost relationship is continued internally, except that it is now complicated by the experience of loss itself: the baby's anger at being abandoned, guilt at having (perhaps, it imagines) caused the abandonment. What is internalized is of course not the objective reality of the lost person, but the baby's image and experience of that person. Thus, the earlier such loss and internalization occur, the more primitive, fragmented, and powerful the mother that is internalized. And the more traumatic the loss, the "worse" the internalized "bad mother" will be, and the more the internalized image and relationship will be rigidified and insulated against modification by further experience. Similar, if less severe, results can be expected if instead of losing the mother, the baby merely experiences a serious "failure of dependability" in her, or their relationship is otherwise seriously disturbed.[61]

A second way of discussing the consequences of disturbances in the relationship between infant and mother is as a failure to integrate the self, so that it remains split into several partial persons. Since integration of the self into a single, continuing person depends on and develops gradually with awareness of the mother as a continuing person neither wholly good nor wholly bad, interruption of this process of coordinated growth can leave a permanently divided psyche, its parts more or less

---

59. Sigmund Freud, "Mourning and Melancholia," in *Standard Edition* 15: 249.
60. Erikson, *Childhood*, 58.
61. Freud, "Mourning," 245; Winnicott, *Playing*, 102.

insulated from each other. In particular, it may leave the psyche divided into a "bodily" self that is active in the world and in relationship to other people, but is experienced as false or unreal, and a "mind" part that is experienced as the true self, but somehow unrelated to body, the world, and other people.[62] The one acts, the other—the real self— merely observes. Laing puts it this way:

The individual experiences his self as being more or less divorced or detached from his body. *The body is felt more as one object among other objects in the world than as the core of the individual's own being.* Instead of being the core of his true self, the body is felt as the core of a *false self,* which a detached, disembodied, "inner," "true" self looks on at with tenderness, amusement, or hatred as the case may be.

Such a divorce of self from body deprives the unembodied self from direct participation in any aspect of the life of the world. . . . The unembodied self, as onlooker at all the body does, engages in nothing directly. Its functions come to be observation, control, and criticism.[63]

Continuing the infantile mechanism of hallucinating gratification, the baby in effect gives up the pleasure of the body in order to be free of bodily needs that make it dependent; it retreats to the realm of mind where it can be omnipotent, wholly in control. Dinnerstein says it manages thereby "to maintain a fantasy of being safer and more self-sufficient—because less limited and distinct" than it would have to recognize itself to be if it "kept full emotional contact with the needy, imperiled flesh."[64] For the nurturance that unreliable mothers provide, it substitutes the pleasures of fantasy and observation; and a number of psychoanalysts point out the symbolic equivalences that can develop between knowledge and food, learning and eating. Identified with the early primitive, "Devouring Mother," Anton Ehrenzweig suggests, a boy may then sublimate the "feminine oral sadism" she represented to his infant self "into the scientific curiosity and thirst for knowledge" he develops. And he cites Leonardo da Vinci as a case in point. The baby's original pleasure in nursing is transformed into a "devouring" curiosity; he "drinks in" the world through his eyes.[65] Karl Stern adds the converse counterpart: he will accept nothing from others; he refuses to "swallow" anything "on faith."[66]

But the security gained by such psychic mechanisms comes at a high price. Detached as he is from the world, he gives up not merely the "fun-

62. Laing, *Divided Self,* 65; Winnicott, "Ego Distortion," 144.
63. Laing, *Divided Self,* 69.   64. Dinnerstein, *Mermaid,* 136.
65. Ehrenzweig, "Origin," 113.
66. Karl Stern, *The Flight from Woman* (New York: Farrar, Straus and Giroux, 1968), 5.

damental, primitive joy of the body," but also the possibility of creativity, of intimate relationship to others, of effective action, and ultimately of a reliable sense of who he is, of his own existence.[67] For the activity of the false self "is associated with a rigidity of defenses," with compliance and deference to conventional patterns of dominant others; the true self is the only source of spontaneity, creativity, initiative, of "the spontaneous gesture and the personal idea."[68] To the extent that a psyche is so divided, furthermore, the person is incapable of genuine relationships with others: the real self is never engaged, and others are perceived as objects rather than persons. Striving to do without the lost or too unreliable mother, but making this desperate effort for autonomy at too early a stage of its own development, the baby is bound to construe autonomy solipsistically and thus to try to do without external relationships altogether. But precisely this undermines genuine self-reliance and the capacity to take care of oneself in the world. For, paradoxically, as John Bowlby says, an "essential ingredient" in the "truly self-reliant person" is the

capacity to rely trustingly on others when occasion demands and to know on whom it is appropriate to rely. A healthily self-reliant person is thus capable of exchanging roles when the situation changes: at one time he is providing a secure base from which his companion[s] can operate; at another he is glad to rely on one or another of his companions to provide him with just such a base in return.[69]

The person split into real and false self, with only the latter part active in the real world, thus not only refuses to recognize his own worldly achievements or relationships as real, but also in fact dooms himself to ineffectiveness. Having thus cut himself off from the realization of self that spontaneous expression, effective action, genuine relationship can offer, the divided person may lose any firm sense of his own continuity over time and extension in space, of his personal identity. The self experienced as true increasingly retreats into fantasy and detached "observation of the transactions of the false self and others, [while] the false-self system is felt to encroach more and more, to make deeper and deeper inroads into the individual's being."[70]

To counter this progressive loss of the sense of self and effectiveness, the person so divided may engage in obsessive "activism," constantly

67. Dinnerstein, *Mermaid*, 122; Winnicott, *Playing*, 102.

68. Winnicott, *Maturational Process*, 144–46; *Playing*, 102.

69. John Bowlby, *Separation: Anxiety and Anger*, vol. 2 of *Attachment and Loss* (New York: Basic Books, 1973), 359–60.

70. Laing, *Divided Self*, 143.

undertaking displays of energy and achievement to prove his own reality, yet never succeeding in the proof because worldly actions can only be those of the false self. Underlying such persistent efforts to prove autonomy, again, is a fear of passivity, of dependence, of sensibility and need. Stern calls this the "problem of activism," manifested in the "man of restless energy, the hustler and go-getter," who shies "away from the pleasure of 'receiving,' from accepting tenderness, from all forms of passivity. . . . There is an air of restlessness about such men . . . an air of endless drive and ambition."[71] The drive is restless and endless because no apparent success can quench the real, underlying need; for each worldly achievement is ascribed to the false self. "At the bottom of it all," says Stern, lies "a maternal conflict and rejection of the feminine," an effort to deny dependence on the mother by identifying with her, constructing an "inner" mother to replace her.[72]

There is, then, the psychic "strategy" of withdrawal into the mind, the abandonment of worldly action, yet somehow linked with a compulsive overactivism. The two are opposite sides of the same coin. As Ehrenzweig says, "Mythology is full of strangely paired male couples," one the clever but impotent observer, the other "the manly, unintellectual hero."[73] He mentions Loki and Thor, Hagen and Siegfried, Odysseus and Achilles; we will of course be reminded of Hephaestus and Ares, and of Ligurio and Callimaco in *Mandragola*. These pairs are two halves of a single self, split apart because of an extremely early and intense identification with the mother, Ehrenzweig suggests, though he does not explain. He says that their relationship is homosexual in nature, and, because they are parts of a single self, narcissistic. "The exhibitionistic, self-destructive hero and the already castrated oral-sadistic voyeur (scientist) represent two types of homosexual attitude."[74]

Again many of these features are suggestive in terms of Machiavelli's texts. The fear of dependence; the superhuman, threatening matriarch; themes of oral aggression and the dangers of nurturance; the fantasy of rescue through the intervention of paternal power; the split hero, the pairing of obsessive activism with voyeuristic withdrawal into the mind, all these are familiar themes.

But psychoanalytic theory, even in the schematic versions presented here, leaves one with a confusing array of possible interpretations of the psychic significance to be attached to the fox and its two rival images. The theories range from essentially Oedipal interpretations organized

71. Stern, *Flight*, 1–2.   72. Ibid.
73. Ehrenzweig, "Origin," 120.   74. Ibid., 119–20.

around fear of the punitive father, to others focused on fear of the mother, in which the father may even appear as a rescuing agent. Yet the Oedipal accounts also somehow depend on the absence of the father during the early years. The theories stressing fear of the mother are, in turn, subdivided between those, like Slater's, that locate the disturbance relatively late and construe it in sexual terms, and those, like Klein's and Dinnerstein's, that locate it in infancy and construe it in terms of separation anxiety. The former stress the absence, distance, or failure of the father, which leaves a boy with no alternative to his relationship with his mother: no escape from its demands, no alternative model for identification, no support for his efforts at autonomy. The latter stress the early loss of the mother, or an equivalent trauma in her nurturing function that makes her seem fundamentally unreliable, so that the baby makes too early and rigid an attempt at autonomy. They describe the consequences variously as too early or rigid an internalization of the mother, a fragmentation of the self, or a withdrawal from body and world into the mind.

It may be fruitful, however, to combine Kleinian or Dinnersteinian psychological theory with Slater's sociology. For the social circumstances he describes not only give boys in the Oedipal period reason to fear their mothers in essentially sexual terms but also make unlikely those boys' successful working through of any psychic conflicts originating in the oral period, in the infantile relationship to the mother. The actually ambivalent and unconsciously resentful mother of Slater's account would tend to reinforce and perpetuate infantile fantasies of the devouring matriarch. Such a combined account might make more sense of Hephaestus, in particular, than can Slater's theory alone, and more sense of Leonardo than Freud's classic Oedipal interpretation.

Nancy Chodorow has argued that in societies such as Slater describes, where sex roles are sharply differentiated and women are regarded as inferior but are assigned complete charge of childrearing, the infantile issues of nurturance, dependence, and integrated selfhood will tend to merge, for boys, with the Oedipal issues of gender identification.[75] In the first place, a mother deprived of other adult gratification may introduce Oedipal and sexual issues into her relationship with her son(s) earlier and more intensely than one who has adult satisfactions— either personal or public—available.[76] As Slater also suggested, the mother's needs may impose both sexually tinged demands and gender-

---

75. Nancy Chodorow, *The Reproduction of Mothering* (Berkeley: University of California Press, 1978), 181–82, 185.
76. Ibid., 107, 196.

based ambivalence on top of the earlier problems of autonomy from maternal nurturance, so that these problems are less likely to be successfully worked through.

In the second place, a boy lacking contact with a father or other "second" person of his own gender, but nevertheless expected (by his mother as well as other people) to assume his gender role, lacks both a concrete model and a supporting sponsor for his task. "Boys in father-absent and normally father-remote families" have to "develop a sense of what it is to be masculine through identification with cultural images of masculinity," through fantasy and abstraction.[77] Lacking a concrete model, they must define themselves negatively, in opposition to the mother and the "feminine" traits in themselves. Lacking the external support of a masculine adult in their struggle, they must fight all the more desperately against not merely the mother's actual power and ambivalent demands, but even more against their own desires and traits: the desire to regress and remain dependent, the Oedipal desire for the mother, and the traits that they have acquired by identification with her. In order to be assured of autonomy, they must prove their masculinity, yet not in relation to the mother as sexual object. They develop a tremendous personal stake in the socially available gender definitions: that there be a distinct masculine realm, that it be superior to the feminine, and that they be admitted to it; yet they remain intensely ambivalent about it.

Freudian and Kleinian theories are simultaneously individualistic and universalistic. They purport to tell us about the development of an individual suffering a personal psychic trauma in any society—or, at any rate, of any male suffering such a trauma in any society with a generally Oedipal family structure, or where infants are tended by females. Slater's theory, by contrast, is sociological; within a generally Freudian framework, it purports to explain psychic development in a particular (type of) society. For present purposes, which concern symbolic interpretation rather than causal explanation, the former theories would be most apt to suggest the (almost) universal psychic meanings of Machiavelli's themes, the latter their specific significance for the men of Renaissance Florence—if, indeed, the social conditions of Renaissance Florence resembled those Slater ascribes to ancient Athens. Whether or to what extent they did, must thus be the next concern.

77. Ibid., 176, 182.

CHAPTER EIGHT

Sociological History

What were the actual circumstances of family life in Machiavelli's world? What were relations between the sexes and child-rearing practices like? What was the practical, lived meaning of gender, generation, and family? Was there, in particular, anything like the patterns of family life hypothesized in the various psychological theories we have surveyed? It might seem that at least a rough answer to these questions should be readily available from standard sources; but that turns out not to be so, for the standard sources flatly disagree.

Some, like Jacob Burckhardt in his *Civilization of the Renaissance in Italy*, praising the Renaissance as the birth of human individuality and achievement after the dark ages, regard it also as a period of liberation for women and enlightenment in domestic relations. In Renaissance Italy, Burckhardt claims, "women stood on a footing of perfect equality with men."[1] Like men, they could gain recognition as unique, memorable individuals; in historical accounts they began to appear as having "nearly all a distinct, recognizable personality" and "taking their share of notoriety and glory."[2] At least in the upper classes, they were educated like men. Further, the period's "thoughtful study of all questions relating to social intercourse" promoted a freer and more equitable domestic life. "Even the intercourse with courtesans seems to have assumed a more elevated character."[3] Clearly, the women and children of Machiavelli's time were experiencing a liberation.

1. Jacob Burckhardt, *The Civilization of the Renaissance in Italy* (New York: Phaidon, 1950), 240.
2. Ibid., 241.
3. Ibid., 243, 242.

But if one turns then to Philippe Ariès's *Centuries of Childhood*, one finds Renaissance women experiencing a decline in status and opportunity, and family life becoming increasingly autocratic. "We know," Ariès declares, "that from the end of the Middle Ages on, the power of the wife steadily diminished."[4] Husbands and fathers "maintained and even increased the authority" in the family they "had been given in the eleventh and twelfth centuries," partly as a result of legal changes: the "substitution of the law of primogeniture for joint ownership and the joint estate of husband and wife." In the fourteenth century begins "a slow and steady deterioration in the wife's position in the household," terminating in the sixteenth century when the husband and father is "finally established as a sort of domestic monarch."[5]

Further consultation of authorities at this level of generality does not resolve the conflict but only intensifies it. Some stress medieval misogyny, the Church's vision of woman as a descendant of Eve, representative of the flesh and agent of sin, at best a "necessary evil," quite possibly lacking an immortal soul.[6] Such sources of course think the Renaissance "freed and raised the dignity of women," bringing a "remarkable rise" in their status, giving them "a new freedom and a wider importance," so that they were "frankly accepted as equals in the business and pleasure of life."[7] Indeed, one phenomenon of the Italian Renaissance was the *virago*—a term then used, we are told, with complete admiration: the woman warrior who wore armor, led troops, and fought for political domain.

But are these "feminine" or "masculine" ideals? The term *virago*, for instance, is formed like *virtù* on the root *vir*, man; and means literally a surrogate man.[8] These ideals are certainly different from those of the

4. Philippe Ariès, *Centuries of Childhood*, tr. Robert Baldick (New York: Random House, 1962), 355.

5. Ibid., 356, citing P. Petiot, "La famille en France sous l'Ancien Régime," *La Sociologie comparée de la famille contemporaine* (Colloques du C.N.R.S., 1955).

6. William Boulting, *Woman in Italy* (London: Methuen, 1910), 8. Joseph and Frances Gies, *Life in a Medieval City* (New York: Thomas Y. Crowell Company, 1969), 55. Edith Sichel, *The Renaissance* (New York: Henry Holt, 1914), 129–39. Julia O'Faolain and Lauro Martines, eds., *Not in God's Image* (New York: Harper & Row, 1973), 129–32. Harold Nicolson, *Good Behaviour* (Boston: Beacon Press, 1960), 108.

7. J. Lucas-Dubreton, *Daily Life in Florence in the Time of the Medicis*, tr. A. Lytton Sells (New York: Macmillan, 1961), 222; Richard A. Goldthwaite, "The Florentine Palace as Domestic Architecture," *American Historical Review* 77 (1972): 1009; Lucy Ingram Morgan, "The Renaissance Lady in England," (Ph.D. diss., University of California, 1932), 13–14. Cf. also E. Rodocanachi, *La Femme Italienne a l'époque de la Renaissance* (Paris: Librairie Hachette, 1922), 278; Goldthwaite, *Private Wealth*, 263; Will Durant, *The Renaissance* (New York: Simon & Schuster, 1953), 575, 582; Rachel Annand Taylor, *Aspects of the Italian Renaissance* (Boston: Houghton Mifflin, 1923), 160–62.

8. Kathleen Casey, "The Cheshire Cat: Reconstructing the Experience of Medieval Women," in *Liberating Women's History*, ed. Berenice Carroll (Urbana: University of Illinois Press, 1976), 245.

Middle Ages, but that very fact has led other interpreters to characterize the Renaissance as honoring masculinity, and the medieval period as cherishing the feminine. The very Churchmen who condemned woman as Eve, these interpreters point out, also conceptualized the Church itself as a woman, maternal and protective: "One Mother, prolific with offspring: of her we are born, by her milk we are nourished, by her spirit we are made alive."[9] Indeed, "whatever the virtues and deficiencies of actual mothers may have been" in the period centering on the eleventh century, one historian says,

maternal example and maternal values were dominant in the lives and ideals of those children of whose experience we have some knowledge. . . . By contrast with this emphasis on the maternal figure and her influence, fathers and their relations with their children assume a more modest and sometimes ambiguous place in our sources.[10]

From the beginning of Christianity, woman was not merely Eve the corruptress but also Mary, the mother of God's only begotten son. And while early Christianity centered on the masculine trinity of the Father, the Son, and the Holy Ghost, as medieval culture developed, the Virgin Mary moved increasingly into prominence. The medieval Church was "wholly given up to" the Marian cult, Henry Adams maintained, and the Virgin filled

so enormous a space in the life and thought of the time that one stands now helpless before the mass of testimony to her direct action and constant presence. . . . Society had staked its existence, in this world and the next, on the reality and power of the Virgin; it had invested in her care nearly its whole capital, spiritual, artistic, intellectual and economical.[11]

Nor was this cult merely abstract, Adams said: "All of the literature and history of the time proclaim" the extent to which "this worship elevated" the actual status of women in society.[12]

The Renaissance is then seen as terminating this medieval appreciation of womanhood; it "admired masculinity" and was "masculine in temper, through and through."[13] Yet another authority sees the Church as "genuinely sympathetic" to women only in the early Middle Ages,

9. St. Cyprian (d. 258), *de unitate*, 5, cited in Peter Brown, *Augustine of Hippo* (Berkeley: University of California Press, 1969), 212. Brown also cites similar passages from St. Augustine.

10. Mary Martin McLaughlin, "Survivors and Surrogates," in *The History of Childhood*, ed. Lloyd de Mause (New York: Psychohistory Press, 1974), 127–28.

11. Adams, *Mont-Saint-Michel*, 100, 249, 252.

12. Ibid., 250; cf. Gies and Gies, *Life*, 55.

13. Crane Brinton, *A History of Western Morals* (New York: Harcourt, Brace, 1959), 250; Taylor, *Aspects*, 159–60; Erikson, *Young Man Luther*, 67, 71; Lucas-Dubreton, *Daily Life*, 223; John Gage, *Life in Italy at the Time of the Medici* (New York: G. P.

and as increasingly misogynist in the "late medieval" period.[14] The late medieval secular literature of chivalry and courtly love is similarly subject to conflicting interpretations. Some authorities, like Denis de Rougemont, see it as a false idealization of abstract woman: the essence of chivalric love is the unattainability of the beloved.[15] More recent scholars, like Joan Kelly-Godol, present medieval courtly love as genuinely sexual, voluntary, based on mutuality between men and women, and "very much at variance with the patriarchal ideal." Only later and specifically in Italy was it transformed into misogynist, abstract idealization of woman as the unattainable love-object.[16] Renaissance humanism, reviving Platonic ideals, then meant a still further withdrawal from women, marriage, and the body. Yet those commentators who associate the Marian cult and the medieval idealization of women with actual feminine social power sometimes construe humanism, too, as a continuation of this respect for femininity, which "reinforced the influence of woman and secured her on her pedestal."[17]

Was she comfortable on her pedestal? At this level of abstraction and generality the picture is decidedly confusing. Not only do ideals and cultural self-interpretation bear a very complex relationship to actual social practice; they may be its accurate reflection, a compensatory denial or escape, an ideological distortion, hortatory prescription, traditional

---

Putnam's Sons, 1968), 179–80; Lauro Martines, "A Way of Looking at Women in Renaissance Florence," *Journal of Medieval and Renaissance Studies* 4 (Spring 1974): 24.

14. Susan Mosher Stuard, ed. *Women in Medieval Society* (Philadelphia: University of Pennsylvania Press, 1976), 8, 10.

15. Denis de Rougemont, *Love in the Western World*, tr. Montgomery Belgion (New York: Harcourt, Brace, 1956). Cf. David Hunt, *Parents and Children in History* (New York: Basic Books, 1970), 70; Susan G. Bell, ed., *Women from the Greeks to the French Revolution* (Belmont, Calif.: Wadsworth Publishing, 1973), 123. It has been suggested that the "infinitely desired and unattainable" lady of courtly love whose "soul-filled glance brings Christmas every day" is a symbolic representation of the unattainable mother so central in the lives of medieval churchmen, a secular version of the Virgin Mary. Already in the eleventh century, the first secular romance, *Ruodlieb*, portrays the mutual devotion of a young knight, obliged to seek his fortune in distant lands, and his widowed mother, who ends up begging him to remember her in her unfortunate state, left twice widowed, "once by your father and for the second time by you, my son" (McLaughlin, "Survivors," 134). Herbert Moller interprets all the worshipped ladies of chivalry on this pattern, as maternal symbols, projections of childlike fantasies, particularly the fearful fantasy of being abandoned or rejected (Herbert Moller, "The Meaning of Courtly Love," *Journal of American Folklore* 73 [1960]: 39–52). But compare C. S. Lewis, *The Allegory of Love* (London: Oxford University Press, 1967); and David Herlihy, "Land, Family, and Women in Continental Europe, 701–1200," In Stuard, *Women*, 23.

16. Joan Kelly-Godol, "Did Women Have a Renaissance?" in *Becoming Visible: Women in European History*, ed. by Renate Bridenthal and Claudia Koonz (Boston: Houghton Mifflin, 1977), 152.

17. Boulting, *Woman*, 27.

reiteration of a reality long since superseded in practice, and so on.[18] But in addition, social practice itself varies with place, social class, and specific time period. It is necessary, therefore, to narrow and specify the inquiry as much as the sources permit.

❖   ❖   ❖

The focus, then, is sociological facts about women, children, and the family in Florence in Machiavelli's own lifetime and that of his parents. For orientation, begin with a review of what little is known about Machiavelli's own personal and family life. He was born in Florence in 1469 and died there in 1527.[19] His father, Bernardo, born about 1432, was a lawyer who apparently did not practice much. He seems to have loved books and to have been something of a humanist. There exists a dialogue by Bartolomeo Scala, a humanist and first chancellor of Florence under the Medici and for some years under the republic, in which Bernardo Machiavelli appears as one of the participants.[20] Niccolò's mother was a widow when she married his father and nine years younger than he. Niccolò was the third of four children, having two older sisters and a younger brother, born when Niccolò was six.

Ridolfi claims that Niccolò's relationship to his father was friendly and teasing, "almost brotherly," but cites no evidence; there does exist an amusing poem composed by the boy for his father.[21] Of his relationship to his mother, nothing is known; a later relative of hers claimed that she composed religious verse and dedicated some of it to her son. From Bernardo's notebook we learn that when Niccolò was seven he began to study with a teacher of grammar, and when he was ten he was sent to live with another teacher to learn calculation on the abacus. At twelve he was sent to study Latin.[22]

The Machiavellis in earlier generations had been active in Florentine public life, having supplied the city with some fifty-four priors and twelve *gonfalonieri*. In the time of Cosimo de'Medici, Girolamo Machiavelli was jailed, tortured, and executed for his republican convictions.[23] And in 1424 Francesco Machiavelli, three generations before

18. Kelly-Godol, "Did Women Have a Renaissance?" 140, 144.

19. This biographical information is drawn from Ridolfi, *Life*; Pasquale Villari, *The Life and Times of Niccolò Machiavelli*, tr. Linda Villari (London: T. Fisher Unwin, 1898); and Cesare Olschki, ed. *Libro di Ricordi di Bernardo Machiavelli* (Florence: Felice le Monnier, 1954).

20. Felix Gilbert, *Machiavelli and Guicciardini: Politics and History in 16th-Century Florence* (Princeton: Princeton University Press, 1965), 318–19.

21. Ridolfi, *Life*, 34–35.

22. Olschki, *Libro*, 31, 45, 103, 138.   23. Ridolfi, *Life*, 2.

Niccolò, wrote in condemnation of tyranny and praise of civic virtue and a citizen militia: "The enjoyment of freedom makes cities and citizens great; this is well-known. But places under tyranny become deserted by their citizens and engage in their extermination."[24] There is no evidence concerning how much Bernardo and Niccolò knew about their family background; Niccolò once wrote in a letter that the well-known Pazzi family was not superior to his own if justly weighed.[25]

By Bernardo's time the Machiavellis had become urban and middle-class. Although he was still entitled to use the family coat of arms and still owned a rural estate in addition to several houses in Florence, Bernardo belonged to an impoverished branch of the family; he was relatively poor and becoming poorer. Although Niccolò's father fell ill of the plague when the boy was eleven, both his parents lived on into his adulthood, his mother dying when he was twenty-seven, his father four years later. Only then did Niccolò himself marry. Eventually he and his wife had seven children, two of whom died in infancy. His diplomatic career kept him much away from home; his younger brother, who had joined the Church, managed his business concerns when Niccolò was abroad. Niccolò's few personal letters suggest a concerned and affectionate family relationship, but he is known to have had at least one and probably several love affairs. His letters to male friends often refer to such liaisons, or to time spent in the houses of courtesans.

That is just about all that is known of Machiavelli's own family life. But since—as already stressed—the interest of this book is not psycho-biographical, its focus must include his contemporaries and their parents: his audience and subject matter. How typical or atypical was his experience, and what else is known or can be conjectured about theirs? Begin with relations between the sexes in education and intellectual life, and in public life and law, turn then to marriage and sexuality, and finally to children and child rearing.

Certainly the increase in literacy characteristic of the period and the higher value attached to education in general and classical learning in particular were shared to a significant extent by women, at least in the upper strata of society.[26] It is not clear, however, how much of this repre-

24. Baron, Crisis, 386.
25. Ferrara, Private Correspondence, 2.
26. Boulting, Woman, 43, 46; Paul G. Ruggiers, Florence in the Age of Dante (Norman: University of Oklahoma Press, 1964), 103; Rodocanachi, Femme, 29; Richard C. Trexler, "The Foundlings of Florence 1395–1455," History of Childhood Quarterly 1 (Fall 1973): 261; Nino [Giovanni] Tamassia, La Famiglia Italiana nei Secoli Decimoquinto e Decimoseste (Milano: Libraio della R. Casa, 1911), 45–46; Boulting, Woman, 45; Durant, Renaissance, 582; Rodocanachi, Femme, 23. On the curriculum of these schools, see Mary Agnes Cannon, The Education of Women During the Renaissance (Washington, D.C.: National Capital Press, 1916).

sents a change from medieval life. In the city of Troyes in 1250, "well-to-do women know how to read and write and figure; some even know a little Latin."[27] Although women are not admitted to the universities, there are occasional intellectual women and female poets; "among the landed gentry, women are better educated than men."[28] And there is evidence that this last may have been generally true in the noble class of the twelfth century.[29]

Still, advanced education for women evidently became more common in the Renaissance. Many upper-class women not merely learned to read but studied Latin and Greek, history, and sometimes science and mathematics. Clearly the spread of humanism played a role in this development. A number of Italian Renaissance princes employed humanists as tutors for their daughters, and Vittorino da Feltre taught girls as well as boys at his famous humanist school in Mantua.[30] To be sure, this must have meant that many girls who might formerly have been schooled by women now had male humanists for their teachers and were thus placed "under male cultural authority."[31] There came to be a number of notable women scholars in the fifteenth and sixteenth centuries.[32] Women of the upper or upper middle classes, although not becoming poets or scholars, might write some verse in their free time, often in a religious vein, as Machiavelli's mother is reported to have done.[33] Machiavelli's father's notebook has entries concerning expenditures for the education of Niccolò and his brother but no corresponding entries for his sisters.[34]

Once one turns from education and intellectual life to other aspects of society, the new freedom of Renaissance women becomes seriously problematic. Certainly there were, as Burckhardt stressed, outstanding individual women who became famous in their own right, even in realms traditionally reserved for men. But those women who became

27. Gies and Gies, *Life*, 52–53.

28. Ibid., 52–53, 55.

29. Grundmann, "Die Frauen und die Literatur," *Archiv für Kulturgeschichte* (1935): 133–34, quoted in McLaughlin, "Survivors," in de Mause, *History*, 125. But cf. David Herlihy, *Women in Medieval Society* (Houston: University of St. Thomas, 1971), 14.

30. Bell, *Women*, 182; Gage, *Life*, 79; Alfred Wilhelm Otto von Martin, *The Sociology of the Renaissance* (London: Kegan Paul, Trench, Trubner, & Company, 1944), 72; Morgan, "Renaissance Lady," 14–15.

31. Kelly-Godol, "Did Women Have a Renaissance?" 151–52.

32. Boulting, *Woman*, 317; see also 319; and Isidoro Del Lungo, *Women of Florence*, tr. Mary C. Steegman (London: C. Patto and Windus, 1907), 181; Morgan, "Renaissance Lady," 30–31; Rodocanachi, *Femme*, 30; O'Faolian and Martines, *Not in God's Image*, 181.

33. Lungo, *Women*, 20, 180; F. Gilbert, *Machiavelli and Guicciardini*, 320; Christopher Hare (pseud. for Mrs. Marian Andrews), *The Most Illustrious Ladies of the Renaissance* (London: Harper and Brothers, 1911) 57, 281–312; Gies and Gies, *Life*, 201–2.

34. Olschki, *Libro*, 31, 45, 103, 138.

scholars or rulers or warriors were exceptional. They appeared almost exclusively in the wealthy upper class, particularly in the newly risen, self-made upper class.[35] For the most part, they assumed their heroic roles only in exceptional circumstances, when their husbands or other male relatives were absent, incapacitated, or dead.[36] And—of particular importance for our purposes—the exceptional, heroic women were almost never found in Florence.[37] That city was mercantile and industrial, and with the exception of a few female poets and scholars, its women seem often to have been literate, but in no sense public figures.

The public and formal organization of Renaissance Florence was thoroughly patriarchal. This was partly a continuing legal inheritance from ancient times, but in important respects Renaissance conditions for women seem to compare unfavorably with medieval ones. Contrary to Burckhardt, a recent historian notes "how frequently women appear in the medieval record" and in how "wide [a] variety of functions."[38] Feudal women generally "could inherit and hold land, honours, and offices like men," although, as in the Renaissance, some of these privileges were available to them only when their husbands were absent or dead.[39] This was particularly likely to be the situation in the crusading period; and in the early Middle Ages the woman accordingly played "an extraordinary role in the management of family property . . . and social customs as well as economic life were influenced by her prominence."[40]

Italy, however, was "reluctant and late in developing a true knighthood on the French pattern," and Lombard law there continued to limit, "though it could not entirely restrict, the freedom of the woman in the administration of land."[41] What matters most for Florence is the status of medieval women of the urban merchant and artisan classes, for instance in guilds. Most medieval guilds were restricted to men, but

35. von Martin, *Sociology*, 73.

36. Ruth Kelso, *Doctrine for the Lady of the Renaissance* (Urbana: University of Illinois Press, 1956), 2; see also 31, and Martines, "Way of Looking," 16–17; Boulting, *Woman*, 58, 317; Lucas-Dubreton, *Daily Life*, 104.

37. Lungo, *Women*, 2, 181; Morgan, "Renaissance Lady," 24; Walter B. Scaife, *Florentine Life During the Renaissance* (Baltimore: Johns Hopkins Press, 1893), 82.

38. Stuard, *Women*, 4.

39. Eileen Power, "The Position of Women," in Bell, *Women*, 170; see also Herlihy, *Women*, 10; Kelly-Godol, "Did Women Have a Renaissance?" 149; Morgan, "Renaissance Lady," 14; Boulting, *Woman*, 36; Ariès, *Centuries*, 355; Gies and Gies, *Life*, 53; Sue Sheridan Walker, "Widow and Ward: The Feudal Law of Child Custody in Medieval England," in Stuard, *Women*, 161.

40. Herlihy, "Land," in Stuard, *Women*, 13; but cf. Jo Ann McNamara and Suzanne Wemple, "The Power of Women through the Family in Medieval Europe, 500–1100," in *Clio's Consciousness Raised*, ed. Mary Hartman and Lois W. Banner (New York: Harper & Row, 1974), 103–18, esp. 112–13.

41. Herlihy, "Land," in Stuard, *Women*, 32.

"some of the crafts in the cities were opened to women," a few even dominated by women.[42] Even the guilds normally closed to women almost always made "exception for the craftsman's wife and daughter, who [were] expected to help in the workshop."[43] But "certain key guilds would not admit women under any circumstances"; in Florence, in particular, "in the one branch of manufacture that already deserved to be called an industry, wool-making," women were never admitted to the "greater guilds"—those with the greatest wealth and power.[44] Even where women were admitted to membership, many guild regulations discriminated against them, they were "not always invited to the organization's social gatherings," and no guild seems ever to have elected a woman to its highest office.[45]

Participation in public economic life and guild membership are of particular importance in Italy because they were also the basis for access to political life.[46] But even in those guilds that had female members, their names "did not even appear on the matriculation lists conferring eligibility for civic office."[47] More detailed research, one historian judges,

would almost certainly confirm the observation that Italian women outside the wool industry made a massive contribution to the economy at managerial as well as laboring levels, yet still failed to gain direct access to power.[48]

Although there were some changes increasing the power of women in business, in most respects their legal and economic position and their role in public life declined in the late Middle Ages and the Renaissance. "The tendency, as the Middle Ages progressed, was toward a lessening of the public activity of women, a lower place in ecclesiastical opinion, fewer roles in guild organizations, and less agricultural administration if not less agricultural labor."[49] The power and status of women was probably always more limited in Italy than in the North, but

42. Barbara Sinclair Deckard, *The Women's Movement* (New York: Harper & Row, 1975), 194. See also A. Abram, "Women Traders in Medieval London," in Bell, *Women*, 152–58; Gies and Gies, *Life*, 175.
43. Power, "Position," in Bell, *Women*, 163, 176. See also John Howard Lawson, *The Hidden Heritage* (New York: Citadel Press, 1950), 57; Gies and Gies, *Life*, 53, 175–78; Diane Hughes, "Domestic Ideals and Social Behavior: the Evidence of Medieval Genoa," in *The Family in History*, ed. Charles E. Rosenberg (Philadelphia: University of Pennsylvania Press, 1975), 131.
44. Casey, "Cheshire Cat," 229.
45. Gies and Gies, *Life*, 179–80; Casey, "Cheshire Cat," 232.
46. Meiss, *Painting*, 59.
47. Casey, "Cheshire Cat," 233, citing A. Briganti, *La donna e il diritto statutario in Perugia, secoli XIII e XIV* (Perugia, 1911), 41–43, 49, 53, 61–62.
48. Ibid. See also Gies and Gies, *Life*, 53.
49. Stuard, *Women*, 9; J[ohn] R[igby] Hale, *Renaissance Europe: Individual and Society 1480–1520* (New York: Harper & Row, 1972), 126. See also Hunt, *Parents*, 70–71.

the kind of economic and political power that [was held by] feudal noblewomen in the eleventh and twelfth centuries [in the North] had no counterpart in Renaissance Italy. . . . The exercise of political power by women was far more rare than under feudalism or even under the traditional kind of monarchical state that developed out of feudalism.[50]

A Renaissance Italian woman, furthermore,

could transact no legal business without the assent of both her father and husband or of trustees. In some States . . . she might not enter a law-suit in her own name or do violence to modesty by appearing personally at a trial.[51]

Forence, we are told, was the most restrictive of all the Italian cities.[52] A Florentine statute of 1415, for instance, provides that "a married woman with children cannot draw up a will in her own right, nor dispose of her dowry among the living to the detriment of her husband and children."[53] A wife did generally recover her dowry if her husband died intestate, but while he lived, it was he who controlled it and was entitled to the income from it.[54] Aside from her dowry, if a woman's husband died without leaving a will, "invariably . . . the claims of kindred came before those of the wife."[55] In general in Italy, real property always went to men in preference to women.[56] There were some special legal protections for women, but even the special benefits often indicated the women's inferior status and relative unimportance. Thus, for example, if a man convicted of a crime was banished from the city, the women of the family were permitted to stay.[57]

Above all, with respect to family relations, the "European wife" in general "*lost* authority" in the Renaissance by comparison with the thirteenth and prior centuries, and in Italy the male head of a family had "virtually unlimited authority" over his wife and children.[58] He

50. Kelly-Godol, "Did Women Have a Renaissance?" 148.

51. Boulting, *Woman*, 314; Tamassia, *Famiglia*, 202–3, 210, 272.

52. Rodocanachi, *Femme*, 291–94.

53. O'Faolain and Martines, *Not in God's Image*, 145.

54. Stanley Chojnacki, "Patrician Women in Early Renaissance Venice," *Studies in the Renaissance* 21 (1974): 189–92.

55. Boulting, *Woman*, 315; see also Gage, *Life*, 180; and O'Faolain and Martines, *Not in God's Image*, 147–48; Stanley Chojnacki, "Dowries and Kinsmen in Early Renaissance Venice," in Stuard, *Women*, 175.

56. Chojnacki, "Patrician Women," 186–87.

57. Ibid.; Lungo, *Women*, 24, 27; Guido Biagi, *Men and Manners of Old Florence* (London: T. Fisher Unwin, 1909), 98; Scaife, *Florentine Life*, 84–85; Hale, *Florence*, 94. John R. Effinger, *Women of the Romance Countries*, vol. 6 of *Woman: In All Ages and In All Countries* (Philadelphia: George Barrie and Sons, 1907), 121.

58. William J. Goode, *World Revolution and Family Patterns* (Glencoe, Ill.: Free Press, 1963), 368; Giuseppe Martinelli, *The World of Renaissance Florence*, tr. Walter Barwell (London: Macdonald and Company, 1968), 90; see also Luigi Barzini, *The Italians* (New York: Atheneum, 1965), 199–203; Durant, *Renaissance*, 587; Tamassia, *Famiglia*, 201–2.

could, for example, inflict corporal punishment on them, put his daughter into a cloister against her will, lawfully kill his wife if she committed adultery.[59]

Marriages were arranged, in the Renaissance as in the Middle Ages, and regarded as "major family decisions. They involved the transfer of property and the realignment of social rank; they often had political implications."[60] Naturally this was most true among those who had property: the pattern of arranged marriages was less pervasive "the lower the position in the social scale."[61] Marriage was a duty to the family, and the wishes of the bride and groom were almost entirely irrelevant to it. The partners certainly should, and probably often did, develop a genuine mutual affection; but marriage was considered incompatible with romantic love.[62] Arranged marriages as such, of course, may constrain young men as much as young women. Indeed, we are told that the men of the Renaissance married reluctantly and as late as possible, giving up their bachelor freedom only out of a sense of familial duty.[63] In the Italian pattern of arranged marriage of this time, however, girls would seem to have had far greater reasons to be reluctant; marriage was not an egalitarian institution.[64]

59. Boulting, *Woman*, 312, 315; Deckard, *Women's Movement*, 196–97; Rodocanachi, *Femme*, 321. Cf. Natalie Zemon Davis, *Society and Culture in Early Modern France* (Stanford: Stanford University Press, 1975), 145, 313 n. 37.

60. Gene Brucker, ed., *The Society of Renaissance Florence, A Documentary Study* (New York: Harper & Row, 1971), 28; see also Gene Brucker, *Renaissance Florence* (New York: John Wiley and Sons, 1969), 91–92, 99; Lauro Martines, *The Social World of the Florentine Humanists 1390–1460* (Princeton: Princeton University Press, 1963), 58–59, 61; Martines, *Lawyers*, 94; Durant, *Renaissance*, 578; Lucas-Dubreton, *Daily Life*, 101, 230; Marie Alphonse René de Maulde la Clavière, *The Women of the Renaissance: A Study of Feminism* (New York: G. P. Putnam's Sons, 1905), 21–27. Historians disagree about whether this pattern changed during the Renaissance in Florence: Goldthwaite, *Private Wealth*, 263; Martines, *Social World*, 58; cf. Boulting, *Woman*, 27. Cf. also Kelso, *Doctrine*, 166; Conor Fahy, "Three Early Renaissance Treatises on Women," *Italian Studies* 11 (1956): 31; Morgan, "Renaissance Lady," 16–17.

61. Boulting, *Woman*, 58; see also Maulde la Clavière, *Women*, 29; Martines, *Social World*, 58; Rodocanachi, *Femme*, 57; Hughes, "Domestic Ideals," 136; Tamassia, *Famiglia*, 150–51; Natalie Zemon Davis, "Ghosts, Kin and Progeny: Some Features of Family Life in Early Modern France," *Daedalus* 106 (Spring 1977): 106–7. In medieval Genoa, artisan marriages seem to have been freer from family pressure and more egalitarian between the sexes (Diana Owen Hughes, "Urban Growth and Family Structure in Medieval Genoa," *Past and Present* 66 [1975]: 21–25).

62. Kelso, *Doctrine*, 165; Maulde la Clavière, *Women*, 22–23; Power, "Position," in Bell, *Women*, 168; Lewis, *Allegory*, 13, 35.

63. Durant, *Renaissance*, 578; Maulde la Clavière, *Women*, 33–35. Leon Batista Alberti, *The Family in Renaissance Florence*, tr. Renée Neu Watkins (Columbia: University of South Carolina Press, 1969), 112.

64. Thus it seems Boulting is wrong to claim that with respect to arranged marriage, "men are no better off than women" at this time (*Woman*, 27). The earliest known Renaissance poems by a woman are lamentations for the youth sacrificed to family tyranny in unhappy marriages (Lungo, *Women*, 20).

Marriages were arranged primarily by the fathers of the young couple, although in at least some cases the mothers also played active roles in helping to select a bride for their sons.[65] The legal power lay with the father. The family of the bride was expected to provide a dowry, and the amount of the dowry was a central concern in the marriage arrangement. Dowries gradually increased in size, particularly in the fourteenth and fifteenth centuries, in all of Italy, until eventually they were limited by law.[66] In 1424 the Florentines, ever interested in good business investments, founded "an insurance office to provide for dower, which was copied by many Italian cities."[67] Poor families might be unable to dower all of their daughters and be forced to choose which might marry and which must become nuns. The decision had to be reached early; typically a father might deposit money toward his daughter's dowry when she was six.[68] Machiavelli's father made such deposits for the dowry of one of Niccolò's sisters.[69]

Girls were married at an early age. Some authorities say that this was the case in the Middle Ages as well in Europe generally, but it does not appear to have been so in medieval Florence. At least according to fifteenth-century sources, Florentine girls in the twelfth and thirteenth centuries were typically married in their twenties.[70] But in the fourteenth and fifteenth centuries, girls were officially marriageable at twelve, and in practice the customary age seems to have been somewhere between fourteen and seventeen. For a girl to remain single much after the age of eighteen was considered a disgrace.[71]

65. The role of the fathers is stressed in Brucker, *Renaissance Florence*, 91; Boulting, *Woman*, 51; Kelso, *Doctrine*, 78, 91; and Ruggiers, *Florence*, 99, and no doubt it was generally dominant; but, for instances of maternal involvement, see Chojnacki, "Dowries and Kinsmen," in Stuard, *Women*, 176, 184–85; Hare, *Most Illustrious Ladies*, 51; Lungo, *Women*, 194, 196, 231, 282; Morgan, "Renaissance Lady," 26.

66. David Herlihy, "Life Expectancies for Women in Medieval Society," in *The Role of Woman in the Middle Ages*, ed. Rosemarie Thee Morewedge (Albany: State University of New York Press, 1975), 12; Hughes, "Urban Growth," 194; Chojnacki, "Dowries and Kinsmen," in Stuard, *Women*, 173–91; Martines, *Lawyers*, 94; Tamassia, *Famiglia*, 266–310.

67. Boulting, *Woman*, 62.

68. Richard C. Trexler, "Le célibat à la fin du Moyen Age: Les religieuses de Florence," *Annales. Économies, Sociétés, Civilisations* 27 (November–December 1972): 1342.

69. Olschki, *Libro*, 42, 47.

70. Boulting, *Woman*, 75; Lungo, *Women*, 18–19; Durant, *Renaissance*, 578; David Herlihy, "Some Psychological and Social Roots of Violence in the Tuscan Cities," in *Violence and Civil Disorder in Italian Cities 1200–1500*. UCLA Center for Medieval and Renaissance Studies, contribution 5, ed. Lauro Martines (Berkeley: University of California Press, 1972), 152; Giovanni Morelli, *Ricordi*, 111–12, quoted in David Herlihy, "The Tuscan Town in the Quattrocento: A Demographic Profile," *Medievalia et Humanistica*, n.s. 1 (1970): 93. Medieval husbands may nevertheless have been older than their wives; compare Dante, *Paradiso* 15.103.

71. Chojnacki, "Patrician Women," 192; Gage, *Life*, 26; Klapisch, "L'enfance," 106, 112, 116; Christiane Klapisch, "Household and Family in Tuscany in 1427," in *Household*

On this point some remarkably detailed information is available from a Florentine tax census taken in the year 1427, five years before the birth of Machiavelli's father. That census, recently subject to careful analysis by several social historians, shows that 86 percent of the women beween the ages eighteen and twenty-two who were not in nunneries were married or widowed, and an astonishing 95 percent of women between the ages of twenty-three and twenty-seven who were not nuns were or had been married.[72] Men, by contrast, were marrying later and later, so that there was an increasing disparity in age between bride and groom.[73] Of couples marrying in Florence in 1427, grooms *averaged* from thirteen to fourteen years older than their brides; a similar age difference was found among the six thousand married couples whose ages were recorded, and 97 percent of all husbands were older than their wives.[74] Of the more than one thousand babies born in Florence that year, the average age of the mother was twenty-seven, that of the father, forty; in many families the father was as much senior to the mother as she was to their newborn infant.[75] Machiavelli's sister was married when she was fourteen; and, as already noted, his mother was nine years younger than his father and a widow when she married him.[76] As one might expect given such a disparity of ages between marriage partners, wives tended to outlive their husbands, and there were a large number of surviving widows in Florence.[77] Research on other Italian cities of the period suggests that such widows often wielded considerable economic power; their large numbers tended to enhance the actual socioeconomic power of women, if not their status.[78]

Prior to marriage, "the *jeune fille* was secluded," being kept at home

and Family in Past Time, ed. Peter Laslett and Richard Wall (Cambridge: Cambridge University Press, 1972), 272; Trexler, "Célibat," 1342; Herlihy, "Tuscan Town," 91–92; David Herlihy, "Mapping Households in Medieval Italy," *Catholic Historical Review* 58 (April 1972): 1–24; David Herlihy, "Vieillir à Florence au Quattrocento," *Annales. Économies, Sociétés, Civilisations* 24 (November–December 1969): 1346; Hughes, "Urban Growth," 27; Richard C. Trexler, "In Search of Father: The Experience of Abandonment in the Recollections of Giovanni di Pagolo Morelli," *History of Childhood Quarterly* 3 (Fall 1975): 230–31, 234.

72. Herlihy, "Tuscan Town," 91. On necessary caution in the use of these *catasto* data, see Christiane Klapisch, "Fiscalité et démographie en Toscane (1427–1430)," *Annales. Économies, Sociétés, Civilisations* 24 (November–December 1969): 1317.

73. Martines, "Way of Looking," 23; Alberti, *Family*, 112.

74. Klapisch, "Household," 272; Herlihy, "Tuscan Town," 92; Herlihy, "Vieillir," 1346.

75. Herlihy, "Vieillir," 1342; Tamassia, *Famiglia*, 161–62, 197–98.

76. Olschki, *Libro*, 99.

77. Martines, "Way of Looking," 23; Chojnacki, "Patrician Women," 192; Klapisch, "Household," 272–73; Klapisch, "Fiscalité," 1333; Herlihy, "Tuscan Town," 95, 99–101.

78. Chojnacki, "Patrician Women,"; Chojnacki, "Dowries and Kinship," in Stuard, *Women*, 176–91; Hughes, "Domestic Ideals," 141.

except for visits to church and never being allowed on the street unaccompanied.[79] Again, this was surely less true among the lower classes. Once married, women were expected to be faithful and chaste; and though some undoubtedly were not, the killing of a wife "*per causa d'onore*" was regarded as justifiable, indeed laudable. Marital fidelity was not expected of husbands; and wives often accepted their husbands' bastard children into their home to be raised with their own.[80] Courtesans, prostitution, and (male) homosexual activity were familiar phenomena, the latter reportedly being particularly widespread in Florence.[81] The young bride, then, previously sheltered and "used to obeying her mother" at home, moved at the moment of her marriage into a strange household where she would be subordinate to her husband's will, expected to be obedient, chaste, and humble. Typically she was "rather timid at the outset: melancholy, out of her element and listless— *oziozetta*," suffering "pangs of longing for her mother and family."[82]

Once married, the Florentine Renaissance wife seems to have been more restricted to the home than her medieval counterpart. As already noted, the medieval woman "played an active and dignified part in the society of her age."[83] The artisan's wife in the town often worked at a trade; aristocratic wives were socially and economically influential; and in general, women "do not appear to have been 'privatized,' that is, relegated to a domestic existence where their functions are determined by, or subordinated to, their sexual capacities."[84] This familial participation in the public world was encouraged by the lack of clear physical boundaries between the domestic domain and those of economic and public activity. The medieval house was typically open to the street at ground-floor level; artisans did their work there, and in upper-class homes there might be shops and a market, even a chapel, downstairs and always a *loggia* open to the street. The actual living quarters, more-

79. Morgan, "Renaissance Lady," 15; see also O'Faolain and Martines, *Not in God's Image*, 167; Gage, *Life*, 185; Boulting, *Woman*, 39–43, 47–48; Rodocanachi, *Femme*, 46–50; Durant, *Renaissance*, 575, 582; Lucas-Dubreton, *Daily Life*, 111–12; Iris Origo, *The World of San Bernardino* (New York: Harcourt, Brace & World, 1962), 64–65.

80. Compare note 59 above, and Rodocanachi, *Femme*, 308; Durant, *Renaissance*, 575; Alberti, *Family*, 99; Tamassia, *Famiglia*, 199–208; Hale, *Renaissance Europe*, 134–35; Kelly-Godol, "Did Women Have a Renaissance?" 140, 156–57; Iris Origo, *The Merchant of Prato* (London: Jonathan Cape, 1960), 168–69.

81. Herlihy, "Vieillir," 1349; Brucker, *Society*, 190–206; Ridolfi, *Life*, 259 n. 32; Boulting, *Woman*, 293–311; Lucas-Dubreton, *Daily Life*, 231–35.

82. Lucas-Dubreton, *Daily Life*, 104; see also O'Faolain and Martines, *Not in God's Image*, 187; Alberti, *Family*, 198, 208; Klapisch, "L'enfance," 116; Origo, *World*, 56, 59; Trexler, "In Search," 232.

83. Power, "Position," in Bell, *Women*, 180.

84. Stuard, *Women*, 4, 7, 13; Hughes, "Domestic Ideals," 127.

over, were "austere, often cramped," so that they "pushed their inhabitants outdoors, into the family enclave" downstairs.[85] In short, "there was a constant penetration of street life" into the house, so that women participated in production and public activity because "the private and public worlds were not . . . clearly demarcated."[86] Artisan households may have been different; at least in medieval Genoa, artisans settled individually rather than in extended family districts and used the church square for their public life. Yet Genoan artisan women had if anything more of an active share in informal public life than their aristocratic counterparts.[87]

But "in the late Middle Ages conditions conducive to women's public participation began to disappear in the Italian city-states."[88] As urbanization advanced and the bourgeoisie became increasingly numerous and wealthy, their women were "liberated" from the necessity to work at their husbands' trades and instead assumed more exclusive control over the household. In the bourgeois family of Renaissance Florence, the wife was expected to stay at home, obey her husband, and tend to his domestic needs.[89] Wealthy widows may have continued to exercise economic powers, but women in general had no public life. The bourgeois ideal, at least, was for a strict separation of functions between husband and wife. Thus a character in Alberti's moralistic dialogue on the family declares:

It would hardly win us respect if our wife busied herself among the men in the marketplace, out in the public eye. It also seems somewhat demeaning to me to remain shut up in the house among women when I have many things to do among men.[90]

And so it appears to have been in Florentine practice; women "did not often attend public meetings of men; nor did they go out into the streets and squares to argue over civic matters."[91] No woman is listed among those Florentines who met with Machiavelli in the Rucellai gardens to discuss literature, philosophy, and politics.[92]

85. Hughes, "Domestic Ideals," 121.
86. Goldthwaite, "Florentine Palace," 983; see also Lawson, *Hidden Heritage*, 57; Gies and Gies, *Life*, 34.
87. Hughes, "Domestic Ideals," 125–26, 136, 138.
88. Stuard, *Women*, 5.
89. Biagi, *Men*, 68; Boulting, *Woman*, 128–39; Lungo, *Women*, 107, 218; Hare, *Most Illustrious Ladies*, 41; Kelso, *Doctrine*, 106–7; Ruggiers, *Florence*, 99; Rodocanachi, *Femme*, 303–5; Hughes, "Domestic Ideals," 121.
90. Alberti, *Family*, 207; see also O'Faolain and Martines, *Not in God's Image*, 188; Kelly-Godol, "Did Women Have a Renaissance?" 140–41.
91. Martinelli, *World*, 88; Effinger, *Women*, 120; Kent, *Household*, 79.
92. Albertini, *Florentinische Staatsbewusstsein*, 74–89.

There was, indeed, in this period in Italy and specifically in Florence, an increasing privatization of family life. By contrast with medieval patterns of communal participation and the extended family,

in fifteenth century Florence the fragmentation of the family frequently reached the point at which each man established his own independent household and possessed his own property privately . . . even brothers did not necessarily live under one roof or share living expenses unless through financial necessity . . . or because of unusually strong personal bonds.[93]

In the census of 1427, 92.5 percent of the households in Florence included only a nuclear family with at most a bachelor uncle or widowed aunt. Only among the upper classes did several nuclear families sometimes share a dwelling.[94] Households in the Tuscan countryside were larger, and there the older, extended-family pattern continued.[95] But in the city, the conjugal family was the primary residential and economic unit.[96] This change is recognized in the legal definition of the family; and it is reflected as well in the *ricordi* of the fourteenth- and fifteenth-century Florentines, which are no longer concerned with relations beyond the immediate nuclear family.[97] As Richard Goldthwaite maintains, "The modern conception of family . . . has one of its first manifestations here and certainly it was a distinctive feature of Florentine society at the time."[98]

This privatization or nuclearization of the family was dramatically

93. Goldthwaite, *Private Wealth*, 257; on the medieval Florentine family cf. David Herlihy, "Family Solidarity in Medieval Italian History," in his *Economy, Society and Government in Medieval Italy* (Kent, Ohio: Kent State University Press, 1969), 173–79; in Genoa, according to Hughes, artisan families were already nuclear in the medieval period ("Domestic Ideals," 116, 125). Francis William Kent has challenged Goldthwaite's findings, arguing that lineage or extended families still played a large role, especially in the upper classes, and that even in those households that were nuclear families "cannot have been 'isolated' in the modern sociological sense" (*Household*, 230–31). He acknowledges, however, that more than half of the households in the three upper-class lineages he studied were nuclear families, and in another one-sixth one person lived alone (ibid., 26). See also Herlihy, "Mapping," 5–13.
94. Herlihy, "Vieillir," 1341; Klapisch, "Household," 279; Goldthwaite, "Florentine Palace," 997, 1003.
95. Christiane Klapisch and Michel Demonet, "'A uno pane e uno vino,' La famille rurale toscane au début du XVᵉ siècle," *Annales. Économies, Sociétés, Civilisations* 27 (July–October 1972): 873–901; Herlihy, "Vieillir," 1341; Herlihy, "Tuscan Town," 88, 98; Herlihy, "Mapping," 12, 14; Klapisch, "Household," 275; Hughes, "Urban Growth," 4–5; David Herlihy, "Family and Property in Renaissance Florence," in *The Medieval City*, ed. Harry A. Miskimin, David Herlihy, and A. L. Udovitch (New Haven: Yale University Press, 1977), 23.
96. Martines, "Way of Looking," 21; Hughes, "Domestic Ideals," 116.
97. Goldthwaite, *Private Wealth*, 265.
98. Ibid., 263. No doubt this was part of the generally narrower "sense of family boundaries" said to have developed in most of early modern Europe (Davis, "Ghosts," 100). But cf. Kent, *Household*; and Herlihy, "Mapping," 15, 18–19.

visible, as both Goldthwaite and Gene Brucker have pointed out, in the new Renaissance architectural style.

In earlier times a man's actual residence was not well defined architecturally: he might share a building or even live with other members of his family, and the entire clan occupied a number of indistinguishable buildings forming a conglomerate whole around the family tower. By the fifteenth century, however, men lived apart, renting houses or building their own.[99]

There was a tremendous amount of new building in Florence from the second half of the fourteenth century to the beginning of the sixteenth, and the new buildings increasingly reflected the Renaissance family structure; they were "the aesthetic articulation of the physical isolation of a man's household from all others."[100] The new buildings displaced medieval shops and decreased the open life of the streets; they were "designed to shield their occupants from contact with the adjacent street. Families no longer assembled in the public loggia, but in the interior courtyard."[101] There was a growing elaboration and elegance of interior space, and whereas the *loggia* had been open to the community, the courtyards "were built by and for single households, or nuclear families."[102] Windows were placed so that one could not see out into the street or be seen.[103] Thus at the same time as the household contracted to the nuclear family, it also closed itself off and turned inward; the new architecture "signalled the family's . . . withdrawal from the community life of the neighborhood," a withdrawal "into a new realm of privacy."[104] The women living in these new houses, then, were increasingly confined to the private world of the household and the nuclear family. And while Herlihy suggests that this constriction of the family might have "forced" its members "to turn their attention outward, to seek in the world beyond the family essential economic and moral supports," his examples are all of men.[105]

Certainly for Florentine women of this time as for the women of an-

99. Goldthwaite, *Private Wealth*, 258; Brucker, *Renaissance Florence*, 264–65. See also Goldthwaite, "Florentine Palace," 983; Goldthwaite, *Building*, 15–16, 98, 102–3, 110; Gies and Gies, *Life*, 34. Again, in Genoa medieval artisans already "settled individually rather than in extended family districts" (Hughes, "Domestic Ideals," 125).

100. Goldthwaite, "Florentine Palace," 977; Goldthwaite, *Private Wealth*, 258. Again Kent disagrees (*Household*, 228, 230).

101. Brucker, *Renaissance Florence*, 264; Goldthwaite, "Florentine Palace," 988.

102. Brucker, *Renaissance Florence*, 265; Stuard, *Women*, 5; Goldthwaite, *Building*, 104.

103. James Bruce Ross, "The Middle-Class Child in Urban Italy," in de Mause, *History*, 207.

104. Brucker, *Renaissance Florence*, 265; Goldthwaite, "Florentine Palace," 988, cf. 997, 1008–9.

105. Herlihy, "Mapping," 18.

cient Athens, the one sphere of exclusive power was the household, including the care of young children. Although the husband and father had legal control, and generally took charge of finances and the earnings of the family's livelihood, "the citizen's wife took entire charge of the house, and it was deemed unmanly for the husband to poke his nose into every corner."[106] Again this may not be true of lower-class families, where the labor power of women would be needed along with that of the men just to provide food and shelter. But it apparently was typical of the bourgeois Renaissance home.

With one important exception to be discussed shortly, Florentine mothers had complete charge of young children to the age of about seven and typically continued to have charge of girls even after that.[107] Girls from poor families were often put out, at between eight and eleven years of age, as servants to a wealthy family that would later dower them.[108] Boys at the age of seven or eight passed into the care of their fathers, and sometimes out of the house altogether, for apprenticeship or education, as Machiavelli himself was sent to study with a master of the abacus when he was ten, though his schooling had begun earlier.[109] Male children were unequivocally preferred; one might say that the main function of marriage was to provide a male heir for the family. Some thought conception of a female to result from defective sexual intercourse.[110] A son was a source of prestige and wealth; the birth of a daughter raised the prospect of having to procure a dowry for her.

Apparently mothers were often reluctant to let their sons go forth into the masculine world.[111] Where fathers remained alive, a struggle sometimes developed between the parents over the education of the son, at the dangerous intersection, as it were, of feminine and masculine realms of power. Where a tutor was brought into the house for the boy, he might become a participant in this struggle: the tutor, a servant in

106. Boulting, *Woman*, 142; see also Lungo, *Women*, 276; Barzini, *Italians*, 201–3; Martinelli, *World*, 86; Alberti, *Family*, 207–8; Tamassia, *Famiglia*, 46; Origo, *World*, 58; cf. Origo, *Merchant*, 159.

107. Maulde la Clavière, *Women*, 72, 74; Kelso, *Doctrine*, 14; see also Rodocanachi, *Femme*, 16; Ross, "Middle-Class Child," in de Mause, *History*, 211; Tamassia, *Famiglia*, 260; Alberti, *Family*, 49–50.

108. Klapisch, "L'enfance," 112–13.

109. Lungo, *Women*, 99; Maulde la Clavière, *Women*, 75; Martinelli, *World*, 90; Tamassia, *Famiglia*, 48; Trexler, "In Search," 238, 245; Alberti, *Family*, 62–63; Gage, *Life*, 69–71. But Klapisch gives fourteen as the age of apprenticeship ("L'enfance," 113). See also Olschki, *Libro*, 103.

110. Klapisch, "L'enfance," 108. See also Boulting, *Woman*, 165; Hare, *Most Illustrious Ladies*, 5, 163; Lucas-Dubreton, *Daily Life*, 104; Rodocanachi, *Femme*, 1; Origo, *World*, 52; Gage, *Life*, 25, 28–30; Ross, "Middle-Class Child," in de Mause, *History*, 205–6; Tamassia, *Famiglia*, 266; Trexler, "In Search," 234; Trexler, "Foundlings."

111. For instance, Gage, *Life*, 70. Cf. Effinger, *Women*, 120.

the household, symbolically representing the outside, secular, masculine world and its ruthless ways; the mother fighting for a continuing personal, as well as moral and religious, influence over her boy.[112] In the Florentine moralistic literature on family life, fathers are warned against neglecting their sons for political and business concerns, and mothers are seen as likely to spoil their children, give their sons effeminate habits, and smother any sign of *virtù* in them.[113]

Finally, one must mention one other important feature of Florentine child-rearing patterns in this period, a feature having no counterpart in Slater's account of ancient Athens. In both bourgeois and upper-class households in Renaissance Florence, newborn infants were immediately turned over to a wet nurse or *balia*; it was "the universal custom."[114] Almost all of the new moralists of family life advised against it but then went on at once to give detailed advice on the selection of a wet nurse. In the Middle Ages, wet nurses had been widely used by the upper classes, but in the Renaissance the custom seems to have spread to the rising bourgeoisie as a matter of prestige, "a symbol of gentility."[115] Thus an early biography of the philosopher Marsilio Ficino says of his father that although he was poor, "we must believe that he lived decently since he sent his children out of the house to be brought up by a *balia*."[116] Although some wet nurses were brought to live in the home of the infant, and some resident slaves were used as wet nurses, the most common Renaissance pattern in Florence seems to have been to send the infant to live in the *balia's* home; no doubt this was partially due to the

112. Hare, *Most Illustrious Ladies*, 69; Boulting, *Woman*, 171–72; Scaife, *Florentine Life*, 83. Cf. Maulde la Clavière, *Women*, 76, on France.

113. Alberti, *Opere*, 1: 40, and Matteo Vegio, *De educatione*, both quoted in Herlihy, "Some Psychological and Social Roots," in Martines, *Violence*, 139–40; Alberti, *Family*, 62–63; also note 144, below.

114. Origo, *Merchant*, 199–200; see also Biagi, *Men*, 67; Origo, *World*, 60; Boulting, *Woman*, 165–67; Gies and Gies, *Life*, 61–62; Rodocanachi, *Femme*, 12; Alberti, *Family*, 215; Trexler, "In Search," 226, 229, 231, 234; Ross, "Middle-Class Child," in de Mause, *History*, 184–96. Wet nurses were apparently used by the wealthy ancient Greek upper classes at least to some extent, although Slater does not mention them; they were not generally used. Willystine Goodsell, *A History of Man and the Family*, rev. ed. (New York: Macmillan, 1934), 107; W. K. Lacey, *The Family in Classical Greece* (Ithaca: Cornell University Press, 1968), 170; Robert Flaceliere, *Daily Life in Greece at the Time of Pericles*, tr. Peter Green (London: Weidenfeld and Nicolson, 1965), 88; Sister Mary Rosaria, "The Nurse in Greek Life" (Ph.D. diss., Catholic University of America, 1917), 9–18; Pomeroy, *Goddesses*, 81, 169.

115. Ross, "Middle-Class Child," in de Mause, *History*, 186; see also 187, and McLaughlin, "Survivors," in ibid., 115–17; Gies and Gies, *Life*, 61; Boulting, *Woman*, 150; Hughes, "Domestic Ideals," 131; Barbara Kaye Greenlief, *Children Through the Ages* (New York: McGraw-Hill, 1978), 42.

116. Quoted in Raymond Marcell, *Marsile Ficin (1433–1499)* (Paris, 1958), appendix 2, 694, which, in turn, is quoted by Ross, "Middle-Class Child," in de Mause, *History*, 217 n. 12.

more constricted and private living patterns of bourgeois families. Most typically the child was literally farmed out, the wet nurse being "generally a peasant woman living at a distance."[117] Infants generally stayed with the *balia* until the age of two.[118] In rich families, girls were put out to wet nurses longer than boys.[119] Sometimes, to be sure, mothers nursed their own infants for a time; it was considered a sign of special maternal devotion and sacrifice.[120] There was considerable concern about selecting a good and healthy *balia*, and it was not unusual for infants to be moved repeatedly from one wet nurse to another.[121] Machiavelli's correspondence reveals that at least two of his children were put out to wet nurses, one of them being placed with a nurse inside the city a week or two after birth.[122] Machiavelli's father's notebook contains no entries about wet nurses, though it covers a period including the infancy of Niccolò's younger brother. Thus whether Niccolò himself had a wet nurse, rural or urban, must remain a mystery, along with the intriguing question of whether his adult banishment from Florentine politics to his farm might have carried the additional humiliating implication of being returned to the world of nursing infancy.

❖   ❖   ❖

What, then, are the overall conclusions to be drawn from this motley collection of information? To begin with the status of women, there seem to have been improvements in some respects and decline in others, considerable change under way in both directions, and considerable tension and conflict about that change. Women had increasing educational opportunities, and there were notable individual women of recognized achievement in mainly masculine realms of enterprise. Yet these women were exceptional and rarely found in Florence. The mainly bourgeois women of that city seem to have been educated but decisively subordinate to men in legal status, social prestige, and the formal institutional structure of family life. Typically they were much younger

117. Ross, "Middle-Class Child," in de Mause, *History*, 184. See also Greenlief, *Children*, 42; Hunt, *Parents*, 103; Klapisch, "L'enfance," 110–11; Trexler, "In Search," 226; Goldthwaite, *Building*, 107. For Machiavelli's fictionalized Castruccio, a foundling, the adoptive parents brought a wet nurse into the house (G 535).
118. Ross, "Middle-Class Child," in de Mause, *History*, 195, 184–85; Lawrence Stone, *The Family, Sex and Marriage in England 1500–1800* (London: Weidenfeld and Nicolson, 1977) 426, 430; Trexler, "In Search," 231, 234; but cf. Greenlief, *Children*, 42, who says up to fourteen years.
119. Klapisch, "L'enfance," 110–11.
120. Ross, "Middle-Class Child," in de Mause, *History*, 187–88; see also Hunt, *Parents*, 105–6.
121. Ross, "Middle-Class Child," in de Mause, *History*, 188, 192.
122. Machiavelli, *Opere* 6: 118–19; Ridolfi, *Life*, 326 n. 22.

than their husbands and increasingly confined to private life, as the family became more nuclear and domestic architecture more enclosed. Surely this contraction of household life must have brought, as Goldthwaite suggests, "a more intensive cohesion" within the nuclear family. More doubtful, however, is his further suggestion that it also brought "a liberation of women," a "remarkable rise" in their "status," allowing them to be "partners" and "companions" to their husbands.[123] Martines maintains, to the contrary, that "it is obviously true that women were more strictly confined to the family and to household tasks."[124] It does seem likely that relations within the nuclear family—between husband and wife and between parents and young children—would become more intense in this new setting. No doubt this would make possible great involvement and affection, but great involvement and affection are likely to be accompanied by great ambivalence. In medieval Genoa, husbands in artisan families, which already lived in the new, nuclearized pattern, tended to beat their wives, while husbands in the extended-family, aristocratic household did not, directing violence instead against male relatives.[125]

Certainly the women of Florence were not as severely or as universally disadvantaged as those of ancient Athens. Many were educated, and some at least must have known about the bold *viragos* and accomplished women in other Italian cities. Though not married as young as Athenian girls or confined as severely, they were much younger than their husbands and were denied the husbands' social and sexual freedom. As in Athens, the young bride passed through a period of depression. Bourgeois Florentine women, moreover, were probably more confined than their grandmothers had been, more exclusively thrown back on the resources of the household for emotional gratification. Thus, given the conflicting changes taking place—the increasing liberation of some women and the confinement of others, the increasing education with restricted opportunities—one might predict a "revolution of rising expectations" among the women, a sense of dislocation and disappointment.[126] Although objectively less deprived than Athenian women, Florentine women may well have been more resentful, for what matters here is relative, not absolute, deprivation. On the other hand, at least for the Slater thesis, what matters particularly is *un*conscious resentment, and

123. Goldthwaite, *Private Wealth*, 262–63.
124. Martines, "Way of Looking," 17.
125. Hughes, "Domestic Ideals," 127.
126. The phrase is from Forrest D. Murden, "Underdeveloped Lands: 'Revolution of Rising Expectations,'" *Foreign Policy Association. Headline Series*, no. 119 (September 20, 1956).

Florentine women may well have been more aware of their anger at male privilege than were their Athenian counterparts. We do not really know much about what the women thought and felt. But there is considerable overt expression of the men's conflicted feelings over relations between the sexes in this period. At the same time that the status of women was being called into question and the structure of the family changing, social conditions also tended to undermine the security of traditional masculine roles. It is, after all, a truism to observe that the Renaissance involved a dissolution of traditional authority, a fragmenting of social ties in which each man became free to make his own way and prove his own worth but thereby also became required to do so. It is not that the manliness of the Renaissance—military violence or business competition—was somehow less "masculine" than that of the Middle Ages—knighthood, monkhood, or the administration of a feudal estate. Rather, the value of the new ideals and the manner in which they were to be properly pursued, and therefore their power to ratify and validate a man's life, were in doubt, no longer guaranteed by any tradition, and had themselves to be proved. There were no longer unquestioned masculine roles available. As Crane Brinton points out, the fifteenth and early sixteenth centuries were

the only period in the history of the West when the male wore very tight lower garments ("hose"), with a conspicuous codpiece, which was often ornamented. This fact "proves" nothing but symbolizes a great deal. The man of the Renaissance admired masculinity, one may hazard, but was a bit uncertain as to whether he had it; hence he must display what he undoubtedly had.[127]

This anxiety about masculinity is, in turn, reflected in the men's response to the new roles and claims of women. That response, as Ruth Kelso says, was pervasively one of

alarm that women were breaking out of bounds and needed to be kept or set back in their place. The facts of life—women's inferiority to men in position and power, their dependence upon men for protection and support, their ignorance—were in the way to be flouted and therefore in need of explanation, iteration, and defense. . . . There was a real antagonism.[128]

Already the women's new interest in books, while supported by some men, was disturbing to many others; and literacy was only the tip of the

127. Brinton, *History*, 250. But hose were mainly worn in Germany; Hale, *Renaissance Europe*, 133. See also Casey, "Cheshire Cat," 238. This is also the period when the corset is introduced for women; it was invented, interestingly enough, by one of the new "liberated" women herself, Catherine de Medici; see Emily James Putnam, *The Lady* (Chicago: University of Chicago Press, 1970), 169.

128. Kelso, *Doctrine*, 10.

iceberg. How much more threatening were the examples of women succeeding like men in realms defined as masculine? David Hunt says,

Men were unable to account for these instances of feminine achievement. In some cases—when women intervened in political affairs, for example—this activity was seen as a kind of aberration, a sign of the decadence of the times.[129]

Thus he argues that the "contempt and condescension" that "superficially inform" men's view of women at the time "tend to shade off into an unmistakable apprehension."[130] The inversion theme of dominating, shrewish wife and henpecked husband, already familiar in medieval literature, now emerges as a favorite topic in popular culture. Behind this humorous "battle," John Rigby Hale suggests, lay fears of "a darker form of domination."[131] Not only did woodcuts and engravings dwell "alarmingly on famous cases of men being dominated by women: Adam tempted by Eve, Samson shorn by Delilah, Holofernes decapitated by Judith . . ." but also in crucifixion dramas of this time, women were

introduced as gleefully forging the nails for the cross, and . . . a misericord could portray a woman heaving a man off to perdition with a rope around his genitals. Fear of woman's sexuality seems to have been widespread. . . . The bourgeois literature of the time harps on the theme of women devouring, pestering, exhausting their husbands.[132]

One does not find in Renaissance Florentine art or literature great mythologized feminine figures comparable in splendor, power, or rage to those of ancient Greece. But there is the revival of fortune as a significant figure. One might also note the Italian revival in this period of the ancient war goddess Bellona, to replace or supplement the male Mars, specifically as a symbol of the new and more brutal weapons of large-scale destruction.[133] But Bellona does not seem to have been a significant symbol in Florence, whose special relationship to Mars remained undisturbed.[134] One also finds the strong revival of triumphantly masculine figures: a renewed interest in Hercules, for example, specifically as dominating female forces, including fortune. Or the revival of the cult of Joseph in fifteenth-century religious art, sometimes explicitly as "lord and master of the mother of the lord and master of all."[135]

129. Hunt, *Parents*, 73.
130. Ibid., 73–75; Casey, "Cheshire Cat," 236.
131. Hale, *Renaissance Europe*, 128–29; Casey, "Cheshire Cat," 237.
132. Hale, *Renaissance Europe*, 129–30.
133. J[ohn] R[igby] Hale, "War and Public Opinion in Renaissance Italy," in *Italian Renaissance Studies*, ed. Ernest Fraser Jacob (London: Faber and Faber, 1960), 105–7.
134. Ibid.
135. Panofsky, *Hercules*, 164–66; Shapiro, "'*Muscipula Diaboli*,'" 29, quoting John Gerson (1363–1429).

In short, there seems to be uneasiness and conflict over sexual roles. In Alberti's dialogue on the family, typical of the genre some commentators take to demonstrate the new happy domesticity and feminine freedom, a leading character explains that he locks his books and records and those of his "ancestors" away from his wife "almost like sacred or religious objects" and always tries "to make sure" that she knows no "more of my secrets than I care to impart."[136] And though another character earlier calls the love between husband and wife "greatest of all" and "a union" to be described as "true friendship," there are repeated warnings against the "madness of sexual love."[137] The concluding speaker is most concerned with the question of who is master in the house: who will obey whom, which is an issue of manhood.

> Some I see quite unwisely suppose that they can win obedience and respect from a wife to whom they openly and abjectly subject themselves. If they show by word and gesture that their spirit is all too deeply lascivious and feminine, they certainly make their wives no less unfaithful than rebellious. Never, at any moment, did I choose to show in word or action even the least bit of self-surrender in front of my wife. I did not imagine for a moment that I could hope to win obedience from one to whom I had confessed myself a slave. Always, therefore, I showed myself virile and a real man.[138]

As for childhood and relations between the generations, here, too, one can expect that feelings would become both more intense and more conflicted as the sphere of family life contracted. Oedipal conflicts, for example, should be more intense in a nuclear than in an extended family situation.[139] In addition, we have seen certain particular features of the Florentine family that would complicate the Oedipal situation. On the one hand, the large differential in age between husbands and wives might well intensify Oedipal rivalry, as mothers might be closer in age to their sons than to their husbands. On the other hand, precisely because of the age differential, as well as the wife's exclusive control over the household, one might expect relatively little actual paternal pressure on sons.[140] Fathers lived in a different world. And in a time of rapid social change such as the Renaissance, parental authority—particularly the authority of those parents who are much older than their children—

136. Alberti, *Family*, 209–10.
137. Ibid., 98, 103–4; see also, 45–46, 51, 109–10.
138. Ibid., 216–17.
139. This idea is explored in Herlihy, "Vieillir," 1342–45, 1352. See also Hunt, *Parents*, 107–8.
140. Hunt, *Parents*, 107–8; Herlihy, "Vieillir," 1342.

tends to be weakened. The aged father is distant; what he has to teach his sons is not relevant to their lives; and he is more likely to die before his son reaches adulthood. In the mercantile classes of Florence, fathers might often be absent for extended periods on business. Medieval fathers were perhaps also often absent from home, but the medieval extended family offered surrogate adult males, and this would not be the case in the isolated nuclear household of Renaissance Florence.[141] Florentine moralists frequently eulogized the loving bonds between fathers and sons, but this may well have been an idealized fantasy to compensate for actual deprivation. Alberti, the most outstanding of these writers, was illegitimate, the product of an unstable marriage, and himself never married or fathered. The father of Giovanni Dominici, another such writer, died before Giovanni's birth.[142]

Mothers and children were thus often each others' only or main resources. David Herlihy observes, "The young mother had every opportunity to lavish her interest, her care, and her most intense feelings on her children."[143] Accordingly, Dominici found it necessary to condemn "the flood of feelings, indeed the excess of sensuality which the Florentine mother permitted herself toward her children."[144] The children, too, have nowhere else to turn, no other model than the mother.

The weakness of the father's physical or affective presence was bound to favor the development of what psychoanalysts call a "symbiotic" relationship between mother and child. In a relationship of this kind, each of the partners feels incomplete and unable to live happily without the other.[145]

Yet one must add, both partners also long (ambivalently) for freedom. In such a situation, children of both sexes are likely to identify with the mother as the only significant adult presence; if sex roles are nevertheless strongly differentiated in the society in a way that is linked to status, boys will be torn between that identification and the social (and maternal) pressure to "be a man," to be unlike the mother. Such boyhood identification with the mother might help account, Herlihy suggests, for the Florentines' notorious military inability, and the men's reluctance to marry (which also helped perpetuate the social pattern).[146] The absence of strong paternal pressure on male children may also help to account,

141. Herlihy, *Violence*, 152; Herlihy, "Vieillir," 1342.
142. Herlihy, "Mapping," 16–17. See also Martinelli, *World*, 91; Boulting *Woman*, 172–73; Lungo, *Women*, 58; Hare, *Most Illustrious Ladies*, 67; Alberti, *Family*, bk. 1; Trexler, "In Search,"; Randolph Starn, "Francesco Guicciardini and his Brothers," in *Renaissance Studies in Honor of Hans Baron*, ed. Anthony Molho and John A. Tedeschi (Dekalb: Northern Illinois University Press, 1971), 411–44.
143. Herlihy, "Vieillir," 1343; my translation.
144. Ibid., 1344.   145. Ibid.   146. Ibid., 1344–45.

he says, for Renaissance men's sense of buoyance and open opportunity.[147] In any case, rather than an intensified classical Oedipal situation with a strong and domineering father, Florentine family life seems
to have been characterized by a relatively distant or absent father and
an isolated mother in intense relationship with her small children—the
situation Slater saw in ancient Athens.

But this picture is still incomplete without some effort to assess the
impact of the wet-nurse system. It is certain that such a system must
have profound psychic implications, but far from obvious what those
implications might be. *Balia*s in Florence characteristically were poor
women, nursing the children of others for money, rather than from any
attachment to the child. Often they also had an infant of their own, and
heavy work to do as well. In the early fifteenth century, some women
actually abandoned their own infants—especially girl babies—at the
foundling home in Florence, in order to become wet nurses to earn
money.[148] James Bruce Ross suggests that under such circumstances,
*balia*s and their families were likely to have resented and neglected their
small charges, who were, of course, "wholly dependent upon the *balia*."[149] The "conclusion seems undeniable," Ross says, "that the life of a
child in these first two years or so may well have been precarious and
pitiable." Another historian has found evidence of such neglect in the
texts of lullabies from the time.[150] David Hunt has reached similar conclusions about sixteenth-century France. Citing the high infant mortality rates of the period, he suggests that there was a genuine problem
about securing enough food for infants.

Those who survived must have been the ones who learned how to seize with
particular ruthlessness the nourishment which a not overly generous adult
world made available to them. Only an aggressive development, an exaggera-
tion of the infantile modes of getting and taking, would allow those infants to
acquire enough food to live.[151]

Accounts of children in this period, Hunt says, always describe them as
rapacious. But of course this is not, or not merely, because they were
rapacious; "the great difficulty experienced in getting enough food into
the child's belly" makes sense "only if we picture the specifically economic factors overlaid with a set of disturbing fantasies about children
at the breast."[152] Hunt says that the nursing relationship is never seen in

147. Ibid., 1352; Herlihy, "Mapping," 18.
148. Trexler, "Foundlings," 274–75.
149. Ross, "Middle-Class Child," in de Mause, *History*, 190–91.
150. Klapisch, "L'enfance," 110; Greenlief, *Children*, 43; Stone, *Family*, 101–2.
151. Hunt, *Parents*, 119; see also, 101, 103; Stone, *Family*, 81.
152. Hunt, *Parents*, 122.

the literature of this period as symbiotic or as pleasurable for the mother, but as a struggle in which the infant drains off "white blood" from her and leaves her depleted. The wet nurses are wanted to relieve and protect the mother.[153]

To be sure, one must allow for the possibility that conditions were markedly different in Italy—where babies are traditionally adored and welcomed—than in France. Surely some *balias* came to care for the infants they nursed, and some children retained an affectionate relationship in later life to the women who had nursed them in infancy. In medieval Genoa, some aristocrats—more women than men—left bequests to their wet nurses in their wills, even calling them "mamma."[154] No comparable study of Renaissance Florence is available. In the early fifteenth century, Florentines "were quick to blame the wet-nurses for malice" in cases of infant death at the city's foundling home.[155]

In any case, the images of infant rapacity and maternal debilitation must be juxtaposed to the marked moralistic concern in this period with domesticity and family life. As with relations between husband and wife, so with those between parents and children, most commentators take this uplifting and admonitory literature as a sign of objectively improving conditions: the Renaissance was coming to care about right family relationships. As Goldthwaite has recently reminded us, in fifteenth-century Florence,

in personal letters, diaries and *ricordanze*, sermons, moral tracts, humanist literature and poetry, much thoughtful attention is given to the sentiments of conjugal and maternal love and to the bliss and moral value of family life.[156]

Similarly, in the representational art of the time, one is struck by

the fascination, almost the obsession, with children and the mother-child relation that is perhaps the single most important motif in Florentine art during the first century of the Renaissance, with its *putti*, its children and adolescents, its secularized madonnas, its portraits of women.[157]

Ross, however, suggests that these artistic and literary images of sweet childhood, far from reflecting a happier family life, are fantasies serving to compensate for actual infantile deprivation. The Renaissance depictions of the madonna and child, he says,

153. Ibid., 120–21.
154. Hughes, "Domestic Ideals," 131–32.
155. Trexler, "Foundlings," 279; see also Trexler, "In Search," 229, but note that this particular infant was an orphan, the wet nurse in fact a foster mother throughout his childhood.
156. Goldthwaite, *Private Wealth*, 262; see also Klapisch, "L'enfance," 118–22.
157. Goldthwaite, "Florentine Palace," 1009; see also Meiss, *Painting*, 61.

portray a large, sometimes enormous, well-fed, chubby baby boy, usually nude
and often active, its masculinity displayed prominently (even if the genitals are
sometimes lightly veiled over) in various positions of intimacy with its young,
beautiful, tender—if sometimes sad, and often adoring mother. . . . Actually a
child at this age . . . was probably lying swaddled and immobile, and often mis-
erable and underfed, at the mercy of a wet-nurse.[158]

In the abstract and a priori both explanations seem equally plausible,
and only a skilled and detailed examination of both the art and its circumstances could decide between them.

Hunt suggests that the demand that children be put out to nurse was
imposed by the father, who "buys a clear Oedipal victory, keeping the
mother to himself."[159] This speculation receives some support from Slater's suggestion that men in such a society prefer young, boyish women
to maternal ones as their sexual partners. Importantly relevant also
would be the belief, noted by Lawrence Stone with respect to seven-
teenth- and eighteenth-century England, that while a woman is nursing,
she should not engage in sexual intercourse, as it is bad for her milk; the
rich, he says, took wet nurses into their homes to make sure the nurse
remained chaste.[160] The father's sexual access to the mother thus would
depend on the *balia* system. Hunt adds that since the wet-nurse system
was linked to social status,

the decision to employ a nurse was as much as anything a sexual triumph for
the father, not only within the family but also in terms of a wider network of
social relationships.[161]

It marked his superior social power relative both to the *balia*'s husband
and to other men who could not afford *balia*s. However, women might
be as socially ambitious for their family's status as men. And a system in
which babies of both sexes are sent out to nurse, although it may be
imposed by fathers who want to keep the mothers to themselves, cannot
be classed as simply Oedipal in intent.

To the infant, Hunt maintains, the wet-nurse system conveyed the
message "that his mother's breasts were forbidden and that his father
did not want him around."[162] But this is not likely to have been the message received initially, for the infant must first of all have experienced
the *balia* as "mother"—as the significant, nurturant person in his life.
And whether her care was generous and loving or neglectful and vicious, the return to his actual parents must have been experienced as a

---

158. Ross, "Middle-Class Child," in de Mause, *History*, 199; see also Greenlief, *Children*, 43–44.
159. Hunt, *Parents*, 107.   160. Stone, *Family*, 427.
161. Hunt, *Parents*, 108.   162. Ibid.

banishment from home (and from the breast) to a new life among strangers. For a middle-class Florentine boy, returning "home" at the age of two is likely to have meant not merely weaning, but a fundamental change in social experience: leaving a rural, extended-family household where masculine figures were much in evidence and where he himself was nursed, to enter an urban, nuclear household dominated solely by a resentful woman, a stranger who refused to nurse him. The change may also have coincided with toilet training.

At the minimum, one would imagine, such a pattern must have meant a sharp periodization in the life of a Florentine boy: an early nursing period either golden or tortured as the case might be, a second period of confinement and discipline in the care of a new and possibly ambivalent and resentful "mother," and then the transition outward into the father's more public and masculine world. No matter how kind the *balia* might have been and how golden the period of her care, it would presumably be tainted in retrospect by the fact and manner of its ending. The *balia*'s disappearance might be resented as a desertion, proving that she had been unreliable all along; or it might be experienced as a guilty loss—a consequence of or punishment for infant rage or greed, especially since loss of the *balia* coincided with weaning; or it might conceivably be blamed on the new mother, who had displaced the *balia* and made her disappear. If the *balia* had been cruel or neglectful, then presumably no matter how loving and kind the second, real mother might be, her care could never fully overcome the powerful initial negative impression of "mothers," nor undo its psychic damage.

Simply in terms of common sense, one would not be surprised to find children who have been reared in the wet-nurse pattern as practiced in Florence coming to resent women—at least large, older, powerful, "mother"-like women—and to regard them with deep suspicion, as changeable, unreliable, and treacherous. One would not be surprised to find a continuing later fear of dependence on (such) women and of anything resembling feminine nurturance; the unthinking, trusting bliss of the nursing infant was, after all, what put him into the mother's treacherous power.

For those who want to go beyond such commonsense interpretations, psychoanalytic theory offers, as we have already seen, some depth-psychological interpretations of what a *balia* system might mean psychically. Early loss of the mother, we learned, whether through death or some important "failure of dependability" will lead to her internalization by the infant, in the forms in which that infant experienced her, complicated by the grief, rage, and guilt felt over her loss. This early loss, internalization, and struggle for autonomy, might then presumably be followed by the kind of experience Slater hypothesizes: the first "mother" who had proved unreliable being followed by a second who made intense and ambivalent demands on her male children.

To conclude this chapter, one may cite as illustration of many of these themes the private journal of a Florentine merchant living a century before Machiavelli, recently reported by Richard Trexler. The merchant, Giovanni di Pagolo Morelli, was an orphan, his father having died when he was three, his mother when he was four (which of course makes his childhood as unusual as Leonardo's). His father, moreover, had been semiorphaned himself as well, and he was raised by a wet nurse, whom he remembered as hateful and cruel. The theme of abandonment, Trexler says, is "the most pervasive element" in Morelli's *ricordanze*.[163] But Morelli's attitude is not the same toward the two parents who "abandoned" him: all the blame for his fate is put on his mother and women, all his yearning for rescue directed toward his father and men.

Trexler says the account displays "a deep-seated resentment of women."[164] Morelli feels that he has been "much oppressed by fortune."[165] He judges that his own wife, like his mother and grandmother, "cannot be relied upon" to remain with her children and care for them.[166] And he observes if a man's wife should turn out to be "minimally wise, little loving, vain, lecherous, a wastrel," that would not be surprising, for "there are many such [women]" in the world.[167]

For protection against the untrustworthy woman and the untrustworthy world she epitomizes, Morelli recommends the autonomy of isolation: strive to need no one beyond yourself, rely on no one. As Trexler puts it, "the world is a jungle in which one is only safe if one is powerful enough not to *need* friends."[168] Morelli himself writes, "Never trust anyone. Make everything clear, and more so with a relative and with a friend than with outsiders, but with everyone. Write everything down."[169] Orphans, in particular, receive the astringent advice: "Above all, if you want to have friends and relatives, don't need them." And, like Machiavelli, Morelli counsels prudently that in this world one cannot hope for clean hands: "One has to think of those remedies which are the least evil."[170]

As in Machiavelli's thought, however, despite the cynical warnings against trust and dependence, there are subordinate themes of hero worship, the imitation of greatness, and a powerful longing for mas-

163. Trexler, "In Search," 226.   164. Ibid.
165. Ibid., 244; also 245.   166. Ibid., 226.
167. Ibid., 235.   168. Ibid., 226.
169. Ibid., 236.   170. Ibid., 235.

culine rescue. Morelli "defines himself through his father and . . . son," Trexler says, and his "account may be characterized throughout as a search for the father."[171] He speaks of "the love and charity" of fathers for their sons, "which is infinite," and writes in detail of all the services a father performs for his sons. As a "remedy for the young orphan, or rather the youth reared without a father," he recommends finding a substitute male to emulate; if no suitable living man is available, an ancient Roman will do as a model to which to assimilate your manliness:

Exert yourself to associate and be domestic with one or with more excellent men [who are] sage and old and without vice. And watch his modes of operating in words, in counsel, in the way he orders his family and his things. Take his lead, imitate him, and thus follow him and try to make yourself like him, keep him always present in your mind, and when you do something, mirror yourself in him. . . . You will always be comforted by his image. And as you can take example from a live man, you can in the same way or just a bit less take example from a capable Roman or another capable man whom you have studied.[172]

Women being unreliable, Morelli's idealized image of a father is, Trexler observes, "highly maternal in nature"; ideally, "fathers should rear children themselves."[173] And Morelli is deeply dissatisfied with himself for having failed in his masculine obligations toward ancestors and progeny. "His own inadequacy," Trexler says, forms another "major motif in the *ricordanze*. Having created an ideal father who overcame all obstacles," Morelli feels that by comparison he himself is contemptible, that he "had been inadequate to both his father and his son."[174]

Now, Morelli lived a century before Machiavelli, and the circumstances of his childhood were surely atypical, as were those of the childhood of Leonardo da Vinci. Most Florentines were neither orphans nor illegitimate children raised by their mothers alone. Yet the material of this chapter suggests that in a way—in terms of infantile experience—the typical Florentine boy of Machiavelli's day may indeed have been "orphaned" at the age of two from the family of his *balia*. It further suggests that he was then relocated in a household much as Slater describes, totally dominated by a mother who may well have had good reason to feel neglected by her husband and resentful of men. But what is the significance of all this for Machiavelli's thought? It is time to return to the texts and their interpretation.

171. Ibid., 225.   172. Ibid., 237–38.
173. Ibid., 226.   174. Ibid., 227.

CHAPTER NINE

Family Origins: Rome and "Beginnings"

Psychological theory and the peculiarities of Renaissance Florentine so-cial life help to illuminate what one might call the family drama implicit in Machiavelli's thought. Centrally concerned about autonomy, Ma-chiavelli frequently conflates the various senses of "being a man," so that he equates humanness not just with adulthood but, even more im-portant, with masculinity. Civilization, liberty, law, politics, history, cul-ture, the whole *vivere civile* that constitutes the world of adult human autonomy are then understood as male enterprises won from and sus-tained against female power—the engulfing mother, the captivating maiden, the vindictive wife—woman as the "other," symbolizing all that man is not, or wishes not to be. The struggle to sustain civilization and republican liberty thus reflects the struggle of boys to become men.

Machiavelli explores many different versions of this family drama, and many alternative strategies for the embattled male, each of them ul-timately unsatisfactory, so that manhood remains fragmented among them. They are all unsatisfactory because being human and adult is not in fact equivalent to being male; and although the realization of au-tonomy may be partly stimulated, it is ultimately undermined by men's fear of women. The misogynist striving for autonomy may be energetic, even frantic, but it is self-defeating. Yet Machiavelli also offers a dif-ferent vision: an understanding of humanness that is not tied to gender, an understanding of autonomy as mutuality, which could apply as much to sexual as to political relations, an understanding of maturity not as an escape from the mythical engulfing mother (nor from the mythical rescuing father) but as a transcendence of these mythologizing distortions themselves—distortions of parents, of authority, of self.

Machiavelli offers that vision, yet he is not able to sustain it. Again and again *machismo* and misogyny, invoked in the name of autonomy, win out against it.

As it has emerged so far from Machiavelli's texts, the family drama begins somewhat as follows: once upon a time there may have been a good and nurturing mother with whom one lived in blissful unity, but that was so long ago and ended so badly that she is now at most a distant dream. There are hardly any images of such a benevolent mother in the texts; at most she can be inferred, for instance from the relations between animals and nature. "In the beginning," Machiavelli says, following Polybius, "men [*uomini*] . . . lived . . . in the fashion of beasts," and "The [Golden] Ass" reveals something of what that means: beasts live in perfect harmony with nature. She teaches them what is healthful for them to do and eat and spontaneously supplies them with "all her good things."[1] They are "content" with what she has to offer, "happy," and free of "anxiety." Yet even in Circe's world that blissful absorption is fraught with ambiguity. The praise of the animals' condition comes from a pig, after all; and is expressed in terms approximating the animal to the human world, even including *virtù*. Yet the animals' condition clearly is not a desirable option for man; a life "on all fours" in Circe's palace is captivity.[2] It means a loss of "liberty," a forgetting of "human things," a "vanquishing" of human "vigor [*virtù*]."[3] It is a dependent, and not a human, life.

Even more important, the initial blissful unity proves to be unreliable. The fickle nature of the nurturing mother is soon revealed (or perhaps one committed some grave fault oneself—biting nature's generous breast as a result of the first stirrings of human greed and ambition—causing her to depart?). She disappears, leaving man to begin his (human) life "in weeping" and "devoid of all protection." Being human means having to provide for oneself through "art," by the power of one's own "hands and speech."[4] The initial unity, if it ever existed, is permanently lost, so that the only real possibility is to struggle forward, toward autonomy.

It is, however, a struggle. To be devoid of protection is not to be autonomous; and though the child may be abandoned, it is neither alone nor free. The nurturing matrix has vanished, but another mother has

1. *Discourses* 1: 2 (G 197); Machiavelli, *Opere* 1: 131; "[Golden] Ass," ch. 8, lines 46–108 (G 770–72).
2. "[Golden] Ass," ch. 2, line 147 (G 756).
3. Ibid., lines 24–36 (G 753); ch. 4, lines 112–38 (G 761).
4. Ibid., ch. 8, lines 95, 130 (G 771–72).

taken her place. Less dreamlike and more definite in outline, she is not merely unreliable but downright malevolent. Though she does not nourish, this second mother is no more willing to permit autonomy than the first; she wants to infantilize and emasculate men, to keep them forever in her power. She is therefore the enemy of all things man-made; and the world created by men's "hands and speech" is their refuge from her. Domination by women thus means childishness, bestiality, and dependence, while the masculine world sorts with adulthood, humanity, and autonomy. The latter is the world of the *vivere civile*: of culture and history, of politics and "fighting by laws." It offers the possibility of mutuality among peers, instead of domination and dependence, for all its members are adult and share responsibility for maintaining and defending it. All of them bear arms in a citizen militia to protect their world, as roofs or shade trees shelter the "soft" human enterprises of civilization. This civic, human world is what is at stake in the battle of the sexes, men's shared struggle not merely against the real women whom they encounter, but even more against the larger feminine force: nature, fortune, or whatever her name.

It is, on the whole, an unequal struggle, for the feminine force has powerful weapons that she has implanted in the men. Natural appetite and entropy draw men back toward reabsorption into the womb and dissolution of the separate self. Men grow weary of the effort and anxiety of maintaining civilization. They yearn for the pig's mud-wallow and the infant's regular feeding. Even worse, the very impulses that stimulate men's quest for autonomy can turn into limitless, destructive cravings that defeat the quest. Sexuality, for instance, draws men out of childhood toward adulthood and masculinity; yet in the form of excessive lust it pits them against each other, enervates them, and returns them to feminine domination. Ambition and acquisitiveness, too, draw men out of nature's power. Able to foresee future needs, men use their hands and speech to construct an artificial order and to seize what is not naturally supplied. Being discontent in dependence, they seek autonomy. Yet avarice and ambition, pursued excessively or in the wrong way, are also the weapons of nature and fortune in men. They are the multilimbed "furies" sent by that "hidden power . . . in the heaven" that is "to man's being by no means friendly." They are the "appetites" that "destroy our states," so that "one goes down and another goes up" on fortune's wheel.[5]

5. "Tercets on Ambition," lines 25–42, 64 (G 735–36).

Not only are natural need, sexuality, ambition, and avarice all ambiguous in this way, both stimulating and undermining autonomy, but the whole opposition between nature and culture as respectively feminine and masculine is still too simple to capture Machiavelli's vision. For though the *vivere civile* is continually threatened by female forces, it also presupposes an underlying connection with them; it must provide for natural needs and enlist natural energy. Even while fighting the possessive domination of the (second) mother and guarding against her (and particularly the first mother's) unreliability, men must somehow reach back to the original nurturing source if their effort at autonomy is to succeed. Civilization, politics, history are human enterprises built in opposition to natural impulse and entropy; yet they must acknowledge, use, and transform rather than reject or deny the forces they oppose.

In the first place, men's animal passions must be enlisted in the cause of the *vivere civile*, or they will destroy it. The story of Alexandria epitomizes the point: only a fool would locate a city intended for his glory where future citizens could not make a living. Machiavelli wants to understand the real foundation of the actual civilization human beings have sometimes achieved, not some fancied utopia for angels; he seeks the "*verita effettuale della cosa*." It is "very natural and normal" for men to want possessions, to have sexual desires, and to be ambitious.[6] "Since no man has power to drive [these impulses] out of himself," the task of civilization is precisely to channel such needs and impulses. Only where they "lack an outlet for discharging themselves lawfully" do they "take unlawful ways that make the whole republic fall."[7] Human beings who would make their history must begin where they are, work with what is at hand, accept as given what they cannot change. Even when the Founder is thought of as a sculptor imposing form on matter, he must still take the material's natural characteristics into account.

The point is made most explicitly in Machiavelli's essay on language— whose authorship is, however, in dispute—which defends the Florentine dialect against Dante's charge that it is unsuited to poetry and high culture. Machiavelli has no use for a deracinated poetry and high culture out of touch with the sources of their own creativity. Dante himself, he proves in the essay, constantly used the Florentine dialect, and its vitality helped to make his poetry great. A great poet is nurtured in

6. *Prince*, ch. 15 (Machiavelli, *Opere* 1: 65); ch. 3 (G 18); letter to Vettori, 31 January 1514–[1515] (G 961).

7. "Tercets on Ambition," line 163 (G 739); *Discourses* 1: 7 (G 211).

his native language; it is the "foundation and source" of his creativity, "producing" his genius.[8] He "writes as though in love with it."[9] A man's native land is explicitly assimilated to nature and fortune in the essay. And injuring one's native land (as Dante criticized Florence) is not merely the equivalent of "parricide" but also "more criminal" than striking "one's father *or mother*."[10] Dante's example shows that "art can never hold aloof entirely from nature," and "it is impossible for art to surpass nature."[11]

But there are complications here, in addition to the essay's uncertain authorship. Machiavelli does say "parricide," suggesting the native land as male parent only, though he then adds "father or mother." He praises the Florentine dialect as "powerful enough to subdue, and not be subdued by," what it borrows from other languages, by contrast with the "effeminate lasciviousness" of the language of the Papal court.[12] Even more fundamentally, language and culture are human artifacts, part of the masculine enterprise of civilization. What does it mean, then, for Machiavelli to cite them as underlying sources of creativity associated with nature and fortune? Is the natural somehow changeable, so that the artifice of one generation becomes part of the next generation's nature?

Even aside from this essay, Machiavelli obviously thinks that while the enormous power of feminine agencies like nature and fortune threatens human autonomy, it can also be tapped and used for the human enterprise. Though inimical to human *virtù*, these forces themselves have a kind of power, perhaps even *virtù*, of their own. That is the point of Machiavelli's famous invocation of the centaur in conjunction with the passage on the lion and the fox. Ancient writers, he says, taught that Achilles and other ancient princes were brought up by Chiron the Centaur; they were given a teacher who was "half animal and half man," so that they might learn to "adopt the nature of either animal or man," as needed. For the way of fighting "according to the laws" that is "suited to man" is "often not sufficient."[13] Similarly, the Founder should be a foundling, reared by bees or wolves.

"Myth-images of half-human beasts," like that of the centaur, Dorothy Dinnerstein says, express the truth of our human species' nature: we are internally inconsistent, both continuous with and distinct from

8. Niccolò Machiavelli, "A Dialogue on Language," in *Machiavelli. Literary Works*, ed. by J[ohn] R[igby] Hale (London: Oxford University Press, 1961), 190, 189.
9. Ibid., 185.		10. Ibid., 175, 178, my italics.
11. Ibid., 185, 187.		12. Ibid.
13. *Prince*, ch. 18 (G 64–65).

other species and the rest of nature in "mysterious and profound" ways.[14] Political leaders need to be educated by centaurs because in politics and history people fashion the *vivere civile* both out of nature and against it, both by fortune and against it. Politics is a border-zone of continual interchange and frequent combat. Insofar as we begin as animals, only animal instinct and need can supply the energy for transforming the animal into the human. There is no other source. Machiavelli tends to associate these natural roots of our humanity with the feminine, the human with the masculine. So he perceives the feminine as the source and the ultimate conclusion, stronger than the entire masculine enterprise; yet it remains for him less "honorable," because it is incompatible with individuation and freedom.

Passages like that about the centaur, no doubt, are what lead Felix Gilbert to argue that Machiavelli teaches "a return to life according to man's inherent natural instincts."[15] The imitation of ancient Rome, he says, signifies a return to nature; and man can become strong only by accepting his membership in nature as his "fate." Animals have a "pristine genuineness" that in man has been "weakened by reason." To achieve "control" of his world, therefore, man must return to an animallike state, "to a level of instinctiveness where he becomes part of the forces surrounding him."[16] Yet though there is some textual support for such a reading, it cannot be fully correct. There is nothing in Machiavelli about the "weakening of instinct by reason," nor is there much hope for "control" of the world. And, above all, nature and instinct are no simple, unambiguous sources of regeneration. Most of the time they signify the opposite of human *virtù* and autonomy; they are dangerous and seductive and men must struggle against them. Far from being identified with them, moreover, ancient Rome may be Machiavelli's most powerful resource against their threat.

Acceptance of our animal nature and continued contact with it are indeed of central value to Machiavelli, a source of energy and perhaps even of *virtù*, but they are also fraught with danger. Contact with these feminine powers is essential, but it can be safely achieved only under the most stringent masculine safeguards. The mother cannot be left behind, for her powers are inside men. The struggle to use those powers without succumbing to them is thus continual, requiring the utmost resources of masculinity.

14. Dinnerstein, *Mermaid*, 2.
15. F. Gilbert, *Machiavelli and Guicciardini*, 192.
16. Ibid., 197.

❖   ❖   ❖

By greed, developing sexuality, and above all, ambition, the boy-child
is motivated to seek escape from maternal domination, to move toward
the masculine and human world, away from dependence. But, on the
whole, he cannot hope to succeed in this quest by himself. The feminine
powers he faces are too strong, too insidiously allied with his own desires. If he is to succeed, he will require one or another form of external
masculine support. A boy's emergence from childhood is the work
of men; fathers guide their sons out of the household and initiate
them into the public world. The boy who does not have a father and
cannot find for himself some substitute source of male sponsorship is
doomed. Indeed, it often seems that only a patriarchal father of superhuman strength and authority would be any match for the mother's terrible power.

Yet once the rescue from matriarchy has been effected, so powerful a
father turns out himself to be a new threat to the boy's developing manhood. The father's fierceness, essential to his function as rescuer, also
endangers the boy himself and constrains his independence as severely
as the mother did. Once having matured to sufficient strength in the shelter of the father's masculinity, the boy will have to escape or remove this
patriarchal power, too, if he is to attain autonomy. What is supposed to
follow patriarchal rule, of course, is the fraternal band of citizens in the
vivere civile, each of them no more than human but by their pooled
masculinity jointly able to sustain civilization. But the vision is fragile.
Connected with the transition from patriarchal to fraternal power are
not only serious problems—political, logical, and psychological—but
also something like an inversion of Freud's "return of the repressed."
While the rescuing father may be mortal, the dangerous mother is apparently eternal, and as soon as he is removed from the scene, she is
once more a threat. Even if a superhuman Founder wrests an area of
human autonomy from nature for future generations of men, they still
must deal daily with her regressive pull and with fortune's control over
the outcome of events. The struggle is endless.

The goal is autonomy; autonomy means adulthood; adulthood requires getting away from mother; and so autonomy comes to be identified with masculinity and misogynistically defined. But defined in that
way, it becomes humanly unattainable. The goal is mutuality in the
vivere civile, but so long as it is pursued in terms of gender, the chosen
means instead reproduce domination and dependence. Every avenue of
masculine defense against feminine power in Machiavelli's thought

turns out to be a dead end; manhood remains split into fragments that cannot be reconciled or even ordered. Consider a summary catalogue of man's various hopes and weapons in the struggle against femininity, keeping in mind that such a list is bound to impose an artificial neatness that distorts the texts. What are the masculine resources in Machiavelli's family drama?

First, doing without a mother. This idea occurs in several forms, the first of which is a mother who is from the outset nonnurturant, so that one is never deceived about her character nor rendered dependent. As nurturance makes men vulnerable, early deprivation might strengthen them. Fortune "afflicts" those whose *virtù* she wants to develop, and necessity is such a rejecting (and therefore beneficent) mother. By preventing sensuality and laziness, "necessity makes *virtù*."[17]

Second, parthenogenesis. If one could do without parents altogether, though unprotected, one would also be free of domination. The image of the foundling Founder expresses this possibility. Lacking both maternal nurturance and paternal sponsorship, he must in effect generate himself and be from the outset wholly autonomous. That is what qualifies him to make a break in the causal chain of history and launch genuine novelty among men.

Third, nurturance from a male. Since autonomy sorts with masculinity, it might be achieved if one could avoid women altogether, if one could be born from a father and nurtured by him alone. Cities and other human institutions have such a purely masculine birth. From a male source, nurturance seems less dangerous. Although almost no nurturant mothers appear in Machiavelli's texts, kind and nurturant fathers are not unusual, nor are they presented as engulfing.[18] They are nevertheless a problem. For the father who nurtures so that feminine power need never appear is hard to distinguish from the weak father unable to protect his sons against that power when it does appear.

Fourth, failing such avoidance of the early, nurturing mother, the growing boy may try to struggle against her power on his own, playing out the Oedipal relationship in the father's absence. Here the protagonist is no longer a helpless infant, and the issue no longer nurturance; he must try to please or conquer her sexually by his budding manhood. Here one finds the classic confrontation between *virtù* and fortune of

---

17. Machiavelli, *Opere* 1: 309; this is my translation, cf. 355; Machiavelli, *Discourses*, ed. Crick, 307; Machiavelli, *Prince*, tr. Ricci, 316.

18. Fathers may nurture with masculine, that is, symbolic food, as the ancients "feed" Machiavelli in his study; letter to Vettori, 10 December 1513 (G 929).

The Prince: the winning of fortune's favor, perhaps by cuffing and mauling her; the seizing of her daughter by the hair; the effort to please her
by going limp when she wants to do all, becoming audacious when she
is in a mood to be mastered. Such employment of sexuality can save
man from his regressive wishes for nurturance, yet it is likely to leave
him still enmeshed in feminine power. For sexual conquest is likely to
entail sensual pleasure or even affection, which weaken men and cast
them into a new dependence. Fortune's favors, moreover, are always
only temporary; the ultimate power remains hers.

Fifth, a kind of sublimated conquest—sexual or nutritive—the retreat into the mind and intellectual life. By withdrawing from the bodily
self that requires nurturance and desires sexual gratification, one might
become invulnerable to feminine power or even able to outwit it. This is
the way of the fox, prudently discerning fortune's "designs" in order to
"assist in weaving" them, but only in thought. This alternative again
seems to offer man a kind of autonomy yet leaves him really still in feminine power.

If early maternal nurturance is unavoidable, and sexual or intellectual
confrontation of feminine power on one's own proves impossible, some
form of external masculine support will be required. Thus there is *sixth*,
discipline, a category that overlaps with others in the list to some extent. *Disciplina* is a kind of man-made functional equivalent of the rejecting mother. By the imposition of external controls, man may be protected against his own cravings for passivity and nurturance, making it
safe for him to take what women have to offer. Roman discipline saved
that city's soldiers from succumbing to the pleasures of conquered
Capua; and fictionalized Castruccio defends his womanizing by saying
"I have taken her, not she me."[19] Similarly, in founding a city, discipline
can make safe a fertile site, securing access to nurturance without femi-
nization. Discipline also controls the divisive effects of lust, greed, and
ambition, imposing limits on the "nature of men."[20] Discipline, moreover is more reliable than mere natural ardor or spirit. Inquiring why
the French seem "more than men" at the beginning of a battle but "become less than women" as the fighting continues, Machiavelli answers
that the French army lacks *virtù* because it depends on natural ardor
(*furore*) without the reliable order that discipline would introduce.[21]
Often, indeed, it seems that the more severe the discipline, the better

19. *Discourses* 1, 19 (G 381); "Life of Castruccio" (G 556).
20. *Prince*, ch. 29 (G 257). See also "Tercets on Ambition," lines 94–117 (G 737).
21. *Discourses* 3: 36 (G 510). See also *Art of War*, bk. 1 (G 581); bk. 2 (G 608, 611);
bk. 6 (G 679, 694); bk. 7 (G 718).

secured masculine autonomy will be, as in Machiavelli's praise of pagan religion for strengthening men by its "blood and ferocity" while Christianity makes them "weak and effeminate"; or in the remarkable last chapter of the *Discourses* in which Rome is saved from the conspiracy of wives by its readiness "to punish" even large numbers in "terrible" ways.[22]

Discipline, however, is not self-generating, and Machiavelli pictures it in two rather different ways, depending on the agency by which it is imposed. The two possibilities correspond, roughly, to the images of Founder and Citizen. There is thus, *seventh*, the saving father. His discipline is the discipline of armies, allowing no internal conflict, eliminating all sensual gratification, directing punitive rage against internal deserters as well as external enemies. The saving father appears as a deus ex machina to rescue men by his ferocity, which he uses both to control their regressive and divisive passions and to defeat the mother.

In an important sense for Machiavelli, if men fail to escape the suffocating maternal embrace, it is the fault of weak or absent fathers "who do not protect us."[23] Again and again he says that if men lack *virtù*, their leaders are to blame: "The sins of the people are caused by the princes."[24] Yet Machiavelli is always an activist: if no saving father seems to be around, men who want autonomy must seek one out. If suitable guardians and models are lacking in their own time, they must seek among the great forefathers of the ancient world. Renewing contact with the ancient supply of *virtù* can strengthen contemporary men in their struggles.

External support and discipline can also come from a different source, however. Instead of the rescuing father there is, *eighth*, membership in a fraternal community. Here each relatively weak individual is aided by the pooled masculinity of his peers, and discipline is mutually imposed. To the cyclical, entropic power of nature and the capricious power of fortune, men counterpose human institutions multiplying their individual *virtù* and extending it through time in a network of mutually supportive relationships, each citizen both assisted and restrained by the others. Through such institutions suited to a "truly free and law-abiding" order, men can "overcome" the "malice" of fortune, for "good

22. *Discourses* 2: 2 (G 331); 3: 49 (G 527–29).
23. *Prince*, ch. 26 (G 94); letter to Vettori, 26 August, 1513 (G 926).
24. *Discourses* 3: 29 (G 493). Cf. 1: 21 (G 246–47); *Art of War*, bk. 7 (G 723–24); letter to Guicciardini, after 21 October 1525 (G 987). Machiavelli obviously does not mean "sin" in the Christian sense; cf. *Prince*, ch. 12 (G 48); *Discourses* 2: 18 (G 374); 3: 38 (G 516).

laws make good fortune."[25] The shared discipline of republican Citizenship, then, is the final male resource against feminine power. Yet its origins are a mystery, and its continued maintenance against internal corruption and external attack is highly problematic. Even fraternal Citizens fail to escape nature's and fortune's power for long.

❖   ❖   ❖

The Citizen vision of manhood, however, is not merely one in a catalogue of male defenses against the feminine, although Machiavelli often presents it in these terms. It also contains an altogether different understanding of autonomy, no longer defined in terms of masculinity and the threat of female power. It offers the elements of a radically distinct way of coming to terms with sexual and generational relations. Stressing mutuality, that vision suggests ways of conceiving human adulthood that are independent of gender, in which parents are no longer mythologized but recognized as simply human, like the self. It suggests the possibility of genuine internal conflict that nevertheless observes civil limits, of genuine gratification that is nevertheless human rather than merely animal, that is safe without punitive discipline. Instead of being harshly repressed, passion and need are to be transformed, enlisted in the civic enterprise, enlarged by ties to others and to principle. Instead of the barren site, the untouched apple tree, the exclusion of women, there is a vision of autonomous mutual nurturance. Animals and infants must be fed, by nature, by a mother, or by a master; adult human beings are those capable of caring for themselves and for others. More than once Machiavelli equates public freedom with the capacity to feed oneself.[26] Political, like personal, autonomy must be rooted in the natural and requires relationships with others, but these need not imply dependence if all are providers and responsible agents, jointly free. That vision is an alternative to the entire family drama.

It is accessible, however, only insofar as the family drama can truly be left behind, and infantile conflicts outgrown. The mutuality within difference that this vision entails, the tolerance for ambiguity and uncertainty, the capacity to trust fallible others and be oneself trustworthy, are all rooted in that "basic trust" Erikson locates in the infant's earliest relationship to its mother: the first, fundamental sense that world-mother-self is capable of providing reliable gratification. Without the capacity for judicious—limited but genuine—trust, bestiality and pa-

25. *Florentine Histories* 3: 5 (G 1148); *Discourses* 1: 11 (G 225). See also *Florentine Histories* 5: 1 (G 1232).
26. *Discourses* 1: 16 (G 235); "[Golden] Ass," ch. 8, lines 94–96, 130 (G 771–72).

triarchy cannot be transformed into citizenship; the mother—that is, their own unresolved preoccupation with the mother—will hold men captive in the family drama.

The remainder of this chapter and the next retrace once more Machiavelli's struggle with that drama—both the struggle to secure masculinity within the family drama and the struggle to escape from that drama altogether to a different understanding of autonomy. This time the struggle will be traced through the texts in terms of birth and rebirth, particularly of cities. That is, however, a more problematic undertaking than the tracing of images of men and women and their relationships; and some words of caution are needed at the outset.

Machiavelli has little to say explicitly about relations between parents and children; images of childhood are few, even in his literary works and letters. Still, he does speak of cities, religions, and other institutions as having a birth (*nasciamento*), as well as parents or a parent. But there is considerable difficulty about identifying the gender of such composite bodies and their parent(s). Cities and states are normally of feminine gender in the Italian language, and when such institutional structures were personified in Machiavelli's time, they were usually presented as female (as, indeed, they still are). Yet man-made institutions in general, and the civic association in particular, are preeminently masculine enterprises for Machiavelli, wrested from and threatened by feminine powers. Rome, for example, was surely for Machiavelli the most masculine, *virtù*-suffused enterprise ever achieved by human beings. Yet when he personifies Rome as having a birth, he refers to it as its founder's "daughter."[27]

If any feature can be said to typify the literal birth of animals and of human beings, it is embodiment: their conception by two parents of opposite sexes, gestation in the female's body, and physical emergence from it. Yet when Machiavelli speaks of the birth or parenting of composite bodies, at least of those having a "free" origin, no mother is in evidence. Rome may be a daughter, but she has only one parent: a father. Indeed, according to the argument of this book, the "birth" of a city or other human organization should be the very opposite of a "natural" event: a masculine artifice, founded *against* the stream of natural growth and decay.

Moreover, when Machiavelli turns to the renovation of cities by recovering their origins, though he calls this being "born again," further difficulties are raised. For if the point is achieving autonomy, the mo-

---

27. Ibid., 1: 11 (G 223).

ment of physical birth can hardly serve as its epitome, nor can return to
that moment symbolize renewal of autonomy. At birth, the infant is
helpless. In terms of autonomy, not birth but maturity should be the
healthy condition to which one seeks to return. Furthermore, Machiavelli conceives of such a rebirth as a return to masculinity, not to the
maternal domination associated with infancy. "Empires begin with
Ninus," held to be "a man divine," and they "end with Sardanapalus,"
who was "found among the serving maids like a woman who dis-
tributes flax."[28] Political origins are infused with the Founder's virility,
while corruption consists in a falling away from *virtù* and is generally
the work of feminine powers, for instance, through their introduction
of foreign substances into the body. Accordingly, Machiavelli says that
composite bodies are liable, like simple bodies, to a gradual accretion of
"superfluous matter" necessitating periodic "purgation" if they are
to remain healthy.[29] Such purgation, which takes them back toward
their origins and can mean a rebirth, is also explicitly a renewal of their
virtù. This seems to counter or at least complicate Machiavelli's images
of cities as female and of Rome as a daughter. But in any case, if origins
are masculine, they can hardly be construed by analogy to infancy.

Finally, composite bodies include not only cities but also religions.
The Christian Church, too, had a birth and parentage. It, too, was frequently personified as female in medieval and Renaissance thought.
Machiavelli does not explicitly personify the Church; but I shall suggest
that it is best understood as a feminine agency in his thought, akin to
Circe, fortune, and nature. What could justify interpreting cities as en-
dangered masculine enterprises but the Church as an endangering feminine force, when both are personified as female in Renaissance thought
and classed as composite bodies by Machiavelli?

These difficulties might together be taken to doom the attempt to
understand Machiavelli's discussion of cities and religions in familial
terms, perhaps even the attempt to analyze the sexual and psychological
dimensions of his thought at all. But one need not give up so easily. The
catalogue of masculine resources for the defense of human autonomy
suggests that the purely masculine "birth" of cities and the ambiguities
about their gender and their embodiment might reflect a family life distorted by wishful fantasy, made "safe" for autonomy by removal of the
female from the scene. Only a purely masculine birth, such fantasies
might be saying, can generate human autonomy. And cities might then

28. "[Golden] Ass," ch. 5, lines 88–93 (G 763).
29. *Discourses* 2: 5 (G 341).

be masculine creations, masculine enterprises, even though themselves female. Something of this sort still seems to be true in modern thought: the "fatherland" is personified as feminine. What makes it a "father-land" is not that it *is* a father, but that it is the land *of* the (fore)fathers, founded by and belonging to fathers.

To be sure, the city as female would not then be the dangerous, powerful matriarch that threatens men. Instead, it would have to be seen as the symbol of tamed femininity. It would be the obedient daughter, sprung like Minerva full-grown from the Founder's (or the theorist's?) head without the intervention of body or woman. And she would be properly grateful to him to whom she owes "her birth and her education," like the ancient Virginia, obediently prepared to let her father take away the life he had given her, if that should prove necessary for protecting his honor and the civic enterprise.[30] By the time the Founder turns her over to his heirs, she would have become the dutiful matron, like the ancient Lucretia, prepared to kill herself to protect men's honor and political order against her own dangerous femininity. All this, however, is highly speculative. A certain skepticism and caution are therefore required in turning now to Machiavelli's treatment of the childhood of cities: first their "beginnings" in general, then the birth of Rome and of the Roman Republic, then that of Florence to which Rome was parent, and finally the "return to beginnings" that is a rebirth and a recovery of *virtù*.

❖   ❖   ❖

Machiavelli begins the *Discourses* with the topic of beginnings. The preface warns of the danger inherent in human innovation, and it is followed by a first chapter on the "beginnings [*principii*]" or "origin [*nasciamento* (birth)]" of cities in general and Rome in particular.[31] Machiavelli first distinguishes between cities built by those native to the place and those built by foreigners, then subdivides the latter category into two: a city "built by foreigners originates [*nasce*] either with free men or with those who depend on others." A city has a "dependent birth" if it originates as a colony or at the behest of a prince who does not intend to live there. It has a "free birth" if a people "either under a prince or of themselves" are forced "to abandon their native land and find a new seat," whether by conquest or in a previously uninhabited place.[32]

30. Ibid., 1: 11 (G 223); 1: 40 (G 282); 1: 47 (G 287).
31. Ibid., 1: 1 (G 192); Machiavelli, *Opere* 1: 125.
32. *Discourses* 1: 1 (G 192, 193); Machiavelli, *Opere* 1: 126.

Autonomy of origins is thus fundamental, and it is a matter neither of whether the city is founded by natives or foreigners nor of whether the government is republican or monarchical, but of whether the city is born as part of some larger political body. Either a native or a foreign founding can be a free birth, and whether one considers Rome as founded by Aeneas, a foreigner, or Romulus, a native, what matters "in either case" is that Rome "had a free beginning [*principio*], without depending on anyone."[33] That is the source of the greatness and liberty of Rome, by specific contrast with Florence, whose dependent origins more or less doomed it to factional weakness.[34] Cities that "are by origin [*origine*] not free" are only rarely able to "make great progress," for they cannot "make other advances than the kindness of the sovereign allow[s]."[35]

If his real concern is free versus dependent origins, why does Machiavelli begin with the seemingly irrelevant distinction between native and foreign origins? Harvey Mansfield has argued that the purpose is to allow Machiavelli to discuss the principles by which to choose a site for the city and that the question of site, like the entire first chapter, really concerns "the scope and use of human choice."[36] In terms of this book's rather different concerns, that phrase suggests autonomy and dependence, or rather, dependence on an implicit nurturing mother versus reliance on an explicit Founder figure. The fortune of a city, Machiavelli says, is determined by the *virtù* of its Founder (*"colui che ne e stato principio"*). His *virtù* is "known in two ways: the first is the choice of its site, the second the establishment of its laws."[37] The laws must deal with the problems of greed, ambition, and entropy that do the work of fortune; the choice of site concerns nurturance.

Machiavelli contrasts "fertile" and "barren [*sterili*]" sites. A "barren" site is a nonnurturing mother like necessity, forcing men into early autonomy if they are to survive at all and thus fostering their *virtù*. "Forced to keep at work and less possessed by laziness," men would "live more united" on a barren site, having less "cause for dissensions" than on a fertile one.[38] But a "barren" site cannot supply the resources a city needs for its growth; it might suffice if men were "content" to live

33. *Discourses* 1: 1 (G 195); Machiavelli, *Opere* 1: 129.
34. *Discourses* 1: 49 (G 296).
35. Ibid., 1: 1 (G 193). See also 1: 49 (G 295–96); Machiavelli, *Opere*, 1: 126.
36. Harvey C. Mansfield, Jr., "Necessity in the Beginnings of Cities," in Parel, *Political Calculus*, 112, 115–116. See also Harvey C. Mansfield, Jr., *Machiavelli's New Modes and Orders* (Ithaca: Cornell University Press, 1979), 28–32.
37. *Discourses* 1: 1 (G 193); Machiavelli, *Opere* 1: 126.
38. Ibid.

on what is their own (*del loro*) "and were not inclined to try to govern [*comandare*] others," in other words, if they were like animals or infants satisfied with what nature offers.[39] But men being as they are, they "cannot make themselves safe except with power," and power requires the greater resources offered by a fertile site. A fertile site, however, tends to make "men lazy and unfit for all vigorous [*virtuoso*] activity." Fortunately, the enervating power of fertility can be overcome by an artificial substitute for natural barrenness: discipline. The founder must "arrange that the laws force upon" the citizenry "those necessities" that would otherwise be imposed by a barren site. This is where Machiavelli tells the story of Alexandria; he introduces that story and sums up the discussion of site with the sentence: "I say, then, that it is the more prudent choice to build in a fertile spot, when by laws that fertility is kept within proper limits."[40] Allan Gilbert explains in a footnote that Machiavelli obviously must have meant that the *influence* of that fertility must be kept within proper limits, which is clearly right logically (since laws cannot affect the fertility of the soil, and Machiavelli does not mean to limit this source of strength) but may be wrong psychologically. Fertility offers nurturance, and the fertile site is an active, dangerous power requiring restraint. The Founder must assure the future citizens' *virtù* by mastering the maternal danger, first by choosing—and to that extent, controlling—the site that will become the citizens' "naturally" beloved native land, but even more importantly (since in fact he should choose the more rather than the less dangerous site), by imposing laws that make masculinely safe the citizens' continued access to nurturant fertility.

Machiavelli then distinguishes between those cities to which, "either at their beginning or not long afterward, laws have been given by a single man and at once, like those that were given by Lycurgus to Sparta," and cities that get their laws "by chance and at several times."[41] Somewhat surprisingly, Rome turns out to belong to the latter category. Machiavelli then presents an account, largely borrowed from Polybius, of the origin of governments among men, and of the cycles through which they pass, from monarchy to tyranny to aristocracy, and so on, ending with praise of a "mixed" government like that of Rome, which "partakes of all" the good forms and is thus "more solid and more stable."[42] He concludes that although Rome did not have a Lycurgus at the outset, her laws were perfected by "chance [*caso*]" as a result of the healthy political

---

39. Ibid. (G 194); Machiavelli, *Opere* 1: 127.   40. Ibid.
41. *Discourses* 1: 2 (G 196).   42. Ibid. (G 199).

"discord between the people and the Senate." Thus "if Rome did not gain the first fortune, she gained the second."[43]

This leads into a discussion of the development of Roman liberty in terms of healthy political conflict, by contrast with the factional strife characteristic of Florence. Articulating the Citizen image of manhood, this series of chapters culminates, after the theme of Florentine factionalism is struck, with the introduction of the Founder image for organizing or renovating a republic. This brings Machiavelli to Numa Pompilius, who was chosen as Romulus's successor and founded Roman religion, for which, Machiavelli says, Rome was even more "under obligation" to him than to Romulus.[44]

Not until Book 3, when he turns to individual deeds of greatness that benefited Rome and to the theme of renovation, does Machiavelli mention the second birth connected with Roman development, the overthrow of the Tarquin monarchy and the establishment of the republic by "Brutus, the father of Roman liberty."[45]

Now, Livy, Machiavelli's source, construes the story of Brutus in familial metaphors as a crisis of adolescence rather than of gender. In its childhood, he suggests, Rome needed parental restraint, but having matured under that control and become ready for liberty, it needed someone to overthrow the monarchy that had become corrupt as Rome matured. All of the earlier Roman monarchs down to Tarquin the Proud, Livy says, were good for Rome and "contributed to the city's growth." They "were all, in their way, successive 'founders' of Rome." Moreover, it was essential for the kingship to have lasted as long as it did, or Rome would not have survived to maturity. It is worth quoting Livy's observations on Brutus's act of liberation at some length:

It cannot be doubted that Brutus, who made for himself so great a name by the expulsion of Tarquin, would have done his country the greatest disservice, had he yielded too soon to his passion for liberty and forced the abdication of any of the previous kings. One has but to think of what the population was like in those early days—a rabble of vagrants, mostly runaways and refugees—and to ask what would have happened if they had suddenly found themselves protected from all authority by inviolable sanctuary, and enjoying complete freedom of action, if not full political rights. In such circumstances, unrestrained by the power of the throne, they would, no doubt, have set sail on the stormy sea of democratic politics, swayed by the gusts of popular eloquence and quarrelling for power with the governing class of a city which did not even belong to them, before any real sense of community had had time to grow. That sense—the only

43. Ibid. (G 200–201); Machiavelli, *Opere* 1: 134.
44. *Discourses* 1: 11 (G 223–24).
45. Ibid., 3: 1 (G 423).

true patriotism—comes slowly and springs from the heart: it is founded upon respect for the family and love of the soil. Premature 'liberty' of this kind would have been a disaster: we should have been torn to pieces by petty squabbles before we had ever reached political maturity, which as things were, was made possible by the long quiet years under monarchical government; for it was that government which, as it were, nursed our strength and enabled us ultimately to produce sound fruit from liberty, as only a politically adult nation can.[46]

No profound analysis is required to detect the family metaphor in this passage: authority is prerequisite to freedom, in politics as in family life. Small children need the "restraint" that their parents provide, lest they be "torn to pieces" by the violence of their own "passion." There is nothing mechanical or automatic about the achievement of "maturity"; it must be "nursed" and given "time to grow." If the child "expels" its parents "too soon" and achieves "premature liberty," the result will be "disaster." On the other hand, while the period of immaturity lasts, Rome is not yet adult or at liberty; only by Brutus's act does it become "a free nation . . . subject not to the caprice of individual men, but to the overriding authority of law."[47] Brutus, moreover, is clearly given mythic status to represent Rome itself in this passage. The opening sentence suggests that he has lived through all, or at least many, of the earlier monarchical reigns, always lusting after liberty but continually restraining his impulse; the "population" of Rome has changed, but Brutus was always there, waiting.

In Livy's telling, the tale is generational: Brutus liberates himself and Rome from the no longer needed parental control. His story is Oedipal, and Livy's family clearly contains two parents of opposite sexes, one imposing restraint and the other "nurs[ing] strength" so that "love of the soil" will eventually enable the community to "produce sound fruit." No comparable passages concerning Brutus can be found in Machiavelli. He does echo Livy's judgment that Brutus acted at just the right time, but for the reason that if the rebellion had been delayed Rome would have "become weak and without energy," for the "corruption" of her kings would soon have "extended through the members" of the body politic.[48] Though a father is explicitly mentioned, and a generational struggle between males suggested, no mothers are in evidence. And while Livy relates at length the story of Lucretia, whose rape by the King's son and subsequent suicide were the occasion for Brutus's launching of the republican revolution, Machiavelli has little to say

---

46. Livy, *Early History*, 89; Livius, *History* 2.1.1–7.
47. Ibid.
48. *Discourses* 1: 17 (G 238).

about Lucretia, and what he says is ambiguous. Though citing her as one example of "how a state falls because of women," he also maintains that Tarquin the Proud was overthrown not because "his son raped Lucretia, but because he broke the laws of the kingdom and governed tyrannically."[49]

Should one conclude that for Machiavelli, unlike Livy, familial images are not relevant to the story of Brutus and the establishment of republican liberty? Or that they are relevant in a different way, the mother having, as it were, been pushed into the background by the initial founding? Certainly Tarquin the Proud seems to exemplify what Machiavelli said more generally, following Polybius, about the decline of monarchy into tyranny and its subsequent overthrow: that "the heirs quickly degenerated from their ancestors" and fell into "lavishness . . . lust and . . . every other sort of licentiousness."[50] Lucretia—prepared to kill herself to uphold patriarchal honor even though she is innocent of any crime—seems the very essence of tamed, domesticated femininity. Yet her rape indicates the incipient breakdown of the masculine discipline that domesticated her. If the fathers can no longer control the sons, the feminine power will once more break out to fragment the civic order, pitting citizens against each other over women, wealth, or status. It is time for a renewal of masculine discipline if *virtù* is to be preserved. Thus Brutus, the rebel against patriarchal authority, is also in a deeper sense an agent of masculinity. In killing the Tarquin "father," and later his own sons, Brutus preserves the order of the forefathers—not, however, as a patriarchy, but as a fraternity in the *vivere libero*.

What seems to interest Machiavelli most about Brutus is neither the rape of Lucretia nor the overthrow of the king, but two personal accomplishments that make him specifically relevant to Machiavelli's own experience: his foxy success in hiding his rebellious intentions until he was ready to act and his ruthless willingness to kill his own sons in order to preserve the new republic. The former might be read as a possible justification for Machiavelli's own prudent inaction and even willingness to serve the Medici; the latter—which Machiavelli exaggerates far beyond the implications of the story as Livy tells it—contrasts with Soderini's fatal weakness in the face of antirepublican opposition. Brutus seems a successful example of a fox who turned into a Founder or at least renovator, an apparent fox who was after all able to father free men, who could master fortune by adapting his way of proceeding to changing

49. Ibid., 3: 26 (G 489); 3: 5 (G 427).
50. Ibid., 1: 2 (G 197).

times. In Brutus, fox and Founder are joined, so that he holds out the promise of wholeness: the possible reunion of the various fragments or rival images of manhood. And the historical Brutus did found the republic.

Yet because he is a Founder, Brutus's capacity for political paternity, for protecting his political sons against the feminine, is measured by his ruthless readiness to slay his biological sons, in dramatic contrast to the weakness of Tarquin and Soderini. Although Machiavelli does not share the gratuitous and dissociated bloodthirstiness of some earlier Florentine humanists and condemns rather than praises parricide, he surely does dwell on filicide as a criterion of greatness. Children are—as we still say—hostages to fortune. Nurturant kindness toward them puts a man into her power. Thus a certain Biagio del Melano—no great Founder, yet cited as exemplary in his courage—trapped with his children in a burning fortress, threw them down to the enemy as a sign that he would never surrender, saying: "Take for yourself these goods that Fortune has given me and that you can take from me; those of the spirit, where my fame and honor lie, I shall not give to you nor will you take them from me." [51] Machiavelli calls it "a deed truly worthy of the antiquity so much praised."

Biagio, however, actually was saving his children's lives by his action. Brutus saved his political "sons" by killing his biological ones. In a way, therefore, the most gratuitously ruthless example of child murder for political purposes in Machiavelli's texts is accomplished by a woman, Caterina Sforza, a true Renaissance *virago*. It, too, seems to fascinate Machiavelli; he tells it twice and refers to it a third time. The enemies of Caterina's husband had killed him and captured her together with her six children. As they besieged a fortress of hers, she persuaded them to let her go inside and tell the castellan to surrender, leaving her children outside as hostages. But once inside, Caterina refused to surrender. Challenging her enemies from the castle wall to do their worst, she bared "her genital members" to them, shouting that she "still had the means for producing more children." [52]

This incident really happened; Machiavelli did not invent it. Indeed, it may have held special significance for him precisely because he had later encountered Caterina personally as a diplomat and been dramatically outfoxed by her. His first diplomatic mission was to her court, and

51. *Florentine Histories* 4: 12 (G 1199).

52. *Discourses* 3: 6 (G 444). See also *Prince*, ch. 20 (G 80); *Florentine Histories* 8: 34 (G 1430); "First Decennale," lines 241–43 (G 1450); *Art of War*, bk. 7 (G 706).

she made a fool of him in the negotiations, finally dismissing him while she nursed her ailing youngest child.[53] A woman with enough *virtù* to sacrifice her own children, it seems, gains a fierce and fascinating power, for she inverts the conventional female role of nurturance and makes manifest what fearful men have always suspected lies hidden beneath it.[54] To protect his children against such vengeful "maternal" power, a man would have to be strong enough to match its strength; filicide is the criterion.

This is surely not the only meaning of paternal filicide for Machiavelli. In the background, one suspects, there also lie the various biblical tales of paternal sacrifice of sons as a measure of higher love, from the story of Abraham and Isaac, which underwent a great revival of interest in the Renaissance, being featured, for example, in the famous 1402 bas relief in Florence by Ghiberti; to the story of Christ himself, God's "only begotten son," given to mankind to be crucified because "God so loved the world." A father's willingness to sacrifice his son indicates an extraordinary measure of faith or love.

Politically, the paternal killing of sons also seems to involve a shift from the private and familial projection of self into the future through offspring, to the impersonal, public, "fathering" of citizen-sons. Thus Machiavelli praises Titus Manlius, later called Torquatus, who put to death his own son for disobeying an order, "because his way [was]

---

53. Caterina Sforza was six years older than Machiavelli and famous for her beauty and courage. She was an illegitimate child, legitimized at the age of eight. But in that same year her father was assassinated. She outlived three husbands; two of them were assassinated and the third died of natural causes. Each time she managed to save herself, her children, and her estates and to take terrible revenge against the assassins and their relatives. Once, when she was twenty-five and her husband lay ill at Imola, word came that their palace master at Forli had murdered the governor and seized the castle. The Countess rode all night to Forli, managed to regain the castle, immediately rode back to Imola with the palace master as her prisoner, and the next morning gave birth to a child. The incident cited in the text occurred the following year. Once, when accused of complicity in the assassination of one of her husbands, the Countess responded that, thank the Lord, neither she nor any other Sforza had ever found it necessary to hire assassins when they wanted someone dead. She was also a student of medicine and magic. The French named an artillery piece after her. Her firstborn son became a *condottiero* and was hired by Florence as a mercenary. When his contract came up for renewal, the young Machiavelli, in his second year of public service, was sent to negotiate the matter. But he was no match for her. It is not clear from sources I have seen whether, in dismissing Machiavelli, she was literally suckling, or merely tending to, her sick child. That child must surely have been her youngest son, later known as Giovanni delle Bande Nere, in whom the aging Machiavelli placed his last hopes of rallying the forces of Italy against the north European invaders (letter to Guicciardini, 15 March 1525–[1526] [G 994–95]). Caterina Sforza was defeated by Cesare Borgia a few years after making a fool of Machiavelli, which may have been another reason for the latter's inordinate admiration for Borgia, discussed in the next chapter. On Caterina Sforza, see Hare, *Most Illustrious Ladies*, 229–56; Ridolfi, *Life*, 26–27; Roeder, *Man*, 137–47; Villari, *Life*, 235–39.

54. *Discourses*, 1: 9 (G 218).

wholly for the benefit of the state and [did] not in any respect regard private ambition."[55] Castruccio, too, is made to give up personal procreation for a higher masculine loyalty. And, most strikingly, Machiavelli praises Romulus for killing his brother in order "to advance not his own interests but the general good, not his own posterity but the common fatherland," even though Romulus's "own posterity" does not seem at stake in the matter.[56]

One can see, then, how in various ways Machiavelli might regard the capacity for killing one's own sons as a measure of greatness, autonomy, and public spirit. Yet one cannot help asking: who would himself want to have such a father? Terrible indeed must be the needs and fears that would produce such an image of paternity, make such a father seem desirable. And it would be surprising if a man could seek such a father without ambivalence. The "choice" between a strong but murderous father and one who is gentle but weak is a recurrent theme in Machiavelli's work. Again and again, one might say, he is driven to conjure up his own murderer as the only hope for his protection.

There are images of kind and caring fathers in Machiavelli's works, and he himself seems to have been such a parent. One of the passages in *Clizia* that is Machiavelli's own creation, without counterpart in the ancient play from which *Clizia* is drawn, describes the "good" bourgeois father: he starts his day by going to mass; he serves as the representative of his household toward the outside world, for instance going out to buy "provisions for the day"; he spends his day usefully at business or public life, doing "his accounts" in "his office at home," conducting "business in the public square, in the market, with the magistrates," or joining with other "citizens in serious conversation." He is "serious, steadfast, and cautious." At the end of his day, he dines "pleasantly with his family" and afterwards devotes himself to his son, advising and teaching him "to understand men, and by means of various examples, ancient and modern . . . how to live." Not least of these examples is the father himself, the fine "ordering" of whose life is admired by all the household so that they all would be "ashamed not to imitate [him]."[57] Now, obviously, one cannot assume that everything a Machiavellian character says in a play represents the author's ideals—the father's going to mass, for instance, is suspect—but much of what the passage says about fathering is echoed in Machiavelli's thought about the tasks of authority: a "serious, steadfast" concern for the welfare of those in

---

55. On her *virtù, Art of War*, bk. 7 (G 706).
56. *Discourses*, 3: 34 (G 506); 3: 22 (G 482).
57. *Clizia*, act 2, sc. 4 (G 835–36).

one's charge, the responsibility for initiating them into the world of men, the presentation of a worthy example for emulation.

These appear to have been Machiavelli's own goals as a father as well. Familial references in Machiavelli's correspondences are scarce, but one of his most frequent complaints about his exclusion from office is that it renders him useless to his family, unable to provide for his children's future.[58] He writes frequent letters, full of care and concern, to his nephew, a merchant in the Levant, whom he regards almost as his own child, admonishing him to "keep healthy and do your duty."[59] To his own son, Guido, he writes urging that he "work hard and learn letters and music," which would "give pleasure to me and bring prosperity and honor to yourself." Offering himself as a model, Machiavelli writes, "If God grants life to you and to me, I believe that I can make you a man of standing, if you wish to play your part as you should."[60]

Though admonitory and perhaps by modern standards a little pompous, these images of fathering nowhere suggest violence or intimidation. Yet Machiavelli is uneasy about whether such gentle paternity is sufficiently strong to provide protection. Caring for children and political greatness are "an almost impossible combination."[61] Not only did political failure leave Machiavelli helpless to protect his own children, but as "father" to the Florentine militia, he may well have felt some responsibility for the deaths of some four thousand militiamen at Prato.

But above all at stake in the question of gentle, weak fathers was Machiavelli's attitude toward Soderini, whether to "condemn" that law-abiding and naive leader whose overthrow brought disaster to Florence and to Machiavelli himself. As already mentioned, in discussing Brutus's willingness to kill his sons, Machiavelli invokes the contrast with Soderini, who "believed that with patience and goodness he could overcome the longing of Brutus's sons to get back [into power] under another government."[62] One also recalls Machiavelli's first letter to Soderini in exile, linking his situation to the dilemma of fierceness versus kindness in leaders and the question of whether men can change their characteristic ways of proceeding to master fortune. Although the letter begins by assuring that Machiavelli understands the "compass" by which Soderini is navigating, "and if it could be condemned, which it

58. Letters to Vettori, 10 June 1514 (G 945); to Vernacci, 19 November 1515 (G 964); to Vernacci, 25 January 1517–[1518] (G 969).

59. Letters to Vernacci, 26 June 1513 (G 913–15); to Vernacci, 20 April 1514 (G 944); to Vernacci, 8 June 1517 (G 965); to Vernacci, 5 January 1517–[1518] (G 968).

60. Letter to Guido Machiavelli, 2 April 1527 (G 1006).

61. *Florentine Histories* 8: 36 (G 1434).

62. *Discourses* 3: 3 (G 425).

cannot, I would not condemn it," it continues somewhat illogically that *"consequently"* Machiavelli himself sees

not with your mirror, where nothing is seen but prudence, but with that of the many, which is obliged in political affairs to judge the result when they are finished, and not the management when they are going on.[63]

Yet Soderini's failure to abandon prudence, become ruthless, master fortune, and save the republic cannot be condemned because it was only human. Men "cannot command their natures" and that is why fortune continues to hold them under her "yoke."[64]

Years later, when Soderini was living in Rome, Machiavelli hesitated to visit that city because he felt he could not do so without visiting Soderini, yet such a visit would surely damage his chances for employment with the Medici.[65] As Felix Gilbert has pointed out, "Machiavelli had to be reminded" by his friend Vettori that his feelings of obligation to Soderini were somehow excessive, that Machiavelli had after all been elected to office years before Soderini became *gonfaloniere*.[66]

There was ample reason in Machiavelli's own political experience for his distrust of weak fathers, and for ambivalence in that distrust. But these experiences do not account for his image of strong authority, for the fact that often the only alternative he can envisage to weakness is murderous—specifically filicidal—repression. Machiavelli's own suppressed rage at Soderini, one suspects, feeds the murderous fierceness of the Founder. But whatever his own psychology, the missing link in the texts is once more the feminine threat: like Soderini, the weak father fails to protect not only the "good" sons from the "bad" but also the whole masculine enterprise from enfeebling and divisive feminine power. To rescue the sons from the matriarch's clutches a father must be a match for her; the real test of his adequacy to the task is whether he, too, is a killer of sons. That terrible paradox emerges most clearly, however, in the childhood of Florence, rather than in that of Rome.

63. Letter to Soderini, January 1512–[1513] (G 895).
64. Ibid. (G 897).
65. Letter to Vettori, 10 December 1513 (G 930).
66. F. Gilbert, *Machiavelli and Guicciardini*, 172–73.

CHAPTER TEN

Family Origins: Florence and the "Return to Beginnings"

The story of Florence's birth and growth is different from that of Rome's, for Florence had neither a great Founder like Romulus (or Aeneas) nor a great liberator like Brutus. Florence is also less mythical than Rome, therefore less admirable and more problematic, but also more strongly tied to reality and to self. If Rome means the (fore)fathers, Florence means "we, ourselves." Accordingly, it is in the story of Florence that the struggle among Machiavelli's political realism, his mutualist vision of republican liberty, and his misogynist authoritarianism becomes most intense. For the lesson of Florence seems to be that republican liberty can arise only under the protection of a father murderous toward his sons (who thus destroys it); can be renewed only by imitating such a father (and thus by self-destruction); can survive domestic factionalism only by authoritarian discipline (which destroys it); and can withstand international attack only by expansionist militarism (which again destroys it). All roads are blocked. Yet Machiavelli refuses to accept that conclusion, for a viable *vivere civile* has sometimes been achieved; he will not give up on self, Florence, reality, freedom.

The problems begin with Florence's birth, for the city's historical origins were already both controversial and symbolically significant long before Machiavelli's time. An early foundation myth pictured Florence as originating with the soldiers of Julius Caesar, as part of the Roman Empire and thus of the universal empire, reflecting the hierarchical order of God's universe. As Hans Baron and J. G. A. Pocock have pointed out, that myth was revised in the beginning of the fifteenth century, in the patriotic republican fervor accompanying Florence's struggle against the duke of Milan.[1] Humanists like Salutati and Bruni attributed the founding of Florence to the Roman Republic instead of the empire. Although Caesar had earlier been considered admirable because an emperor, and his assassin Brutus accordingly a traitor, in this republican period Brutus was glorified and Caesar condemned as a tyrant. In a later work, Bruni "was disposed to look even further back, to consider Florence affiliated to the Etruscan city republics which had flourished before Roman domination of the peninsula."[2]

Machiavelli's account of Florentine origins begins in Etruscan times, yet he ascribes the city's founding to Rome; he gives a number of different versions. In his *Florentine Histories*, the story begins with the Etruscan city of Fiesole, located on a hill for security, but having its market below in the plain beside the Arno River for convenience of transport. After the Roman conquest of Carthage "had made Italy secure," this market became a permanent settlement, called Villa Arnina.[3] Then the Romans sent colonists to Fiesole, and at least some of these settled near Villa Arnina; their settlement came to be called Florence (*Firenze*). Thus the question of who founded Florence depends as much on what counts as the beginning of this "composite body" as on when these various events took place. In the *Florentine Histories* Machiavelli says that the city "had her origin [*principio*] from Fiesole and her growth from [Roman] colonies."[4] The security that allowed Villa Arnina to grow on the unprotected plain was provided by the Roman Republic; the first colonies were sent by Sulla, others after Caesar's death. But then Machiavelli sums up: "Whatever the cause of her origin [*origine*], she began under the Roman Empire."[5] In the *Discourses* he says that Florence was "built either by the soldiers of Sulla or perhaps by the inhabitants of the mountains of Fiesole, who, trusting in the long peace that began in the world under Octavian, came to live in the plain by the Arno" but that in any case it "was built under the Roman Empire."[6] And, as already noted, he classifies Florence as one of those cities that "are by origin not free" and therefore "rarely . . . make great progress."[7] Having from the outset "always lived under the control of oth-

---

1. Pocock, *Machiavellian Moment*, 52; Baron, *Crisis*. See also Harvey C. Mansfield, Jr., "Party and Sect in Machiavelli's *Florentine Histories*," in Fleischer, *Machiavelli*, 245n; David Weinstein, "The Myth of Florence," in *Florentine Studies: Politics and Society in Renaissance Florence*, ed. by Nicolai Rubinstein (Evanston, Ill.: Northwestern University Press, 1968), 15–44.
2. Pocock, *Machiavellian Moment*, 52.
3. *Florentine Histories* 2: 1 (G 1081).   4. Ibid.; Machiavelli, *Opere* 7: 138.
5. *Florentine Histories* 2: 2 (G 1082); Machiavelli, *Opere* 7: 140.
6. *Discourses* 1: 1 (G 193).   7. Ibid.

ers," Florence never took effective responsibility for its own life. The city remained "humble [*abietta* (abject)], without planning for herself." Thus the political difficulties that continually beset Florence were ultimately the fault of her founders: "Difficulties like hers have always existed for all those cities whose beginnings were like hers."[8]

So, while locating Florence's origins in Etruscan Fiesole, Machiavelli also says that it was founded by Rome and, as a colony, had dependent origins. While sometimes suggesting the late Roman Republic as a parent, he says explicitly that the empire founded Florence. Evidently there are symbolic and political issues at stake that go beyond questions of historical fact. The identification of one's origin and ancestors is part of a self-definition, of who "I" am or "we" are. In any case, Machiavelli clearly thinks that Florence's parental "protection" came at a high price, leaving the city severely damaged and unfit for autonomy.

But Machiavelli also offers an alternative version of the story, in which Florence is otherwise identified, the stress is placed on the city's Etruscan origins in Fiesole, and the relationship with Rome is very differently presented. For Fiesole was one among a number of self-governing cities in Tuscany that Rome destroyed. Before the coming of the Romans, Machiavelli says in Book 2 of the *Discourses*, Tuscany was "powerful," "religious," and "vigorous [*piena di virtù*]."[9] Tuscany had "her own customs and her native language," and her cities "were all free" and "lived with . . . equality."[10] They formed themselves into an egalitarian alliance in which no city had preference "in authority or in rank" over the others. Together they "had great power on sea and on land," so that from the Tiber to the Alps "men submitted to their arms."[11] Thus the cities of ancient Tuscany, including Fiesole, achieved the "utmost glory of authority and of arms, and . . . highest reputation in manners and religion."[12] But "all this achievement" was eventually "wiped out by the Roman power," or rather, it was "first decreased by the French [*Franciosi* (the Gauls)], then destroyed by the Romans."[13]

If Florence originated in Fiesole of Tuscan ancestry, then it had a "free" origin and must itself take responsibility for its political failures. Yet its early achievement and autonomy were wiped out by superior military force. Indeed, what gave the Romans the most difficulty in conquering Tuscany was "the love that in those times" the self-governing

8. Ibid., 1: 49 (G 296); Machiavelli, *Opere* 1: 242.
9. *Discourses* 2: 5 (G 341); Machiavelli; *Opere* 1: 294.
10. *Discourses* 2: 5 (G 341); 2: 2 (G 328); 2: 4 (G 336).
11. Ibid., 2: 4 (G 335–36).   12. Ibid. (G 339).
13. Ibid., 2: 5 (G 341); 2: 4 (G 339); Machiavelli, *Discourses*, ed. Crick, 288; Machiavelli, *Opere* 1: 291.

Tuscans "had for their freedom, which they defended so stubbornly that never except by the utmost vigor [*virtù*] could they be subjugated."[14] Evidently Roman *virtù* was able to overcome Tuscan *virtù*; and, as already observed, the long-term result was that Roman conquests steadily reduced the quantity of manliness in the entire Mediterranean world.[15]

One might suppose, then, that being a Florentine patriot and a republican lover of liberty, Machiavelli would hate the ancient Romans. Instead he admires them inordinately. Here one comes close to the troubled heart of Machiavelli's complex thought, where politics meets gender: his tendency to choose for the rescue of the self and what it cherishes devices likely to destroy them. Indeed, that sometimes seems his very criterion for rescue: only that which destroys "us" is capable of saving "us," because only it will be a match for the ultimate threat, the feminine force.

Why does Machiavelli counsel his fellow Florentines to imitate ancient Rome, rather than ancient, free, self-governing, virtuous Tuscany? Leo Strauss says that it is because not enough information was available on the ancient Tuscans, the historical records having been—as Machiavelli points out—almost totally destroyed, so that "no choice" was "left to Machiavelli except to return to ancient Rome."[16] As to this, the origins of the self may be lost in the same antiquity as (and together with) the first nurturing matrix, and inaccessible for the same reasons. But this is unlikely to be the whole answer, since, as Strauss himself notes, one finds throughout Machiavelli's thought a significant "tension between his Roman patriotism and his Tuscan patriotism," perhaps equivalent to the "tension between his Italian patriotism and his Florentine patriotism."[17]

There is one passage where Machiavelli does recommend the imitation of ancient Tuscany instead of Rome; and its context allows exploration of the issues at stake. In Book 2 of the *Discourses*, he compares three ways of organizing the foreign relations of a self-governing republic: the Roman, that of ancient Athens and Sparta, and that of the Tuscan cities. The Romans made alliances in which they always reserved to themselves "the seat of authority and the reputation of command."[18] As a result, their allies soon "found that without realizing it they had subjected themselves with their own labors and their own

14. *Discourses* 2: 2 (G 328); Machiavelli, *Opere* 1: 279.
15. *Art of War*, bk. 2 (G 622–23); *Discourses* 3: 43 (G 522).
16. *Discourses* 2: 5 (G 341); Strauss, *Thoughts*, 93. Also, of course, there was no Livy who dealt with ancient Tuscany.
17. Strauss, *Thoughts*, 80–81.
18. *Discourses* 2: 4 (G 337).

blood." Athens and Sparta simply conquered their neighbors outright, turning them into subjects rather than allies. The ancient Tuscan cities formed an egalitarian alliance, carrying over into their foreign relations the mutuality and reciprocity that characterized their republican domestic politics.

This three-way comparison, however, must be read against the background of a dichotomous contrast earlier in the *Discourses*, between the Roman and the Spartan way in foreign affairs (though in that earlier contrast Sparta is linked with Venice rather than Athens). The earlier contrast concerns the choice between a state that remains fortified in its own territory and one that expands. The theme of the contrast is that a relatively small and self-contained state can enjoy "the true good government [*vivere politico* (political life)] and the true calm of a city," but only if there is tranquility in foreign affairs.[19] For such a republic, expansion is a "poison," because the state is too weak to hold what it might seize. "Conquests based on a weak state are its total ruin."[20] Thus states like Sparta and Venice are drained rather than strengthened by military victory abroad, because they try to hold more and more territory with their own, unaugmented forces.[21] Rome, by contrast, invited or forced the people of conquered neighboring cities to move to Rome, and thus strengthened itself. As in nature, Machiavelli says, a "slender stem" cannot "bear up a large limb," so a weak republic that expands is like a tree with "a branch larger than its trunk, which . . . is broken down by the least wind."[22]

Thus a self-contained free republic could survive only if it were content to be relatively small, to remain within its boundaries "without ambition," and if it were secured against foreign invasion, for instance by having a location that is "naturally strong and so fortified that no one will believe he can quickly conquer" it.[23] The republics of Germany "by these methods are living free and have so lived for some time," but only because of "special conditions," mainly the symbolic figure of "the Emperor, who, though he does not have forces, yet has such reputation among them" that as a mediator he "quickly gets rid of all strife."[24] One cannot count on such circumstances to last, "since all human affairs are in motion and cannot remain fixed."[25] Consequently it is after all "es-

19. Ibid., 1: 6 (G 210); Machiavelli, *Opere* 1: 145.
20. *Discourses*, 1: 6 (G 210).   21. Ibid., 2: 19 (G 380).
22. Ibid., 2: 3 (G 335). See also 2: 30 (G 411) where the "trunk" turns out to be the citizen militia.
23. Ibid., 1: 6 (G 210).
24. Ibid., 2: 19 (G 379).   25. Ibid., 1: 6 (G 210).

sential" to organize republics on the Roman model lest they become "effeminate"; states should choose "the most honorable courses" and organize "in such a way that if necessity causes them to grow, they can keep what they have taken."[26]

In this bipolar discussion, then, the choice is between the "honorable" and expansionist Roman way and the "effeminate" and weak way of Sparta and Venice. "I believe it is impossible to balance these affairs," Machiavelli says, "or to keep exactly [to the] middle way."[27] Florence, furthermore, is explicitly classed with Venice as having pursued the wrong policy and been weakened by its conquests.

In the later discussion, however, there is a viable third alternative: the ancient Tuscan way, which is (at least in one interpretation) the proto-Florentine way. The method of Sparta and Athens, who conquered their neighbors outright, is dismissed as "totally ineffective." But while Machiavelli again finally chooses the Roman way of unequal alliances, here the Tuscan alternative of an egalitarian league is recognized as a contender with genuine merits. It allows for only limited expansion, but it does have two advantages: "first, you do not easily draw wars down on yourself; second, all you take, you keep easily."[28] When a league of free cities like that of the ancient Tuscans reaches sufficient strength for its members' defense, "it does not strive for more dominion, both because necessity does not force it to gain more power and because it sees no profit in conquests."[29] The Tuscan method, then, is one requiring self-limitation; it cannot produce an empire such as Rome achieved, but it can provide secure self-government for communities that value their own freedom above the glory of conquest.

In this context, although he asserts that "clearly" because of its possibilities for unlimited growth, "the right method is that of the Romans," Machiavelli immediately adds that "if the imitation of the Romans seems difficult, that of the ancient Tuscans ought not to appear so, especially to the present Tuscans."[30] The Tuscan method, one recalls, did secure "the utmost glory of authority and of arms" for the Etruscan cities until they were conquered by Rome. To class oneself as a "modern Tuscan" rather than a son of ancient Rome, then, is in a way to accept second best, and yet it seems a genuine alternative with distinct advantages. It means accepting limitation and risk, abandoning the hope for total security; it means accepting mutuality, abandoning the ambition for unique glory. Yet it may be within our reach, as we now are. It im-

26. Ibid. (G 211).   27. Ibid.   28. Ibid., 2: 4 (G 337).
29. Ibid. (G 338).   30. Ibid., 2: 5 (G 339).

plies a certain judicious acceptance of the self and its limited, merely human reality.

Florence itself is an imperial power, and Machiavelli is aware that Florence does to other cities what Rome once did to it, though he thinks Florence does it ineffectively. On this topic his ambivalence between cruelty and kindness is extraordinarily intense, as he views the world now from the perspective of the victim, now from that of the imperial power. Sometimes he says that the best policy for an imperial city is to keep its subject cities happy; but it turns out that "best policy" means the one most effective for domination. At other times he advocates ruthless repression of subject cities but argues that this is actually kinder to them in the long run. Thus he sometimes says that Pistoia accepts Florentine rule "willingly" because toward that city "the Florentines have always conducted themselves like brothers" rather than "enemies," and if they had done the same toward their other subject cities they would have "tamed" them and would now "be lords of Tuscany."[31] At other times he says that Florence "allowed the ruin" of Pistoia by fearing to be called cruel, by contrast with Cesare Borgia, whose "well-known cruelty . . . reorganized the Romagna, united it, brought it to peace and loyalty."[32] And sometimes what seems to be crucial, as in the meditations on cruelty and kindness, prudence and boldness, is that the imperial power be able to change with the times and act decisively, now to repress and now to reward its subject cities. Rome, unlike Florence, "never used indecisive measures."[33]

When he advocates repressive cruelty, Machiavelli invokes generational metaphors, not merely calling subject cities that rebel "wicked" and saying that they "sin," but comparing them to "parricides." Paternal "honor consists in being able and knowing how to punish" such rebellious sons, because there is "no other remedy than to destroy them."[34]

The issue here is not so much whether Machiavelli "really" favors repression or kindness or decisive changeability as imperial policy, but rather the image of politics that he presents. The subject cities are like children, to be treated kindly when they are good because that is the most effective method of control, or cruelly punished for their own good when they disobey, because only such repression can control their parricidal passions. Yet at the same time, imperial policy really aims at

31. Ibid., 2: 21 (G 385). See also 2: 23 (G 389); 2: 25 (G 399); *Florentine Histories* 2: 38 (G 1133); 7: 25–26 (G 1368–71); "Tercets on Ambition," line 124 (G 738).

32. *Prince*, ch. 17 (G 61). See also *Discourses* 3: 27 (G 490); also G 1441.

33. *Discourses* 2: 23 (G 389; see also 391).

34. Ibid. (G 390).

the welfare of the imperial city; if its subjects are children, they have a cruel and selfish parent, nor are they ever intended to reach adulthood. What the alternatives do not include here is any genuine mutuality or reciprocity among peers. Politics here concerns domination, who rules whom, and "government is nothing other than holding your subjects in such a way that they cannot harm you or that they do not wish to."[35] The only significant question is how to dominate rather than be dominated.

But perhaps these really are the only alternatives in international relations? Perhaps among states there can only be victims and victimizers, so that the only effective defense is aggression? Perhaps the only hope for the survival of a free republic practicing a politics of mutuality and limits at home, is exploitive expansion abroad? Sometimes Machiavelli says so:

It is impossible for a republic to succeed in standing still and enjoying its liberties in its narrow confines, because if she does not molest some other, she will be molested, and from being molested rises the wish and the necessity for expansion.[36]

This is a zero-sum world, one can gain security only as others lose it.

The desire for defending its liberty [makes] each party try to become strong enough to tyrannize over the other. For the law of these matters is that when men try to escape fear, they make others fear, and the injury they push away from themselves they lay on others, as if it were necessary either to harm or to be harmed.[37]

Yet Machiavelli does say "as if" in that last clause, and he uses the subjunctive. He cannot fully accept the pessimistic implications of such a view. Perhaps victim and victimizer may not be the only two alternatives after all? Not only does that choice run counter to Machiavelli's central teachings about politics within the city, but the repressive vision is inadequate even in international relations. He knows the costs of war, "repulsive, horrible, and unnatural," leaving the "earth wet with tears and blood, and the air full of screams, of sobs, and sighs."[38] He knows that Florentine imperialism does to that city's neighbors what Rome once did to Florence, destroying their liberty and their *virtù*.[39] And he knows that in the end this means a decline in overall *virtù* and the cor-

35. Ibid. (G 389).
36. Ibid., 2: 19 (G 379). See also Letter to Vettori, 10 August 1513 (G 919).
37. *Discourses* 1: 46 (G 290); Machiavelli, *Opere* 1: 235–36.
38. "Tercets on Ambition," lines 153, 157–59 (G 738).
39. *Discourses* 3: 12 (G 460); 2: 21 (G 385); *Florentine Histories* 2: 38 (G 1133).

ruption of the imperial power itself. Having destroyed the *virtù* of others, Rome "could not maintain her own."[40]

Thus from time to time the third alternative, limited in its expansionist ambitions and in the security it offers, seems the most desirable choice. Many a "man has complained about" the smallness of his territory, Machiavelli says in "The [Golden] Ass," and proceeded to expand it by conquest, only to find "after the fact" that he has done so "to his own ruin and damage."[41] This was precisely Florentine experience: having "extended her power to the lands round about and become great and vast," now she finds herself weaker than before; instead of feeling secure, she now "dreads everything."[42] The German cities, by contrast, "live secure through having less than six miles [of territory] round about."[43] In the same vein, Castruccio, for all his militaristic *virtù*, on his deathbed tells his adopted son that he would have preferred to leave the boy "a smaller state" with "fewer enemies and less envy . . . without doubt more secure and more solid."[44]

Occasionally, then, Machiavelli does take seriously the possibility that the "we" of Florence is Tuscan rather than Roman. Even after the Roman founding or conquest of the city, when Florence "freed herself from the Empire," if only she had adopted the right form of government, Machiavelli says, "I do not know what republic, modern or ancient, would have been superior to her."[45] Florence was one among those "new states born [*nacquono*] among the Roman ruins" that "showed such great ability [*virtù*]" and "were so united and so well organized that they freed Italy and defended her from the barbarians."[46] Was this, then, the real birth of Florence? And did it involve any parents? And again, why does Machiavelli not invite his fellow citizens back to this, apparently adequate, Tuscan *virtù*? Even in his own time, he will occasionally concede, the Florentines show such "courage," "organization," and "equality" as would support the "*vivere civile*"; indeed, Florence is "a subject very suitable for taking this form."[47] Yet the republic fell, Florence is corrupt and weak, and seems unable to save itself. It must find sponsorship in a greater than merely human manliness.

40. *Art of War*, bk. 2 (G 623); Machiavelli, *Opere*, 2: 394.
41. "[Golden] Ass," ch. 5, lines 56–57 (G 762).
42. Ibid., lines 67–69 (G 763). See also *Discourses* 1: 53 (G 305).
43. "[Golden] Ass," ch. 5, lines 61–63 (G 762).
44. "Life of Castruccio" (G 553).
45. *Florentine Histories*, preface (G 1032).
46. Ibid., 5: 1 (G 1233); Machiavelli, *Opere* 7: 326.
47. *Discourses* 1: 55 (G 309); "Discourse on Remodelling" (G 107). See also Machiavelli, *Opere* 1: 257.

Roman republican *virtù* defeated Florentine republican *virtù*; that proves the superiority of the former and suggests that Florence must learn from its conqueror if it is to become autonomous. Yet both logically and psychologically this is dangerous terrain, inviting "identification with the oppressor"—that paradoxical last-ditch effort of the defeated and demeaned to save a remnant of self by joining their destroyers.

Sometimes Machiavelli seems to hold up Rome as a standard and sponsor not just in spite of but because of its ruthless destruction of Florentine liberty and *virtù*. His treatment of Rome and Tuscany in this regard recalls the dilemmas of foxiness: the danger of losing the self among its many masks and of identifying too much with those enemies whose thoughts one is trying to penetrate. Machiavelli's attraction to Cesare Borgia, enemy of Florence and diplomatic outfoxer of Machiavelli himself has been mentioned, together with the remarkable copy of a Borgia letter in Machiavelli's handwriting, signed with a painstaking imitation of Borgia's signature. Similarly, Machiavelli selected as his fictional hero and patriarchal spokesman in the *Art of War* a mercenary papal captain who had served both the French and the Spanish in Italy. He chose as the hero of a laudatory fictionalized biography a general who defeated Florentine troops in battle; indeed, Machiavelli's account dwells on a fictionalized version of that battle.[48] When praising the Romans, by contrast with the Florentines, for giving "the generals of their armies plenary power," he illustrates with the example of Fabius, who on his own and without authorization defeated Tuscany.[49] And more generally, as Strauss has pointed out, Machiavelli has a penchant for praising the leaders of states that ravaged Italy, such as the Spanish king, Ferdinand the Catholic, and the French king, Louis, even giving them advice on how they might have enhanced their conquests.[50]

Although it makes sense to learn from those who succeeded where you failed, sometimes including your enemies, that policy also entails the danger of coming to side against yourself and the values you wanted to defend. It is not easy to draw the line here between effectiveness and masochism. But at the point where—to paraphrase the notorious remark by an American officer in Vietnam—one "is forced to destroy" the self "in order to save it," clearly something has gone wrong.

---

48. "Life of Castruccio" (G 548–51); G 564; *Florentine Histories* 1: 26 (G 1065).
49. *Discourses* 2: 33 (G 417–18).
50. Strauss, *Thoughts*, 323–24.

❖   ❖   ❖

Though the birth of Florence, like that of other cities, seems to have
been an entirely masculine accomplishment, and though Florence also
lacked a Founder such as those who built Rome or Sparta, still it might
be said to conduct its struggle for autonomy in relation to two parents
of opposite sexes. Harvey Mansfield has pointed out that "the origins of
Florence must be seen in the decaying empire and the growing Church
that give it protection."[51] He speaks of these as the "ancient" and the
"modern" Rome and notes that Machiavelli blames them both for Florentine dependence: "Florence began as a colony of ancient Rome and
now continues as a colony of modern Rome."[52] In the terms of this
study, the former being the very essence of fatherhood, the latter might
be considered the role of dangerous, infantilizing mother.

But there are difficulties about identifying the Church as such a malevolent matriarch. For one thing, Machiavelli never personifies the
Church explicitly. It is true that generally when the Church was personified in medieval as well as Renaissance thought, it was presented as
feminine.[53] And while the figures directing the Church were of course
male, in Machiavelli's Florence the mother was often the stronger religious influence in the home. For Machiavelli, religions, like cities,
are man-made "composite bodies"; and as with cities, this leaves the
Church's gender in doubt. Should it be classed as a "daughter," like
Rome, or another masculine enterprise furthering civilization? Or is it
different from cities?

Machiavelli himself suggests at one point that, like cities, the Church
may have had masculine vigor at the outset but degenerated into effeminate corruption; it is the fault, he says, of the "worthlessness [viltà
(cowardice, meanness)]" of certain men who made a "false interpretation" of Christianity, "according to sloth and not according to vigor
[virtù]."[54] The "foundations" of the Church were obviously very different from its "present habit."[55] Only the powerful renovating influence of Saints Francis and Dominic, bringing Christianity "back toward
its beginnings," has counteracted the "improbity of the prelates and the
heads of our religion" from utterly ruining it and causing the Church to
"disappear."[56]

51. Mansfield, "Party," in Fleischer, Machiavelli, 239.
52. Ibid., 238. Machiavelli calls the Church "Roman" in the Discourses (1: 12 [G 226,
228]).
53. Cf. above, chapter 8, note 9.
54. Discourses 2: 2 (G 331); Machiavelli, Opere 1: 283.
55. Discourses 1: 12 (G 228).
56. Ibid., 3: 1 (G 422).

In its present condition, at any rate, the Church seems to be a feminine force at least in this sense: it emasculates men and ruins states in the same ways women do. For one thing, it purveys hypocrisies and fairy tales about human conduct that Florentine mothers also try to instill in their children: that virtue means not glory but humility, that the meek shall inherit the earth, that one must keep one's word, forgive one's enemies, and so on. Whoever tries to live by such teachings will remain incapable of autonomy and—as Soderini's example shows— will endanger the autonomy of anyone associated with him. The many naive believers are exploited by the few corrupt hypocrites; the Church has made the world "prey" for "wicked men."[57] It is in revulsion against such hypocritical teachings, no doubt, that Machiavelli would wish Florence to have a preacher who knows the road to hell.[58]

Not only is the Church a purveyor of childish naiveté and, at least in its upper ranks, hypocritical, but it also saps men's vigor by teaching "that without effort on your part God fights for you, while you are idle and on your knees."[59] The Church teaches "humility, abjectness, and contempt for human things, and its ceremonies are mild," by contrast with the "blood and ferocity" that filled the ceremonies of ancient pagan religion, which honored "worldly glory" and human things. Through such teachings the Church "has ruined many kingdoms and many states"; it has made men "weak" and "effeminate," with the result that there are "fewer republics than in ancient times" and men "do not have such great love for freedom as then."[60]

Indeed, the Church seems the polar opposite of martial *virtù*, undermining men's ability to defend themselves by "their own arms." Since weapons are "unsuitable to . . . an ecclesiastic," Churchmen are, like women, forced in time of danger to "summon a powerful man to defend" them; and they induce the same unmilitary and unmanly dependence in others.[61] Thus the foundling Castruccio, adopted by a priest and his widowed sister and destined by them for the Church, preserved his *virtù* only by rejecting these adoptive parents as soon as he dared. At fourteen, as soon as he "began to get a little courage in respect to [the priest] and not to fear [the sister] at all," he apprenticed himself to a general, nominating him to be his "true" father.[62]

---

57. Ibid., 2: 2 (G 331).
58. Letter to Guicciardini, 17 May 1521 (G 971–72).
59. "[Golden] Ass," ch. 5, lines 115–16 (G 764).
60. *Discourses* 2: 2 (G 331).
61. *Florentine Histories* 1: 39 (G 1078); *Discourses* 1: 12 (G 228).
62. "Life of Castruccio" (G 535; cf. 553).

Finally, the Church therefore threatens the integrity of the body politic, just as women do, both fragmenting it internally and introducing
alien, poisonous forces. Like fortune, it uses men's ambition and other
drives to pit them against each other, to keep states "divided"; and,
being like women, forced to rely on the arms of others, it summons into
the state "outside help—which is one of the chief starting-points for imminent slavery."[63] The Church thus displays that paradoxical quality
which femininity generally represents to Machiavelli: a despicable weakness that turns into an insidious, overwhelming strength, a strength that
can destroy but cannot create autonomy. "Not powerful enough to take
possession" openly, it nevertheless succeeds in keeping any region
where it is active from uniting "under one head."[64]

Against this apparently feminine and certainly effeminizing power,
Machiavelli, being himself weak, deploys his foxy skills to expose
Christian hypocrisies; but he also summons up the protective fathers of
ancient Rome. Against the power of Church teachings he invokes the
authority of Roman patriarchy, in the same manner as, in the words of
Robert Denoon Cumming, the Renaissance more generally "secured
some of the confidence it needed for the enterprise of being a renaissance" from the ancient thought it resurrected, for example, from the
"ancient cyclical theories of history (such as Polybius')," which enabled
it to "make a clean break away from the Middle Ages, by dropping
them into the trough of the cycle that had intervened since Antiquity."[65]
By translating, imitating, commenting on and adapting ancient writers,
Machiavelli not only deploys their authority against Church teachings,
but also allies himself with them. Thus he hopes to share their prestige
in the eyes of others, and himself gains reassurance about the correctness of his own views. Clearly he both learns from and manipulates
Livy's history, sometimes uncritically adopting Livian presuppositions,
occasionally explicitly challenging Livy, and sometimes altering Livy's
teachings for his own purposes without acknowledging that he does so.
Even more clearly, Livy and other ancient historians make possible Machiavelli's contact with what is for him the greatest ancient authority:
that of ancient political actors, for whom he puts on his "garments regal
and courtly" and with whom he is "not ashamed to speak about the
reasons for their actions."[66]

63. *Discourses* 1: 12 (G 228); 3: 26 (G 489). See also 1: 12 (G 228–29); *Florentine Histories* 1: 9 (G 1046); *Prince*, ch. 12 (G 50).
64. *Discourses* 1: 12 (G 229).
65. Robert Denoon Cumming, *Human Nature and History*, 2 vols. (Chicago: University of Chicago Press, 1969), 1: 101. See also Strauss, *Thoughts*, 108, 141, 144; Cassirer, *Individual*, 99.
66. Letter to Vettori, 10 December 1513 (G 929).

But the ancients are not merely an intellectual authority, or counter-authority, for Machiavelli; they also serve as exemplars of a more manly way of life. Their military discipline, specifically their successful use of a citizen militia, their capacity to sustain vigorous political conflict that does not degenerate into factional strife, their fierce religion oriented toward worldly glory, and above all, their *virtù* are to serve as models for modern men's emulation. In short, Machiavelli resurrects the Roman fathers to free his weak contemporaries from the clutches of the mother Church, and to make men of them.

Yet paternal ancient Rome, as he also shows, was murderous toward its offsprings' *virtù*. Nevertheless—or rather, precisely for this reason—Machiavelli regards it as capable of rescuing modern men. The tensions of that by now familiar paradox are revealed once again in his extraordinary vacillation in allocating blame between the ancient and the modern Rome for the lamentable condition of modern men, Italy, and Florence.

At first he blames the weakness of modern men and the fragmentation of Italy on "the Church alone."[67] In *The Prince* he says that "as soon as" the Pope got temporal power in Italy, the region became "divided" and began its disastrous reliance on mercenary soldiers.[68] In *The Discourses*, similarly, his first claim is that "the Church . . . is the cause" of Italian debility, and "we Italians are indebted to the Church and not to any other" for "the great disunion and the great weakness" that have made the region prey to "whoever assails" it.[69] Later, pondering why modern Italians do not love freedom and fight for it as their ancestors did, he "concludes" that the "cause" is the same one that makes modern men less "hardy [*forti* (strong)]."[70] He "believes" that this cause "is the difference between our religion and the ancient."[71] Yet within two paragraphs he has changed his mind and blames ancient Rome instead: "Still I believe that the cause of this is rather that the Roman Empire with her arms and her greatness wiped out all the republics and all the self-governing communities."[72] There then follow two chapters about the Roman conquest of free Tuscany and about the relative advantages and costs of the Tuscan way of conducting international relations, by self-limitation and mutuality. Then comes a chapter about how conquerors try to destroy all memory of the conquered civilization, its main example being how "the Christian sect" wiped out almost all reminders of "the Pagan sect." But that example again leads Machiavelli to draw a

67. *Discourses* 1: 12 (G 228).   68. *Prince*, ch. 12 (G 50).
69. *Discourses* 1: 12 (G 229).
70. Ibid., 2: 2 (G 330–31); Machiavelli, *Opere* 1: 282.
71. *Discourses* 2: 2 (G 331).   72. Ibid. (G 332).

concluding parallel between that triumph of the Church and the ancient Roman destruction of Tuscan *virtù*.[73]

Evidently the issue of which Rome to blame is very troubling. Insofar as the Church is the enemy and is feminine, one might suggest, identification with the Roman forefathers holds out hope of rescue. If both parents must be acknowledged as equally threatening to the self and its autonomy, then no rescue can be expected and "we" must try to save "ourselves" by our own, merely human "hands and speech."[74] Insofar as the Church is to blame for the weakness of modern men, their rescue by resurrected forefathers is more likely to seem both necessary and possible. Insofar as those Roman forefathers are equally or more to blame, the self-help of Citizen mutuality is more likely to appear as the only hope. Perhaps that is why, also, the peer equality of the Citizen image tended to vanish on the topic of religion: the Church symbolizes overwhelming feminine power, and misogyny undermines (even as it also partly stimulates) the capacity for mutuality that underlies Citizen autonomy.

❖   ❖   ❖

Machiavelli does not deal in psychological categories; the concept of identification is one that we anachronistically bring to his work. He is, however, deeply concerned with a closely related category: imitation (*imitazione*). Most men, he says, "almost always walk in the paths beaten by others and carry on their affairs by imitation," and imitation of the right models is his remedy for modern weakness and corruption.[75] Yet he also assigns the greatest glory to innovation, and himself claims to be an innovator. Commentators have noted the apparent inconsistency but do not agree on its interpretation. I shall suggest that it arises from ambiguities in the concept of imitation itself, ambiguities that make it a particularly suitable mirror for reflecting, once more, Machiavelli's conflicting images of manhood. Two ambiguities, in particular, require attention here: that between the imitation of methods and of character, and the paradox involved in imitating innovation.

Sometimes when Machiavelli urges the imitation of the ancients, he seems to have in mind the acquisition of skills and techniques that leave the imitator's self essentially unchanged and simply add to his store of tools for effecting his preexisting purposes. "There cannot be great difficulty, if only your family will use the methods of those whom I have set

73. Ibid. 2: 5 (G 340–41).
74. "[Golden] Ass," ch. 4, line 130 (G 772).
75. *Prince*, ch. 6 (G 24).

up as your aim," he tells Lorenzo de'Medici in the concluding chapter of *The Prince*.[76] Such imitation of methods plays a role particularly in military affairs:

The prudent prince reads histories and observes in them the actions of excellent men, sees how they have conducted themselves in wars, observes the causes for their victories and defeats, in order to escape the latter and imitate the former.[77]

Similarly, in *The Art of War* Machiavelli, both in his dedication and through his chief spokesman, Fabrizio, expresses the desire "to bring military practice back to ancient methods" by "imitation."[78] This kind of imitation is the way of the fox: by detached observation one discerns which techniques work and can then pick and choose in terms of one's own purposes. One's own self, remaining essentially unchanged in the learning process, is never at risk, as a skillful diplomat can make limited identifications with the powerful enemies among whom he must move, discerning their goals and strategies without being deflected from his. Imitation is like the acquisition of goods; one can learn effective techniques as well from the evil as from the good and can pick from each model precisely those techniques that work well in a particular situation. Accordingly, the imitation of methods is associated with the hope (which Machiavelli repeatedly indulges and repeatedly rejects) of overcoming the power of fortune by being a chameleon—taking from the cruel Emperor Severus "those methods essential for founding" and from the kind Emperor Marcus "those suitable and splendid for preserving a government long established and firm."[79]

But there is also a different kind of imitation, appearing even in *The Prince* but central to *The Art of War* and especially the *Discourses*: the emulation of character rather than the acquisition of methods. Here one does not merely add techniques to one's repertoire but models oneself on a great man of the past, as Scipio "shaped himself" on the model of Cyrus "completely in chastity, affability, courtesy, and liberality."[80] In hoping to restore the *virtù* of ancient Rome, Machiavelli is seeking for a recovery not merely of specific military or political techniques but of a certain kind of human character, a way of life. For all its talk of methods, *The Art of War* is aimed at the restoration of citizens who "love one another," who "honor and reward excellence," who "live without

76. Ibid., ch. 26 (G 94).
77. Ibid., ch. 14 (G 56–57).
78. *Art of War*, preface (G 567); bk. 7 (G 722). See also *Art of War*, bk. 1 (G 572).
79. *Prince*, ch. 19 (G 76).
80. Ibid., ch. 14 (G 57).

factions," who "esteem private less than public good," and who do not "despise poverty."[81]

In such imitation the imitator's self is transformed: instead of merely acquiring tools, picking whatever seems to work, he yields his very self up to a chosen hero, for transformations that his present self cannot fully control or foresee. Indeed, such emulation need not be deliberately undertaken; it can befall us when we encounter some exemplary authority. Thus it is the means by which great Founders and renovators are able to induce *virtù* in others: "Their example is so powerful that good men wish to imitate them, and the wicked are ashamed to live a life contrary to theirs."[82]

Machiavelli's praise of imitation, in characteristic Renaissance fashion, is itself an imitation of ancient authors. But for ancient thinkers, imitation was always unambiguously a question of character rather than of technique. The political leader was to serve as a model of virtue because he was in the public eye, and the way to be such a model was by cultivating the true reality behind the public appearance. The "crucial rule" for achieving public glory "is to *really* be what is one's interest to *appear* to be to others."[83] Thus the ideal statesman

should be assigned almost no other role and duty besides this single one which includes all the others, of never relaxing his effort at self-improvement and self-examination, or urging others to imitate him, and of holding himself up—by means of the luminousness of his mind and life—as a mirror for his fellow-citizens.[84]

In the ancient Greek understanding, we are told, the public self was the real self; there was no gap between public appearance and reality, so that public life was a privilege, not a duty, and privacy a deprivation.[85] In the decline of the polis that was no longer the case, and the gap between appearance and reality in politics was as problematic to Thucydides as to Machiavelli. In Roman thought, although the self was never wholly equated with its public role, the stress being rather on dutiful self-sacrifice than on self-fulfillment in public life, still the performance of public duty was the way to achieve genuine virtue. By disciplining oneself and emulating earlier greatness, one might ultimately fuse with one's public role.

81. *Art of War*, bk. 1 (G 572).
82. *Discourses* 3: 1 (G 421).
83. Cumming, *Human Nature*, 2: 27, quoting Cicero, *De Officiis*, 2.43.
84. Ibid., 28.
85. Arendt, *Human Condition*, 24–27 and chs. 4 and 5 passim.

In Machiavelli's time all this has become much more problematic, as the gap widens between what is taught about virtue and what people actually do. Machiavelli sees his world as lacking greatness of character in the Roman—let alone the Greek—sense, and he is concerned not just to condemn that world but to transform it. Thus, insofar as he shares the ancient belief in emulation, he must look to ancient models; yet he cannot simply imitate the ancient doctrine, for living models of such greatness are not readily available.[86] Machiavelli both draws authoritative support from the ancients and revises their teachings for his own times. Thus he both is and is not imitating them, both is and is not teaching what—and as—they taught.

Although he advises the "prudent" man to imitate greatness, he reserves the ultimate "glory" for Founders—actors who initiate something unprecedented. And he himself claims to have entered "upon a path not yet trodden by anyone," despite the extraordinary risks always attending the introduction of "new institutions [ordini (orders)]" among men—risks that he compares to those of geographic exploration.[87] Others should imitate; Machiavelli himself will innovate like the truly great. And yet, is this not an imitation of ancient innovation?

It is not just that Machiavelli presents himself as an exception to the conduct of most men or the advice he gives prudent men. Rather, the concept of imitation itself is ambiguous when put to his purposes. Though imitation is an ancient doctrine imitated by Machiavelli, and though he says that "excellent men . . . in the past" modeled themselves on still earlier great men, the ultimate model at the end of the chain extending backward through time must of necessity be an innovator rather than an imitator, an unmoved mover. Modern men can achieve greatness by imitating the Romans, but what made at least the early Romans great is that they imitated no one. Without any prior model, without any sponsoring father, "by themselves they knew how to find means"; and their "method" was "so much the more wonderful in that before Rome there was no instance of it."[88] Their method thus grew out of their own character; one may try to imitate that method, or that character, but the advice to imitate their innovativeness is inherently

---

86. There may still have been *virtù* somewhere on earth, e.g., among the Turks, but it would hardly have done for Italian emulation; *Discourses* 2: preface (G 322).

87. *Discourses* 1: preface (G 190–91); *Prince*, ch. 6 (G 26); *Florentine Histories* 7: 24 (G 1368); Machiavelli, *Opere* 1: 124.

88. *Discourses* 2: 4 (G 339). The Florentines, by contrast, having destroyed the *virtù* of their nobility, followed the *ordini* and the fortune of others; *Florentine Histories* 1: 39 (G 1079); Machiavelli, *Opere* 7: 135.

paradoxical. What will count as "doing as the Romans did"? Insofar as their true greatness lay in innovating, one can imitate them only by not imitating anyone.

Indeed, Machiavelli emphasizes that men already imitate ancient greatness, but in the wrong things and in the wrong way. They imitate ancient art rather than ancient manliness, and they imitate style rather than substance. Imitating abjectly, they do not aim high enough and thus fail to make contact with the saving power of ancient *virtù*. They must be encouraged to

> act like prudent archers, who, seeing that the mark they plan to hit is too far away and knowing what space can be covered by the power [*virtù*] of their bows, take an aim much higher than their mark.[89]

In imitating the prudent archer, they will find the courage to aim high, to imitate greatness. For though the ancients "were exceptional and marvellous, nevertheless they were men."[90] That, Machiavelli says at the outset of both the *Discourses* and *The Art of War*, is why he writes: to give the men of his time real access to ancient *virtù*. They read and admire Livy, but they do not achieve a "true understanding" of what he relates, do not get from it "that profit for which they should seek acquaintance with books."[91] They do not succeed in bringing Livy into real connection with their own lives; they playact at being Romans, but the early Romans were not playacting.

Thus Machiavelli is constantly driven to two incompatible teachings about the forefathers: that they were very great indeed, almost superhuman, and that they were like "ourselves" and not beyond the reach of imitation. If the model is too close, too much like the present self, emulating it will bring no change. If it is too distant, imitation will seem impossible or will take the form only of playacting. Men have a choice about the model for their emulation, and it entails the choice of a future self, along with its appropriate "father." Are "we," for example, the offspring of the ancient Romans or of the ancient Tuscans? This choice, between Machiavelli's "Roman patriotism and his Tuscan patriotism," is indeed related, as Strauss suggests, to that "between his Italian patriotism and his Florentine patriotism," but in inverted order. As Rome was imperial conqueror to Tuscany, so Florence is to the cities around her, and potentially or in fantasy to all of Italy. The choice between Roman

---

89. *Prince*, ch. 6 (G 24–25); Machiavelli, *Opere* 1: 30. See also *Art of War*, preface (G 566–67); bk. 1 (G 570–72); *Discourses* 1: preface (G 190); 2: preface (G 324).

90. *Prince*, ch. 26 (G 94). See also *Discourses* 1: 11 (G 226); 1: 39 (G 278); 1: 58 (G 315).

91. *Discourses* 1: preface (G 191).

and Tuscan forefathers, implying a choice of future self, is importantly related to the issue of Florentine imperialism. If Florence regards its paternity as Tuscan and tries to become what the Tuscans were, it is not only liable to eventual conquest by some modern Rome but is in effect forced to recognize its kinship with the surrounding cities it might otherwise feel justified in exploiting. They are to Florence as the Tuscan proto-Florence once was to Rome—virtuous republican victims. To them, Florence is as Rome once was to proto-Florence: an exploitive conqueror spoiling "the sheepfolds of others." Choosing Tuscan ancestry, Florence would have to identify with its own victims; but Roman ancestry implies the conquest of proto-Florence, the end of its autonomy and *virtù*. Either choice of rescuing forefathers implies self-destruction.

So the two ambiguities in the concept of imitation converge in the problem of autonomy. The imitation of technique which seems, in foxy terms, to safeguard autonomy precludes that change in character and that real engagement with the world which might yield real autonomy. The latter, it seems requires precisely that transformation of self which the fox fears; it requires emulation of character. But the imitation of character as a means to autonomy is inherently paradoxical; it means copying those who copy no one. It implies both sameness and radical difference between model and imitator. Insofar as the stress falls on the sameness, on the model's merely human fallibility, the hope of rescue and radical transformation is lost. Insofar as the stress falls on difference, on the model's extraordinary greatness, imitation will seem impossible, will degenerate into playacting, will be a false piety disguising secret resentment, or will even imply identification with the oppressor and destruction of the self that he was to rescue. The imitation of radical difference cannot result in the mutuality that practical, human, political autonomy requires. So long as the point of imitation remains rescue, it blocks rather than serves autonomy.

What the imitation of heroes is for individuals, renovation or the "return to beginnings" is for cities and other institutions: a salutary contact with earlier generativity that simultaneously disciplines ambition, makes safe the acceptance of nurturance, replaces corruption with *virtù*, and restores autonomy. The topic is addressed most explicitly in the third book of the *Discourses*, which opens without a preface directly into the claim that religions and republics need often to be "brought back toward" their "beginnings [*principii*]," which is equivalent to being "born again [*rinascere*]."[92] Machiavelli calls such institutions "composite" or "mixed bodies [*corpi misti*]" having a "communal life," as distinct from "simple bodies" like those of animals or individual people.[93] All things "in the world" have only a limited existence that must come to an end. But those that succeed in moving "through the entire course ordained for them by Heaven" do so by not letting their "bodies" get "into confusion." They keep their bodies "in the way ordained" for them or allow only those changes that are "to their advantage."[94]

For composite bodies, in particular, those changes are advantageous that take "them back toward their beginnings," recovering thereby "some goodness" through which they had initially gained their "growth" and "reputation." In a way, this need for frequent revitalization in human institutions is the central theme of the whole of Book 3, which opens with the idea of composite bodies and both opens and closes on the analogy between political and medical health. Political corruption, Machiavelli says at the outset, is a "daily" accretion of poisonous matter "which necessarily kills the body" unless there is an intervening "cure," as the "doctors of medicine say."[95] And Book 3 closes with the reminder that keeping a republic free "requires new acts of foresight every day" as "cures" for "sicknesses that have to do with the government," such sicknesses as the matrons' conspiracy to "poison" Roman manhood, which was foiled by the Roman capacity for "terrible" punishment.[96] From the first chapter to the last, the returning of composite bodies to their beginnings is explicitly associated with masculinity and the recovery of *virtù*; the decline into corruption is associated with women, nature, and fortune.[97]

But how are these metaphors to be interpreted? Why is the return to "birth" a masculine affair, and what does Machiavelli really mean by the return to beginnings? With respect to states, one might at first suppose that he intends a return to their initial constitution or governmental form or legal structure. But that is not the case. On the contrary, although renewal may well require institutional change, the forms and laws that were suitable at a community's founding are unlikely to be suitable for its renewal out of corruption. The "order [*ordini*]" and the laws established at the "origin [*nasciamento*], when men were good, are

92. Ibid., 3: 1 (G 419); 1: 17 (G 240); Machiavelli, *Opere* 1: 179, 379.
93. *Discourses* 3: 1 (G 419); 2: 5 (G 341). Walker's translation—"composite"—seems better; Machiavelli, *Discourses*, ed. Crick, 385; Machiavelli, *Opere* 1: 379, 293.
94. *Discourses* 3: 1 (G 419).   95. Ibid.
96. Ibid., 3: 49 (G 527–28).
97. Ibid., 3: 1 (G 419); 3: 9 (G 453); Machiavelli, *Opere* 1: 380.

no longer applicable when they have become wicked."[98] This is most evident when the renewal takes the form of a liberation, as in Brutus's overthrow of the Tarquin monarchy and establishment of the republic. This paradigm of renovation meant precisely the alteration of a constitution to an unprecedented form.[99] Despite his borrowing of Polybius's cyclical theory of recurrent governmental forms, then, Machiavelli is not talking about a return to prior laws or institutions.

Besides the matter of institutions, Machiavelli has two other ways of talking about the return to beginnings: in terms of terror and of self-recognition. Both are tied to memory, the recovery of a forgotten past. Concerning terror, he says that unless something happens frequently "to bring the penalty" for crime back to men's "memories" and "renew fear in their minds," they will gradually but soon "take courage to attempt innovations and to speak evil."[100] So renovation requires frightening them back into obedience, "inspiring such terror and fear in the people" as the initial Founder inspired when he first "punished those who" did "wrong." Machiavelli mentions a number of punitive executions that performed this function in Rome.

Strauss suggests that in Machiavelli's conception of the return to beginnings, a still more fundamental threat and terror lie behind this fear of punishment:

Machiavelli's return to the beginning means return to the primeval or original terror which precedes every man-made terror . . . the terror inherent in man's situation, to man's essential unprotectedness.

Strauss means, I take it, that Machiavelli wants to make men doubt the existence of a benevolent God, perhaps even to replace God with the devil, or at any rate with the doctrine that all is permitted. Strauss continues, "The primacy of love must be replaced by the primacy of Terror if republics are to be established in accordance with nature and on the basis of the knowledge of nature."[101] But when Machiavelli speaks of man's essential unprotectedness, it is in contrast to the harmonious life of animals in symbiosis with mother nature, available to man only at the price of dependence and captivity in Circe's palace. That Machiavelli was hostile to Christianity, at least in the form it took in his time, is no secret. However, nature is not exactly the basis of his alternative, but another mythical feminine force threatening civilization. Nevertheless, Strauss's suggestion can be interpreted in gender terms as im-

98. *Discourses* 1: 18 (G 241); Machiavelli, *Opere* 1: 180.
99. Accordingly, Brutus closes the chapter (*Discourses* 1: 18 [G 243]).
100. Ibid., 3: 1 (G 421).
101. Strauss, *Thoughts*, 167.

plying that Machiavelli's return to the beginning means a return to the terrifying feminine power that preceded every other including that of the patriarchal Founder; that establishing the *vivere civile* requires a return to the nurturance involved in that earliest condition; yet that such a return can be rendered safe for men and for the *vivere civile* only under the most stringent safeguards of masculine discipline. But in that case, while the terror involved in the return to beginnings—both the original terror of unprotectedness and the saving terror of the murderous Founder's discipline—may be necessary, they are not in themselves sufficient for establishing the free civic life.

Terror, it has been argued, can only cow men into obedience, make of them dutiful soldiers who abstain from the fruit of the apple tree in their midst. If, however, autonomy depends on an active, fraternal citizenry, then the single, patriarchal enforcer is at best transitional, at worst a hindrance to its achievement. And if he is to serve as a transition, his terrifying power must be combined with inspiring virtue; he must serve as a model for emulation. But the emulation of innovation is problematic; the choice of forefathers is problematic; how patriarchal domination can ever produce republican fraternal autonomy is problematic.

Indeed, the entire *Discourses* might be considered an extended meditation on this logically, politically, and psychologically troublesome transition from the apparently necessary autocratic leader to the desired republican self-government, from paternity to fraternity. Book 1 might be said to contemplate patriarchal Rome and the great Founders like Moses and Romulus as ideals. Book 2 treats the relationship between Rome and ancient Tuscany, the Roman versus the proto-Florentine way, and thus begins to suggest that the patriarch might be a threat to "us" and "our" liberty. Book 3 begins with Brutus, who is of course a father, but the father of Roman liberty, and thus also a rebel against bad fathers. From Brutus, who knew how to "play the fool" until the time was right for action, Book 3 moves on to the topic of conspiracy and the overthrow of autocrats to establish liberty; and its announced overall topic is the role of leadership, of great men, in the maintenance of the *vivere civile*. Yet Brutus and other republican leaders merely continue the mystery of the transition, so long as they and their role are construed in patriarchal terms.

There may, however, be another way to think about the return to beginnings, and the role of terror and memory in that return—a way more compatible with *vivere civile* and the Citizen image of manhood. Perhaps one should construe the forgetfulness that gradually corrupts a composite body as reification: a coming to take for granted as "given" and inevitable what in fact is the product of human action. Thus people may come to consider their civic order beyond their choice or control and, therefore, beyond their responsibility, secure without any special effort on their part. Then each may feel free to poach on the public spirit—or the public-serving habits—of others, behaving as if someone else were in charge and losing touch with his own stake in public life. When the polity is "left to heirs," it soon reverts to *rovina* (ruin) for "heirs quickly degenerated from their ancestors."[102] Then what Strauss calls the "primeval or original terror which precedes every man-made terror" might be something like the existential fear inherent in recognizing the full extent of human responsibility, the fragility of human order and its dependence on our commitment. From that perspective, the return to origins would be a return not to the initial institutions but to the spirit of origins, the human capacity to originate. Or rather, since that capacity is never extinguished but only forgotten, a return to awareness of it, as it may be felt in a time of political crisis, in what Pocock has called "the Machiavellian moment."[103]

Machiavelli insists that the actual founding or renewal of a state must be the work of a single man of overwhelming *virtù*; Romulus and Brutus had to act alone. Yet he also acknowledges that Rome "did not gain the first fortune [but] gained the second," because not one but a series of great founders established the liberty of the Roman Republic: not just Romulus (or Aeneas) and Brutus, but Numa, as well as the various Tarquins prior to the Proud, as well as the political interaction of the Roman people and nobility.[104] "New necessities were always appearing," making it imperative "to devise new laws" if liberty was to be preserved; "every day" new acts of *virtù* were needed.[105] So the civic life requires "not merely two able rulers in succession but countless numbers to follow one another," and a republic is precisely the form of civic organization most likely to produce such a succession of able leaders.[106] Nor is leadership alone sufficient, for it must find support in popular *virtù*. Thus Brutus's conspiracy would have been of no effect if the people had been corrupt. As Strauss says, Machiavelli eventually reveals that "foundation is, as it were, continuous foundation" and is carried on jointly by many.[107]

102. *Discourses* 1: 10 (G 222); 1: 2 (G 197).
103. Pocock, *Machiavellian Moment*, vii–ix, 3, 52–55, 486, 503, 545–46, 551.
104. *Discourses* 1: 2 (G 200).
105. Ibid., 1: 49 (G 295, 297); 3: 49 (G 527).
106. Ibid., 1: 20 (G 246).
107. Strauss, *Thoughts*, 44.

Such passages suggest a way of understanding foundation, and hence also the renovating return to beginnings, that is more consonant with the Citizen image of manhood and the *vivere civile*. Here one would see republican citizens as themselves co-founders of the civic order in which they live, which they sustain and augment and pass on to future generations. Insofar as they are able to see themselves and each other in association accurately, they recognize that what now sustains their civic order is not some posthumous power of an original patriarchal Founder over them, but simply they themselves in their shared commitments and interactions. Instead of imagining a Founder as different in kind from themselves, the source of a sacred order with which they may not tamper, they realize that civic order was begun by human beings essentially like themselves, but that they nevertheless want to sustain (much of) it *as if* sacred, because of the values and benefits it secures. So they become co-founders of the order with each other, with the original founder(s), and with all the generations in between, taking responsibility for and exercising choice about the order in which they live and into which they initiate the next generation.

From this perspective, believing in the superhuman Founder and seeking to imitate him by dutiful obedience rather than by discovering one's own capacity to found are not merely failures to recognize the actual origins of one's community and its tradition, but also failures in self-knowledge. Such a line of thought is supported by Machiavelli's other way of talking about the return to beginnings, besides institutions and terror, namely as a recovery or recognition of self. Discussing the renovation of composite bodies, Machiavelli says that what is "necessary" for "men who live together in any organization" is that they frequently "examine themselves."[108] The Italian text is *si riconoschino*, which Sergio Bertelli glosses as *esaminino se stessi*; so the return to beginnings evidently is to be understood as a self-examination or self-recognition, perhaps even the mutual recognition of each other by citizens, or their presentation of themselves to each other for recognition (*riconoscere* [to recognize oneself; to declare oneself; to recognize or acknowledge each other as legitimate]). In the next sentence, Machiavelli speaks also of examining "the record [*conto*]" of the citizens.

Not only is the return to beginnings a recovery or renewed recognition of self, or a mutual recognition among citizens, but it is a return to initial "goodness" and "*virtù*." And while these do here imply vital en-

108. *Discourses* 3: 1 (G 420); Machiavelli, *Opere* 1: 381.

ergy, the source of "growth and reputation," they also imply something like genuine virtue. For the return to beginnings is explicitly a return to "religion and justice," as well as to public spirit. Moreover, renovation is a return to the *principio*. And *principio*, a word derived from the Latin *principium*, has the (to us) dual meaning found also in the Greek *arche*, of both the beginning or initial cause and the fundamental principle.[109]

Thus a republican interpretation of the return to beginnings as a de-reification and continuous mutual co-founding would not exactly imply the terror of confronting meaningless chaos. Goodness, justice, principle, and self are not chaos. Though the return to beginnings is, in a sense, an experience of such existential terror—the realization that only we human beings sustain civilization and order—at the same time it is also a recognition of our human capacity to sustain them. In the beginning lies not chaos, but human capacity: of parents to nurture, of children to mature, of human beings to repair (some of) what they damage, to create and sustain civilization. And if the discovery of this capacity in ourselves is a self-recognition, it is accompanied by a simultaneous discovery of our particular, historically shaped selves, and the particular, historically shaped way of life of our community. We are human selves, capable of choice and action, precisely insofar as we are part of a human culture which has, in our time and in us, a specific, determinate form that cannot be wished away but must be recognized if we are to act. Its recognition, our self-recognition as particular selves, empowers us as creative actors and thus empowers our self-recognition as human beings. For individuals as for human communities, this means a re-discovery of the preexisting but somehow obscured, distorted, or forgotten reality of self: its inescapable history together with its capacity for change.

No doubt, that capacity also entails the genuine possibility of destroying, wrecking, invoking chaos; but that is not what Machiavelli is recommending. The community, like the choosing self, already exists in its historical particularity. Both can be changed, and some changes will be an enhancement of self, a return to fundamental principles. Becoming aware that one has a choice about one's habits and commitments need not mean abandoning them but may equally well lead to their re-endorsement, to holding the same commitments in a new way. Unlike Hobbes, Machiavelli does not maintain that *any* order whatever is better than none because all are equally arbitrary and equally necessary;

109. *Discourses* 3: 1 (G 419–20); Walker, *Discourses*, 2: 148.

and unlike modern existentialists he knows that all choices are not possible at all times. Not just any change is a real possibility at any given time, for individuals or for a community, and not just any change will be a renewal of fundamental principle, of self. Thus, such an understanding of the return to origins would require initiative, but it would also require receptivity and respect, even piety, toward the true principles of the community, the true bases of the self, the true achievements of ancestors.

In what sense, then, is such a return to *principio* a rebirth? Given Machiavelli's time and place one must of course think here primarily of the Christian eschatological symbolism of redemption, the "rebirth" of the soul that is saved. Machiavelli must have been aware that he was invoking that symbolism, even as he turned it to his own—Strauss would say diabolical, but I have suggested secular, political—purposes. In the Christian understanding, the conversion experience both is and is not like a (second) birth, ambiguous as the Machiavellian return to beginnings is ambiguous. It is like a birth, first, because it is powerfully transforming; afterwards one is changed, as if a different person. Characteristically, further, it is experienced as a sudden and powerful transition, no merely incremental growth from the old into the new self; or rather, as in birth, there is a long preparatory period, a sudden and traumatic transition that marks the emergence of the new self, and then a continuing further growth and development of what has emerged. The Christian symbolism further suggests a return to the innocence of childhood, a release from accumulated guilt and resentment, a wiping clean of the slate. The reborn Christian, accordingly, will look to his unsaved contemporaries like a fool, a ninny, an infant; so different from theirs will be his standards and conduct. To be saved means to "become as little children." Yet what is born in this Christian rebirth is not in fact an infant, but a fully formed human self with a developed personality, a person capable of choice and responsible action, altogether free and yet—or rather, because—dependent on God.

What is "born" in the Machiavellian return to beginnings, too, is the integrated human self. The transition is not the one in which the infant's body emerges from the mother's and begins its separate metabolism, but that by which the dependent infant and child, more animal than human, produced and shaped by its circumstances rather than shaping them, becomes a person, a moral being capable of choosing, creating, action, responsibility. Of course this does not happen all at once. It is a gradual process of maturation, although it may be marked by one or several dramatic transitions: public ceremonies and rites of passage, pri-

vate experiences of existential freedom, or of religious or other conversion, dramatic moments of taking responsibility for oneself. The conceptual difference between infant-animal and adult-human, however, is
stark and may seem to demand a dramatic and perhaps inexplicable
chronological and logical transition. That transition can be symbolized
as a birth, the true beginning of a separate, unique, human self. Communities, too, may be thought of in such terms, as having a distinct and
perhaps traumatic founding, even though of course the people involved
existed before that moment, were to some extent already interrelated
and, at the minimum, sufficiently of one culture that they could commu-
nicate, and even though their real membership in a lasting community is
never a total merging, nor achieved at a single moment, but developed
and proved through history.

If this is indeed the sort of "birth" Machiavelli had in mind, one can
see why he might construe it as an entirely masculine affair. In his society, the transition from dependent childhood to responsible adulthood
and citizenship was made only by boys and mediated only by men; and
the household world of childhood was dominated almost exclusively
by women, who were also largely confined to it. Even in our society—
perhaps in any society with differentiated sex roles where childcare is a
female function—growing up tends to mean getting away from mother,
so that father is likely to seem its agent. Thus Thoreau, for example,
distinguished between the "mother tongue" suited to thoughtless prat-
tle and the "father tongue" which is "noble," "reserved and select," and
in which grown men express serious personal convictions.[110]

But though the plausibility of construing the rebirth into autonomy
as masculine is evident, so are its costs. Insofar as we remain caught up
in infantile fears and fantasies, experiencing mother as a mysterious
force instead of a person, we are all likely, first, to confuse autonomy
with masculinity, and, second, to imagine autonomy and what threatens
it in such overwhelming terms that it seems hopelessly out of reach. For
both reasons, we are likely to act in ways that undermine actual autonomy and to flee from fantasied feminine engulfment into actual patriarchal domination. And so the misogynist way of construing autonomy damages not merely the women it excludes but also the men it
is meant to liberate.

A metaphor of birth that denies the mother and the body is bound to

<hr>

110. The passage is meant to distinguish primarily between speech and writing, between oral and literary culture; but Thoreau blurs that distinction when he adds that "we
must be born again in order to *speak* [the father tongue.]" Henry David Thoreau, *Walden*
(Boston: Ticknor and Fields, 1854; reprint, New York: Harper, 1965), 75.

distort whatever it was meant to illuminate. The physical transitions by which cells become a new viable being and a child is born and the psychic transitions by which a dependent infant becomes a responsible adult are gradual, complex, and profoundly mysterious. The conceptual differences between objects and living beings, between the animal or infant shaped by causal forces and the human person who chooses, judges, and acts are stark. In construing the latter, logical distinctions in terms of the former, chronological processes, one fails to see that all the conceptual aspects remain simultaneously present in human adulthood. The second birth into autonomy must be both a transcendence and an outgrowth of the first; the responsible human self both a transcendence and an outgrowth of the animal self. To construe birth without females and without the body is to deny essential aspects of the self, and thus of what it means to be human.

PART V

Meditations on Machiavelli

CHAPTER ELEVEN

Action and Membership

As a political theorist, Machiavelli is difficult, contradictory, and in many respects unattractive: a misogynist, frequently militaristic and authoritarian, uncomplimentary about human nature. What nevertheless makes him worth taking seriously is that his works contain an understanding of politics, autonomy, and the human condition, which is profoundly right in ways that really matter. That understanding consists of a set of syntheses holding in tension seemingly incompatible truths along several dimensions. It is therefore difficult to articulate and to sustain, and Machiavelli does not always sustain it. But the understanding is there, and even when he loses the syntheses he is a better teacher than many a more consistent theorist, because he refuses to abandon for very long any of the aspects of the truth he sees. Thus he manages to be both political and realistic even while articulating a theoretical vision of human achievement.

This concluding pair of chapters, therefore, frequently refer to the ideas of a thinker called "Machiavelli at his best" and offer an account of how and why the historical Machiavelli diverged from those ideas. In the process, these chapters also make some suggestions about the relevance of those ideas for our time. For all these reasons, these concluding chapters are more speculative and personal, less grounded in evidence, than the rest of this book.

At his best, Machiavelli formulates an understanding of human autonomy that is activist without megalomania, insisting on our capacity and responsibility for choice and action, while nevertheless recognizing the real limits imposed by our historical situation. He understands the open-ended, risky quality of human interaction, which denies to politics the sort of control available in dealing with inanimate objects. Yet he insists that the risks are worth taking, are indeed the only way of securing what we most value. He also formulates an understanding of autonomy that is highly political. He assumes neither the solidarity postulated by organic theorists nor the atomistic, unrelated individuals postulated by social contract theorists. Instead, he focuses on the way in which citizens in political interaction continually recreate community out of multiplicity. He formulates an understanding of autonomy, finally, that is neither cynical nor hortatory, but realistic: tough-minded about political necessities and human weaknesses without being reductionist about our goals and potentialities. Justice, civility, and virtue are as real, in that understanding, as greed and envy, or as bread and air (though of course people often say "justice" when they are in fact speaking of mere interest or expediency).

Although he rarely cites Aristotle and probably had only contempt for the Thomistic Aristotelianism he is likely to have encountered, Machiavelli's best understanding of politics is importantly reminiscent of Aristotle's teaching that man is a political animal, meaning not that people are always found in a *polis*, but rather that, first, politics is an activity in which no other species engages and, second, engaging in it is necessary to the full realization of our potential as humans.[1] For Machiavelli as for Aristotle, this means that we are neither beasts nor gods, neither mere products of natural forces nor beings with unlimited power. We are capable of free agency, but always within the bounds of necessity. We are the products but also the makers of culture, law, and history. We develop our humanness only in the company of others, yet our sociability is never automatic but rather requires effort and care. Finally, for Machiavelli as for Aristotle, our political nature is a function of our unique capacity for judgment. The human being is the *polis* animal because it is the *logos* animal, capable of speaking, reasoning, distinguishing right from wrong, and thus of freely chosen action.

In terms of Machiavelli's conflicting images of manhood, the right understanding of human autonomy he offers is closest to the image of the fraternal Citizen. Yet it transcends the misogynist vision and manages to combine the commitment to republican, participatory politics with the fox's deflation of hypocritical and empty ideals, as well as the appreciation of authority, tradition, and generativity associated with the Founder image.

1. I do not mean to suggest that Machiavelli's and Aristotle's political thought run parallel in all important respects; obviously they do not.

This best, synthetic Machiavelli holds in tension apparently incompatible truths along at least three interrelated dimensions of what it means to be human, political, and autonomous; dimensions so fundamental to these topics that any political theory must address them, if not expressly, then by implication. Autonomy is problematic for creatures such as ourselves in relation to the past, in relation to our contemporaries, and in relation to nature, both around and within us. It is problematic in relation to the past because we are the creatures of history. Our present situation and our very selves are shaped by the past. What can freedom mean for such a creature? Call that the dimension of action. Our autonomy is problematic in relation to our contemporaries because harmony among us is not automatic, as among the insects. We are distinct individuals with often conflicting needs and desires, yet we are also products and shapers of shared societies. Call that the dimension of membership. Our autonomy is problematic in relation to nature because we are both rooted in the natural and capable of transcending it, because we have bodies that need food and shelter and are mortal, and psyches, minds, or spirits that render us capable of distinguishing and choosing right from wrong, good from evil, just from unjust. But what is the relationship between natural need or drive and standards of judgment, and what is the basis of those standards—convention, nature, or some transcendent source? Call this the dimension of judgment. A right understanding of autonomy requires synthesis along all of these dimensions, and that is what Machiavelli at his best has to offer.

Yet Machiavelli often loses the synthetic tension along one or another dimension and falls into that endless circling among incompatible alternatives which Hegel associated with "bad infinity."[2] And the psychological and familial themes he employs, though they partly support, ultimately tend to undermine, those syntheses. To be sure, those syntheses are problematic and unstable also because each of the dimensions involves fundamental philosophical problems built into the very structure of our conceptual system, perhaps of our human nature. The dimension of action involves the problem philosophers sometimes call the "freedom of the will"; the dimension of membership, that of "universals and particulars"; the dimension of judgment, the problem of "value relativism" or "'is' and 'ought.'" These are surely among the most formidable, difficult problems ever taken up by philosophers. And Machiavelli was no philosopher; he was not interested in resolving such

2. Georg Wilhelm Friedrich Hegel, *Wissenschaft der Logik*, 2 vols. (Nürnberg: J. L. Schrag, 1812–16; reprint, Frankfurt am Main: Suhrkamp, 1969), 1: 152–56, esp. 155.

problems nor particularly self-conscious about them. This is both a strength and a weakness. Precisely because he is not a philosopher, Machiavelli never leaves political reality for very long; but by the same token, he is also not fully aware of the conceptual or philosophical difficulties that complicate his theorizing.

The syntheses are problematic not only philosophically, however, but also politically. Machiavelli demanded of himself that his theorizing be relevant to the political realities of his time. Politically, the dimension of action requires that theory guide us about "what is to be done," help us to delineate here and now those things that we must accept as "given" from those that are open to change by our intervention. The dimension of membership requires, politically, that theory speak to power and plurality, that it not merely articulate abstract truths but make them relevant to an audience that has—or could generate—the power actually to do what the theory suggests must be done. And the dimension of judgment requires, politically, that justice and right be tied, if not to expedience, then at least to possibility; what is truly impossible cannot be politically right. The political realities of Machiavelli's situation, as was remarked at the outset, were extraordinarily troubled and intractable. The real difficulties facing Florence, and particularly Florentine republicanism, were just about overwhelming, seeming to defy even the best understanding that political theory might devise. In demanding of himself that his theory address those realities, Machiavelli was sometimes forced into utopian fantasies and enraged distortions—the very kinds of theorizing he rightly condemned in others.

But even when allowance has been made for the philosophical difficulties of the subject matter and the political difficulties of his situation, it nevertheless remains true that Machiavelli's best synthetic understanding is frequently further undermined by the personal and familial themes he himself invokes. The very metaphors and images he employs to convey his insights repeatedly distort or destroy those insights. Whether this is because of his own psychic needs and conflicts, or because of his effort to address the psychic vulnerabilities of his audience, must remain ultimately undecided. What matters is to understand the connections between political and psychological considerations in the texts.

❖   ❖   ❖

Mankind is the species that makes itself, not just biologically as every species perpetuates its kind, but culturally, through history. Human beings are born less completely developed toward adulthood than any other creature. Thus their development is shaped more by the particular circumstances into which they are born; and those circumstances are less purely natural, more cultural and social than those of any other species. Using our capacity for language and abstract thought, and our opposed thumbs and ability to make tools, we produce a material and nonmaterial culture that forms the environment in which the next generations of humans grow up. Thus to be human is to be the product of a particular society and culture, which is the product of past history. Yet to be human is also to have a share in making history, transmitting, preserving, and altering culture, shaping society. It is we who enact the forces that shape us. As Hobbes said, man is both the "matter" and the "artificer" of "commonwealth," of community and civilization.[3]

Those facts pose a mystery, or rather, whole clusters of mysteries: philosophical, political, psychological. How can a product of causal forces also be a free agent capable of action, creativity, responsibility—to be praised and blamed for its choices and deeds? What does it mean to say that this person *did that*, is responsible for it, could have done otherwise? On what basis do we make such judgments? Every action has antecedents and every person a past, so is an action really different from an event, a person from an object? What will count as initiating something new rather than just continuing preexisting processes? Do these distinctions mark something objectively real in the world, or are they merely conceptual conventions that we impose arbitrarily and, in the end, inconsistently? These are among the questions with which social and ethical philosophers must deal.

But the political theorist is not merely, or not exactly, a philosopher. Philosophy investigates those aspects of the human condition that could not be otherwise and that are so basic we are ordinarily not even aware of them. But politics concerns matters that might well be other than they are; it concerns the question "what shall we do?" Insofar as it directs itself toward matters that cannot be changed, it is misguided and will fail. Politics is the art of the possible. To theorize about politics, then, is not exactly like philosophizing about the human condition or the nature of being. Political theory does teach us about fundamental necessities, not merely those that are given to all humans in all ages but also those that are merely inescapable for *us*, here and now; but it does so with reference to, and in order to distinguish them from, those other matters that are subject to our choice and power, with regard to which we might successfully act. Thus the political theorist is concerned not

3. Hobbes, *Leviathan*, 19.

merely with the philosophical problem of whether humans can ever break the causal chain of history to make a new beginning, but even more with the political problem of how and where and with whom we might take action, given our present circumstances. He delineates, one might say, "what has to be accepted as given" from "what is to be done."

But this delineation is not really as simple as the drawing of a line between unchanging regions. For the political world is composed of human activities and relationships and habits, all of which are anchored in human thought. Change people's understandings of themselves and their political world, and they will change their conduct, and thereby that world. The political theorist is thus always a teacher as much as an observer or contemplator, and to the extent that his teaching succeeds, his subject matter will alter. So the distinguishing of necessities from possibilities is less like the drawing of a line than like a *Gestalt* switch: a reconceptualization of familiar details so that realities we feel we have always known suddenly become visible for the first time, familiar things suddenly take on a new aspect.

We live our ordinary lives in the particular and the concrete, largely unaware of our remote connections to people we never see, the long-range and large-scale consequences for others of what we do, for us of what they do. On the whole, we know how to use the resources at hand for the immediate tasks we face, how to do what we must daily do. But the factual particulars among which we live can be organized and interpreted by many different theoretical schemas. That is why, as Machiavelli says, "the people" may be deceived "in judging things in general," but they "are not so deceived" about "particular," "specific things," "things individually known."[4] It is not so much that we do not see the forest for the trees, as that more than one theoretical forest is compatible with the many trees among which we live. The political theorist, one might say, invites us to a new organizing schema for making sense of our concrete reality. If we accept the invitation, our familiar world will seem changed, and as a result we shall live differently in it. Yet whether we accept the new schema will depend on whether it makes sense of what we already know, makes meaningful what was before confused, chaotic, or intractable.

Obviously this will depend both on the truth of a theorist's vision and on his power as a teacher. Nothing is harder than to get people really to *see* what has always been before their eyes, particularly since such a changed vision will have implications for action (which may make un-

4. *Discourses* 1: 47 (G 291–93).

comfortable demands on them) and interest (which may make it offensive to those who now hold privilege and power). Thus the political theorist faces a special problem of communication: in order to be understood, he must speak in terms familiar to his audience, from within a conceptual framework and an understanding of the world that they share. Yet he wants not to convey new information to them, but rather to change the terms, the conceptual framework through which they presently organize their information. It may seem an impossible task; and political theorizing accordingly has its dangers, from ridicule to martyrdom. Yet sometimes it does happen that people are ready for a new understanding, when the old explanations no longer make sense, the old rules no longer guide, the old procedures no longer produce satisfactory results, the old ceremonies no longer sanctify. Then a new vision—the right new theoretical vision—may "take" among a large audience and even produce basic political change.

Every political theory must expressly or by implication take its stand on these matters, since every theorist has both something to say and some reason for saying it. He wants to convey to an audience some truths, some matters he hopes people will recognize as "given," so that about other matters they will subsequently act differently than they now do. Even the most radical or relativistic theorist thus teaches respect toward something, and even the most conservative or pessimistic hopes by his teaching to produce some change.

❖ ❖ ❖

The idea of fortune in the largest sense—not just the personification of fortune as woman, but that figure together with her various (partial) equivalents, such as nature and opportunity, and their male counterplayers, such as *virtù*, the Founder, and the *vivere civile*—this whole configuration of ideas is Machiavelli's particular response to these perennial problems of political theory. Fortune in this largest sense is his way of relating man the "maker" to man the "matter" of "commonwealth," of relating action to necessity and initiative to tradition. It is his way of addressing an audience in terms they will understand about a changed understanding of their political world that would—if they accepted it—bring them to change their conduct, and thereby their world. What are the consequences of this particular way, Machiavelli's way, of doing it?

Machiavelli presents a political universe that is neither a fixed, sacred order nor a meaningless accident. We face neither eternally valid abstract standards of right that it is our duty to try to approximate, nor inevitable forces moving to predestined goals, nor yet a randomness that defies understanding and effort. Coping with necessity is neither a worshipful seeking nor a scientific predicting. Nor is it a throw of the dice. Instead, it is like dealing with a person—a difficult, unpredictable, even sometimes malevolent person, to be sure, and one larger and more powerful than ourselves, but nevertheless a being with personality like ours, intention like ours, moods and foibles like ours, open to influence to some extent and in some ways, just as we are, yet never wholly within our control. That being can be known as any person can, which is to say, imperfectly, but sufficiently to make the effort worthwhile. The kind of knowledge that will be relevant here will be the kind we have of people, knowledge that leads us to expect the unexpected. It will involve not primarily causation and technical control, but relationship, intention, communication, meaning.

But Machiavelli's fortune is neither merely a person nor just any person; and the personification of our relationship to the universe was hardly an invention of Machiavelli's. The medieval Christian conception of the world, for example, was also personalized, a relationship to the Father, the Virgin, Christ, and the many saints. Yet it was a very different conception from Machiavelli's. For God was not merely a father, but also the creator of the world, ultimately beyond human comprehension. He presided over an order beyond human influence in which fortune was a relatively minor figure.

Machiavelli's fortune, by contrast, is part of no righteous eternal system, subordinated to no male divinity. She enacts not some predestined justice, but her own whims. But by the same token she is open to human influence, not through prayer or supplication, but rather through courtship, manipulation, and bold challenge. Above all, she is female and thus simultaneously inferior and dangerous.

The conception of fortune as responsive to human effort, the revival of *virtù* as symbolizing that effort, and the specific interpretation of that symbol in terms of virility were widespread in the Renaissance. But it is Machiavelli who presents man's relationship to the outcomes of human action in terms of sexual conquest—less violent than rape but more forceful than seduction. Thereby he not only anthropomorphizes and sexualizes the givens and the outcomes of human action in history but invests them with those specific desires, fears, and attitudes his male readers already bear toward woman—as unreliable nurturer, as sexual object, as "other." The consequence is both empowering and constraining; it promotes the striving for autonomy yet renders that goal inaccessible.

Personifying fortune in this way means that the boundaries between necessity and possibility in Machiavelli's world are above all changeable, subject to the whims of fortune on the one side and human effort on the other. What has to be accepted as given varies, for him, with the particular situation and with our own capacities and efforts. We are never all-powerful, but always subject to countless necessities. Yet the limits are always partly up to us to determine, expanding and contracting as we vary in skill, energy, and imagination.

Most of all, Machiavelli is an activist, urging us to hopefulness and effort. In drawing the line between what had to be accepted as given and what might be changed, Machiavelli had to address a mixed audience: many of them discouraged about the possibilities for action, others active enough but only in private concerns, particularly the pursuit of wealth, a few driven by ambition to activity in the public sphere, but in a hubristic and selfish manner that only increased the chaos and corruption of public life. His task thus was to rouse men to action, but to action that recognized some limits to human capacities, that did not assume perfect certainty or unlimited human power. So Machiavelli's activism is of a peculiar kind. It is founded in no promise of guaranteed success or mastery, no alliance with providence or historical necessity. If anything, it is founded in challenge rather than promise. Against Christian otherworldliness, Church hypocrisy, Stoic withdrawal, bourgeois acquisitiveness, factionalism and envy, Machiavelli summons his contemporaries to *virtù* and to glory. In the cause of community welfare and political liberty, he tries to enlist their concern for manliness, their fear of dependence, their craving for sexual gratification. Machiavelli's ultimate challenge to his contemporaries is to shame them: stand up, and act like a man!

The image of fortune as woman, then, challenges men in terms of their masculine identity: she is there for the taking—if you're man enough. The political universe is meaningful and manageable, yet the image cautions that not just any action will succeed and prepares men for possible failure. It thus challenges what Machiavelli called "ambition," without promoting the excessive ambition entailed in imagining humans as having godlike power.

And yet, the image also has more indirect implications with almost the opposite effect. Machiavelli's was a time when sexual and familial relationships were in flux and were the focus of considerable conflict. We know, in addition, that certain features of Florentine family life at the time were likely to intensify infantile conflicts. Appealing to the pride in masculinity of men who grow up in such circumstances is likely to be rhetorically effective; but it is also likely, first, to reinvigorate and import into political life the anxieties that trouble their relations with women: their fear of the feminine, their need to prove manliness, and as a consequence, violence, hero worship, relations of command and obedience. Second, insofar as relations between the sexes are troubled by unresolved infantile conflicts, invoking woman means invoking mother and tends to return men to childhood fears and fantasies, trapping them in their own past. That is likely to stir up and import into political life fears of trust and nurturance, yearnings for omnipotence and merging, misleading fantasies of what adulthood means. Machiavelli undermines the very teaching he wants to convey by appealing to his audience's desire for manliness and thereby also summoning up childishness: fantasies of huge engulfing mothers and rescuing fathers, relationships of domination and submission, an unstable combination of cynicism and exhortation, and misleading conceptions of action, membership, judgment, and autonomy. The appeal to *machismo* can move men all right, particularly men troubled about their manliness, but it cannot make them free.

❖   ❖   ❖

The problem of action concerns human creativity and our relationship to the past, issues Machiavelli confronts in the image of the Founder, in the authority of ancient Rome, and in the doctrines of imitation and the "return to beginnings." Yet each of these topics remains itself problematic, and specifically so in relation to familial and sexual themes. The Founder image, meant to solve the mysteries of creativity in history, merely reexpresses them. The Founder is the very essence of generative authority, yet must murder his sons. He is supposed to make men out of babies or beasts, yet must assure that they do not themselves aspire to Founder status. He, the solitary patriarch, is supposed to serve as inspiration for fraternal mutuality. Possibly the transition from patriarchal domination to the *vivere civile* is to be made by a liberating Brutus. Yet Brutus is himself a problematic Founder figure, his conspiracy effective only if the citizenry are already free in all but a formal sense.

The Founder is a myth, as Machiavelli the fox well knows, and thus cannot be a genuine solution to any problem in the real world. Yet the problem he is meant to solve—how to "get there from here"—*has been solved* from time to time in the real world. People have been formed into communities, barbarians civilized, republics founded, corrupt institutions renewed. There must be ways to do it. Though there are no

Founders, capital *F*, there are sometimes founders, people who act so that the world is creatively altered after their passing. The image of the Founder, however, blocks rather than facilitates understanding of what human founding is really like. Conjured up as a counterweight to the mythical feminine power, it remains an escapist fantasy, for the mythical proportions of both threat and rescuer dwarf any merely human achievement. Meant to comfort the self, the Founder is actually a fantasy of self-denigration. Instead of empowering, it leaves people helpless, "blaming the princes" for their fate.

The doctrine of imitation and the "return to beginnings" are similarly ambiguous and may be read in terms of either paternal rescue or one's own generative capacities. Thus, imitating the Romans can mean copying their forms and formulas, or it can mean, like them, copying no one. Returning to beginnings can mean recovering terror to renew reluctant obedience, or it can mean dereification, recovering the self—both its capacities and its real commitments. The one reading offers escape from the engulfing matriarch, but only at the price of self-annihilation, whether through merger or murder. The other is genuinely empowering but liberates only at the price of risk. Read in the latter way, founding can be understood as a universal human potential, so that every moment is an opportunity for initiative (though the options are always limited), and every citizen is a potential (co-)founder. Then the Founder image appears as a symbol of the human capacity for action, but a misleading symbol. For if founding is a shared human capacity, it is neither solipsistic nor a creation ex nihilo.

Even the wisest and most charismatic founding fathers are leaders of persons, not molders of material; their authority is the capacity to induce the free actions of other persons. This is not a denial of ancestral authority but the extension to ancestors of that manner of leadership Machiavelli called "the way of freedom." From this perspective, it is precisely the "irreverent" questioning of inherited tradition, the insistence on one's own equal freedom to choose and change, that constitutes true reverence, recognition of one's origins, and renewed contact with the founders. It is true reverence, first, because creating something valuable and lasting is a much more magnificent achievement for fallible human beings than it would be for divinities. It is true reverence, second, because unquestioning dutiful obedience means an implicit denigration of the self by comparison with the sacred ancestors. Therefore it masks a hidden resentment and rebellion; inside the Founder image lurks the fox. And, third, the implicit self-denigration is a partial denial of one's own capacities—to judge and change, but therefore also to defend and augment the tradition. Adults with full awareness of their powers and responsibilities are more effective guardians of what is to be preserved than dutiful children.

To repeat, such an understanding of ancestors and action is offered by Machiavelli but also blocked by his invocation of mythical engulfing mothers and rescuing fathers. For the personal and psychological counterpart of the political theory problem of action is our relationship to our parents: the human problem of growing up. For the small child, adults are indeed larger than life, authors of timeless, sacred, and unchangeable rules. The child feels by turns helpless in their power and omnipotent by assimilation to them. It regards the rules as sacred, although it has not mastered them, but is in fact ready to accept any innovation presented to it as authoritative.[5]

Growing up means acquiring a more realistic view of authority, both the authority of parental figures and that of the principles and practices by which one's community lives. At the same time it also means becoming oneself competent at those practices and capable of parenting others. It means becoming a master of the rules, a responsible custodian and interpreter of the inherited culture. To the extent that our growing up is troubled or incomplete, traces of the earlier understanding remain in us all and are likely to be evoked by certain images and situations, particularly in times of stress.

The transition from total subservience under a godlike authority to autonomous liberty, so problematic in Machiavelli's political argument, thus does take place in normal psychic development, but as shift in perception, not in reality. The small child normally perceives in ways that in an adult might be called myth and reification. Parents are not really gods; indeed, the psychological theory examined in this book suggests that such infantile images are more likely to linger into adulthood in proportion as actual parenting was inadequate, the parents absent or unreliable. In any case, the sense in which the transition is a psychic reality does not make it politically feasible. Citizens, or even privatized adults who might become citizens, are not children. And while no doubt we all need authority, adults do not need the kind of authority parents exemplify, and particularly not the kind exemplified by the small child's images of parents. The projection of those images into politics can only distort political reality.

But recognizing that parents are merely human, like oneself, and that

5. On the child's understanding of rules, see Jean Piaget, *The Moral Judgment of the Child*, tr. Marjorie Gabain (New York: Collier Books, 1962), esp. 13–109.

our conventions are humanly made must not be confused with the hubristic suppositions that one had no parents, that our conventions have no authority, or that *every* option is open to us, here and now. Growing up is not the transition from regarding parents as demigods to regarding oneself as a demigod, but the acceptance simultaneously of the human powers and limitations of self and parents. Reification and hubris are equally childish. Growing up means coming to terms with this ambiguous authority of the past: that it is not sacred beyond our challenge, yet that it is *in* us, and without it, we would not be who we are.

To say it another way, growing up means coming to terms with the arbitrariness of the past. Though history is humanly made, it is inescapable. The past is given; the future is open to our action. We are "thrown" into the world, as Heidegger puts it, suggesting a random cast of dice, into some particular time, place, and circumstances not of our choosing. Yet only the unique configuration of circumstances and events that are my life could have made me. We begin helpless and unindividuated; only by being initiated into some particular culture do we become human individuals, capable of autonomy. So my origins, arbitrary as they are, must be accepted, for they are the preconditions of my capacity for choice and action.

That is what Nietzsche called *amor fati*, learning to love the accidents that have befallen us, to redeem them as sacred, by our will. It is an extraordinarily difficult doctrine to articulate. It does not forbid tampering with authoritative tradition but says that we *cannot* change what is past. The will cannot act on the past, Nietzsche says, and martyrs itself in trying. We act always in the present, but all too often the real motivation of our action is the wish to undo some past event, rather than to alter its results in the present. Nietzsche called such backward-looking action "reaction," because it was not free; and he said it was the product of weakness and *ressentiment*. Freud called it neurotic and said that neurotics expend vast inner energy continually trying to obliterate something in the past that cannot be obliterated because it is graven in the self. This cripples them and makes their actions ineffectual. Only if one can—in one sense—wholly ratify as if sacred everything in the past and thus everything about the world and oneself is one free to act effectively to change what—in another sense—needs changing about them.

But ratifying the past as if sacred does not mean imagining it as sacred. On the contrary, it requires recognizing the historical past as a product of human controversy and choice, at every step actually or potentially political. In Machiavelli's terms, we must not worship the an-

cestors and ape them but connect their achievements to our own potential. The past that to us looks so inevitable—partly because it is past
and therefore for us inescapable—was for past actors a series of opportunities and choices, often fought out in political controversy, in which
some won and others lost. And all that welter of conflicting views, policies, efforts is our heritage. In recovering the past and seeking out ancestors, we thus have some choice about whom to seek and how to see
them—whether, for example, our origins are Roman or Tuscan, and
what the choice implies for us now.

Both Nietzsche and Freud thought, paradoxically, that enslavement
to the past could be cured only by the right sort of recovery of the past.
For Freud, neurosis is cured by remembering the past that was repressed
into the unconscious. Nietzsche's metaphor is digestion: to be free for
action one must deal with the past in a way that incorporates it, once
and for all, and be done with it. Machiavelli speaks not in such psychological and personal terms, but characteristically in political ones, yet
his teaching is much the same.

The political counterpart of what Nietzsche called *ressentiment* Machiavelli called corruption. Corrupt people are obsessed with past
injustice, desiring vengeance more than any direct gratification. "The
reward they desire from victory is not . . . glory" but rather "the satisfaction of having conquered the others."[6] Thus when they come to
power they kill or exile their enemies, making laws "not for the common profit but altogether in favor of the conqueror."[7] Their real desire
being to undo the past, which is impossible, they cannot let the past go
or look rationally toward the future. They would rather "go back over
past things" endlessly than "provide for future ones" in ways designed
to "reunite, not to divide the city."[8] So they launch escalating feuds or
even ally themselves with their own state's enemies abroad. No law is
"more dangerous for a republic," says Machiavelli, "than one that
looks back for a long time."[9]

But a different sort of "looking back for a long time," one that renews
contact with origins and founders and recovers the self, is also Machiavelli's cure for such factional resentment. Only, as already argued,
this curative looking back can be understood in either of two ways: the
one misogynistic and ultimately crippling, the other genuinely liberating. Developing the former understanding, Machiavelli, like Nietzsche,
links resentful factionalism with femininity. Resentment is the passion

---

6. *Florentine Histories* 3: 5 (G 1146).   7. Ibid. (G 1140).
8. Ibid., 4: 14 (G 1202).   9. Ibid., 3: 3 (G 1143).

of the effeminate; factional vengeance is the weapon of fortune within men. So the cure seems to lie in renewed contact with the saving masculinity of forefathers, who will impose murderous discipline. But that cure fails in its liberating intent, for it leaves people still trapped in the past, reliving instead of resolving childhood conflicts.

Alternatively, the curative recovery of origins and ancestors can mean recognizing one's kinship with their great, but human, achievement. It can mean recovering simultaneously one's own capacity to judge and change or augment what they created, and one's commitment to that creation which constituted both self and community. This would leave autonomy linked still with adulthood, but no longer with gender; the past would liberate not from feminine but from mythologized parental power. Here, however, the problem of action merges with those of membership and judgment, for an individual is not really free to change the traditions of his community by himself, and not just any action we take will be a right action. Even though free to create, we are nevertheless bound to be reverent toward something already given, and respectful of others with whom we must act if our action is to have political meaning.

❖   ❖   ❖

Concerning the problem of membership, Machiavelli is neither a contractarian nor an organicist. He takes it for granted that we are somehow both distinct individuals, each unique and capable of action, and yet objectively interconnected, achieving individuality only in interaction with others. What really interests him, as always, is politics: the possibility of an active, intentional membership enabling us jointly to take responsibility for our objective interconnections, the large-scale consequences for each other of what we are actually doing. Particularly in the Citizen image of manhood, he sees politics as the activity by which free individuals, already objectively interdependent in a society but (therefore) also at odds in terms of interest, need, outlook, desire, repeatedly make themselves into a community, restore and redirect their community, defining it and themselves in the process. Politics thus both partly presupposes and creates both individuality and communal ties.

In deliberation and political conflict citizens are forced to bring their individual or class interests and "humors" into relationship with the interests and "humors" of others, producing a renewed recognition of their interdependence and shared membership. In the process, old connections are discovered and new ones made, and all are reminded of their stake in the community, in its policies and the ways those policies are made, in its ways of life and ethos, and in each other. This is neither a transformation of self-interest into dutiful self-sacrifice to something external called "the public," nor a mere refinement of self-interest to the longer-range and more rational, but something like a redefinition of the self, an enlarged awareness of how individuality and community are connected in the self.

This political struggle involves both power and principle, each side mustering what power it can, yet also appealing to the other in terms of law, right, justice, and the common good. Indeed, in the *vivere civile* might and right are interrelated, for law and justice are themselves partly resources of power; and, conversely, a purely abstract "right" that serves no community needs and can muster no community support is politically ineffectual and wrong. Because we are simultaneously both distinct and connected, politics always simultaneously concerns both the distribution of costs and benefits among competitors, and the nature and direction of their shared community, both "who gets what, when, why" and "who we are." Every law or policy allocates, advantaging some and disadvantaging others; but every law or policy also affects their shared common life and the principles for which they stand. Neglecting either aspect is naive and potentially disastrous. Neglect the former aspect, and you are likely to be exploited under cover of attractive slogans about the public good or to formulate unrealistic policies that do not work. Neglect the latter, and you court "corruption"; your political community is likely to dissolve into factions, each poaching on a public good and on principles for whose maintenance it takes no responsibility.

For Machiavelli at his best, the real point is not some unified harmony at which politics theoretically aims, but the activity of struggling toward agreement with and against each other, in which citizens take active charge of the historical processes that would otherwise direct their lives in hidden ways. And that activity is no mere courtly dialogue, but a genuine conflict, in which needs and important interests are at stake. Without passion and struggle there can be no liberty, but only reification, habit, and drift. Yet political conflict must also always be kept within limits; politics is not civil war. The struggle must be kept open and public, rather than clandestine and private. It must involve a genuine appeal to principle, to what is reasonable and what is just; the public and principled aspect of politics must be kept lively in it. And citizens must be kept aware of their interdependence, their shared stake in fair rules and right principles, the civil limits (*i termini civili*) that forbid wiping out their opponents. These requirements are both prerequisites for and products of a healthy politics (which is one reason why the initial founding of a *vivere civile* is such a puzzle).

The essential element in membership so understood is mutuality; politics is not the domination of some by others, but a relationship among peers; the *vivere civile* means neither to dominate *superbamente* nor to serve *umilmente*. It resembles that outlook Kant later discerned as fundamental to morality: the recognition of other human beings as persons capable of action, like oneself, as members of the "kingdom of ends," not to be exploited for one's own purposes like objects but to be encountered in dialogue as peers with purposes of their own. Yet politics is not morality, and the reciprocity required of citizens lacks the intimacy of moral relationship; political deliberation is not dialogical but multivocal and impersonal. Although citizens must certainly share some degree of commonality to be and remain one community, there is room for much difference and conflict among them; and the mutuality politics requires is a recognition of similarity within difference, a peerhood that does not presuppose total equality, a capacity to continue to live and act with others who are substantially, even offensively, different from oneself.

Instilling this capacity for mutuality within difference is a crucial part of Machiavelli's effort at the political education of his factional fellow Florentines. But the sexual and familial imagery he invokes again partly undermines this effort by calling up images of domination and fears of dependence. The counterpart in personal and psychological life of the political theory problems of membership is our relationship to the "other": to someone we recognize as simultaneously like ourselves and yet dangerously different. It begins with the task already discussed, of learning to see our parents as human, as persons like ourselves; but it continues into relationships with our contemporaries. To relate actively, without masochistic resentment and yet within civil limits, with a recognition of mutuality, to persons defined as significantly different, in conflict with oneself, requires a certain self-confidence and tolerance for ambiguity. The "other" threatens the psychic integrity of the self. Whoever is excessively anxious about internal unity, purity, and consistency, who finds it difficult to acknowledge the "other" inside the self—parts of the self that seem alien, dangerous, in conflict with the rest—is likely to project that otherness onto external groups and persons defined as different, and therefore to deny mutuality with them. Ascribing to such external "others" forbidden parts of the self, we then relate to those others as we feel about those parts of the self. This happens in ethnocentrism and in many cultures' treatment of aliens and outgroups. It happens also between social classes and races, particularly as privileged and dominant groups project forbidden wishes onto subordinated groups, denying their humanity or at any rate their equality, perceiving them as simultaneously contemptible and dangerous: childish, passionate, physical, irrational, uncanny, mysterious. So white Americans tend to see people of color, so gentiles tend to see Jews, so the rich tend to see the poor, so men tend to see women.

Relations with the opposite sex are perhaps the most common and certainly the most intimate example of this encounter with the "other," of the difficulties in achieving mutuality within differences.[10] The difficulty exists for both sexes, but, on the whole, men are in the role of the dominant and privileged group here. Women tend to signify infantile relationships for us all, because the care of children is assigned mainly to women in our culture. But it is only for men that the infantile comes to be associated with "the opposite sex," that group and those individuals encountered as fundamentally different. In Dorothy Dinnerstein's terms, insofar as a boy's infantile relationship with his mother remains unresolved and unworked through, he is likely to project it onto his perceptions of all—or all significant, or all motherly, or all authoritative—women; and that relationship is more difficult for a boy to work through than for a girl precisely because he is socially constrained to keep mother at arm's length as "other," as fundamentally different from the self.[11] To the extent that our infantile experience remains unmodified, Dinnerstein says, we all perceive "the threat to autonomy which can come from a woman . . . as more primitively dangerous, than any such threat from a man"; thus we may even welcome male domination as "a reasonable refuge" from the female. "We come eventually, of course, to resent male authority, too," but not wholeheartedly.[12] Thus Dinnerstein says that when we abandon the risks of free self-government for the security of some "male tyranny, the big, immediate thing we are feeling the need to escape is not freedom," but our recollections and fantasies of that "earlier, and more total tyranny" of the mother's power, as experienced by the infant.[13]

Consequently, men's definition of the female as radically "other" both stimulates and undermines their struggle for freedom.

---

10. For the first formulation of the idea in these terms see Simone de Beauvoir, *The Second Sex*, tr. H. M. Parshley (New York: A. A. Knopf, 1961), esp. 57, 129. See also Philip Mason, *Prospero's Magic: Some Thoughts on Class and Race* (London: Oxford University Press, 1962).

11. Dinnerstein, *Mermaid*, 107.

12. Ibid., 112, 175. See also, 161, 178.   13. Ibid., 187.

Even in the efforts [misogynist] man makes to *overthrow* male tyranny—male tyranny over males, that is—he rests on the vassalage of woman. Reassured that he has the original despot under control, he can play with the notion of emerging from under the wing of the new one.[14]

But he can only play with that notion rather than effectively pursue the goal, because his feeling of strength is unstable.

He is drawing strength from the subservience of woman for a struggle against the tyranny of man; but he can keep woman subservient only with the strength he draws from the sponsorship of the male tyrant. . . . He is balancing terrors, dependencies, against each other; the balance keeps tipping and he keeps slipping back into the patriarchal trap.[15]

Accordingly, relations between the sexes can be taken as one measure of the capacity for mutuality, and thus for the type of citizenship Machiavelli envisages. That is, I think, what Marx meant in claiming that the "species being" of humanity is "sensuously manifested, reduced to an observable fact" in the relationship between the sexes. From this relationship, he thought, one can judge the "whole level of development" of a people,

the extent to which man's natural behaviour has become human, or the extent to which . . . his human nature has come to be natur[al] to him. In this relationship is revealed, too, the extent to which man's need has become a human need; the extent to which, therefore, the other person as a person has become for him a need—the extent to which he in his individual existence is at the same time a social being.[16]

The relationship between the sexes is suffused with natural animal drives and primitive psychic impulses; to the extent that it is nevertheless a civilized, moral relationship of mutuality, each recognizing and indeed needing the other as a person, an end rather than a mere means, our animality has been humanized. This humanizing transformation has occurred only to the extent that the civilized and moral type of relating has become a fulfilling expression of physical and psychic impulse, rather than a duty reluctantly performed.

Similarly, Hannah Arendt has suggested a correlation between the attitude men take toward women and their understanding of human action and politics. She sees that correlation exemplified in Christian thought by the choice between the two biblical versions of the creation story. Thus she says that Paul, for whom "faith was primarily related to

14. Ibid., 196.
15. Ibid., 196–97.
16. Robert C. Tucker, ed. *The Marx-Engels Reader*, 2d ed. (New York: W. W. Norton, 1978), 83–84.

salvation . . . insists that woman was created 'of the man' and hence 'for the man'" (1 Cor. 11:8–12), while Jesus, "for whom faith was closely related to action," cites Genesis 1:27: "he which made *them* at the beginning made them male and female" (Matt. 19:4).[17] Arendt does not elaborate, but the point is clearly related to her observation that action, the human capacity to create relationships and make history, always presupposes a context of plurality, "because we are all the same, that is, human, in such a way that nobody is ever the same as anyone else who ever lived, lives, or will live." This plurality within likeness "is specifically *the* condition—not only the *conditio sine qua non*, but the *conditio per quam*—of all political life."[18]

Certainly in Machiavelli's texts, misogyny works to undermine the vision of political liberty. Yet if one seeks to generalize about actual politics, no simple equation between free politics and mutuality between the sexes will do. Given the frequency with which actual participatory republics in history—examples of what Machiavelli would have called the *vivere civile*, from ancient Athens to modern Switzerland—have excluded or even severely oppressed women, one can hardly argue that democracy presupposes sexual equality, let alone that mutuality between the sexes would promptly produce a just and democratic polity. Even in the psychological and sociological theories examined in this book, the relevant variable is not actual relations between men and women, but how the citizen-men and the child-rearing women feel about those relations. In the second place, a free and participatory political life depends on a lot more than the psychic state of the citizens; that can surely be at most one factor among many economic, social, and cultural considerations. And, in the third place, as Machiavelli's writings indicate, the appeal to *machismo* really can move men toward intense bonds with their fellow males, and toward energetic, heroic action. However, the action so motivated is not likely to be coordinated with any public good, and the bonds so motivated are likely to require a rigid, authoritarian discipline.

Misogyny, overtly directed only against women, is also and necessarily directed against parts of the male self, since virtually every man was once mothered by a woman and began the formation of his self in relation to her. Needing therefore to expunge or deny those parts of the self they experience as feminine or childish, men who are anxious about their masculinity will be severely limited in their capacity for genuine

17. Arendt, *Human Condition*, 8n.
18. Ibid., 8, 7.

mutuality—for the combination of trust with conflict—even in relation to other men. Unable to trust beyond their immediate circle of family and friends, unwilling to acknowledge their interdependencies, they would likely lead privatized lives—not, of course, confined to the household like their women, but concerned with business, for instance, or family status.

If such men do move into public life, they do so in order to escape and deny their private selves, the vulnerabilities of the body and their troubling relations with women and children in the household. Fleeing their bodily and domestic selves, they march out to ravage "the sheepfolds of others." To the extent that they feel threatened by "inner" conflict, psychic or political, they will lack that capacity for limited struggle among peers that differentiates citizenship from civil war, political dispute from the factional disintegration of a community. And so their community is likely to be an army, women safely excluded, the apple tree dutifully left untouched, and their mortality and private particularity left behind as they turn their rage outward against a (psychically) safely external "other." Theirs, in short, will be a zero-sum world in which the only possible conception of public life is of domination; they will be either fragmented and thus vulnerable to the domination of others or unified and dominated by a single commander for the purpose of dominating others.

Machiavelli's writings never transcended the conventional misogyny of his time. Like the other men of Renaissance Florence, he had virtually no experience of women as citizens or peers, though he had at least some significant experience of the exceptional woman *virago*, notably in his disastrous early diplomatic encounter with Caterina Sforza. This book has tried to show that his failure to deal with the "otherness" of women as a worldly, realistic difference rather than an uncanny and threatening mystery is not merely unfortunate for women—whose cause he might otherwise have given some early, though doubtless futile, assistance—but also has profound consequences for his teachings about men, about humanness, politics, and autonomy. Because he could not think (or at any rate, did not write) about women as fellow citizens but instead rested even his republican politics on a misogynist ideal of manliness, his own metaphors and images constantly cast doubt on what he most wants to teach. Two great failures of mutuality, one might say, flaw his best vision of political relationship, the one a sin of omission and the other of commission. The one is his exploitation of—his failure to challenge—the misogyny of his time; the other is his militarist imperialism, his failure to extend into international relations the vision he fashioned of political life within a community. This book has argued that the two are intimately interrelated.

As with the problem of action, so with that of membership, Machiavelli's sexual and familial imagery, meant to challenge men out of their concern with private, household matters of wealth and family into the more "manly" realm of political life, also has the opposite effect, arousing images of domination and submission and undermining that capacity for mutuality which citizenship requires. There is, moreover, this difference between the two cases: while Machiavelli's best understanding of action does represent adulthood, an overcoming of childishness and an acceptance of mature powers and responsibilities, the same cannot be said of his association of political membership with masculinity. Adults are more fit for citizenship than children. Men are not inherently more fit for citizenship than women and will appear so only in a society where women are confined to household and private affairs and denied access to public life. Thus while the equation of humanness with adulthood can lead to distortion if interpreted in terms of an anxious and defensive understanding of adulthood, the equation of humanness with masculinity is distorting not just in terms of an anxious and defensive understanding of masculinity, but in terms of any understanding of masculinity at all. Men who deny the humanity of women are bound to misunderstand their own.

CHAPTER TWELVE

Judgment and Autonomy

The problem of judgment grows out of the relationship of what is distinctively human to what is natural: our own bodies and animal instincts as well as the natural world around us, out of which we construct civilization, technology, morality, politics. The latter, in turn, imply standards for action and judgment, right and wrong ways to do things, good and evil conduct. The status of those standards is a mystery, a cluster of mysteries. The problem of action earlier raised the question of what constitutes the "beginning" of a community or an individual, how causation and the animal turn into the capacity for action and the human. Now come these closely related questions: How does the causally determined natural turn into the moral and political, capable of choosing right from wrong, of judging and being judged? What is the origin of concepts such as justice, virtue, civility, honor, and the practices connected with them? How does any human individual make the transition? And what, accordingly, is the status of our norms of right conduct and judgment, the basis of their validity? Are they merely conventional? Or are they anchored in nature or in some transcendent authority guaranteeing their validity?

Such philosophical questions become politically acute in times like Machiavelli's, when there is a great disparity between the inherited ideals and standards, on the one hand, and people's actual activities, needs, and feelings, on the other. Traditional forms and ceremonies are experienced as empty, and they no longer sanctify. Traditional rules virtually guarantee failure, for there is "such a difference between how men live and how they ought to live that he who abandons what is done for what ought to be done learns his destruction rather than his preservation."[1] Inherited theories no longer make sense of the world, and actual practice remains chaotic, inconsistent, untheorized. It may be time for new theory, for the (re)creation of value and meaning. But where are they to come from?

The political theorist is not merely an observer but also a teacher, a bridge builder offering a new vision of the familiar world and trying to make it accessible to people through and despite their old ways of seeing. But how does one teach in such times of dislocation in judgment and action? Confronted by such conditions, a theorist may feel that the most urgent task is to destroy the remaining pretensions of existing ideals and unmask those who exploit them. Moved by a yearning for truthfulness, a rage at the prevailing hypocrisy, he may speak in the cynical mode, teaching that ideals are fraudulent devices, not merely conventional but foisted by the powerful on the credulous. He may, that is, equate truth telling with the systematic description of current, exploitive, and hypocritical practice.

Or he may, instead, choose the other side of the gap between ideals and practice, cleaving to the standards to which others only pay lip service—or to some different, perhaps historically earlier, set of ideals—and exhort his audience to live up to those standards. But if the corruption of the time has gone very far, neither of these modes of teaching is likely to be effective. The cynical mode may win popularity but can offer no cure, for it tells only a partial truth and can neither restore nor replace the old commitments. Yet exhortation is likely to fall on deaf ears, for everyone has learned to ignore the familiar cant of preachers and teachers, since taking it seriously so frequently means disaster "among so many who are not good."

Machiavelli is sometimes drawn to each of these modes: cynical in the image of the fox, hortatory in relation to the Founder. Yet at his best he transcends and synthesizes both into what one may justly call a political and humanist realism: a truth-telling theory that perceives in the objective world not only the corrupt and exploitive practices currently pursued, but also their disastrous results, and therefore also the potential practical reality that ideals have. He seeks to theorize the *verita effettuale della cosa*, but that includes human achievement and potential along with human failure and corruption.[2]

1. *Prince*, ch. 15 (G 57–58).
2. At least in this respect, Martin Luther faced the same problem in the north of Europe as Machiavelli faced in the south. Striving to become a monk, he was obsessively scrupulous and plagued by doubt, unwilling to make the hypocritical compromises customary in his time. His superiors prescribed the traditional exercises: fast, pray, perform rituals. If you behave like a monk, in time faith will come. But Luther could not accept

The cynical theorist, one might say, wants to define human nature by what is most basic in us, to find a secure foundation on which to build: *"Erst kommt das Fressen, dann kommt die Moral."*[3] The hortatory theorist, by contrast, defines human nature by what is highest in us, our capacities for transcendence. Machiavelli ultimately rejects both alternatives and the choice between them. At his best, he retains the cynical fox's animus against utopian, empty, and hypocritical ideals, but not the conviction that all ideals are of necessity like that. He retains the foxy premise that standards of right are human artifacts, and thus cannot be legitimated by their origins, but not the conclusion that they must therefore be illegitimate. His deepest commitment here, as on so many topics, is to action, but responsible, creative action: glory. We are the creatures capable of transforming what is basic into what is glorious. That capacity makes possible real but limited—limited but real—human greatness, and so it defines our responsibilities. Precisely because ideals are humanly made, leaving their care and maintenance to some transcendent power amounts to a failure of responsibility. Yet precisely because some ideals promote an objectively better life for human beings than do others, the cynical refusal to judge and act is equally a failure of responsibility.

But here again the sexual and familial imagery Machiavelli invokes tends partly to undermine his teaching. Challenging his audience to a manly acceptance of the burdens of human self-fashioning, his imagery often makes that task seem more than human, suggesting a flight into either cynicism, excusing us from the effort, or submission to some rescuing father who will make the effort for us.

Machiavelli teaches that ideals like virtue and honor, justice and civility—both how we conceive them and how we practice them—are humanly determined. The goals people pursue, the standards by which they judge and act, are shaped by their upbringing, training, and experi-

---

that solution, feeling that the performance of ritual acts without faith was itself sinful—in effect, hypocrisy toward God—and could produce only more sin, never salvation. Confronting the gap between ideals and practice, he insisted on cleaving to the former; and his personal solution turned out to be meaningful for much of Europe. Machiavelli would have scoffed at the proposition that the problems he was addressing were theological in nature, yet he too refused to settle for hypocrisy, to live with the gap between ideals and practice. And he, too, associated the recovery of meaning, value, and virtue with a renewed and more direct access to true paternal authority.

3. "First comes food, then the moral." But the impact of Brecht's *"Fressen"*—the German verb for the way animals eat—is lost in translation. Bertold Brecht, *The Three-Penny Opera*, sc. 6, "Second Three-penny Finale: What Keeps Mankind Alive?"

ence, what Machiavelli in the largest sense calls *educazione*. This includes parental example and admonition, schooling, the discipline of law and public authority, military discipline, religion, and the whole way of life (*modo del vivere*) into which members of a community are initiated.[4] Yet each of these shaping elements is itself subject to human choice and sustained only by effort. All of them were arranged better in ancient times than in corrupt modern Florence.

Some conclude that consequently Machiavelli must also teach that there is no absolute, objective right and wrong, such standards being merely conventions and the only absolute being our origin in nature, which makes no moral distinctions. Indeed, there are passages in Machiavelli supporting such a reading, for the vision of the fox is a cynical vision. But this is not his final or his best position. Rather, he wants to maintain that although man-made and sustained only by effort, ideals enacted are as real as any natural phenomenon. The tyrant is "deceived by a false good and a false glory," which is to say that the difference between false and real glory is as objective as any other fact about which some may be deceived.[5] No mere convention can change such deception into truth. The ideals and practices we create are anchored on the one side in natural need and capacity, on the other side in their practical consequences for human life.

These questions can be fruitfully explored in Machiavelli's treatment of the great Ciompi Rebellion, the revolt of Florence's wool workers, "the poorest of the people." At the height of his account of the rebellion, Machiavelli presents an invented speech he ascribes to a man identified only as "one of the most fiery and of greatest experience among" the rebels.[6] It is a cynical speech, in effect claiming that all property is theft, all power domination, every relationship exploitative and concluding that the workers should take by force whatever they can, in order to dominate and exploit their former masters.

By "nature," the speaker argues, all men are equal; some claim to be of ancient and noble lineage, but that is mere convention, "for all men, since they had one and the same beginning, are equally ancient." The fundamental reality is nature; all else is mere convention and as superficial as clothing on the body.

Strip us all naked; you will see us all alike; dress us then in their clothes and the[m] in ours; without doubt we shall seem noble and they ignoble, for only poverty and riches make us unequal.

4. *Discourses*, 2: 2 (G 331); 3: 27 (G 490); 3: 31 (G 500); 3: 43 (G 521); 3: 46 (G 525); Machiavelli, *Opere* 1: 496, 501.
5. *Discourses* 1: 10 (G 220); 1: 53 (G 302).
6. *Florentine Histories* 3: 13 (G 1159–60) for this and the following quotations.

Poverty and riches, moreover, are both equally unnatural, for "God and Nature have put all men's fortunes in their midst," so that wealth goes to those who take it. In the resulting struggle, theft is more effective than work, "the bad arts" more effective than "the good."

Indeed, great wealth, power, and status are always illegitimate at their origin, "attained . . . by means of either fraud or force." Only the "rapacious and fradulent" ever emerge from poverty, only the "unfaithful and bold" from "servitude." Small crimes may be punished, but "great and serious ones are rewarded"; and the successful conqueror, whatever his means, is never "disgraced" by what he has done. After seizing what they want "with trickery or with violence," the conquerors "conceal the ugliness of their acquisition" by imposing a legitimizing terminology of ideals. Under such "false title," their ill-gotten gains come in retrospect to look "honorable" to the credulous exploited. Thus the wool workers should not be either "frightened" or "shamed" by the invocation of terms like "noble" and "ignoble," by appeals to conscience or to "ill fame," the judgment of others. All of these are mere conventions deployed by the winners to fool the losers. One must look behind ideals and conventions, including religion, to the natural realities of physical life: "When people fear hunger and prison, as we do, they cannot and should not have any fear of hell." Those who heed the call of "conscience" are naive, disappointingly inadequate as "men," since their credulity prevents them from acting. "Spirited men" act boldly to seize "the opportunity that Occasion brings," that is "offered . . . by Fortune."

On this basis, the agitator teaches the wool workers not merely that they should act, but specifically that they ought "to use force" whenever they "get the chance." Since all power is illegitimate in origin, relations of domination and exploitation are the only possible ones. The only issue is who will be on top, and the speaker urges the wool workers to take their turn, so that the former masters "will have to complain of and fear you," as the wool workers now complain of and fear their masters.

Here is an eloquent formulation of the view that "beginnings" are illegitimate, a return to nature and the body and to force. Anything beyond force, fraud, and the physical is mere convention externally imposed for exploitative purposes. But does Machiavelli mean it? The speech is written with verve and relish; one imagines Machiavelli enjoyed its writing. It is peppered with familiar Machiavellian maxims, suggesting a continuity with the main body of his works. And it is, of course, an invention, inserted in the *Florentine Histories* without any logical necessity.

But Machiavelli frames the speech in disparaging commentary. He says that it was made "in order to arouse" the workers and succeeded in "greatly inflam[ing] their spirits, which were of themselves already hot for evil."[7] The person in the Ciompi Rebellion for whom Machiavelli expresses admiration is not this anonymous (though "experienced") speaker, but Michele di Lando, a real historical figure who became the leader of the rebellion in its later stages but resisted the extreme claims of the poor, "determined to quiet the city," and who "publicly proclaimed that nobody should burn or rob anything."[8] Machiavelli says that Michele di Lando surpassed all others in his time "in courage, in prudence, and in goodness," and that he deserved "to be numbered among the glorious few who have greatly benefitted their native city."[9]

It is not obvious what to make of Machiavelli's praise for Michele di Lando and of the moderate framework in which the cynical speech is set. His letters indicate that Machiavelli felt constrained in writing the *Histories* by the fear of offending the powerful, particularly the pope who had commissioned the work. So it is in principle possible that the moderating framework is deception, the speech expressing his real views and teachings.

That interpretation becomes impossible, however, if one recalls the overall theme of the *Florentine Histories*, Machiavelli's investigation of why the Florentine Republic, unlike the Roman, was always unstable. His explicit answer to that question, it will be recalled, concerns factions, "unreasonable and unjust" demands, and a failure to observe limits in dealing with the opposition. Indeed, the preface to the book of the *Histories* that deals with the Ciompi Rebellion attributes Florentine weakness to the fact that whenever any group or faction gained power in the city, it tried to destroy its opponents utterly, making laws "not for the common profit but altogether in favor of the conqueror."[10]

Although the speech does invoke something like courage ("spirited men") and "honor" and does mention the hope of having "more liberty . . . than in the past," and although it mentions the wool workers' complaints about the masters' "avarice" and "injustice," it does not really, consistently address the ideals implied in such words.[11] It addresses only conquest and revenge, a simple inversion of past oppression, not liberty but what Machiavelli in the preface to the next book of the *Histories* identifies as "license." Florence, he says there, has never been well organized, having had at most a "semblance of republican government," fluctuating as its rulers and constitutions varied,

---

7. Ibid. (G 1159, 1161).   8. Ibid., 3: 16 (G 1166).
9. Ibid., 3: 17 (G 1168).   10. Ibid., 3: 1 (G 1140).
11. Ibid., 3: 13 (G 1161, cf. 1160); 3: 12 (G 1158).

not between liberty and slavery, as many believe, but between slavery and license. The promoters of license, who are the people, and the promoters of slavery, who are the nobles, praise the mere name of liberty, for neither of these classes is willing to be subject either to the laws or to men.[12]

In a city that can rightly "be called free," by contrast, there is reciprocity between opposing classes and groups, and an awareness of common membership in an association valuable to all.

By these criteria, the speech to the wool workers is licentious, advocating a politics without limits or mutuality, and counseling the workers to exploit the public life for their private advantage by threatening "damage" to "the city."[13] The speaker acknowledges that the consequence of the kind of politics he advocates is "that men devour one another," but he can envisage no alternative. On the contrary, precisely from the observation that men devour each other he concludes they should therefore use force whenever they can.[14] The speech thus displays a fundamental inconsistency characteristic of the fox's cynical stance. It employs terms like *fraud* and the conventional contrast between "bad" and "good" ways of getting ahead, "bad" and "good" men. Yet it also insists that standards of good and bad are based on fraud and force, all equally exploitive. If the world is as the speaker claims, the conventional terms and distinctions are meaningless, and he is not entitled to their use. Thus it does not fully make sense to claim that moral standards originate in exploitation and fraud, for the latter terms already imply the existence of standards; if there is no such thing as virtue in mere nature, there is no such thing as fraud, either.

Not only is the speech incoherent in this sense, but there is also a problem, given the speaker's premises, about the nature of collectivity in his audience or in the city. "You see the preparations of our adversaries," he says, "let us get ahead of their plans."[15] Thus he presents two opposed collectivities: "we" and "they." Hitherto "they" ruled "us"; soon "we" shall dominate "them." It is taken for granted that "I" gain if "we" win. But what will be the relations among "us" if all human power is based on force or fraud? If what the speaker says is true, then surely the audience ought to be as suspicious of his motives as of the masters', and indeed of each other's as well. The only "natural" unit, it seems, is the isolated individual. There is no reason for anyone among the oppressed to suppose that he will gain even private liberty if "our side" wins, for all that unites "us" is our common oppression, which will disappear when "we" win. Having won, or perhaps already in the

12. Ibid., 4: 1 (G 1187).   13. Ibid., 3: 13 (G 1161).
14. Ibid. (G 1160).   15. Ibid. (G 1161).

process of winning, we shall do what men have always done: "devour one another." Yet if we do not trust each other, we cannot win; as the speaker points out, it is precisely because the masters are "disunited" that "we" have hopes of seizing power now: "Their disunion will give us the victory."[16]

Despite its eloquence, despite its use of Machiavellian idiom, then, the speech to the wool workers is not an articulation of Machiavelli's views, both because he does distinguish between truth and fraud, benefit and exploitation, and because he believes in and teaches about the value of collectivity based on a well-founded mutual trust that is not naive. The fact that standards are human artifacts does not make them fraudulent or illegitimate, for such notions are themselves the products of standards. Still, how any conventional creation can be (or become) more than arbitrary does pose a mystery, like the mysteries of how matter can be (or become) animate, how animal can be (or become) human, how individuals can be (or become) collectivity.

❖   ❖   ❖

Another approach to that mystery, the apparent opposite of cynicism, is the edifying exhortation to duty. It, too, attracts Machiavelli, yet is ultimately rejected by him. And though opposed to cynicism in a way, it is actually cynicism's flip side: inside the Founder image lurks the fox. Consider the famous charge leveled by Edmund Burke against the *philosophes*, that their irreverent questioning of authority would soon destroy "all the pleasing illusions which made power gentle and obedience liberal," leaving mankind exposed in all its "naked, shivering nature." What sort of illusions? Burke illustrates: to the *philosophes* "a queen is but a woman, a woman is but an animal—and an animal not of the highest order."[17]

Calling such beliefs "illusions," Burke ratifies through his choice of word the cynical view he means to oppose, that a queen is nothing more or other than an animal. To believe otherwise is to hold an illusion, he says, but one with vitally important practical consequences. Where such illusions are believed, power will actually be gentle and obedience liberal. Indeed, the urgency of Burke's larger argument makes clear that he thinks even more—the survival of civilization itself—is at stake in such illusions. Why, then, does he insist that people must believe *illusions* to preserve the very tangible and *unillusory* benefits civility and

16. Ibid. (G 1160; cf. 1161) and Mansfield, "Party," in Fleischer, *Machiavelli*, 262.

17. Peter J. Stanlis, ed., *Edmund Burke: Selected Writings and Speeches* (Garden City, N.Y.: Doubleday, 1963), 458.

culture bring to all? Why cannot those benefits directly motivate a knowing, disillusioned civility?

Several answers are possible here, all part of Burke's argument at some point. First, there is the problem of human passion. People—or at least most people, or people of certain social classes—lack sufficient self-control to do what is prudentially in their best interest, unless it is reinforced by certain illusions that engage stronger passions than prudence ever can. Second, even in merely rational and prudential terms, while everyone clearly benefits from civilization, an individual might perhaps benefit even more if *everyone else* were moral and civilized, while he alone was consummately selfish. Third, the prudential outlook itself, which calculates consequences in terms of costs and benefits, may require a character structure tending to undermine morality and the public good.

To some extent, Machiavelli shares each of these views. He says that most men will "be good" only out of fear; that most people want only security and gain rather than glory; that anyone introducing important innovations must manipulate popular illusions, because "many good things are known to a prudent man that are not in themselves so plainly rational that others can be persuaded of them."[18] And yet Machiavelli also at times envisions a secular reverence achieved without reification, a human autonomy that is neither dependent on illusion nor further by hortatory preaching. Maurice Merleau-Ponty calls it a political "principle of communion" and says that "by putting conflict and struggle at the origins of social power," Machiavelli "did not mean to say that agreement was impossible," but only "meant to underline the condition for *a power which does not mystify*, that is, participation in a common situation."[19]

At his best, Machiavelli envisions a free politics of citizens holding themselves and each other to the civil limits defined by their particular tradition, a tradition they recognize to be conventional yet honor or alter as conscious "co-founders." They not only live by their principles but choose those principles consciously, and collectively take responsibility for them. Thus Machiavelli anticipates Kant's claim that moral autonomy requires not just acting in accord with principles, but positing those principles for oneself. Kant even calls this positing "lawmaking," but he is speaking metaphorically.[20] Machiavelli, as always most

---

18. *Discourses* 1: 11 (G 225).
19. Maurice Merleau-Ponty, *Signs*, tr. Richard C. McCleary (Evanston, Ill.: Northwestern University Press, 1964), 215, my italics.
20. Immanuel Kant, "Metaphysical Foundation of Morals," in *The Philosophy of Kant*, tr. and ed. Carl J. Friedrich (New York: Modern Library, 1949), 186.

political, thinks that full autonomy requires not just metaphorical legis-
lation in the mind to govern one's own conduct, but literal and public
political engagement by which the members of a community together
continually (re)define their shared way of life.

Such a citizenry cherish their shared *nomos* despite its conven-
tionality and the arbitrariness of its origins, both because it defines who
they now are, and because of the way of life it now secures. Thus they
look to prudential consequences, yet not in narrowly self-interested
ways; they look to glory and the public good, but these ideals have tangible content in their lives; tangible content includes not just profit but
principle. Thus they think in terms of a glory that transcends, yet remains connected with, interest and need; and in terms of a self that is
distinct from others, yet remains connected with them and with principle. The glory is made meaningful by its content of practical gratification; the needs it gratifies are enlarged and humanized by being tied
to glory.

As with respect to action and membership, so too with respect to
judgment, what is needed is synthesis: a transcendence that is also a
continuity. To be human, our standards must transcend the animal, the
natural, the necessary, mere force. Yet to be meaningful for us they must
also retain—and so we must frequently renew—contact with their "origins" in natural need, the body, infancy and its earliest relationships. A
right understanding of the problem of judgment, a reverence without
reification, thus rests as the *vivere civile* does on the mature human capacities for mutuality and limitation, for judicious trust and trust-
worthiness. And since these in turn are anchored in the "basic trust" of
infancy, once again Machiavelli's best teaching is threatened wherever
his imagery evokes misogynist fears and unresolved infantile conflicts.

❖   ❖   ❖

The psychological counterpart of the problem of judgment in political theory is, in Freudian terms, the difference between repression and
sublimation, the former corresponding to superego domination, the
hortatory false piety toward authority associated with the Founder image; the latter corresponding to ego strength and an authority that is
not reified. Freud himself never systematically explicated the difference
between repression and sublimation.[21] Both are possible outcomes of
the encounter of infantile libidinal drives with parents, significant other

21. Sigmund Freud, *Standard Edition*, esp. 11: 53–54, 14: 94–95; but also 9: 161, 171,
175, 187–89, 197; 11: 78, 132–36, 178–90; 14: 245–48; 19: 207.

people, and the world of physical objects and processes. Repression occurs when a forbidden libidinal wish, blocked by the child's fear of punishment, is forced into the unconscious, where it continues to press for gratification. Energy is continually expended in keeping it unconscious, and neurotic symptoms may result from the inner conflict. Alternatively, however, the libidinal drive may be redirected to a substitute goal that is not forbidden, as when sexual energy is rechanneled into artistic, scientific, or cultural endeavor. Here the substitute activity is a genuine gratification that satisfies the libidinal drive, so no continuing expenditure of inner energy is required. Repression concerns the perpetual struggle between id and superego, which the ego attempts to mediate; sublimation concerns how the ego itself is constituted. A certain amount of repression, a certain amount of instinctual renunciation, is inevitable for anyone in any society; indeed, in his later, pessimistic writings Freud argues that neurosis might well be the necessary price for civilization.[22] But without sublimation, without the rechanneling of libidinal energy into acculturation, we could not become human persons at all.

We all begin in infancy, with our instinctual drives. And in a certain mood it may seem that the infant we once were was our only true self, all of its subsequent development a mere overlay of social pressures and external demands. But that does not really make sense, for it would leave the self an impoverished thing indeed. The infant is not yet a developed person, is incapable of action or meaningful choice; its needs and pleasures are infantile. Furthermore, that would mean that the whole development of human culture and history, the self-creation of the human species, was a series of accidents, a process devoid of any agency. If the adult person who acts is only an alien overlay over the core of true self, then not only the true "me" is incapable of action or responsibility, but so were my parents, grandparents, and their ancestors. "Society" shaped us all, but society itself is merely a collection of such nonagents, and no one is responsible for anything.

No matter how radically conceived, the liberation of the true self from alien social impositions cannot mean a return to infancy, for then there would be no self to liberate, no one *there* to take advantage of the liberty, but only total dependence. The *id* is not a self. The initial instinctual drives are essentially the same for all of us at the start of life; what makes us into unique individuals is the living of a human life, or at least the living through of a human childhood. In that sense, the self is a

22. Ibid., esp. 21: 96–97, 103–5, 108, 139, 143–45; and 9: 193; 11: 190.

history much more truly than it is an infant, a body, or an id. Only through our initiation into the cultural world of our parents, ancestors, and peers do we each become capable of particularity as a human self.

To be sure, *some* of the habits and attitudes we acquire in growing up really are and remain alien impositions, and at some point in adolescence or later we may reject them, more or less successfully, as demands that others imposed on us but that we do not ratify. But the self that rejects this or that aspect of its upbringing, of itself, is also a product of that upbringing. It makes no sense to suppose that I might reject as alien every aspect of myself, or even every aspect except those rudiments of self with which I was born. For the very capacity to make such rejections, and the standards by which I make them, are the products of my development. By the time I am capable of choice, undertaking deliberately to change myself or the world, I already am some particular individual person with concepts, commitments, standards, expectations, ideals, some of which may be alien impositions I have been indoctrinated to accept, but not all of which can be.

In that sense, the individuated self, the person capable of responsible action, is the product of convention, not nature; or rather, of the interaction between nature and convention, infant and world. For there is, of course, historical continuity between the infant I once was and the person I become. And my individual psyche, although it is equivalent neither to my body nor to its natural drives and needs, nevertheless can exist only—how should one put it?—in the most intimate, necessary, one-to-one relationship with this particular body. Psychic life remains embedded in physical life. Furthermore, at least some of the social convention internalized as we grow up becomes so fundamental a part of our selves that it is as if natural, a kind of "second nature" that behaves and must be regarded *for us* just like the truly or originally natural. And this second nature includes not merely powers and impulses, but also standards of conduct and judgment, goals, ideals.

Of course we can be and indeed often are wrong about ourselves, about what in us is alien and what must be accepted as given, or even revered as authoritative. We do not always live up to our own standards (that is part of what is meant by standards of conduct); but we violate them only at a price to ourselves.

Although a community is not a person, still, much of this is true of human communities as well. They, too, are formed not just at a moment of "birth" or founding but, on the one hand, have an underlying "nature" that would-be founders must accept as given, and a continuing "natural" life of productive and reproductive needs and activities, and, on the other hand, develop through their history, which they both make and suffer. They, too, might be said to acquire out of that history something like a "second nature"—cultural features so fundamental to the members' character and relationships, that they must be regarded as if natural *for this community*. And this second nature also includes some of the community's standards and commitments. So Machiavelli, for example, speaks of the hereditary ruler as a "natural" sovereign or prince, allegiance and deference to whom has become an unquestioned part of his subjects' very selves.[23] Yet communities, like individuals, frequently have illusions about themselves and their nature; in particular, they frequently have ideological illusions maintained because they serve the interests of some, to the detriment of others and of the whole.

For both individual and community, then, one can say: the self is a product of its history, and thus conventional, yet remains rooted in nature, and part of its arbitrary historical accretion becomes a second nature, defining the very self. Nevertheless, that core may be mistaken and violated by the self in action and judgment. Then there can be moments of insight, in which we recover aspects of the self that have been lost, distorted, or violated. Such moments may be quotidian, or sufficiently dramatic to be experienced as a "rebirth." That means: a starting over afresh because no longer "hung up on" the past; a recovery, therefore, of the self as free actor, of capacities that had been hidden by reification; a recovery, also, of the self as the product of its history and of those parts of that history that had been distorted or disguised.

That way of thinking about Machiavelli's "return to beginnings" appeared already in discussing the problem of action; now a different aspect emerges in the context of judgment. The return to beginnings is a new and right insight into what ideals, standards, and commitments are sacred to us and simultaneously a recognition of our capacity to make—and concomitant responsibility for making, revising, sustaining—them. For the individual, these are moments when "ego comes to be where id was," to paraphrase Freud; moments when repression is replaced by sublimation. For a community, they are moments when the citizens recover awareness of their stake in the public and at the same time redefine the public in terms of justice, thereby becoming free to act effectively as a community instead of being deadlocked in factional strife or resentfully bound to the past in the form of political vengeance. Though a community is not a person, still there are political counterparts to repression and sublimation: the former, a polity of domination,

23. *Prince*, ch. 3 (G 16).

where some make the rules by which others are forced to live; the latter, a polity of mutuality, where the citizens share jointly in self-
government.

❖   ❖   ❖

Machiavelli does not talk in psychological terms, yet he does address
the problem of human drives and natural needs and discuss how they
must be transformed in order to make men fit for the *vivere civile*, to
make animals human. What he says about them differs to some extent,
depending on which sort of need he is considering and which image of
manhood is most salient at the time. But in general, Machiavelli at his
best teaches, first, that human drives and appetites are natural and have
to be accepted; ideals that ignore them are vain. Second, however, too
much of any of these drives, or the wrong way of handling them, destroys civilization and *virtù*; thus they are the weapons of mystical feminine power implanted in men. But, third, their open and direct expression and reasonable gratification is the right way of handling them, the
way to prevent their excesses. His successful synthesis is a vision of sublimation; its failure takes the form of a vision of repression, the punitive
discipline of the Founder.

Machiavelli discusses three groups of such drives: hunger or greed,
ambition with its concomitant aggression, and sensuality or lust. Politically, each of them threatens to corrupt public life through privatization. Ambition, however, is also the source of civilization and a healthy
public life; avarice is more difficult to transform into public terms, and
sexuality Machiavelli mostly leaves to repression (and the occasional
evasion of repressive authority). In each case, the key to transforming
need into value, and private into public, is the capacity to acknowledge
limits. Each natural need must be given its due but must be distinguished from its unhealthy extension into limitless craving, when the
natural need is mediated by anxiety and becomes obsessive and insatiable. The truly human life requires acknowledgment of and provision for
our real needs but is undermined by the distorted extensions of drives
beyond need. Proper provision for needs also helps to prevent such unhealthy extension. So the greatest danger is the denial of human drives,
the setting of ideals for man that are unrelated to his real needs, the sort
of "humility, abjectness, and contempt for human things" that is taught
by the Church.[24]

Ambition, and the closely correlated problem of aggression, are most

24. *Discourses* 2: 2 (G 331).

instructive here. Ambition in itself is not a vice but a normal part of human nature that must be accepted; yet it is also a fury that does evil among men. Were it not for ambition, the desire for mastery, men would never grow up, would never leave the matriarchal household or create civilization and the city. Yet excessive ambition, ambition handled in the wrong way, is also what undermines civilization and politics. The distinctions to be drawn here are between two forms ambition may take, and two ways it may be handled. Direct and relatively self-confident ambition, the desire to grow, to develop one's capacities and be admired for one's achievements—these are all healthy features without which we could not reach human maturity; they are also capable of (intermittent) satisfaction, like any natural hunger. And they are ready, under appropriate conditions, to be channeled toward public ends and thereby to make men genuinely public-spirited; they are capable of producing a right understanding and pursuit of glory. They are to be contrasted to the resentful, envious, self-denigrating, masochistic ambition that knows no limit because it seeks to silence an inner critic who is never satisfied, because it wants to undo the past. Similarly, the open and direct expression of ambition must be distinguished from its indirect and hidden pursuit; the institutions that politicize ambition and make it public, from those that privatize it and drive it underground.

The resentful and insatiable sort of ambition is by its very nature de-politicizing and makes people unfit for citizenship. It leads them to prefer vengeance to success at any other undertaking; thus they court disaster, for instance by inviting foreign forces into the city to support their side in a factional dispute. Where this condition becomes widespread, even men of *virtù* find it almost impossible to pursue the public good, for the resentfully ambitious are filled with envy of other men's glory, "grudging," "ungrateful," ever ready to "censure" and bring others down, even if all suffer as a result.[25]

The wrong sort of ambition can be minimized, and its dangerous effects for political life controlled to some extent, by acknowledging the right sort of ambition as natural, acknowledging the right sort of conflict as healthy, and providing institutional channels for their expression. "The malignant humors that spring up in men" must somehow "find vent," and where they are not permitted "lawful" and open expression, the will find "unlawful" methods of private revenge that produce factions and civil war.[26] Institutions for the public, open ex-

25. "[Golden] Ass," ch. 1, lines 97–99 (G 752); *Mandragola*, prologue (G 778).
26. *Discourses* 1: 7–8 (G 112–16).

pression of ambition and anger, like the Roman institution of "accusations," will minimize both the formation of resentful, private ambition and its danger to public life by forcing all into public channels and exposing false, merely envious charges for what they are. Ambition and aggression then must be acknowledged, even encouraged, and brought out into the open.

The case of hunger and avarice or greed is less clear-cut. Obviously, human beings have bodies that need food; and hunger and the desire "to acquire" are therefore natural and inevitable. Only a fool would locate a city where it might look "glorious" but its inhabitants have no way to make a living. Natural hunger, however, is also capable of (intermittent) satiation through human effort. Its extension into avarice, greed, the insatiable craving for further acquisition for its own sake, is a different matter. It may, in a way, grow out of the natural need, yet it can outweigh even that need itself: the miser will starve himself in order to add to his riches. Avarice is, one might say, natural hunger transformed by anxiety, a vain attempt to provide against all future hunger; it reflects a fundamental distrust of the adult capacity to feed oneself (and others).

Like the resentful sort of ambition, avarice privatizes and sets people in rivalry with each other in destructive ways. Being insatiable, it instigates action without the recognition of limits, of commonality, promoting factionalism in the city and displacing the craving for glory by petty and private goals. Machiavelli's charge against the Florentine bourgeoisie is that there is no "limit or measure to their greed." They "plunder" each other of their goods; they avoid paying their taxes; they "sell justice"; and they "thirst not for true glory but for despicable honors depending on hates, enmities, disputes, factions."[27] Like Churchmen, "men in trade" are incapable of soldiering, the direct expression of aggression; thus they are incapable of autonomy, forced to follow "the Fortune of others."[28] All Florence's "evils," Machiavelli wrote a friend, "proceed from our being in the hands of priests and merchants; neither the one nor the other knows how to manage arms."[29] What is worse, neither understands the meaning of glory, so they pursue the wrong sort of goal.

Ideally, Machiavelli would like to treat this problem in terms of the opposing interests and "humors" of different classes, reintegrated through political struggle. Bourgeois avarice must be tempered by the nobility's military spirit and ambition for glory. But in the absence of a

27. *Florentine Histories* 3: 5 (G 1146).   28. Ibid., 1: 39 (G 1079).
29. Quoted in Ferrara, *Private Correspondence*, 46.

Florentine nobility, he must try to teach men of avarice about the value of glory, an extraordinarily difficult task of theoretical bridge building. For the only appeal the merchants can understand is to self-interest, yet their orientation to avarice and self-interest is precisely what must be overcome. Speak to them of glory, and they cannot hear; but speak to them of interest, and you cannot express your message. So Machiavelli insists, on the one hand, that *virtù* and the *vivere civile* are the only effective ways to secure wealth, that "riches multiply in a free country," and on the other hand, that the concern for wealth privatizes people and tends to destroy *virtù*: "Well-ordered republics" keep "their treasuries rich and their citizens poor."[30] In addition, the topic of avarice is also psychologically more troubling than that of ambition, for ambition draws men away from infantile dependence and is not itself an impulse of sensuality or nurturance. For men troubled about dependence, ambition is thus a "safer" drive with which to deal than either avarice or lust. Sensuality, sex, and lust are, in a way, most difficult of all for Machiavelli. Here there seems to be no way to transmute private into public welfare, and the best that can be hoped for is the imposition of a severe, public discipline in support of monogamy and patriarchy, combined with clandestine private freedom for men to pursue sexual pleasure. The reproduction of the species is of course beneficial to the community as well as individually pleasurable, but Machiavelli is not prepared to argue, in accord with Church teaching, that good men will find their sexual pleasure only in the begetting of legitimate children. Nor is he prepared to challenge the mores of his time by suggesting that species reproduction might be reorganized in ways more consonant with human needs and pleasure. Thus "women" remain, in his theory, the most mysterious and in a way the most dangerous threat. Again, there is not much point in blaming Machiavelli for having failed to challenge the misogyny of his time—a topic that surely would have seemed to him remote from his explicit concerns—yet misogyny repeatedly works counter to his best political teachings.

Concerning judgment, once again Machiavelli summons us to an acknowledgment of our adult human powers and responsibilities; but he does so by summoning males to their manhood. And once again that turns out to defeat as much as to serve his purpose. For insofar as adulthood and full humanity are pursued out of anxiety about dependence, their pursuit will be distorted by childish fantasies and fears, the need to prove what cannot be proved because it is forever in anxious doubt.

30. *Discourses* 2: 2 (G 332); 1: 37 (G 272).

Men anxious about dependence will fear to trust anyone or anything and thus will be inclined toward cynicism. They will fear the feminine "other" inside themselves and will thus be powerfully drawn to hortatory hero worship and to repressive ideals. Fearing nurturance or other sensual gratification except under stringent safeguards of discipline, they will seethe with impotent anger, prefer vengeance to direct gratification, and identify with their—real or fantasied—oppressor, all of which tends to generate a conception of autonomy that blocks access to its real achievement.

❖   ❖   ❖

Machiavelli urged people to assume deliberate, active, collective control over the conditions of their lives. Yet he urged action framed by the recognition of limits: limits on what is historically possible, here and now, and humanly possible anywhere; limits on what is politically acceptable, capable of enlisting the support of fellow citizens; limits on what is right and deserving of true glory. In teaching this delicately balanced multiple synthesis, Machiavelli also articulated a right understanding of that topic so central to Renaissance experience: autonomy.

A wrong understanding of human autonomy, by which Machiavelli himself was frequently tempted but from which he tried to wean us, is as a kind of sovereignty, a self-contained isolation, a solipsistic fantasy of omnipotence. Here, to be autonomous would mean either to be utterly alone, needing no one and nothing outside oneself, or else to be singular in privilege and power—the only person among objects, the only human among animals, the only god among humans—capable of dominating and free to exploit whatever is outside the self.

Machiavelli at his best, by contrast, teaches an autonomy that acknowledges our necessary interdependencies: that human freedom lies not in eradicating or escaping our necessary connections with others like ourselves, but in acknowledging them and using them to liberate us from other, unnecessary dependencies. "If men wish to be free," as Hannah Arendt has said, "it is precisely sovereignty they must renounce."[31] That is the point of Machiavelli's distinctions between liberty and license, between true glory and that false glory by which tyrants are deceived, between genuine autonomy and "doing whatever you want." Both princes and republics he says need "to be regulated by the laws; because a prince who can do what[ever] he wants to is crazy; [and] a people that can do what[ever] it wants to is not wise."[32]

---

31. Hannah Arendt, "What Is Freedom?" in *Between Past and Future*, 165.
32. *Discourses* 1: 58 (G 317).

True autonomy is a matter of accurate self-knowledge and responsible self-government. For both individual and community, it is a matter of getting right the synthesis between our determinant past and our freedom to act, between our objective interconnectedness and our individual agency, between our natural beginnings and our capacity for transcendence. Only through recognizing our particular past and the present world and self it has created do we become free to act effectively. Only in shared political interaction can we come to know accurately, and to take responsibility for, what we are doing. That limits our personal freedom because each of us is only one among many citizens but also expands it because together we can take charge of the social conditions that we collectively create, that would otherwise constrain our individual lives as alien powers. Only by transforming instinct into authority, recognizing the demands of both nature and our human commitments, do we become free simultaneously of and in our necessities.

That is the essence of Machiavelli's understanding of action within a context of necessity, of individual *virtù* within a context of interdependence, of transcendent value as anchored in particular, secular, historical life. The breakdown of synthesis along any one of these dimensions is "corruption": the corruption of passivity, of privatization, of cynicism, but also the corruption of mindless action for its own sake, or of hypocritical exhortation to "public" or "higher" duties that are empty. Along each of these dimensions synthesis has always to be actively made. Yet its making is not arbitrary but requries a certain reverence toward self, world, and ideals. The experience of political action among fellow citizens was for Machiavelli the best way to achieve this sort of self-knowledge. Where that process broke down into corruption, as it always tended to do, the next best hope for its restoration lay in leadership, of the sort employing "the way of freedom." Where even the necessary leadership seemed lacking, or people were so corrupt that available leadership could not help them, there was perhaps an outside chance that political theory might serve. In each case the point was returning people to themselves: to their connection with past and future, to their connection with each other, to their connection with nature and human values, to their capacity for action and a right understanding of the context in which that action must take place.

That is the heart of what Machiavelli has to teach us. Yet he himself was not able to sustain this vision. On certain subjects, such as relations between men and women, he never achieved it; on others, such as international relations, he at most defined a set of problems and questions pointing toward it. Even in discussing the *vivere civile* he was unable to sustain the vision consistently. Where he lost it, the loss was correlated with images and metaphors about sex roles and familial relations; particularly with the fear of dependence and of malevolent feminine power, and consequently with an anxious and defensive stress on autonomy, solipsistically conceived, and *machismo*, whether expressed in the cult of violence, in cynicism, or in submission to a supermasculine leader.

Machiavelli summons us from apathy, private acquisitiveness, and reactive violence to heroism and to glory. How shall we assess that summons? Heroism, like so many familiar and apparently simple concepts, turns out on closer inspection to be a profoundly ambiguous notion. Consider two contrasting views of what it might mean; call them the traditionally "masculine" and the traditionally "feminine" view. In the traditionally masculine view, the summons to heroism is a call to leave behind lower for higher things; to give one's life meaning and purpose by the willingness to sacrifice physical comfort and even life itself for some noble ideal; to leave the household for the public realm, there to express one's unique individuality in connection with something larger and more valuable than self. Without such opportunity to pursue heroism, human life would be impoverished. And so the men march out to war in pursuit of glory.

But now comes the subversive, the traditionally "feminine," view. The women watch the men depart, look at each other, and shake their heads: there they go again, the fools, making themselves feel important with all that fine rhetoric and shiny equipment, pretending to be fierce to hide their vulnerability. They are marching off to kill other people like themselves—and like us!—just so that they can get away from us and the kids for a while. And we are left, as usual, to cope with the true realities: to tend to the children, the harvest, the cooking and weaving that keep bodies alive.

What shall we say of this ancient confrontation of views? Surely there is something right in each. Surely the summons to heroism and glory is often a mask for privilege and exploitation, or for anxious flight from reality. But surely also a life confined merely to the household and care of the body is impoverished. Exclusion from community self-government and a share in making history is a deprivation. To lose or to flee contact with either the public or the private is to lose a part of our humanity. That is as true for the housewife whose life is empty as for her executive husband who imagines that clean shirts appear in his drawer by magic; as true for the alienated worker or apathetic peasant as for the privileged "movers and shakers" who live off of, and are utterly dependent on, the productive labor of others.

Machiavelli at his best summons us to heroism rightly understood: to public action for higher goals that nevertheless serve our natural and private needs, action that recognizes both our vulnerability and our capacity as creators and judges. He strives for, and sometimes achieves, a synthesis of the traditionally "masculine" and "feminine" views of heroism. But insofar as he excludes or encourages his readers to exclude the women and things feminine from the vision, the synthesis is bound to be lost. Heroism becomes *machismo* and embodies the wrong conception of autonomy, as sovereignty and domination. The participatory, republican politics of freedom does coexist in Machiavelli's political theory with protofascism; the key to their complex relationship lies in the metaphor that "fortune is a woman."

Afterthoughts, 1999

The good news is: the art of interpreting the enigmatic Machiavelli is alive and well. Numerous books and essays illuminating his thought have appeared in the fifteen years since *Fortune is a Woman* was published, and the long-standing debates about his political theory continue: ancient versus modern, authoritarian versus republican, sincere and principled versus devious and sinister. There would be neither point nor pleasure in reviewing that literature here, though I shall say a little about some lines of inquiry within it that touch directly on the concerns of this book.

But first, the bad news: my book hasn't made a noticeable dent in the established genres of Machiavelli scholarship. It is something of a maverick, does not fit well into any of those genres. "Provocative," "unusual," "ambitious" the kinder reviewers call it.[1] The reviews also indicate the books' weaknesses, however: some that they point out explicitly, and others—failures of explication—revealed indirectly by their misreadings. They leave me regretful on several counts.

First off, I wish I had been more emphatic about the irrelevance of grammatical gender. The fact that Italian is a gendered language in which the word for fortune is grammatically feminine has just about nothing to do with my argument, since speakers or writers of a gendered language who personify some noun quite often assign it a gender different from the word's grammatical classification. The point being so obvi-

---

1. Arlene W. Saxonhouse, Review of *Fortune is a Woman,* by Hanna Fenichel Pitkin. *Ethics* 105 (1985): 759–61 at 759; Mary G. Dietz, Review of *Fortune is a Woman,* by Hanna Fenichel Pitkin. *Contemporary Sociology* 14 (1985): 215–17 at 215.

ous, I gave it only a single paragraph in the middle of a chapter.[2] That was a mistake, since two reviewers—distinguished Renaissance scholars both—considered it a major problem I had overlooked.

Next, a number of regrets about gender and psychology. It was a serious error in explicating the psychoanalytic literature to have set aside the topic of feminine psychology as too difficult and complex. That surely contributed to the impression formed by some reviewers that I am a "gleefully" castrating man-hater out to condemn Machiavelli as a "misogynist authoritarian" (though others fault me for not condemning him severely enough).[3] Clearly I also should have said more about just how troubles in infancy in relation to the mother might affect a boy's later Oedipal rivalry, since relations between fathers and sons figure prominently in the chapters on cities in the family drama.[4]

Most important, however, are my regrets about the penumbra of vagueness surrounding the book's central concern: the connection between gender relations and Machiavelli's political theory. Although aware of this problem from early in the book's writing, I remained—and remain—unable to do better. There is a clear and explicit disclaimer: this is not a psychobiography and does not allege a causal explanation of Machiavelli's ideas. There are also passages about what the book does allege, but not nearly so clear or explicit. Some reviewers found their way nonetheless, but others were understandably at a loss and jumped to wrong conclusions.

No doubt their difficulties were worsened by my failure to distinguish clearly enough between my own judgments and my efforts to articulate Machiavelli's. Thus several reviewers missed the central point about Machiavelli's three conflicting images of manhood: that he circles endlessly among them because each is unsatisfactory to him (not to me) by the criteria of the other two. My "Machiavelli at his best," by contrast, reflects my judgment (not his). It was not intended to express what Machiavelli "really thought," his "true position," for my argument is precisely that he has no singular true position, that this irresolute quality in the texts is what most needs to be addressed. "Machiavelli at his best" is simply *my* favorite voice in the dialogue—or rather, trialogue—he conducts with himself. It is what, in my opinion, constitutes his greatness, even though it is manifestly not the loudest voice. Here it would

2. See above, 131.
3. Lauro Martines, "Mastering the Matriarch," *Times Literary Supplement* 4270 (February 1, 1985): 113; N. J., Abstract of *Fortune is a Woman*, by Hanna Fenichel Pitkin. *Studies on Women Abstracts* 7 (1989): 317.
4. As Mary Dietz points out; Dietz, Review, 217.

have helped if I had distinguished more clearly within the citizen image of manhood, between the ways in which it shares in that endless circling, as yet another defense against the feminine threat, and its potential for transcending the trilemma.

Despite these multiple regrets, much about this book still seems to me valid and valuable. I remain convinced that Machiavelli's notorious inconsistencies and apparent incoherences must be acknowledged rather than denied; that they are not random but reflect three distinct lines of thought about politics; that each of these lines of thought is tied to a version of manhood in all of that word's multiple connotations: humanness, masculinity, adulthood, autonomy; and that the endless circling among the three lines of thought in the texts is related to the uncanny power unconsciously ascribed to women.

My book's failure to articulate, let alone prove, a clear, singular thesis, I think, in part reflects Machiavelli's irresoluteness, to which I have tried to remain faithful even while providing a synoptic, organizing overview of the textual chaos. The requirement of such fidelity to the texts, paradoxically combined with the need to provide an insightful schema that illuminates and yet preserves the multiplicity, is, I suppose, my basic methodological commitment in studying political theory, and it distinguishes this book from the many more traditional Machiavelli interpretations that do ascribe to him a singular "true view," ignoring or explaining away the textual counterevidence.

As both its title and the dedication to my mother suggest, this book reads Machiavelli in terms of the Woman Question, or—to be more precise—of the symbolic representation of woman, and thus in terms of gender relations. It was the first to do so seriously and at length, though others have since adopted the approach (not, I think, under my influence). The book did not start out with such an intent. Initially it was to be a minor article to enhance my *curriculum vitae* and terminate a frighteningly long fallow period that had followed my last previous publication. It set out to transcribe one of my routine lectures on Machiavelli in an undergraduate course, a lecture concerning his conflicted understandings of manhood. At that time there were only two of these: the fox, based in his own experience, and a vague compound of what later became the citizen and the Founder, derived from his reading and associated with ancient Rome. There was nothing at all about the Woman Question, family, childhood, or gender relations.

As I began trying to turn the lecture into an article, however, it took
on a life of its own that escaped my control. Three developments remain
vivid in my memory, though I am no longer sure in what order they
occurred. The original two visions of manhood complicated themselves
into three; the text sprouted a footnote about family life in Machiavelli's
time; and it suddenly struck me that there was something bizarre, even
cowardly, about me—a woman—criticizing this male thinker in terms
of his conflicts about manliness without ever touching on (my own conflicts about) womanliness or femininity.

The most pressing practical problem was the footnote, which almost
immediately became a pathological growth. Greatly admiring Erik Erikson's psychoanalytically oriented study of Luther, I secretly yearned to
write something comparable, but the requisite information about Machiavelli's childhood simply did not exist.[5] Instead, I thought, I must at
least include a paragraph or a footnote about what was happening at
the time to family structure and child-rearing practices. Ashamed of my
ignorance, I took for granted that historians of the period must know,
so I pulled from my shelves the two books that seemed likely to sum up
that knowledge succinctly, Burckhardt on the Renaissance and Ariès on
childhood.[6] To my dismay, they flatly contradicted one another. Damn!
I would have to go to the library. Once begun, however, the library research went on and on, and the footnote grew. (I recall a lunch with my
then colleague, Norman Jacobson, in which I sought his advice on what
to do with a footnote already longer than the article to which it was
appended.) It took quite a while before I realized that the ungainly
growth might be not a cancer but a pregnancy, that my article was determined to be a book.

This was in the 1970's, when some of my women students were getting involved in what was then called "women's liberation," and specifically in issues of affirmative action at the university. I myself had grown
up, one might say, as a second-generation liberated woman; that is, my
mother fought those battles in Germany in her youth, after the First
World War, and I was one of those privileged exceptions who succeeded
under existing standards and procedures in entering the ranks of an
overwhelmingly male faculty. While I took for granted that ability is
independent of gender, genuinely tried to support my women students,
and regarded myself as politically and socially radical, the Woman Ques-

5. Erikson, *Young Man Luther.*
6. Burckhardt, *Civilization*; Ariès, *Centuries.*

tion was not my passionate, personal cause. In truth, I quite enjoyed being the (almost) only woman among all those men, relishing both the (as I supposed) honor of it and the socio-sexual opportunities. The last thing I would have wanted was to concern myself professionally with "women's issues" as that phrase was then understood: cosmetics and recipes or, at a stretch, welfare policy and school budgets. It was mainly my students who educated me in these matters, although the response of (some of) my male colleagues to the women students' increasing militancy also proved enlightening.

Far from being a militant feminist determined to expose Machiavelli as a male chauvinist pig, then, as some of my reviewers assume, I backed into the Woman Question almost inadvertently in writing this book, more out of loyalty to my father and his profession of psychoanalysis than out of solidarity with my mother or other women. This has left me somewhat uneasy about whether to call myself a feminist, an issue raised for me in connection with this book by Susan Moller Okin's review, about which I shall say a little more at the end.[7]

Turning now to recent scholarly developments tangent to the argument of this book, let's begin with Anthony Parel's *The Machiavellian Cosmos*, which examines the role of astrology in Renaissance thought generally, and for Machiavelli in particular. Astrology was very widely accepted in this period. Parel calls it "the natural philosophy of the day," and argues that Machiavelli, too, "entertained an astrological worldview."[8] The tradition of thought deriving from Ptolemy, one of the "two major figures most influential in setting the background for astrological thought in the Renaissance, . . . divi[ded] astrology into two major parts": the general, concerned with the "fortunes and ethos of nations and states," and the particular, concerned with "the temperaments and fortunes of individuals."[9]

Parel applies this distinction to Chapter 25 of *The Prince*, where fortune is compared first to a river likely to flood, and then to a woman. My book devotes a few pages to trying to puzzle out the problematic relationship between these two images, which have rather different—

7. Susan Moller Okin, "The Roots of Realpolitik," *Women's Review of Books* 2 (January 1985): 15–16.

8. Anthony J. Parel, *The Machiavellian Cosmos* (New Haven and London: Yale University Press, 1992), 1–2.

9. Ibid., 11–12.

even contradictory—implications about how to confront fortune.[10] If fortune is a river, the implication is that one must prepare for bad weather while the sun shines, by building dams and dykes. In terms of character, this requires foresight, the capacity to delay gratification, caution, cold calculation, prudence, and technical skill. If fortune is a woman, by contrast, she must be confronted as a person rather than as material to be worked, and because she is a female person envisioned by Machiavelli as encountering a male, the policies and character requisite for his success are boldness, impetuousness, passion, initiative, and courage (youthfulness helps too, he says). Both kinds of conduct and character can be seen as *virtù;* both reflect Machiavelli's call to manly activism, contrasting to laziness, fatalism, and passivity. Yet the two modes seem almost incompatible, and indeed Machiavelli explicitly says that they are (although whether he saw an incompatibility between the two metaphors of chapter 25 is not clear).

The relationship between the two images of fortune in Chapter 25 presents an interpretive puzzle, then, toward the solution of which Parel makes an important contribution. Following Gennaro Sasso, he focuses on a key passage that marks the transition in the chapter from the river image to the woman image. Noting the trouble that passage has given to editors, who had to paragraph the Italian text, and to translators, who have rendered it into English in a wide variety of ways, Parel suggests an astrological reading. The passage marks the transition by announcing that Machiavelli is now moving from *universale* to *particulare,* in some sense whose specification is the problem. Hitherto the sentence has been read in a logical sense: a topic treated broadly in the first part of the chapter is now to be taken up in detail. But Parel suggests that the central reference is to the astrological distinction between universal and particular fortune—that is, between the fate of nations or states and the fate of individuals.[11]

"Countries and individuals are affected differently by fortune," he says, and Machiavelli's two metaphors "refer to two quite distinct realities."[12] States that want to prosper must treat fortune as if it were a river likely to flood; individuals wanting to succeed should conduct themselves like men confronting a difficult woman. There is no conflict in the chapter, no interpretive problem, as long as one keeps the two contexts properly sorted out.

10. See above, 147–53.
11. Parel, *Machiavellian Cosmos,* 67–70.
12. Ibid., 70, 85.

Next, Parel asserts, for reasons that he does not set forth, that Chapter 25 of *The Prince* is Machiavelli's "final statement on the subject," so that references to fortune elsewhere must be read in accord with Parel's exegetical rule.[13] "It is crucial that we adhere to that distinction," he says, because "to consider otherwise would be to mix categories that should not be mixed."[14] Thus, while "the metaphor of woman marks the high point of Machiavelli's treatment of Fortune as she affects individuals," it has no relevance "to Fortune as she affects countries" and "no application in international politics."[15] In short, woman is not the key to Machiavelli's political theory, for that image applies to only half his concerns, and in a sense to the less political half; the river is at least equally important. The key to the whole is astrology.

I do not mean to construe Parel's argument as an attack on *Fortune is a Woman*. Insofar as he deals with my book, he is actually very kind, taking me to task only for my too curt dismissal of astrological influence in Machiavelli's thought.[16] Parel persuades me that Machiavelli indeed shared in the widespread acceptance of astrology of his time, and I am fully convinced by his reading of the transitional sentence. What troubles me is only the conclusion he draws about how interpreters must handle Machiavelli's two metaphors. Assigning each to a distinct, hermetically sealed sphere and insisting that they do not conflict seems to me not only untrue to the texts, but also almost perversely blind to the larger issues at stake.

In one sense, to be sure, the rigid distinction is a foregone conclusion, an artifact of the two images themselves. The damming or dyking of a river is rarely if ever undertaken by a single individual alone; it conjures up collective endeavor, public policy, states. A woman, by contrast, is herself an individual and thus, at least under conventional assumptions, conjures up confrontation with a man, another individual. But these are metaphors; one must not confuse them with what they are taken to represent. States and other collectivities are very often depicted metaphorically as individuals, sometimes male and sometimes female. "One does not build 'dams' or 'dykes' to avert a personal tragedy," Parel says, which is of course literally true.[17] But individual conduct that resembles the timely building of precautionary dams surely does sometimes avert

---

13. Ibid., 77.
14. Ibid., 70.
15. Ibid., 82–83.
16. Parel does misread one passage, presuming an affirmative answer to a question I posed only rhetorically; ibid., 85; see above, 151–52.
17. Parel, *Machiavellian Cosmos*, 70.

a personal tragedy or promote personal success. Similarly a public policy of boldness and passionate commitment, resembling a rough and impetuous courtship, will sometimes succeed in international relations.

Accordingly, it is not surprising that Machiavelli himself does not consistently observe Parel's rigid boundary. It is true that the river metaphor, which appears rarely, is applied only to states, but fortune as woman is repeatedly applied to states as well.[18] Parel himself introduces an example from the poem on fortune, which he calls Machiavelli's "most comprehensive review of history." Here fortune is explicitly presented as a goddess, who—as Parel reports—"turns states and kingdoms upside down," so that, he adds, "the fortunes of states are due to the actions of this goddess."[19]

Sorting out Machiavelli's use of the two images is made more difficult by the fact, to which I have already alluded, that "fortune" is grammatically feminine in Italian, so that even when it is a river, translators tend to call it "she," and often even to capitalize the word as if it were her name. Indeed, Parel repeatedly does so himself. Nor are they altogether wrong in doing so, for Machiavelli speaks even of the river in anthropomorphic terms, as "angry" and "in fury," and as "directing her [its] fury where she [it] knows that no dykes or embankments are ready to hold her [it]."[20]

More important than these almost technical difficulties, however, is that Parel's neat bifurcation obliterates the central issue at stake for political theory, which concerns the *relationship* between individual and collective fate, between individual action and public policy. Nations and states are made up of individual people, so that what befalls the former has profound consequences for the latter, and the sum of what individuals do or fail to do largely shapes the fate of their collectivity. Of a shallow and uninteresting political theorist it might conceivably be true that he ignores these connections—both conceptual and causal—and treats individuals always in accord with one perspective, states always in accord with a different, incompatible perspective. But it most assuredly is not true of Machiavelli, who was a very great political theorist.

Indeed, precisely Machiavelli, with his interest in leadership, in "princes" (both within principalities and in the sense of principal leader

18. See also Roger D. Masters, *Machiavelli, Leonardo, and the Science of Power* (Notre Dame and London: University of Notre Dame Press, 1996), 302 n 39, where Masters notes the distinction that Parel stresses, but without Parel's insistence on rigid dichotomization.
19. Parel, *Machiavellian Cosmos*, 71.
20. Machiavelli, *Prince*, ch. 25 (G 90).

in republics), military commanders, and conspirators, constantly inter-
relates and sometimes conflates the success of the leader with the rise or
renewal of the state. (Hence his ambiguous concept of *lo stato,* which
hovers in meaning between the polity that the prince leads or holds, and
his status or estate as prince.)[21] Accepting Parel's compartmentalization
would mean missing Machiavelli's almost obsessive concern, throughout
his works and even apart from any metaphors, with adopting the right
style of action for the times (prudence versus boldness, kindness versus
cruelty, and so on) if such characterological versatility is possible for
human beings, or, failing that, with having available the right sort of
leader to suit the times.[22] Thus, while Parel is quite right that "the river-
metaphor is as important as the woman metaphor" for Machiavelli, the
two images do not "refer to two quite distinct realities."[23]

The relationship between these two realities is a profound problem
for Machiavelli, for astrological thought (as Parel shows), and for us.
Since completing this book, I have come to regard that problem as located at the intersection between two deep and intractable philosophical
issues unavoidably joined in political theory: the relationship between
universal and particular (individual and society, citizen and polity, the
possibility and appropriateness of categorizing people), and what is
sometimes (misleadingly) called the "free will problem": how to understand political choice, creativity, action, and responsibility in relation to
historical·conditions and forces, which reflect past action and delimit
present possibilities.[24]

While I quote Machiavelli's "fortune is a woman" and Parel holds
that "the river-metaphor is as important as the woman-metaphor," the
title of Roger D. Masters' most recent book suggests that he has opted
for the other extreme: *Fortune is a River.*[25] It turns out, however, that
he focuses on the river less to displace the woman than to continue a
line of research begun in his last previous book, *Machiavelli, Leonardo,*

21. Pitkin, *Wittgenstein,* 310–12.
22. See above, 158–59.
23. Parel, *Machiavellian Cosmos,* 85.
24. See above, 158–59; Hanna Fenichel Pitkin, *The Attack of the Blob: Hannah Arendt's Concept of the Social* (Chicago and London: University of Chicago Press, 1998),
241–49.
25. Roger D. Masters, *Fortune is a River: Leonardo da Vinci and Niccolò Machiavelli's
Magnificent Dream to Change the Course of Florentine History* (New York, London,
Toronto, Sydney, Singapore: Free Press, 1998).

and the Science of Power.[26] Masters, a distinguished political theorist, has recently turned historian, exploring and extrapolating from Machiavelli's relationship with Leonardo da Vinci and their collaboration on an unsuccessful project to rechannel the Arno River, which flows through Florence and then through Pisa—the enemy of Florence—to the sea.[27] The plan, devised by Leonardo and supported by Machiavelli, had the military purpose of cutting off Pisa's water supply, but Masters holds that it also aimed at more ambitious goals: irrigating the Arno valley and giving Florence navigable access to the sea, and to the new lands recently visited by Amerigo Vespucci.

That both men were involved in the Arno project is well known; that they probably knew each other is widely accepted, though neither mentions the other in extant writings. But Masters argues that they were friends, perhaps even "intimate" friends, and that Leonardo's influence and the experience of the Arno project "particularly shaped" Machiavelli's thought, turning it toward science and technology, and thus toward the modern outlook.[28] Could the mysterious "new way" that Machiavelli declares himself resolved to open by his theorizing, Masters asks rhetorically, have involved "the project of using science and technology—as Leonardo's *Notebooks* show he [Leonardo] thought was possible—to transform the human condition to one of hitherto unimagined convenience, security, and plenty?"[29] It was under Leonardo's influence that Machiavelli "came to use the river as a symbol or metaphor," so that the image of fortune as a river "echo[es] Leonardo's plans to move and tame the Arno."[30] The river is crucial because the friendship was crucial; so, in that sense, for Masters the key to understanding Machiavelli is not woman but male bonding.

26. Masters' *Fortune* thus should not be read as challenging mine, which it mentions only as an item in the bibliography.
27. By "turned historian" I do not mean to suggest that Masters has abandoned political theory, nor that political theorists never write about history, but only that he has actually been doing historical research in primary source material.
28. Masters, *Machiavelli*, 13, 3.
29. Ibid., 190. Masters argues that Machiavelli learned from the failure of the Arno project that technology is not enough, that engineering science must be supplemented by politics, which, however, Masters equates with a "science of power" or "of human nature." In this book, indeed, Masters himself seems to join in trying to further such a science out of ethology, yet he also seems critical of the hubristic modern confidence in science's unlimited potential; ibid., 5, 8, 131, 133, 146, 189, 191, 209, 210, 212; Masters, *Fortune*, 147. In his recent essay, Masters appears to revert to the idea that Machiavelli did share Leonardo's hubristic modern technologism; Roger D. Masters, "Machiavelli's Sexuality: 'Love, be my guide, my leader,'" unpublished paper prepared for delivery at the Annual Meeting of the American Political Science Association (September 1998), 28.
30. Masters, *Fortune*, 208–209. See also Masters, *Machiavelli*, 8.

That way of putting it seems particularly apt in light of the most recent turn in Masters' historical research. At the 1998 Annual Meeting of the American Political Science Association he presented a paper "outing" Machiavelli as a bisexual.[31] This is a remarkable departure for a self-proclaimed follower of the late Leo Strauss, who held—as Masters says—"that a major philosopher's work should be understood on its own terms, without reference to the author's personal experiences or sexual behavior." Machiavelli, Masters suggests, may be the only "legitimate exception" to this rule, justifying the breach of Straussian decorum that Masters commits.[32]

That male homosexuality and bisexuality were widespread in Renaissance Florence, even notoriously so, is not news. That Machiavelli took pleasure in violating conventional pieties in his private correspondence and some of his literary works is evident, as is his predilection for parody, satire, reversal, and inversion. The letters and some of the literary works, moreover, are full of sexual allusions, risqué jokes, and tales of sexual adventure. Masters draws on the recent work of Michael Rocke to argue persuasively that a number of these allusions and stories are homosexual in nature.[33] He also holds—I think less persuasively—that the sexual tales Machiavelli relates, which other interpreters take to be amusing fictions, metaphors, or even lies intended to enhance Machiavelli's reputation among his friends, are factual reports of his own experiences.[34]

What is seriously problematic, however, is that Masters takes Machiavelli's supposed conduct to have been motivated not by sexual desire but by propagandistic purposes. Machiavelli "engaged in overt sexuality for the purpose of shocking others," his promiscuity "an intentional provocation that extended to homosexual as well as heterosexual behavior."[35] What he did amounted to an "exuberant espousal of sexual liberation," the incidents a series of "theatrical events intended" to challenge doctrines of chastity and sexual restraint deriving from both the Christian and the "Socratic" tradition.[36] Machiavelli's orientation was "a thoroughgoing materialism" or naturalism; he sought "to liberate the natural human passions" from pious constraints in order to "redirect them

31. Masters, "Machiavelli's Sexuality."
32. Ibid., 1. See also 27–28 n 63.
33. Michael Rocke, *Forbidden Friendships* (New York: Oxford University Press, 1996).
34. Masters relies heavily on speculation and conjecture, as may be unavoidable, given the scarcity of hard facts.
35. Masters, "Machiavelli's Sexuality," 13.
36. Ibid., 28, 3.

toward this-worldly ends."[37] That is Masters' real justification for his public exposure of Machiavelli's intimate life: "Niccolò's sexuality . . . is important for philosophical reasons," a proposition with which I of course thoroughly agree, though for different reasons.[38]

While Masters' essay, surprisingly, does not mention Leonardo da Vinci, whose sexual deviance Freud discusses, nor suggest an affair between Leonardo and Machiavelli, it does hold that the young Machiavelli had an affair with Giuliano de Medici. Partly on that basis, Masters argues that Machiavelli's real loyalty was not republican, but to the Medici. This would conflict with my view of him as a committed republican (hedged by my insistence on his universal ambivalence), but that debate is a perennial one in Machiavelli studies. Machiavelli was certainly critical of Soderini, as Masters says, but personal loyalty to Soderini must not be confused with commitment to a republican Florence.[39] In any case, the notion that Machiavelli may have been bisexual and have had some homosexual relationships seems plausible, and some of Masters' evidence is persuasive. The possibility would fit nicely into my own argument (which emphatically is not to say that I imagine Masters agrees with that argument).

❖   ❖   ❖

Lastly, a couple of books devoting a chapter or two to Machiavelli, which focus on the figure of fortune and on the Woman Question. Both claim to do so not in order to attack Machiavelli as a misogynist, but in order to explore his—and improve our—understanding of politics; but the lesson each draws differs greatly from that drawn by the other, and from the one I draw.

The first is Arlene W. Saxonhouse's *Women in the History of Political Theory: Ancient Greece to Machiavelli,* which develops an idea about Machiavelli that her review charges my book missed: Machiavelli's "own assimilation to the female figure."[40] Far from being "afraid of the female," Saxonhouse writes, Machiavelli "models himself after her."[41] It is an excellent suggestion, some version of which did cross my mind

37. Ibid., 28, 4. On naturalism, Masters, *Machiavelli,* 2.
38. Masters, "Machiavelli's Sexuality," 27.
39. Masters seems to have changed his mind about whether Machiavelli was a republican; compare Masters, *Machiavelli,* 4–5, with Masters, "Machiavelli's Sexuality," 12.
40. Saxonhouse, Review, 760; Arlene W. Saxonhouse, *Women in the History of Political Thought: Ancient Greece to Machiavelli* (New York, Philadelphia, Eastbourne, U.K., Toronto, Hong Kong, Tokyo, Sydney: Praeger, 1985), ch. 7.
41. Saxonhouse, Review, 761.

repeatedly as I wrote, but which I never took up. I wish that I could have read Saxonhouse's chapter before completing my book, the more so now that Masters' investigations are available. Machiavelli may well have indulged fantasies of himself in fortune's role, nearly omnipotent and free to do as he pleased, to toy with mastering and being mastered by handsome, bold young men without risking any real loss of control.[42]

This is not, however, the line Saxonhouse pursues. What she means by Machiavelli modelling himself on woman or identifying with fortune is that he is changeable, adaptable, shifty, and perfects a "manipulative style."[43] In order to cope with fortune's womanly fickleness, he "adapts, overcomes his masculine nature by becoming like a woman."[44] This is valuable, but also incomplete, for fortune is not exactly like other women. They are adaptable because they are weak; adaptability is the weapon of the weak. But fortune herself is not weak and has no need to adapt to anyone. She may be feminine, but hardly effeminate.

Machiavelli's shiftiness, his "capacity to be many things to many people," which Saxonhouse thinks I ignore, is indeed crucial.[45] I treat it, first, under the rubric of foxiness, one of his three conflicting images of manhood, and, second, through the fact of that conflict itself, and its rootedness in gender issues. That his foxiness, or even his endless circling among the three kinds of manliness, might reflect a partial *feminine* identification even though the visions are of *manliness* is a fascinating idea, highly problematic of course, but well worth trying to work out.

Saxonhouse does not engage it, partly because she stresses only the feminine identification, but also because she takes any conflicting passages or difficulties in the texts to be part of Machiavelli's manipulative shiftyness. He is out to blur distinctions, to promote ambiguity in categories and uncertainty in judgments. In his thought, the fixed order that the Middle Ages took for granted as both natural and sacred, she says, is "to be questioned. Natural hierarchies, clear lines of authority are undermined as Machiavelli confronts his readers with a chaotic world," which can be ordered only by exceptional human effort.[46] Machiavelli's orientation is naturalistic, as Masters also says, but nature "reveals no precise guidelines, no clear standards of evaluation . . . no

42. Compare his possible fantasies about being Cesare Borgia; above, 40.
43. Saxonhouse, *Women*, 155.
44. Saxonhouse, Review, 761.
45. Ibid., 760.
46. Saxonhouse, *Women*, 151.

well-articulated boundaries" for distinguishing categories, social sta-
tuses, or genders.[47] In particular, a world thus "in flux allows men to
become women and women to become men." The fortune figure symbolizes such inversion: "the female as dominant."[48] Sometimes Saxonhouse seems to be saying that the world of Renaissance Florence actually
was like that, a "world of appearances" in which "all is uncertain, subject to manipulation."[49] More often she treats this chaotic flux as Machiavelli's goal. Like Masters, she holds that Machiavelli "intends to startle,
to shock," because he wants to "revolutionalize," to bring about a "fundamental transvaluation," to "overthrow and transform the certainties
on which political thought of the previous two milennia had been
based." That is why he inverts traditional values, confuses good and bad,
virtue and vice, and the two sexes, and renders "the differences between
what had been opposites so ambiguous that we can no longer tell"
what's what.[50]

There is something right about these claims, yet they cannot be the
whole story. Machiavelli surely also insists on the objective difference
between appearance (by which most people are taken in) and reality
(perceived by those who are up close, in the know, like himself). He is
proud of his own realism, by contrast with the utopian hypocrisy of
other theorizing. He takes for granted the objective difference between
effeminate submission and virile activism, and constantly tries to teach
it to others. And the traditional values that Masters and Saxonhouse
think he wants to subvert had been pretty thoroughly hollowed out already in his time and place. Far from denying all standards, he wanted
to replace the traditional ones, which were proving disastrous, with ones
more realistically likely to produce objectively good outcomes, including
not just prosperity and security but also "glory," not to be confused
with "false glory."[51] Not all is flux for Machiavelli.

Sometimes, indeed, Saxonhouse herself sees more positive themes in
Machiavelli, with respect to categories, gender, and politics. Concerning
gender, she says that for ancient thinkers, women symbolized difference,
being considered so radically different from men that they were wholly
excluded "from direct involvement in . . . public affairs."[52] Yet their exis-

47. Ibid., 179.
48. Ibid., 165, 155.
49. Ibid., 180, 173.
50. Ibid., 151, 154. See also 172–73, 180.
51. Machiavelli, *Prince*, ch. 8 (G 36); Machiavelli, *Discourses*, 1:10 (G 220).
52. Saxonhouse, *Women*, 177.

tence as a distinct category of people, and their indispensable reproductive function were undeniable. This had two beneficial consequences, or at least set ancient thinkers a dual "task," which disappears when gender distinctions dissolve. It challenged them to understand community in ways that "incorporat[ed] difference," and to acknowledge limits on politics, limits symbolized by women, the necessary but unpolitical category of people, who stood for human embodiedness, reproduction, and thus "our basic interdependence."[53]

Machiavelli, Saxonhouse says, "destroyed . . . the importance of difference," so that later thinkers no longer faced this dual task.[54] Thus he "helped to set the stage for" modern liberalism, which accords women political rights, but at the price of a debilitating abstraction. Abstracting from all differences among people including the gender difference, liberalism envisions a disembodied, depersonalized, isolated citizen, related to others only contractually, and required to leave his individual, personal self behind in entering the public realm. For Saxonhouse, then, unlike many contemporary feminists and theorists of gay and lesbian life, maintaining two distinct, clearly defined gender roles is a way of defending both "difference"—even "diversity"—and individuality.[55]

It is also apparently a way of defending politics, and here Machiavelli, despite his subversive questioning that destroyed difference, becomes Saxonhouse's ally. For he himself still thinks like the ancients about gender and politics. Women still "underscore diversity" and symbolize "divisions" in the polity for him, which he sees "must be joined" together if the polity is to survive.[56] This political task is symbolized by the erotic encounter between fortune and the man of *virtù*, here definitely masculine. The city's survival depends on political resolution of conflict as the survival of the species depends on heterosexual conjunction. In this context, accordingly, Saxonhouse acknowledges the positive potential in Machiavelli's vision, even in his subversive questioning. He questions "creatively," just as both politics and heterosexual reproduction are creative; they "give life," and "create . . . an order" in the otherwise chaotic world.[57] Along with the terror and chaos Machiavelli introduces, "there is also the opening up of possibilities" for what people "could do or

53. Ibid., 182, 16. See also 11, 177.
54. Ibid., 179.
55. Ibid., 182, 164, 177.
56. Ibid., 164.
57. Ibid., 152, 157.

become," possibilities of "changing roles for men and for women, for princes and for subjects."[58] Saxonhouse does not, after all, seek a return to women's status in the ancient world.

The Latin motto on United States coins, *e pluribus unum*, Saxonhouse rightly observes, "reflect[s] *the* central political problem" that political theory and politics must address: the continual need to recreate a working unity out of continually arising new diversity and conflict, endemic among creatures like ourselves: simultaneously individual and interconnected, free agents and embodied products of a particular growing up.[59] That's my formulation, but it is Saxonhouse's thought, which I heartily endorse. Sometimes, at least, she sees that it is Machiavelli's as well, but her univocal stress on his feminine identification leaves no room for that side of Machiavelli to emerge fully.[60] I think that is why she doubts the existence of my "Machiavelli at his best."

❖   ❖   ❖

Like Saxonhouse and myself, Wendy Brown interprets Machiavelli in terms of fortune and gender issues, but her *Manhood and Politics* announces at the outset, by its subtitle, that it is "a *feminist* reading in political theory."[61] Here, then, is my chance to find out whether mine too is a feminist reading, or whether, in my status as privileged exception, I have betrayed my sisters.

Brown's preface puts gender at the center not merely of her project but of "everything in the human world," since it is all a "gendered construction," but her book is to focus on the "gendered quality" of just two human enterprises: politics and political theory. Their gendered quality, she says at once, is "masculinist," since both enterprises are "socially male constructions," made "by and for" men, or even "perpetrated by masculine dominance."[62]

When she turns specifically to Machiavelli, Brown sees that manhood is his "beacon and his downfall," because his "sharply gendered view of . . . politics" causes him to "subvert some of his own understandings

58. Ibid., 152, 179.
59. Ibid., 182; my emphasis.
60. It is perhaps important that when Saxonhouse speaks about Machiavelli seeing order as humanly created, she construes that creativity as "individual" rather than shared, collective, or political; ibid., 151.
61. Wendy Brown, *Manhood and Politics: a Feminist Reading in Political Theory* (Totawa, N. J.: Rowman & Littlefield, 1988); my emphasis. Brown dedicates her book to her mother.
62. Ibid., ix–xii, 12.

about the political world."[63] His masculinist gender anxiety takes the form of a quest for control, and this is what accounts for the "self-subverting twist in his thought."[64] This coincides gratifyingly with my own account, and occasionally Brown even says explicitly what these passages obviously imply: that there must be something right in Machiavelli's thought as well, something that gets twisted and subverted. Masculinism does not exhaust his political theory. He comprehends "the complex nature of the political realm," and understands that its "fluid, nuanced and strongly contextual" quality makes "control and mastery . . . ultimately impossible."[65]

Like some of Saxonhouse's best insights, however, these are passing remarks that conflict in ways Brown does not acknowledge with her more pervasive central characterization of Machiavelli's thought: that for him, politics is about "control and mastery," "domination," "*over-coming,*" "the raw drive for power" in which "power becomes its own end."[66] Politics is war for Machiavelli, since he "literal[ly] collapse[s] the distinction between" them, and specifically chooses as "*the* paradigm" of political life "the war between the sexes."[67] This is symbolized in the encounter between fortune and the man of *virtù,* which Brown sees simply as a rape. I worry that in such a "feminist" reading, the valuable side of Machiavelli's thought, his unique insights into the nature of politics, are likely to get lost, being fragmented and without systematic articulation.

That worry is much intensified by Susan Moller Okin's review of my book, which generously classes me as contributing to "feminist" scholarship, but tries to save me from myself by excising "Machiavelli at his best."[68] Okin's own book, *Women in Western Political Thought,* a pioneering study published well before my work on Machiavelli, does not deal with him, but her review characterizes his politics as "zero-sum," its "basic principle" being "dominate or be dominated." In our age of nuclear weaponry, Okin says, "nothing could be more important than knowing how to get away from" such an aggressive, masculinist vision of political life.[69]

63. Ibid., 9, 72.
64. Ibid., 87.
65. Ibid., 86.
66. Ibid., 71, 80, 82, 96, 107; emphasis in original.
67. Ibid., 116, 86; emphasis in original.
68. Okin, "Roots," 15–16.
69. Susan Moller Okin, *Women in Western Political Thought* (Princeton: Princeton University Press, 1979); Okin, "Roots," 16.

My contribution to such knowledge, she says, is only obscured by my unfortunate tendency to split Machiavelli into three conflicting visions of manliness or into two distinct versions of the theorist himself: "at his best" and "as a whole." The feminist task is instead to expose and reject the masculinist "flavor" that taints the entirety of his thought. A "stronger and more persuasive case" could then be made for my "major thesis," which is (My thesis! At last, my missing thesis!) "that a society's basic psychic attitudes, rooted in early childhood, affect the limits of its political vision." Machiavelli is all of a piece, his republicanism as zero-sum as the rest of his politics, and inseparable from it. My "Machiavelli at his best" is a "fiction" that gets in the way of the feminist point, which would emerge "more strongly once 'Machiavelli at his best' is buried as he deserves to be."[70] A feminist reading of Machiavelli, then, requires abandoning him as a valuable teacher about politics or anything else. I've been too soft on the old man, too deferential to the tradition.

But what if Machiavelli gets something right, something not easily available elsewhere, something we need but are reluctant to face? What if politics really is zero-sum, always, and would be so even if conducted entirely by women, or by women and men together in a world beyond gender anxieties? What if it is inherently zero-sum *even though* it is not war, and even though it is also, inevitably, in another sense non-zero-sum? Politics, it seems to me, is about conflict—real, serious, sometimes desperate conflict (About Nazis and Jews, say, or Jews and Arabs, or rich and poor). It is about issues and decisions on which people are divided; in the absence of conflict, a matter does not become political. The decisions have consequences that condition people's lives. There are winners and losers.

Of course that is not the whole story. The consequences add up to a shared fate for the polity. All have a shared interest in the principles by which the polity lives and the ways it handles conflict. And sometimes the consequences turn out to benefit all, even those who "lost" in the voting, and sometimes the consequences are disastrous and everyone loses, even the "winners." If you miss either side of this complicated duality, you will get politics wrong. Gender anxiety can blind people (perhaps in our culture particularly men) to the non-zero-sum side of politics, but it can also blind people (perhaps in our culture particularly women) to the zero-sum side.

70. Okin, "Roots," 15–16.

Machiavelli is one of our best teachers in the tradition of political theory about not just the inevitability but the positive value of conflict if it is rightly handled, and about how to handle it. Feminism might need that knowledge. There is a lot to be learned from Machiavelli if, like Saxonhouse (who may or may not regard herself as a feminist), you want creative politics, diversity that can be unified yet protects individuality, opportunities opened for people; or if, like Okin, you are worried about international tensions in a nuclear age; or if, like Brown, you want changes that serve "human life, genuine freedom, and equality."[71] It will not be learned if you read in him only the louder voices in his trialogue, and reject him wholesale on that basis. Feminists have taught us so much in recent years about this danger, about not really listening to someone whom you have defined as the evil and dangerous "Other," and impoverishing yourself as a result.

Brown's book closes with a chapter sketching her own vision of "post-masculinist" politics, which not only coincides at many points with my "Machiavelli at his best," but actually reverts to Machiavelli himself. This time he appears not as a control-and-mastery freak, but as Brown's authority for the claim that "conflict and struggle" are desirable because they make us "strong, powerful, and free." She invokes that authority against those feminists who "idealize and sentimentalize" politics and assimilate it to "the warm ambiance of a quiet nursery," and against the general reluctance of women in our culture to engage in combat or exercise power openly.[72]

The extent to which Brown sees what is of value in Machiavelli heartens me: perhaps I can have my Machiavelli and be a feminist too. Yet Brown does not help me with the Woman Question as much as I had hoped. Her appreciation of Machiavelli is limited, I think, by needing him to exemplify "masculinism," which is what "feminism" opposes. Brown's last chapter contains a brief but truly thoughtful critique of the idea of "female values" that are somehow "essentially feminine," but she nowhere undertakes a comparable critique of "masculinism" or "male dominance."[73] So she continues to hold that our politics and political theory are "perpetrated by masculine dominance," made "by and for" men, though at point after point she shows that this is too simple and too easy. She shows that men are not wholly "masculinist" in their thinking or their conduct, nor women devoid of "masculinism." She

71. Brown, *Manhood*, 210.
72. Ibid., 208–10.
73. Ibid., 190–91.

shows that present arrangements are not really in the interest of men, that men too might gain from their transformation. She shows that women also have a stake in those arrangements and are complicit in their maintenance, and she points out the danger in blaming only the men, so that women seem to lack agency, and appear merely as "subjected and victimized."[74]

In what must surely have been a deliberate choice, Brown calls the politics approached in her last chapter "post-masculinist" rather than "feminist," perhaps because in that context, as a label for the ultimate goal, "feminist" might sound misleadingly, distressingly parallel to "masculinist," as if Brown intended what she in fact condemns: a "simple reversal" in which nothing changes except who's on top.[75] Yet she does not interrogate the concept of feminism, either, when she criticizes the idea of "female values." And when the chapter finally arrives in the last few pages at politics, conflict, and power, Brown is once more in quest of "a distinctly *feminist* theory of political power."[76]

The achievements of the women's movement—in my mother's time and in our own—are real and wonderful, even if much remains to be done. I marvel at those achievements and honor all who worked and struggled to promote them, or indeed to promote justice and freedom more generally, for all. I try to do my bit. But intellectually, I worry. If it is misleading to call the goal feminist, why is it right to call the movement that? If I am a feminist, is my primary duty solidarity (and with whom?) or is the cause furthered better by critique, even of friends, by learning, even from enemies, by thinking even while one acts?

74. Contrast, for example, ibid., ix and 12 to xii and 195.
75. Ibid., 189.
76. Ibid., 209; my emphasis.

Bibliography of Works Cited

Adams, Henry. *Mont-Saint-Michel and Chartres.* 1913. Reprint. Boston and New York: Houghton Mifflin, 1936.

Adams, John Clarke, and Paulo Barile. *The Government of Republican Italy.* 3d ed. Boston: Houghton Mifflin, 1972.

Alberti, Leon Batista. *The Family in Renaissance Florence.* Tr. by Renée Neu Watkins. Columbia: University of South Carolina Press, 1969.

Albertini, Rudolf von. *Das Florentinische Staatsbewusstsein im Uebergang von der Republik zu dem Prinzipat.* Bern: A. Francke, 1955.

Almond, Gabriel A., and Sidney Verba. *The Civic Culture.* Boston and Toronto: Little, Brown & Co., 1965.

Anglo, Sydney. *Machiavelli: A Dissection.* New York: Harcourt, Brace & World, 1969.

Arendt, Hannah. *Between Past and Future.* Cleveland and New York: World Publishing, 1963.

―――. *The Human Condition.* Chicago and London: University of Chicago Press, 1974.

―――. "Truth and Politics." In Peter Laslett and W. G. Runciman, eds., *Philosophy, Politics and Society,* 3rd series, 104–33. Oxford: Basil Blackwell, 1969.

Ariès, Philippe. *Centuries of Childhood.* Tr. by Robert Baldick. New York: Random House, 1962.

Bailey, Cyril, ed. *The Legacy of Rome.* Oxford: Clarendon Press, 1923.

Banfield, Edward C. *The Moral Basis of a Backward Society.* New York: Free Press, 1958.

Baron, Hans. *The Crisis of the Early Italian Renaissance.* 2d ed. Princeton: Princeton University Press, 1966.

Barzini, Luigi. *The Italians.* New York: Atheneum, 1965.

Beauvoir, Simone de. *The Second Sex.* Tr. by H. M. Parshley. New York: A. A. Knopf, 1961.

Bell, Susan G., ed. *Women from the Greeks to the French Revolution.* Belmont, Calif.: Wadsworth Publishing, 1973.

Benjamin, Jessica. "Authority and the Family Revisited, or A World Without Fathers?" *New German Critique* 13 (September 1978): 35–57.

Bernardo, Aldo S. *Petrarch, Scipio and the "Africa."* Baltimore: Johns Hopkins Press, 1962.

Biagi, Guido. *Men and Manners of Old Florence.* London and Leipsic: T. Fisher Unwin, 1909.

Boulting, William. *Woman in Italy.* London: Methuen, 1910.

Bowlby, John. *Separation: Anxiety and Anger.* Vol. 2 of *Attachment and Loss.* New York: Basic Books, 1973.

Brecht, Bertold. *The Three-Penny Opera.* Vol. 2 of *Collected Plays,* tr. by Ralph Mannheim and John Willett. New York: Random House, 1977.

Brinton, Crane. *A History of Western Morals.* New York: Harcourt, Brace & Co., 1959.

Brown, Peter. *Augustine of Hippo.* Berkeley and Los Angeles: University of California Press, 1969.

Brucker, Gene. *Renaissance Florence.* New York: John Wiley and Sons, 1969.

———, ed. *The Society of Renaissance Florence: A Documentary Study.* New York: Harper & Row, 1971.

Burckhardt, Jacob. *The Civilization of the Renaissance in Italy.* New York: Phaidon, 1950.

Cannon, Mary Agnes. *The Education of Women During the Renaissance.* Washington, D.C.: National Capital Press, 1916.

Casey, Kathleen. "The Cheshire Cat: Reconstructing the Experience of Medieval Women." In Berenice Carroll, ed., *Liberating Women's History: Theoretical and Critical Essays.* Urbana, Chicago, London: University of Illinois Press, 1976.

Cassirer, Ernst. *The Individual and the Cosmos in Renaissance Philosophy.* Tr. by Mario Domandi. New York and Evanston: Harper & Row, 1963.

———. *The Myth of The State.* Garden City, N.Y.: Doubleday, 1953.

Clarke, Maude L. *The Roman Mind.* London: Cohen and West, 1956.

Chodorow, Nancy. *The Reproduction of Mothering.* Berkeley, Los Angeles, London: University of California Press, 1978.

Chojnacki, Stanley. "Patrician Women in Early Renaissance Venice." *Studies in the Renaissance* 21 (1974): 176–203.

Cioffari, Vincenzo. "The Function of Fortune in Dante, Boccaccio and Machiavelli." *Italica* 24 (1947): 1–13.

Cumming, Robert Denoon. *Human Nature and History.* 2 vols. Chicago and London: University of Chicago Press, 1969.

Dante Alighieri. *The Inferno.* Tr. by John Ciardi. New York: New American Library, 1959.

Davis, Natalie Zemon. "Ghosts, Kin and Progeny: Some Features of Family Life in Early Modern France." *Daedalus* 106 (Spring 1977): 87–114.

———. *Society and Culture in Early Modern France.* Stanford: Stanford University Press, 1975.

Deckard, Barbara Sinclair. *The Women's Movement.* New York: Harper & Row, 1975.

De Maria, Udo. *Intorno ad un Poema Satirico di Niccolò Machiavelli.* Bologna: Zamorani e Albertazzi, 1899.

De Mause, Lloyd, ed. *The History of Childhood.* New York: Psychohistory Press, 1974.

Dinnerstein, Dorothy. *The Mermaid and the Minotaur.* New York: Harper & Row, 1976.

Doren, A. "Fortuna im Mittelalter und in der Renaissance." *Vorträge der Bibliothek Warburg* 2 (1922–23): 71–115.

Durant, Will. *The Renaissance.* New York: Simon & Schuster, 1953.

Effinger, John R. *Women of the Romance Countries.* Vol. 6 of *Woman: In All Ages and In All Countries.* Philadelphia: George Barrie and Sons, 1907.

Ehrenzweig, Anton. "The Origin of the Scientific and Heroic Urge (The Guilt of Prometheus)." *International Journal of Psychoanalysis* 30 (1949): 108–23.

Engel, Stephanie. "Femininity as Tragedy: Reexamining the 'New Narcissism.'" *Socialist Review* 10 (September–October 1980): 77–103.

Erikson, Erik H. *Childhood and Society.* 2d ed. New York: W. W. Norton, 1963.

———. *Young Man Luther.* New York: W. W. Norton, 1962.

Evelyn-White, Hugh G. *Ausonius, with an English Translation.* 2 vols. London: W. Heinemann; New York: G. P. Putnam's Sons, 1931.

Fahy, Conor. "Three Early Renaissance Treatises on Women." *Italian Studies* 11 (1956): 30–55.

Ferrara, Orestes. *The Private Correspondence of Nicolo Machiavelli.* Baltimore: Johns Hopkins Press, 1929.

Flaceliere, Robert. *Daily Life in Greece at the Time of Pericles.* Tr. by Peter Green. London: Weidenfeld and Nicolson, 1965.

Flaumenhaft, Mera J. "The Comic Remedy: Machiavelli's 'Mandragola.'" *Interpretation* 7 (May 1978): 33–74.

Fleischer, Martin, ed. *Machiavelli and the Nature of Political Thought.* New York: Atheneum, 1972.

———. "Trust and Deceit in Machiavelli's Comedies." *Journal of the History of Ideas* 27 (1966): 365–80.

Freud, Sigmund. *Leonardo Da Vinci.* Tr. by A. A. Brill. New York: Random House, 1961.

———. *The Standard Edition of the Complete Psychological Works of Sigmund Freud.* Ed. by James Strachey. 24 vols. London: Hogarth Press, 1953–74.

Gage, John. *Life in Italy at the Time of the Medici.* New York: G. P. Putnam's Sons, 1968.

Gies, Joseph and Frances. *Life in a Medieval City.* New York: Thomas Y. Crowell Company, 1969.

Gilbert, Allan H. *Machiavelli's Prince and Its Forerunners.* New York: Barnes and Noble, 1968.

Gilbert, Felix. "The Composition and Structure of Machiavelli's *Discorsi.*" *Journal of the History of Ideas* 14 (1953): 135–56.

———. "The Humanist Concept of the Prince and *The Prince* of Machiavelli." *Journal of Modern History* 11 (December 1939): 449–65.

———. *Machiavelli and Guicciardini: Politics and History in 16th-Century Florence.* Princeton: Princeton University Press, 1965.

———. "Machiavelli: The Renaissance of the Art of War." In E. M. Earle, ed.,

Makers of Modern Strategy. Princeton: Princeton University Press, 1944.

Goldthwaite, Richard A. *The Building of Renaissance Florence*. Baltimore and London: Johns Hopkins University Press, 1980.

———. "The Florentine Palace as Domestic Architecture." *American Historical Review* 77 (1972): 977–1012.

———. *Private Wealth in Renaissance Florence*. Princeton: Princeton University Press, 1968.

Goode, William J. *World Revolution and Family Patterns*. Glencoe, Ill.: Free Press, 1963.

Goodman, Paul. *Growing Up Absurd*. New York: Vintage, 1962.

Goodsell, Willystine. *A History of Man and the Family*. Rev. ed. New York: Macmillan, 1934.

Greenlief, Barbara Kaye. *Children Through the Ages*. New York: McGraw-Hill, 1978.

Hale, J[ohn] R[igby]. *Florence and the Medici*. London: Thames and Hudson, 1977.

———. *Machiavelli and Renaissance Italy*. New York: Collier, 1963.

———. *Renaissance Europe: Individual and Society 1480–1520*. New York, Evanston, San Francisco, London: Harper & Row, 1972.

———. "War and Public Opinion in Renaissance Italy." In Fraser Jacob, ed., *Italian Renaissance Studies*. London: Faber and Faber, 1960.

Hare, Christopher [pseud. for Mrs. Marian Andrews]. *The Most Illustrious Ladies of the Renaissance*. London and New York: Harper and Brothers, 1911.

Hartmann, Mary, and Lois W. Banner, eds. *Clio's Consciousness Raised*. New York, Evanston, San Francisco, London: Harper & Row, 1974.

Hegel, Georg Wilhelm Friedrich. *Wissenschaft der Logik*. 2 vols. Nürnberg: J. L. Schrag, 1812–16. Reprint. Frankfurt: Suhrkamp, 1969.

Heitman, Klaus. *Fortuna und Virtus: eine Studie zu Petrarcas Lebensweisheit*. Köln: Boehlau, 1958.

Herlihy, David. *Economy, Society and Government in Medieval Italy*. Kent, Ohio: Kent State University Press, 1969.

———. "Family and Property in Renaissance Florence." In Harry A. Miskimin, David Herlihy, and A. L. Udovitch, eds., *The Medieval City*, 3–24. New Haven and London: Yale University Press, 1977.

———. "Mapping Households in Medieval Italy." *Catholic Historical Review* 58 (April 1972): 1–24.

———. "The Tuscan Town in the Quattrocento: A Demographic Profile." *Medievalia et Humanistica*, n.s. 1 (1970): 81–109.

———. "Vieillir à Florence au Quattrocento." *Annales. Économies, Sociétés, Civilisations* 24 (November–December 1969): 1338–52.

———. *Women in Medieval Society*. Houston: University of St. Thomas, 1971.

Higginbotham, John. *Cicero on Moral Obligation*. Berkeley and Los Angeles: University of California Press, 1967.

Hobbes, Thomas. *Leviathan*. Ed. by Michael Oakeshott. New York: Collier, 1962.

Holmes, George. *The Florentine Enlightenment, 1440–1450*. London: Weidenfeld and Nicolson, 1969.

Hughes, Diana Owen. "Domestic Ideals and Social Behavior: the Evidence of Medieval Genoa." In Charles E. Rosenberg, ed., *The Family in History*, 115–43. Philadelphia: University of Pennsylvania Press, 1975.

———. "Urban Growth and Family Structure in Medieval Genoa." *Past and Present* 66 (1975): 3–28.

Hunt, David. *Parents and Children in History*. New York and London: Basic Books, 1970.

Jackson, Janet Flannery and Joseph. *Infant Culture*. New York: Thomas Y. Crowell, 1978.

Jensen, De Lamar, ed. *Machiavelli. Cynic, Patriot, or Political Scientist?* Boston: D. C. Heath, 1960.

Kant, Immanuel. "Metaphysical Foundations of Morals." In Carl J. Friedrich, tr. and ed., *The Philosophy of Kant*, 140–208. New York: Modern Library, 1949.

Kantorowicz, Ernst. *The King's Two Bodies*. Princeton: Princeton University Press, 1957.

Kelly-Godol, Joan. "Did Women Have a Renaissance?" in Renate Bridenthal and Claudia Koonz, eds., *Becoming Visible: Women in European History*, 137–64. Boston: Houghton Mifflin, 1977.

Kelso, Ruth. *Doctrine for the Lady of the Renaissance*. Urbana: University of Illinois Press, 1956.

Kent, Francis William. *Household and Lineage in Renaissance Florence*. Princeton: Princeton University Press, 1977.

Klapisch, Christiane. "L'enfance en Toscane au début du XVᵉ Siècle." *Annales de Démographie Historique* (1973): 99–122.

———. "Fiscalité et démographie en Toscane (1427–1430)." *Annales. Économies, Sociétés, Civilisations* 24 (November–December 1969): 1313–37.

———. "Household and Family in Tuscany in 1427." In Peter Laslett and Richard Wall, eds., *Household and Family in Past Time*. Cambridge: Cambridge University Press, 1972.

Klapisch, Christiane, and Michel Demonet. "'A uno pane e uno vino,' La famille rurale toscane au début du XVᵉ siècle." *Annales. Économies, Sociétés, Civilisations* 27 (July–October 1972): 873–901.

Klein, Melanie. *Contributions to Psychoanalysis, 1921–1945*. London: Hogarth Press, 1948.

———. *Envy and Gratitude*. New York: Basic Books, 1957.

Klein, Melanie, and Joan Riviere. *Love, Hate and Reparation*. London: Hogarth Press and Institute of Psychoanalysis, 1962.

König, René. *Niccolò Machiavelli*. Erlenbach-Zürich: Eugen Reutsch, 1941.

Kohl, Benjamin G., and Ronald G. Witt, eds., *The Earthly Republic*. University of Pennsylvania Press, 1978.

Lacey, W. K. *The Family in Classical Greece*. Ithaca: Cornell University Press, 1968.

Laing, R. D. *The Divided Self*. Baltimore: Penguin Books, 1970.

Lawson, John Howard. *The Hidden Heritage*. New York: Citadel Press, 1950.

Lewis, C. S. *The Allegory of Love*. London: Oxford University Press, 1967.

Livius, Titus. *The History of Rome*. Tr. by B. O. Foster. 14 vols. London: William Heinemann; Cambridge: Harvard University Press, 1967.

Livy. *The Early History of Rome*. Tr. by Aubrey de Selincourt. Baltimore: Penguin, 1969.

Lucas-Dubreton, J. *Daily Life in Florence in the Time of the Medici*. Tr. by A. Lytton Sells. New York: Macmillan, 1961.

Lungo, Isidoro del. *Women of Florence*. Tr. by Mary C. Steegman. London: C. Patto and Windus, 1907.

Machiavelli, Niccolò. *The Art of War*. Ed. and tr. by Neal Wood. Indianapolis and New York: Bobbs-Merrill, 1965.

————. *The Chief Works and Others*. Tr. by Allan Gilbert. 3 vols. Durham, N.C.: Duke University Press, 1965.

————. *The Discourses*. Tr. by Leslie J. Walker, S. J. with revisions by Brian Richardson. Ed. by Bernard Crick. Harmondsworth: Penguin, 1974.

————. *The History of Florence and Other Selections*. Tr. and ed. by Myron P. Gilmore. New York: Washington Square Press, 1970.

————. *Literary Works*. Ed. by J[ohn] R[igby] Hale. London and New York: Oxford University Press, 1961.

————. *Opere*. 8 vols. Milano: Feltrinelli Editore, 1960–65.

————. *Machiavelli's The Prince*. Tr. and ed. by Mark Musa. New York: St. Martin's Press, 1964.

————. *The Prince and the Discourses*. Tr. by Luigi Ricci. New York: Modern Library, 1940.

Mansfield, Harvey C., Jr. *Machiavelli's New Modes and Orders*. Ithaca and London: Cornell University Press, 1979.

Martin, Alfred Wilhelm Otto von. *Coluccio Salutati und das humanistische Lebensideal*. Leipzig and Berlin: B. G. Teubner, 1916.

————. *The Sociology of the Renaissance*. London: Kegan Paul, Trench, Trubner, Co., 1944.

Martinelli, Giuseppe. *The World of Renaissance Florence*. Tr. by Walter Barwell. London: Macdonald and Co., 1968.

Martines, Lauro. *Lawyers and Statecraft in Renaissance Florence*. Princeton: Princeton University Press, 1968.

————. *The Social World of the Florentine Humanists 1390–1460*. Princeton: Princeton University Press, 1963.

————, ed. *Violence and Civil Disorder in Italian Cities 1200–1500*. University of California at Los Angeles. Center for Medieval and Renaissance Studies. Contributions 5. Berkeley, Los Angeles, London: University of California Press, 1972.

————. "A Way of Looking at Women in Renaissance Florence." *Journal of Medieval and Renaissance Studies*, 4 (Spring 1974): 15–28.

Mason, Philip. *Prospero's Magic: Some Thoughts on Class and Race*. London: Oxford University Press, 1962.

Maulde la Clavière, Marie Alphonse René de. *The Women of the Renaissance: A Study of Feminism*. New York: G. P. Putnam's Sons, 1905.

Meiss, Millard. *Painting in Florence and Siena After the Black Death*. Princeton: Princeton University Press, 1951.

Merleau-Ponty. Maurice. *Signs*. Tr. by Richard C. McCleary. Evanston, Ill.: Northwestern University Press, 1964.

Miller, Jean Baker, ed. *Psychoanalysis and Women*. New York: Penguin, 1973.

Miskimin, Harry A. *The Economy of Later Renaissance Europe, 1460–1600.* Cambridge: Cambridge University Press, 1977.

Miskimin, Harry A., David Herlihy, and A. L. Udovitch, eds. *The Medieval City.* New Haven and London: Yale University Press, 1977.

Mitchell, Juliet. *Psychoanalysis and Feminism.* New York: Pantheon, 1974.

Mitscherlich, Alexander. *Society Without the Father.* New York: Schocken, 1970.

Moller, Herbert. "The Meaning of Courtly Love." *Journal of American Folklore* 73 (1960): 39–52.

Morewedge, Rosemarie Thee, ed. *The Role of Woman in the Middle Ages.* Albany: State University of New York Press, 1975.

Morgan, Lucy Ingram. "The Renaissance Lady in England." Ph.D. diss., University of California, 1932.

Murden, Forrest D. "Underdeveloped Lands: 'Revolution of Rising Expectations.'" *Foreign Policy Association. Headline Series,* no. 119 (September 20, 1956).

Nicolson, Harold. *Good Behaviour.* Boston: Beacon Press, 1960.

O'Faolain, Julia, and Lauro Martines, eds. *Not in God's Image.* New York: Harper & Row, 1973.

Olschki, Cesare, ed. *Libro di Ricordi di Bernardo Machiavelli.* Florence: Felice le Monnier, 1954.

Origo, Iris. *The Merchant of Prato.* London: Jonathan Cape, 1960.

———. *The World of San Bernardino.* New York: Harcourt, Brace & World, 1962.

Panofsky, Erwin. *Hercules am Scheidewege.* Leipzig and Berlin: B. G. Teubner, 1930.

Parel, Anthony, ed. *The Political Calculus.* Toronto and Buffalo: University of Toronto Press, 1972.

Patch, Howard R. *The Goddess Fortuna in Medieval Literature.* New York: Farrar, Straus and Giroux, 1974.

Piaget, Jean. *The Moral Judgment of the Child.* Tr. by Marjorie Gabain. New York: Collier Books, 1962.

Pitkin, Hanna Fenichel. "Justice: On Relating Private and Public." *Political Theory* 9 (August 1981): 327–52.

Plautus. *Casina.* In Henry Thomas Riley, tr., *The Comedies of Plautus,* vol. 2. London: George Bell and Sons, 1895.

Plutarch. *Complete Works.* 6 vols. New York and San Francisco: Thomas Y. Crowell and Company, 1909.

Pocock, J. G. A. *The Machiavellian Moment.* Princeton: Princeton University Press, 1975.

Polybius. *Histories.* Tr. by Evelyn S. Schuckburgh. London and New York: Macmillan and Company, 1889.

Pomeroy, Sarah B. *Goddesses, Whores, Wives, and Slaves.* New York: Schocken Books, 1975.

Prezzolini, Giuseppe. *Machiavelli.* New York: Farrar, Straus and Giroux, 1967.

Putnam, Emily James. *The Lady.* Chicago: University of Chicago Press, 1970.

Rabb, Arthur K. *The Struggle for Stability in Early Modern Europe.* New York: Oxford University Press, 1975.

Ridolfi, Roberto. *The Life of Niccolò Machiavelli*. Chicago: University of Chicago Press, 1954.

Rodocanachi, E. *La Femme Italienne à l'époque de la Renaissance*. Paris: Libraire Hachette, 1922.

Roeder, Ralph. *The Man of the Renaissance*. Cleveland and New York: World Publishing, 1967.

Rosaria, Sister Maria. "The Nurse in Greek Life." Ph.D. diss., Catholic University of America, 1917.

Rougemont, Denis de. *Love in the Western World*. Tr. by Montgomery Belgion. New York: Harcourt, Brace, 1956.

Rubinstein, Nicolai, ed. *Florentine Studies: Politics and Society in Renaissance Florence*. Evanston, Ill.: Northwestern University Press, 1968.

Ruggiers, Paul G. *Florence in the Age of Dante*. Norman: University of Oklahoma Press, 1964.

Sayers, Janet. *Biological Politics*. London and New York: Tavistock Publications, 1982.

Scaife, Walter B. *Florentine Life During the Renaissance*. Baltimore: Johns Hopkins Press, 1893.

Schaar, John H. *Legitimacy in the Modern State*. New Brunswick and London: Transaction Books, 1981.

Schafer, Roy. "The Loving and Beloved Superego in Freud's Structural Theory." *The Psychoanalytic Study of the Child* 15 (1960): 163–88.

Schapiro, Meyer. "'Muscipula Diaboli,' the Symbolism of the Mérode Altarpiece." In Creighton Gilbert, ed., *Renaissance Art*. New York, Evanston, London: Harper & Row, 1970.

Seigel, Jerrold. "Rhetoric and Philosophy in Renaissance Humanism from Petrarch to Valla." Ph.D. diss., Princeton University, 1963.

Sereno, Renzo. "A Falsification by Machiavelli." In Bruce Mazlich, *Psychoanalysis and History*, 108–14. New York: Universal Library, 1971.

Shumer, S. M. "Machiavelli's Republican Politics and Its Corruption." *Political Theory* 7 (February 1979): 5–34.

Sichel, Edith. *The Renaissance*. New York: Henry Holt, 1914.

Slater, Philip E. *The Glory of Hera*. Boston: Beacon Press, 1968.

Stanlis, Peter J., ed. *Edmund Burke: Selected Writings and Speeches*. Garden City, N.Y.: Doubleday, 1963.

Starn, Rudolph. "Francesco Guicciardini and his Brothers." In Anthony Molho and John A. Tedeschi, eds., *Renaissance Studies in Honor of Hans Baron*. Dekalb: Northern Illinois University Press, 1971.

Stern, Karl. *The Flight from Woman*. New York: Farrar, Straus and Giroux, 1968.

Stone, Lawrence. *The Family, Sex and Marriage in England 1500–1800*. London: Weidenfeld and Nicolson, 1977.

Strauss, Leo. *Thoughts on Machiavelli*. Chicago and London: University of Chicago Press, 1978.

Strouse, Jean, ed. *Women and Analysis*. New York: Grossman, 1974.

Stuard, Susan Mosher, ed. *Women in Medieval Society*. Philadelphia: University of Pennsylvania Press, 1976.

Sumberg, Theodore A. "*La Mandragola*: An Interpretation." *Journal of Politics* 23 (1961): 320–40.

Tamassia, Nino [Giovanni]. *La Famiglia Italiana Nei Secoli Decimoquinto e Decimoseste*. Milano, Palermo, Napoli: Libraio della R. Casa, 1911.

Tarlton, Charles. *Fortune's Circle*. Chicago: Quadrangle Books, 1970.

Taylor, Rachel Annand. *Aspects of the Italian Renaissance*. Boston and New York: Houghton Mifflin, 1923.

Trexler, Richard C. "Le célibat à la fin du Moyen Age: Les religieuses de Florence." *Annales. Économies, Sociétés, Civilisations* 27 (November–December 1972): 1329–50.

———. "Florentine Religious Experience: The Sacred Image." *Studies in the Renaissance* 19 (1972): 7–41.

———. "The Foundlings of Florence 1395–1455." *History of Childhood Quarterly* 1 (Fall 1973): 259–84.

———. "In Search of Father: The Experience of Abandonment in the Recollections of Giovanni di Pagolo Morelli." *History of Childhood Quarterly* 3 (Fall 1975): 225–52.

Tucker, Robert C., ed. *The Marx-Engels Reader*. 2d ed. New York: W. W. Norton, 1978.

Villari, Pasquale. *The Life and Times of Niccolò Machiavelli*. Tr. by Linda Villari. London: T. Fisher Unwin, 1898.

Thoreau, Henry David. *Walden*. Boston: Ticknor and Fields, 1854. Reprint. New York: Harper, 1965.

Walker, Leslie J., tr. *The Discourses of Niccolò Machiavelli*. 2 vols. New Haven: Yale University Press, 1950.

Warburg, Aby. *Francesco Sassettis Letztwillige Verfügung*. N.p. 1907.

Weinstein, Fred, and Gerald M. Platt. *The Wish to be Free*. Berkeley, Los Angeles, London: University of California Press, 1969.

Wheelis, Allen B. *The Quest for Identity*. New York: W. W. Norton, 1958.

Whitfield, John H. *Machiavelli*. New York: Russell and Russell, 1966.

———. "Machiavelli and Castruccio." *Italian Studies* 8 (1953): 1–28.

Whiting, Beatrice B. "Sex Identity Conflict and Physical Violence." *American Anthropologist* 67 (December 1965, Supplement): 123–40.

Winnicott, D. W. *The Child and the Outside World*. New York: Basic Books, 1957.

———. *The Maturational Process and the Facilitating Environment*. London: Hogarth Press, 1965.

———. *Playing and Reality*. London: Tavistock Publications, 1971.

Index

Abraham and Isaac, 250
"Accusations," 70, 87, 92, 322
Achilles, 234
Action: ancients discuss, with Machiavelli, 45, 266; and authority, 54; without certainty, 18, 71–72, 150–51, 285–86, 292–93; deferred, 276; "dimension of," 287–99, 306–7, 316, 325; in Founder image, 67; and guilt, 66, 149, 186–89; as human capacity, 8, 99, 186–87, 195, 279–80, 282, 285–99, 304, 307–9, 317–19, 325; and magic, 104–5; without megalomania, 285, 293, 324, 327; and psychology, 186–89, 195–96; theory useful to, 104; and women, 111–12, 119, 131, 135, 143, 165, 168, 294
Activism: and astrology, 161; in Citizen image, 82; Florentine, 14, 19, 293; vis-à-vis fortune, 142, 144, 146, 148, 152, 154; in Founder image, 67–68; Machiavelli's, 22, 103–4, 127, 144, 146, 148, 152, 164, 179, 182, 239, 285, 293, 324; and misogyny, 5, 293–94, 305; psychology of, 179, 182–83, 195, 196, 305
Adam, 132, 221
Adams, Henry, 9, 201
Adams, John Clarke, 32
Adulthood: and autonomy, 236, 240, 299, 306, 322–23; capacities of, 296, 322; as false self, 317; as feeding self, 96, 240, 322; and freedom, 247, 261, 306; as masculinity, 8, 109, 136, 230, 232, 236, 281, 306; misogyny and, 294, 299, 306; transition to, 280–82. *See also* Childishness; Mutuality
Adviser. *See* Counselor
Aeneas, 55, 57, 244, 254, 277
Agathocles the Sicilian, 60–61
Age difference between spouses, 180, 210–11, 218–19, 222
Agis (Spartan King), 20, 58
Alamanni, Luigi, 64
Alberti, Leon Battista, 143, 150, 213, 222, 223
Alexander the Great, 55, 76, 93–94, 100
Alexandria, 94, 233, 245
Alliances: danger in, 19–20, 158–59; Roman manner of, 257, 259; Tuscan manner of, 256, 258
Almond, Gabriel, 48
Ambition: of counselor, 32; and fortune, 145, 158, 165–66; of Italians, 45, 95, 293; of nobility, 84–85, 88, 322; political autonomy promoted by, 90–91, 93, 127, 130–36, 231–33, 236, 320–22; political autonomy threatened by, 37, 115, 119, 127, 129–36, 231–33, 238, 244, 258–59, 262, 266, 273, 320–22; private and public expression of, 59, 92–93, 95, 226, 251, 320–22; sources of, 129, 132–33, 158, 196
Ambivalence, 5; concerning autonomy, 129, 136, 189–91, 223; in family, 219; about Founder, 251; Machiavelli's, 34, 41, 45, 105, 253; concerning manhood, 5, 8, 129, 173; mother's, 182, 190, 197–98, 227–28
Ancestors. *See* Forefathers